Contents

CONSOLIDATING DEMOCRACY IN POLAND

RAYMOND TARAS

WestviewPress

A Division of HarperCollins*Publishers*

"Utopia," from *Postwar Polish Poetry* by Czeslaw Milosz, Translation copyright 1965 by Czeslaw Milosz. Used by permission of Doubleday, a division of Bantam Doubleday Dell Publishing Group, Inc.

Published in 1995 in the United States of America by Westview Press, Inc., 5500 Central Avenue, Boulder, Colorado 80301-2877, and in the United Kingdom by Westview Press, 12 Hid's Copse Road, Cumnor Hill, Oxford OX2 9JJ

Library of Congress Cataloging-in-Publication Data
Taras, Ray, 1946–
    Consolidating democracy in Poland / Raymond Taras.
        p.   cm.
    Includes bibliographical references and index.
    ISBN 0-8133-1463-1. — ISBN 0-8133-1464-X (pbk.)
    1. Poland—Politics and government—1989–   2. Democracy—Poland—
History.   3. Poland—History.   I. Title.
JN6752.T37   1995
320.9438'09'049—dc20   95-30556
                                                                                            CIP

The paper used in this publication meets the requirements of the American National Standard for Permanence of Paper for Printed Library Materials Z39.48-1984.

10   9   8   7   6   5   4   3   2   1

Economic Models After the Command Economy, 227
Socioeconomic Change, 230
Foreign Policy and the International Political Economy, 244
Conclusion, 253
Notes, 255

Tables and Figures

Tables

Figures

Acknowledgments

No one theoretical framework can make sense of such diverse and multilevel phenomena as regime change, separation of power, electoral realignment, and capitalist transformation in a country. Since describing democratic consolidation in Poland requires us to examine these and associated phenomena, I acknowledge the inspiration I have obtained in recent years from several political science theorists. Gabriel Almond renewed my interest in the regime-change framework that orders this study. Philippe Schmitter talked to me about transition moments and democratic consolidation in imaginative ways that the printed word could never do justice to. The late Aaron Wildavsky was as creative a political scientist as there has been, and he confidently led initiates through the grid-group gates of cultural theory. During the summer of 1994 I participated in a seminar on democracy, development, and civil society organized by the Institute for the Study of Economic Culture at Boston University. Its director, Peter Berger, kept the focus on the cultural prerequisites for free-market success. If this book, then, explores a variety of theoretical approaches and recognizes the value of a healthy dose of epistemological relativism, it is because I have been infected by the enthusiasm and have been largely persuaded by the argumentation of these theorists.

I am very grateful to Krzysztof Jasiewicz of the Polish Academy of Sciences and Washington and Lee University for critically reviewing the postcommunist chapters in this book. I also acknowledge the many constructive comments on the manuscript given by an anonymous reviewer. I thank Curt Pendergraft for expert assistance with the graphics. Susan McEachern of Westview Press has offered me consistently good advice and encouragement. Barbara Metzger provided unassailable editing of the manuscript. Jo Ellen Miller has always kindly provided me with professional secretarial support. I gratefully acknowledge their contributions.

An empirical study is only as good as its source material. Whenever I visit Poland, Regina Kacprzyk has considerately set aside a large stack of periodical literature for my use. Julita Wroniak has faced many an embarrassment on my behalf in asking at bookstores for the memoirs of disgraced communist officials. I can count on Tomek Mirkowicz to track down the most obscure books or the wildest rumors. Jan Trzciński has sensitized me to the extraordinary difficulties that an earlier generation of democratic Poles had to face.

When asked what influence Marxism had exerted on him, former British Labour Party Prime Minister Harold Wilson is said to have replied, "I never got beyond page three of *Das Kapital.*" It is an answer my wife, Małgosia, might give if she were asked about the influence of my work on her. I admire her, as well as my sons, Michał and Krzysztof, for doing their own work so well.

Finally, I hope readers will be understanding about the mistakes I have made in this book. I have strived diligently to cross the łs and dot the żs. I have also sought to keep track of the changing names, alliances, and leaders of political parties and of the changing party affiliations of politicians. It is a task conducive to acquiring a neurosis. I am grateful for readers' forebearance.

Raymond Taras

Introduction: Approaches
to Democratization

Scholarly writing about politics in Central and Eastern Europe[1] in recent years has been largely concerned with the *transition* from communism to democracy and capitalism. The historic changes that took place in the countries of the region in 1989 have justifiably inspired extensive research aimed at explaining why the Soviet bloc suddenly crumbled and liberal democracy quickly found many public advocates and few public adversaries. Further archival research, interviews, and surveys need to be conducted to shed as much light as possible on the momentous events that led to the democratic breakthrough.

This book is different. It is primarily concerned with whether, in the Polish case, the transition has led to a stable and consolidated democracy. Questions about which party holds power, who is likely to win the next presidential election, and when Poland can expect to join the European Union and the North Atlantic Treaty Organization are important, of course, and I examine these issues carefully. But to discover the broader meaning of the answers to these questions it seems useful to introduce the dichotomous variable of *consolidated* versus *unconsolidated* democracy. This approach allows me to map clearly what the country has achieved since 1989.

The Explanandum

The test for determining whether democracy has been consolidated is that identified by the political scientist Adam Przeworski: "Democracy is consolidated when it becomes self-enforcing, that is, when all the relevant political forces find it best to continue to submit their interests and values to the uncertain interplay of institutions."[2] A similar definition of consolidation is provided by Scott Mainwaring, Guillermo O'Donnell, and J. Samuel Valenzuela: It occurs when "all major political actors take for granted that democratic procedures dictate government renewal" and that democratic continuity is certain.[3] A more procedure-based definition is contained in Ralf Dahrendorf's view that consolidated democracy occurs

1

when the alternation of political parties in power is both regular and accepted by the contenders.[4] Giuseppe di Palma advocates a minimalist understanding of consolidation as being possible when accords are reached between incumbent rulers and the political opposition.[5] In all these cases, consolidated democracy has to meet procedural criteria and a legitimacy test, that is, whether its rules and constraints are accepted by all politically significant groups. Testing consolidation using these criteria allows us to overcome the tautological fallacy of simply associating consolidation with stability, the passage of time, or the absence of regime reversals.

Focusing on consolidation is important because there is no guarantee that it will occur in a given country. Zbigniew Brzezinski has cautioned that "though the notions of 'democracy' are fashionable, in much of the world the practice of democracy is still quite superficial and democratic institutions remain vulnerable."[6] In examining consolidation in Poland, we need to find out whether democracy has remained superficial and vulnerable in the years since its seemingly indisputable triumph.

This is not to suggest that this book ignores the intriguing issue of the transition *moment*. Indeed, both the empirical studies of and the theoretical literature on transitions are too fascinating to be set aside. In order to be clear about the relationship between the transition moment and democratic consolidation, let me consider a distinction made by Guillermo O'Donnell. For him, the "first transition" occurs when a change is made from the previous authoritarian government to a new democratically oriented one; the "second transition" comes when this initial democratic government is absorbed into the "effective functioning of a democratic regime."[7] The importance of examining the first transition, or transition moment, is self-evident; that of determining the degree of democratic consolidation, the second transition, is more easily overlooked.

It also appears presumptuous to disregard Poland's politics before the first transition. Much has been made of the strong electoral showings recorded by revamped former communist parties in 1993–1994 in the former East Germany, Bulgaria, Hungary, Lithuania, and Poland—nations not otherwise known for their affection for the Leninist party-state. In some cases former communist party politburo members have returned to power, causing us to reexamine research agendas and to give more weight to a research question that was largely ignored after 1989—the question of transition from *what*. In the heady days of late 1989, some political commentators and many ambitious politicians dismissed the legacy of the bankrupt communist regimes. These regimes were regarded either as an aberration in the country's history or as largely irrelevant to its future. Such hastily drawn conclusions come under challenge as we observe the electoral trends emerging in the 1990s. The harsh reality for many participants in the new political and economic system is increasingly the subject of inquiry by Western social scientists.[8] Both subjects—transition from what and the nature of the first transition—are addressed in Chapters 2–4 of this book.

From these preliminary research questions I move to my overriding objective—to describe the second transition, that is, the democratic government and politics of contemporary Poland. I pose a problematic similar to the one that Alexis de Tocqueville set for himself in chapter 9 of *Democracy in America,* entitled "The Main Causes Tending to Maintain a Democratic Republic in the United States." Three general categories are cited in his conclusion: "The first is the peculiar and accidental situation in which Providence has placed the Americans. Their laws are the second. Their habits and mores are the third."[9]

For contemporary Poland as much as for eighteenth-century America, geopolitics, institutions, and political culture count in assessing prospects for democratic consolidation. But this is where the similarity ends. First, I do not pretend even to approximate the magnitude of de Tocqueville's contribution. Second, democracy in late twentieth-century Poland is hardly comparable to the American democracy forged in a much earlier era; indeed, Poland was itself experimenting with constitutionalism when the U.S. founding fathers were praising the virtues of individual rights, federalism, and separation of powers. Third, politics, like economics, is infinitely more complex today and democratic consolidation can only be evaluated within a much expanded multivariate framework.

In Chapters 5 and 6, I identify the institutions of democratic rule in Poland—its constitution, party system, and election results. Questions asked about the much older Western democracies, such as what type of separation of power exists and what electoral mechanisms ensure representative and responsible government, are directed to Poland's young democratic system. While accepting that it would be absurd to compare Poland with de Tocqueville's America, I suggest that politics in Poland today can legitimately be studied alongside the politics of other contemporary European states such as England, France, or Germany. Rather than viewing Poland as an anomaly, counterpoint, or contrast to these countries, it is now appropriate to highlight its essential *comparability* with liberal-democratic states in the West. Many of the features of democracy in this large Central European country have deliberately been modeled on the experience of the West, making the reasons for comparison even more compelling. Those features not patterned on the West have an intrinsic interest of their own that call for our attention.

Comparative analysis that includes Poland can be informed by another objective—examining countries at similar stages of political development. Comparing Poland with other consolidating democracies rather than with established ones provides a different set of measures and expectations about it. Indeed, the comparison of consolidating democracies has sparked both theoretically and empirically driven research.[10]

In summary, with the end of communism students of comparative politics have new research agendas. No longer can we juxtapose democratic political regimes with communist ones as texts in comparative or European politics have traditionally done. Instead we search for commonalities found across states that are committed to democratic development. Although the residuals that still differentiate them are important, they seem overshadowed by the democratic imperative. The field of comparative communist studies is no longer viable except, perhaps, for the examination of the similar problems found in postcommunist societies.[11] Because of the enhanced comparability of states, cross-national research does not need to be limited to a regional or area-studies focus. We now have a potentially larger number of democratic countries to compare in terms of selected variables, and we can largely control for population or territorial size. For example, comparing Polish with Spanish or French politics can enhance our understanding of modern democracies more surely than comparing Polish politics with the politics of neighboring Belarus, Lithuania, or Slovakia. If we accept the widely held view that regional boundaries are becoming more permeable as Europe moves toward greater integration and democratic values become almost universally accepted, then there can no longer be any reason for treating Polish politics as exotic.

Poland as a Discrete Case

To be sure, we should not lose sight of Poland's distinct path of political development, described in Chapter 1. This development has not been linear, nor has it reached any such end point as full democratic consolidation. Like other political transitions from communism in the region, Poland's is incomplete in a number of ways. Prior to the 1995 presidential elections it still lacked a new constitution and had to make do with an interim "Little Constitution," in force alongside sections of the 1952 constitution adopted in the period of high Stalinism. Presidential, parliamentary, and local elections have been held several times, but voter dealignment and realignment is not fully clear. The former communist party has been decimated, extensively reconfigured, and then returned to power, whereas the Solidarity movement has disintegrated. The command economy has given way to an occasionally chaotic economy, and a seeming army of employees of Western accounting, consulting, legal, and appraisal firms has replaced Soviet troops as permanent and symbolic political landmarks in the country.

Like many of the former Soviet-bloc states, Poland is confronted with a number of obstacles impeding full democratic consolidation. Nationality politics, minority rights, and subsystem autonomy remain sensitive issues, although not to the same degree as in neighboring countries, and political parties still splinter, merge, realign, and change names. Governmental coalitions continue to be fluid, and regardless of the composition of the parties, disputes within such coalitions are a permanent feature of the political scene. Bidding and bargaining now pervade political and economic spheres, but many large, still-unprivatized state enterprises remain anomalies. Often they contain a politically embattled and experienced industrial proletariat that regularly calls strikes or organizes antigovernment demonstrations.

Poland's transition process has a number of distinctive characteristics. It was the first country in the region to achieve the democratic breakthrough, with the roundtable agreement of April 1989 that granted formal recognition to the political opposition. But this was a flawed breakthrough in that the ruling coalition received a battery of guarantees—65 percent of the seats in the legislature, its own president, and, some observers allege, tacit arrangements providing leading officials with both political immunity and a golden parachute. In a remarkable irony of history, fully free elections four years later produced a legislature that had almost the same proportion of postcommunist deputies as the 1989 "contract" legislature had assigned communist members—about 65 percent.

In the intervening years, the country tried to make sense of allegations (and counterallegations) made in 1991 that the prime minister (or the president himself) had planned to stage a military coup that would have aborted Polish democracy. These charges came during the stormiest tenure of any of the five prime ministers to serve in this period—the former Solidarity lawyer Jan Olszewski. He also was linked with the release of secret police files that implicated Wałęsa as being a former agent of the communist security police. Wałęsa's swift action to oust Olszewski after these disclosures remains, arguably, the most mysterious of the political events of this period. Had he simply lost confidence in his prime minister, or did he really wish to cover up his past?

There were other manifestations of an imperfectly functioning democracy. Symbolizing the initial immaturity of political actors and the electorate and typifying its early opéra bouffe character was the presidential campaign of the Canadian businessman and Peruvian cable television magnate Stan Tyminski, who forced a runoff in the 1990 elections with longtime Solidarity leader Wałęsa. A year later, a maverick political grouping calling itself the Polish Beer Lovers' Party (Polska Partia Przyjaciół Piwa—PPPP) not only won eighteen parliamentary seats in the October 1991 elections but also quickly split into a serious political group (the Polish Economic Program) and a serious beer-loving faction.

Of more consequence were the president's doomed efforts in 1992 to enact a new constitution that would have created a presidential system. Wałęsa's draft was resisted by parliament, and in its place a compromise provisional "Little Constitution" was passed. Returning to historical irony, it did not seem out of the question that when a new constitution for Poland's democratic republic was proclaimed it might bear the signature of the leader of parliament, who was an excommunist. In fall 1994 another confrontation occurred between Wałęsa and parliament over the matter of the defense minister. The president insisted that defense was a "presidential ministry," that is, that he alone appointed, held accountable, and dismissed the defense chief. Conversely, parliament suspected that the effort to remove the incumbent minister—occurring at the same time that Wałęsa was struggling to have his man head the committee overseeing Polish television—was an attempt at presidential control of the key institutions of society.

As a socialist state, Poland was also unique in the number of political crises it experienced. Crises in 1948, 1956, 1970, and 1980 forced political leaders to resign because of "poor health." Crises in 1968 and 1976 galvanized the intellectual opposition, which became an important political actor for the last two decades of communist rule. Within the supposed monolithism of the Soviet bloc, then, Poland's political development was idiosyncratic and its transition from communism quite unlike that in other countries.

This book offers an analysis of the sometimes bizarre and unique and sometimes universal and path-dependent nature of Poland's transition to democracy. It is a case study of political crisis, choice, change, and consolidation.

Choice of Analytic Framework

Many explanatory variables have been identified as crucial to the making of democracy.[12] In his study of the most recent wave of democratization, the political scientist Samuel Huntington compiles a lengthy, though not exhaustive, list of factors that scholars have singled out as promoting democratization:

- a high overall level of economic wealth;
- relatively equal distribution of income and/or wealth;
- a market economy;
- economic development and social modernization;
- a feudal aristocracy at some point in the history of a society;
- the absence of feudalism in the society;
- a strong bourgeoisie ("no bourgeoisie, no democracy," in Barrington Moore's succinct formulation);
- a strong middle class;
- high levels of literacy and education;
- an instrumental rather than consumatory culture;
- Protestantism;
- social pluralism and strong intermediate groups;
- the development of political contestation before the expansion of political participation;
- democratic authority structures within social groups, particularly those closely connected to politics;
- low levels of civil violence;
- low levels of political polarization and extremism;
- political leaders committed to democracy;

- experience as a British colony;
- traditions of toleration and compromise;
- occupation by a pro-democratic foreign power;
- influence of a pro-democratic foreign power;
- an elite desire to emulate democratic nations;
- traditions of respect for law and individual rights;
- communal (ethnic, racial, religious) homogeneity;
- communal (ethnic, racial, religious) heterogeneity;
- consensus on political and social values;
- absence of consensus on political and social values.[13]

A number of conclusions emerge from this checklist. First, contending theories of democratization are occasionally contradictory; some rest on the presence of certain factors, for example, ethnic homogeneity, others on the absence of these same factors. Further, as Huntington points out, although virtually all factors offer plausible explanations for democratization, each is likely to be relevant to only a few cases. Thus, being Protestant, being a British colony, or not experiencing feudalism circumscribes the number of states that may have been pushed toward democracy as a result of such factors. Some alleged explanatory factors are themselves in need of explanation. For example, the existence of prodemocratic elites inevitably raises the question of the source of this elite orientation. Some variables seem to be as much the outcome as the cause of democracy, such as low levels of civil violence or respect for individual rights.

Moreover, the list excludes, among others, Marxist and post-Marxist theories underscoring the democratization impulse. Marxist theories would highlight capitalist exploitation and deep structures of power in the modern state and post-Marxist ones metaclass forms of domination and the postmaterialist demand for direct participation. A case that substantiates the relevance of post-Marxist theories emphasizing nonclass actors and interests is that of the Zapatista National Liberation Army that emerged in southern Mexico in January 1994, which is not a classic revolutionary Marxist movement but primarily a nonclass movement pressing for the empowerment of Indian groups and the democratization of regional and national politics. Postmodernist explanations are also excluded. Postmodern theorists explore new forms of empowerment that might replace conventional representational structures that, they contend, depict an outside world that does not exist. Their search for new understandings of political self-determination and freedom, identities and consciousness raising, popular control and direct democracy is designed to reassert the primacy of the subject, and of human agency generally, in politics. Whereas postmodernism would stress the interconnectedness, for example, of the democratization thrust and feminists' search for truth and identity, both Huntington's list and his explanation of third-wave democratization ignore this relationship.

Any theory of democratization founded upon the primacy of one factor will appear deterministic, simplistic, and neglectful of the complex realities of late-twentieth-century societies. To be sure, recent history has vindicated Adam Smith in stressing the close relationship between liberty and commerce.[14] Max Weber employed somewhat different logic—arguing that capitalism promoted democracy mainly by separating political from economic power—in reaching a similar conclusion.[15] In the same spirit, Barrington Moore was close to formulating a law of the social sciences when he asserted that there can be no democracy without a bourgeoisie.[16] None of these writers would have overstated their findings, however, and they would undoubtedly have qualified their propositions by noting that the existence of commerce or independent economic power or an entrepreneurial middle class constituted a necessary if insufficient condition of democracy.

Apart from searching for factors that are closely associated with democracy, it is possible to identify general conditions that promote democracy, representing the intervening variables between democracy and its causes. Three contextual variables are widely believed to shape the character of democratic transitions. The first of these is the *historical period* in which the transition takes place. This variable circumscribes the options available to political contenders. Thus, growing interdependence among states in the postwar period began to limit the scope for independent action of any particular government. This was especially true of authoritarian regimes such as communist ones, which were dependent on other states and organizations for development assistance, credits, investment, and trade and therefore could not afford to be seen as politically unstable. The appearance of a police state, the regular occurrence of politically-motivated violence, and the lack of legitimacy of an undemocratic system were likely to produce the very instability that authoritarian rulers feared. In view of the fact that, in the global village created by mass communications, the use of force by a repressive government may be deterred by the threat of the unfavorable media coverage it would occasion, an authoritarian regime may not even be able to apply its most powerful resource—coercion. An authoritarian government's resort to force seems to carry more risks today than when it was regularly used fifty years ago in Stalin's lifetime. The time-dependent nature of the use of force is very clear if we compare the brutal tsarist repression employed in Poland after the failed 1863 uprising with the selective communist repression after the student demonstrations of 1968 or the martial-law crackdown on Solidarity after 1981.

The contemporary historical context also appears more likely to ensure a smooth transition to democracy by late-arriving states because of the presence of a learning curve. Earlier transitions to democracy were the result of tentative, often trial-and-error efforts at producing a stable constitutional outcome, and there was little understanding of the specific political institutions and processes needed to achieve a stable democracy. It is true that, even after the most recent wave of democratic transitions, scholars are still debating what configuration of institutions is most likely to consolidate democracy.[17] Nevertheless, late-transiting states stand to benefit from historical experience; certain institutional formulae have been developed about crafting democracy,[18] and democratic transition-management is now being conducted with greater confidence.[19]

A second contextual variable affecting the transition to democracy is the *level of development* of the nation at the time. Although a democratic transition involves the incorporation of citizens into the political process, the country's level of development may determine which citizens and how many. In the case of Poland, peasants, who have traditionally not engaged in political mobilization, exhibited an uncharacteristic militancy and sense of solidarity that led to the establishment of a peasant-party-based coalition government in fall 1993. Poland's industrial working class has had a celebrated apprenticeship in political activism and was in large measure responsible for the return of the excommunists to power in late 1993. The level of socioeconomic development in Poland, described in Chapter 2, has continued relevance, then, to an understanding of political conflict in the new democratic system.

The third contextual variable affecting the democratic transition has to do with identity politics, specifically, the *relative strength of mass identification with a particular community.* A permanent democratic outcome is more probable where the community as defined by the constitution serves as the primary focus for citizens' own identity. In the three former communist states that had federal systems—Czechoslovakia, Yugoslavia, and the USSR—the transition to democracy was complicated by competing national identities. Nationality politics have played out differently in each of these countries—a velvet divorce leading to two polities with different levels of democratic politics in the case of Czechoslovakia, authoritarianism and/or war in several of the Yugoslav successor states, and neither war nor peace, neither democracy nor dictatorship, in the vast majority of the Soviet successor states. The limited, perhaps even negligible, degree of ethnic schism in Poland has meant that this contextual variable favors democratic consolidation.

Individual factors and sets of conditions do not exhaust the list of units of analysis relevant to democratization. A number of scholars are attentive to the *sequence* in which political and economic change occurs. Two decades ago Robert Dahl concluded that the timing of liberalization and inclusiveness does matter—that early liberalization, allowing for greater subsystem autonomy, promoted democratization whereas large-scale participation in politics preceding the emergence of a liberal pluralist order reduced the chances for a strong democracy (the likely emergence of popular radicalism from such a sequence being at odds with a democratic order).[20] Recently the sociologist John Hall has returned to Dahl's point: "if one virtue of having liberalism prior to democratization is that it encourages moderation on behalf of those entering the political stage, another is that it ensures that the powerful are not unduly threatened: and such reassurance is absolutely necessary if political modernization is to take place at all."[21] Clearly, the sequence in which liberalism and democracy, liberalization and inclusiveness, political and economic reform, and economic stabilization and privatization appear is crucial.

Since I have been stressing the complex, multicausal nature of the democratization process, it is imperative that I locate an analytic framework that is at once sufficiently rigid to order complex and diverse data and unrestrictive: "Models which are unrestrictive are detailed, contextual, and more realistic" than abstract, although they provide less precise estimates.[22] It is possible, of course, to offer a historical narrative of democracy's triumph and communism's collapse without being guided by any theoretical framework, but the result is likely to be unsatisfactory.[23] Philippe Schmitter and Terry Karl, writing of the study of regime change, underscore this point:

> The one thing that *cannot* be done is to take refuge in *empirie*—in the diligent collection of facts without any guidance from theories and models. Given the sheer volume of data, not to mention their frequently contradictory referents, without some sense of priorities and categories for classification no analyst is likely to be able to make much sense of what is going on.[24]

Their advice to former sovietologists is to spend more effort on conceptualization than on diligent data gathering.

A leading candidate for a framework for addressing the complex nature of democratization is structural or system functionalism, arguably the most widely applied analytic model in political science since the 1960s.

System Functionalism
as Explanatory Framework

Forming part of the behavioral revolution in the social sciences in the 1950s, structural-functionalism was not designed to explain democratization processes. Instead, it sought to discover the conditions that make for stability. Every political system, it was argued, had to perform a number of functions, and these functions were most efficiently performed by systems in which structures of representation were well developed. Western democratic systems had perfected many such structures and were, consequently, blessed with political stability.

In time, structural-functionalism underwent much modification, appeared in many variants, and crossed several disciplines. The Polish anthropologist Bronisław Malinowski is often regarded as the originator of functionalism.[25] As did political scientists later, he posited that institutions exist for the purpose of promoting human cooperation and need satisfaction and survive because they contribute positively to a greater cause. The criticism that there is some circularity and teleology in a functional explanation is well founded, but these shortcomings can be overcome through carefully designed research.[26] In a functional explanation, then, "the explanans specifies the function of the explanandum within the larger system and the benefits that the feature confers upon the smooth working of this system."[27] In turn, causal structuralism holds that societies consist of many structures and that both social stability and social change can be explained by the nature of these structures. Social structures acquire causal force "by providing an environment of incentives and prohibitions for various agents within a social system."[28] For example, the structures of property ownership and rights that existed in communist societies are today considered, explicitly or not, as having formed the constricting environment that made regime change a necessity.

Structural-functionalism, first associated with the British anthropologist A. R. Radcliffe-Brown, contends that institutions do more than merely function to meet human needs; their higher purpose is to achieve the functional unity, and therefore maintenance, of the social structure as a whole.[29] In political science, Gabriel Almond similarly noted the interdependence of the political system and its environment; system stability followed from an equilibrium relationship between the polity and its domestic and international environments. System functions included socialization, recruitment, and communication. Process functions consisted of interest articulation and aggregation and policy formulation and implementation. How effectively structures performed these various functions differentiated one political system from another. Whereas in a democracy many institutions took part in carrying out these indispensable functions, only a few, monopolistic structures (according to Almond, almost exclusively the communist party and the bureaucracy) engaged in them in a communist state.[30]

Early criticism of the structural-functionalist approach in political science centered on its giving inordinate weight to processes more common in Western democracies than in Second and Third World countries. In the 1990s we can stand this criticism on its head. In a world celebrating the triumph of Western liberal-democratic values, such bias in the framework has been transformed into an advantage. More than ever it seems that the framework is theoretically well equipped to make sense of Western-type democratization trends in various parts of the world. We set aside here the loaded normative question whether Western democracy should be a desideratum everywhere.

Another general criticism of structural-functionalism was that it valued political stability over political change. As an early exponent of structural-functionalism, Almond responded to criticism of the static, conservative nature of this framework by incorporating processes of political adaptation and change into the research agenda. Influenced by systems theory, which studied the organizational workings of holistic phenomena such as a society or a polity, he and other scholars turned their analytic focus to the way in which the components of a system were interrelated. Rather than elaborating a multicausal model in which all explanatory variables were linked solely to the dependent one, these scholars highlighted the interaction among the variables and therefore sought to link the various elements of a political system to each other.

The Crisis, Choice,
and Change Framework

System functionalism served as the principal, though not exclusive, framework for studying key developmental episodes in a nation's history in a book edited by Almond, Scott Flanagan, and Robert Mundt entitled *Crisis, Choice, and Change: Historical Studies of Political Development*. Published in 1973, the book treated political change as a complex, functional, and positive development that, under given conditions, caused ossified anciens régimes to collapse and dynamic new ones to rise in their places.[31] The original "crisis, choice, and change" (hereafter, CCC) model proposed an elaborate framework that could identify causation through the empirical testing of the *sequence*—and, when statistical or comparative methods were used, the *regularity*—of a variable set a's being followed by a variable set b. In this respect, the CCC model followed generally accepted strictures concerning causality: "The construction of a causal story based on a particular case . . . requires two things: fairly detailed knowledge about the sequence of events within the large historical process and credible theoretical or inductive hypotheses about various kinds of social causation."[32]

For Almond and his collaborators, as important a consideration as discovering causal chains in developmental episodes was drawing together the increasingly self-standing methodological approaches dominant in the discipline of political science in the late 1960s.[33] They identified four general approaches in the discipline—system functionalism, social mobilization, rational-choice, and leadership theory—and stressed that each possessed both strengths and weaknesses. Each approach was closely associated with a particular methodology and theoretical orientation; the practitioner of a particular approach usually had a modest research agenda that focused on only a few key variables and ignored or minimized the impact of others. For Almond, "It is the theoretical integration of these separate methodologies that is the special contribution of the Crisis, Choice, and Change approach. It is not simply a more comprehensive check list of causes of political change."[34] Almond, Flanagan, and Mundt concluded that a framework of analysis that transcended the artifical dichotomies inherent in political science and integrated distinct approaches would combine their separate strengths while overcoming their individual deficiencies.[35]

By combining different methods, the CCC design enabled empirical research to incorporate macro-, system-level phenomena into micro-, individual-level change, to reconcile long-term socioeconomic processes with short-term political events, and to conduct both quantitative analyses and qualitative explanations. The model thus analyzed a broad array of disparate phenomena and stressed the linkages among them, while the common framework of analysis facilitated comparison across historical cases.

The model identified four separate phases of political development and applied different methods of analysis to each of them. Table I.1 lists these phases, the

TABLE I.1 Process Model of Crisis, Choice, and Change

Phase	Process Studied	Method (Scope)	Performance Characteristic
I	Antecedent system	System functionalism	Stability
II	Crisis	Social mobilization and environmental change (long-term, macro-level factors)	Dissynchronization
III	Choice	Coalition theory and leadership analysis (short-term, micro-level factors)	Breakthrough
IV	Resultant system	System functionalism	Resynchronization

Source: Adapted from Scott C. Flanagan, "Models and Methods of Analysis," in Gabriel A. Almond, Scott C. Flanagan, and Robert J. Mundt (eds.), *Crisis, Choice, and Change: Historical Studies of Political Development.* Boston: Little, Brown, 1973, p. 49.

methods used to examine each, the scope of the variables (whether macro-, long-term, or micro-, short-term), and the performance characteristics. Analysis of each phase requires identifying relevant variables and collecting and interpreting specific data. Before describing these phases as they occurred in the case of the democratic transition in Poland, I shall briefly consider the ways in which Almond, Flanagan, and Mundt modified their model so that it might be applied to the study of the regime changes of the 1980s and 1990s.

The 1973 CCC model centered on developmental episodes that constituted systemic crises. These crises were "a challenge to the authority of the constituted decision makers expressed through extralegal means of protest on a scale sufficient to threaten the incumbents' ability to maintain order and continued occupancy of authority roles."[36] In a systemic crisis the constitution and established rules of the game for allocating authority and rewards were under challenge. The effort to resolve such crises invariably moved the political system in a new direction. Systemic crisis was, then, the defining feature of a case. Once such a crisis was identified, research could move backward, historically, to the antecedent system—the features that lent it stability and those that helped weaken it. In addition, analysis would move forward beyond the crisis moment to delineate the features of the new regime.

In order to model the democratic transitions of the 1980s and after, the design of the CCC framework was adapted so as to focus on one central theoretical problematic—the transition from an authoritarian to a democratic regime. In this way the framework would serve as a model that explains regime change. Studying the complexity of the transition to democracy still required a multimethod approach but one that was more "user-friendly" than the previous, behaviorally derived framework.[37] In defense of methodological pluralism, Flanagan and Mundt cited the many cross-national aggregate studies largely carried out in the 1960s to test Karl Deutsch's social mobilization theory.[38] Although these studies confirmed that there was indeed a linkage between economic development and democracy, they were at a loss to explain micro-level changes that had occurred in the attitudes, values, and behavior of individuals. Yet, clearly, such culture shift contributed to macro-level socioeconomic and political change. Similarly, use of only rational-choice or leadership explanations might lead to a depiction of the transition process as the outcome intended by the principal actors, as the only logical outcome, as idiosyncratic, or as the result of short-term forces alone. The CCC theorists warned, therefore, that opting for a single theoretical or methodological approach just because it fit a particular research tradition was bound to provide a partial and misleading explanation of the transition.

The revised CCC project is designed to apply to democratic transitions, and, accordingly, the decision point that now defines the case is the attempt to achieve a democratic breakthrough.[39] This decision point need not be accompanied by systemic crisis and confrontation—the defining feature of the original CCC framework—although it certainly was in the case of Poland. Typically, a breakthrough involves a change in the constitution, the political institutions, the rules of political competition, and the composition of the leadership. Democratic breakthroughs are also typically accompanied by the establishment of limits on the exercise of power and by power sharing between outgoing and incoming elites for a prearranged period of time, between executive and legislative branches, and between national and subnational levels. The principal check on the exercise of political power becomes the verdict rendered by the electorate at regularly constituted intervals.

In addition to instituting competitive elections, a democratic breakthrough usually signifies the loss of some if not all power by the incumbent coalition. Changes in the political rules and power loss are the most visible signs of a democratic transition. In a number of respects these correspond to Robert Dahl's two criteria for democratization, liberalization and inclusiveness.[40] Liberalization indicates an increasing degree of permitted political competition in a system and tends to be subtle, gradual, and often perceptible only over time. Rules controlling dissident activity may be relaxed through either legislative changes or, more often, changes in the way in which the rules are enforced. By contrast, inclusiveness is associated with more abrupt, dramatic changes. Competitive elections ensuring widespread participation are either held or not. Furthermore, in contrast to earlier historical cases of democratization, in which property and gender often figured as criteria of voter enfranchisement, the choice now is between extending meaningful suffrage to all citizens and extending it to none of them.

Democratic transitions involve, then, both incremental, almost imperceptible processes and decisive, dramatic turning points. Although the means—ranging from violent revolution to consensual transition[41]—by which the democratic breakthrough is achieved are relevant to democratization, it is not the defining criterion. More significant is that democratic breakthrough involves changes in elite structures and, furthermore, a societal transformation, for example, the forging of a civil society. If analysis of the first centers on incumbents and their response to the changes taking place in society, the focus of the second is the status of hitherto excluded groups and their struggle for incorporation. The linkage between the two is seen in the shifting balance of political resources held by each and the salience of the policies each espouses. The relationship between state rulers and society can indicate why an attempted democratic breakthrough became an option.

The Four Phases of Analysis

Although each chapter of this book opens with a description of the variables and methods used in the analysis of a particular phase, I shall here briefly identify the phases listed in Table I.1 as they apply to the case of Poland. Phase I concerns the country's antecedent regime, that is, the postwar authoritarian communist system. System functionalism is employed to map out the characteristics of the regime and its basis of power and authority. The analysis focuses on the following variables: (1) the socioeconomic structure, (2) the international environment, (3) the political culture, (4) political groups and social cleavages, (5) the political structure, and (6) the ruling coalition (Chapter 2).

Phase II deals with macro- and micro-level change in the forty-five-year communist period. The overriding objective in the study of this phase is to discover the origins of the political crisis that make the need for regime change compelling and seemingly unavoidable—in short, to locate the sources of later democratization pressures. The regime's long-term economic performance, changes in social structure, and developments in the international arena over this forty-five-year period now become explanatory variables. Value change, cognitive mobilization, culture shift, and the political mobilization of opposition forces are the dependent variables (Chapter 3).[42]

The shift from Phase II to Phase III represents a major change in the mode of analysis. Whereas in Phase II the focus is on long-term factors and the independent variables are primarily socioeconomic, in Phase III short-term factors are central and the independent variables are all political: the resources, issue preferences, skills, and actions of the contenders for political power and the leadership characteristics of the major individual players that conditioned the outcome. The decision point is nested in this phase, so instead of looking at broad patterns of change taking place within society (both on the micro-level of mass attitude change and on the macro-level of social movements and political mobilization), the focus, much narrower, is on key actors. Phase III entails a study of the process of "coalition formation," understood as the need for a pact between incumbents and their chief political opponents. It reviews the choices available to political leaders at a time of crisis and describes for the Polish case how the communists extricated themselves from a crisis while, simultaneously, the democratic opposition opened a path for its entry into the political system. Methods of analysis change in this phase from the interpretation of aggregate trends to rational-choice considerations[43] and examination of leadership personalities and styles (Chapter 4).

Phase II and Phase III methods are grounded in two distinct levels of analysis and two time frames. The levels of analysis are macro-level, societal, and micro-level, individual. The time frames are a long-term component, typically in the form of a liberalization process responding to long-term processes of societal and attitude change and incremental adjustments in a state's legal and institutional structure, and a short-term component that takes the form of major decision points at which key democratizing changes are made in political structures and processes. These time frames correspond to two distinct schools identifiable in the democratization literature of recent years: (1) the "wave" explanation, specifying general ideological trends favoring liberalism, found in the work of writers such as Huntington and Francis Fukuyama,[44] and (2) the technical approach, focusing on elite bargaining, the making of strategic choices, and the crafting of pacts, processes, and institutions, central to the analyses of Przeworski and Schmitter, among others.[45]

Combining two levels of analysis and two time frames, the CCC framework offers us four distinct perspectives on the transition process: (1) long-term, macro-level changes such as economic development and social mobilization, (2) long-term, micro-level changes in the form of attitude change and culture shift, (3) short-term, macro-level changes such as in the international system and the regime's economic performance, and (4) short-term, micro-level change in the resources, issue positions, coalition preferences, and leadership attributes of the contenders. Each of these four perspectives focuses on a different set of variables, and together they advance a comprehensive explanation for a democratic transition. All four perspectives are operationalized in this study of the democratic transition in Poland.

Phase IV deals with the contemporary government and politics of Poland. It replicates the system-functional analysis, this time for Poland's democratized system and its capitalist economy. The analysis revisits the same Phase I mapping categories—the socioeconomic structure, the international environment, the political culture, social cleavages and political groups, the political structure, and the composition of the ruling coalition. A comparison of Phase I and Phase IV system characteristics provides a measure of how much change has occurred between the preexisting and resultant systems: the different social bases, political characteristics, and policy orientations of the two regimes. As surprising as it may seem, in contemporary Poland one hears both the criticism that nothing has really changed from the communist period *and* the criticism that there has been too much change. The extent of political and economic changes becomes clear from the system-functional analysis carried out in Chapters 5–6.

In the case of Poland, the interval between Phase I (the establishment of the authoritarian regime) and Phase III (the attempt at a democratic breakthrough) is approximately forty-five years. Over this period we discover cumulative changes resulting from long-term processes of political mobilization and culture shift that forced democratization as an option upon the embattled incumbents. The post-breakthrough system runs from the end of the Phase III decision stage up to the mid-1990s—an interval of not much more than five years. This is too little time to warrant full confidence about the consolidation of the democratic system, but it is time enough to permit a relatively clear depiction of the Polish Republic's overall shape, structure, and direction.

Adapting the CCC Framework to the Study of Polish Democracy

Three issues related to the use of the CCC framework need to be considered before we apply it to the study of democratization in Poland: causality, the scope of the analysis, and the status of alternative explanatory frameworks.

On the basis of just one case, it is difficult to make confident assertions about the causal relationships underlying a democratic breakthrough. No matter how meticulously we study the Polish example and how well the empirical findings prove to fit the theoretical expectations of the CCC model, any causal claims we may advance will be precarious. They can be assailed as reflecting a form of historical determinism ("why-it-was-necessary" argumentation), ascribed intentionality and agency ("how-it-was-possible" argumentation), triviality, or ex post facto rationalization.[46] While the CCC framework aims at providing causal stories, as noted above, it is used here as an explanatory rather than a causal framework.

Certain associations were of course necessary for the democratization process to unfold in Poland. For example, it has been claimed that Gorbachev's appointment as Soviet leader and the policies he advocated were possible only because Solidarity had earlier demonstrated the widespread desire for reforms in a socialist society, but we can identify indisputable antecedents of Solidarity itself. This social movement would not have been possible without the learning experiences undergone by workers and intellectuals in the 1956, 1968, 1970, and 1976 Polish crises. In turn, we can trace a consequence of the Gorbachev phenomenon: The democratic breakthroughs in Poland and neighboring states would not have occurred as they did in 1989 had it not been for the presence of a benign Soviet leader. Solidarity did not cause the Soviet politburo to appoint Gorbachev in 1985 any more than Gorbachev can be considered the architect of 1989, the annus mirabilis. Yet Solidarity and Gorbachev were necessary antecedents of subsequent developmental episodes.

Instead of causal claims, then, the objective is insight into why events unfolded in one way and not another in Poland. The CCC framework rejects historical or cultural determinism and, instead, assigns importance to the distinct conjunctions of local conditions. Using a "case/narrative approach is thus a move first to a new way of regarding cases—as fuzzy realities with autonomously defined complex properties—and a move second to seeing cases as engaged in a perpetual dialogue with their environment, a dialogue of action and constraint that we call plot."[47] Although preferring complex explanations to strict causal claims, this study also seeks parsimony—"simplifying complexity in a theoretically guided manner."[48] Employing an analytic framework such as the CCC enables us to piece together a meaningful image from scattered evidence and to isolate the key aspects of a case, a process sometimes called data enhancement.[49]

The second aspect of this book's use of the CCC model concerns its scope. The model provides a comprehensive list of factors contributing to democratic breakthroughs, but such a four-phase, multimethod, multivariate framework raises the question what if anything the model leaves out of the analysis.[50] In defense of its broad scope, the authors of the CCC framework point to the characteristics of regime change: "These are enormously complex processes which require the study of both elites and masses, culture and institutions, longer-term processes of change and short-term choices."[51] The overarching, unrestrictive nature of the CCC framework is helpful in studying longer-term processes, and it especially highlights the interconnected nature and interplay of system components—society, economy, and the polity. Moreover, like other qualitative approaches the model consists of a series of ordering concepts, and, as Charles Ragin has stressed, "Without concepts, it is impossible to select evidence, arrange facts, or make sense of the infinite amount of information that can be gleaned from a single case."[52]

Finally, my application of the CCC framework is intended not to exclude but to incorporate other explanatory theories whenever possible. By setting out the many factors that have to be considered in studying regime change, the CCC model invites the use of specific paradigms to address particular issue areas. Thus, important hypotheses derived from a plethora of theories about democratization can be tested. For example, an enormous literature has emerged dealing with transitions—called by Philippe Schmitter, a major contributor to the subject, "transitology."[53] This literature puts forward a myriad of explanations for the movement of so many countries from authoritarian to democratic rule over the past decade. By reviewing such alternative theories we enhance the explanatory power of the CCC framework. Again, in examining Poland's 1989 roundtable negotiations, coalitional analysis can be supplemented by an interactionist framework that highlights the dynamics of bargaining between rulers and opposition. Finally, in describing efforts to institutionalize democracy after the transition, the specialized literature on the new institutionalism and on presidentialism can inform our account. In this way, my application of the CCC framework seeks to make effective use of specialized middle-level theorizing about specific phases and factors.

One problem largely ignored by regime-change theory is whether there can be transition *back to* a preexisting political system. Is today's so-called Polish Third Republic really building upon the interwar Second Republic? The next chapter covers Poland's historical discontinuities and suggests the extent to which the present system has its origin in earlier developmental episodes.

Notes

1. Although I prefer to assign Poland to *Central Europe,* I use that term interchangeably with *Eastern Europe* in this book. To refer to Poland exclusively as part of Central Europe would be retroactively to abandon the conventional terminology used for decades to describe the Soviet bloc. Considering Poland Central European is just one of the competing visions of where its future lies. For an informed introductory discussion, see Timothy Garton Ash, "Does Central Europe Exist?" in T. Garton Ash, *The Uses of Adversity: Essays on the Fate of Central Europe.* New York: Vintage, 1990, pp. 179–213. See also Adam Michnik, "The Two Faces of Europe," *The New York Review of Books,* July 19, 1990.

2. Adam Przeworski, *Democracy and the Market: Political and Economic Reforms in Eastern Europe and Latin America.* Cambridge: Cambridge University Press, 1991, p. 26.

3. Scott Mainwaring, Guillermo O'Donnell, and J. Samuel Valenzuela (eds.), *Issues in Democratic Consolidation.* South Bend, IN: University of Notre Dame Press, 1992, p. 3.

4. Ralf Dahrendorf, *Reflections on the Revolution in Europe.* New York: Times Books, 1990.

5. Giuseppe di Palma, *To Craft Democracies: An Essay on Democratic Transitions.* Berkeley: University of California Press, 1990, chap. 7.

6. Zbigniew Brzezinski, *Out of Control: Global Turmoil on the Eve of the 21st Century.* New York: Collier Books, 1993, p. 216.

7. Guillermo O'Donnell, "Transitions, Continuities, and Paradoxes," in Mainwaring, O'Donnell, and Valenzuela, *Issues in Democratic Consolidation,* p. 2.

8. For example, see Frances Millard, *The Anatomy of the New Poland: Post-Communist Politics in Its First Phase.* Aldershot, England: Edward Elgar, 1994.

9. Alexis de Tocqueville, *Democracy in America.* Edited by J. P. Mayer. Garden City, NY: Anchor Books, 1969, p. 277.

10. I refer to research focusing on specific aspects of the consolidation of democracies in subsequent chapters. An early comprehensive effort is Enrique A. Baloyra, *Comparing New Democracies: Transition and Consolidation in Mediterranean Europe and the Southern Cone.* Boulder: Westview Press, 1987.

11. *Postcommunist* is used in Poland to denote political parties and ideologies that were part of the communist system and have since been overhauled. In Western usage it refers to all the political developments that have followed the communist regime.

12. For an excellent summary of the recent literature on democratization, see Doh Chull Shin, "On the Third Wave of Democratization: A Synthesis and Evaluation of Recent Theory and Research," *World Politics,* 47, no. 1 (October 1994), 135–170.

13. Samuel P. Huntington, *The Third Wave: Democratization in the Late Twentieth Century.* Norman, OK: University of Oklahoma Press, 1991, pp. 38–39.

14. For a succinct exposition of Adam Smith's general theory, see Donald Winch, *Adam Smith's Politics: An Essay in Historiographic Revision.* Cambridge: Cambridge University Press, 1978.

15. Max Weber, "Socialism," in *Weber: Selections in Translation*. Edited by W. G. Runciman. Cambridge: Cambridge University Press, 1978, pp. 251–262.

16. Barrington Moore, *Social Origins of Dictatorship and Democracy*. Boston: Beacon Press, 1966, chap. 7.

17. I review the relevant theories of transition in Chapters 4 and 5.

18. See especially di Palma, *To Craft Democracies*.

19. Confidence in the ability to manage a democratic transition underlay the 1994 U.S. intervention in Haiti.

20. Robert Dahl, *Polyarchy*. New Haven: Yale University Press, 1971.

21. John A. Hall, "Consolidations of Democracy," in David Held (ed.), *Prospects for Democracy: North, South, East, West*. Stanford: Stanford University Press, 1993, p. 277.

22. Gary King, Robert O. Keohane, and Sidney Verba, *Designing Social Inquiry: Scientific Inference in Qualitative Research*. Princeton: Princeton University Press, 1994, p. 50.

23. An example of a historical narrative as opposed to a causal story is Adam B. Ulam's intended magnum opus *The Communists: The Story of Power and Lost Illusions 1948–1991*. New York: Scribner, 1992. It is largely an unstructured, atheoretical account.

24. Philippe C. Schmitter with Terry Lynn Karl, "The Conceptual Travels of Transitologists and Consolidologists: How Far to the East Should They Attempt to Go?" *Slavic Review*, 53, no. 1 (Spring 1994), 184, n. 21.

25. The earliest functionalist analysis of cultural institutions is found in Bronisław Malinowski, *Argonauts of the Western Pacific*. New York: Dutton, 1922, chap. 1.

26. See Jon Elster, *Explaining Technical Change*. Cambridge: Cambridge University Press, 1988, chap. 2.

27. Daniel Little, *Varieties of Social Explanation: An Introduction to the Philosophy of Social Science*. Boulder: Westview Press, 1991, p. 92.

28. Little, *Varieties of Social Explanation*, p. 104.

29. Although he had referred to structural-functionalism as early as in a 1935 article in the *American Anthropologist*, the most detailed exposition came with A. R. Radcliffe-Brown, *Structure and Function in Primitive Society*. London: Cohen and West, 1952.

30. Gabriel A. Almond and G. Bingham Powell Jr., *Comparative Politics Today: A World View*. Boston: Little, Brown, 1984, pp. 5–13.

31. Gabriel A. Almond, Scott C. Flanagan, Robert J. Mundt (eds.), *Crisis, Choice, and Change: Historical Studies of Political Development*. Boston: Little, Brown, 1973.

32. Little, *Varieties of Social Explanation*, p. 30.

33. Gabriel A. Almond, "Separate Tables: Schools and Sects in Political Science," *PS*, 21 (Fall 1988), 828–842. See also his *A Discipline Divided*. Newbury Park, CA: Sage, 1990.

34. Gabriel A. Almond, "The Systematic Study of Democratization," in Gabriel A. Almond, Scott C. Flanagan, and Robert Mundt (eds.), *Crisis, Choice, and Change Revisited*, forthcoming.

35. This account of the motivations for modifying the original CCC model draws on Scott C. Flanagan and Robert J. Mundt, "Adapting the Crisis Choice and Change Model to the Study of Transitions to Democracy," paper presented at the Workshop on Case Studies in Democratization, Annual Meeting of the American Political Science Association, Washington, DC, September 2–5, 1993.

36. Scott C. Flanagan, "Models and Methods of Analysis," in Almond, Flanagan, and Mundt, *Crisis, Choice, and Change*, p. 48. His process model is found on p. 49.

37. To understand the arcaneness of the earlier methodology, see appendix A of *Crisis,*

Choice, and Change on resource and distance estimates, appendix B on the index of polarization, and appendix C on coalition formation measures.

38. Karl Deutsch, "Toward an Inventory of Basic Trends and Patterns in Comparative and International Politics," *American Political Science Review,* 54 (March 1960), 34–57.

39. The operationalization of the revised model (now termed CCC-II) involves case studies of democratic breakthroughs in Brazil, Mexico, Poland (which I analyze in chapter-length form), Russia, South Africa, South Korea, and Taiwan, among others. See Almond, Flanagan, and Mundt, *Crisis, Choice, and Change Revisited.* The description of the re-designed framework comes from Chapter 2 of this book. See also Flanagan and Mundt, "Adapting the Crisis Choice and Change Model."

40. See Robert Dahl, *Polyarchy: Participation and Opposition.* New Haven: Yale University Press, 1971.

41. For theoretical insight on consensual transitions, see Donald Share, "Transitions to Democracy and Transitions Through Transaction," *Comparative Political Studies,* 19 (1987), 525–548.

42. For an example of such research, see Scott C. Flanagan, "Value Change in Industrial Societies," *American Political Science Review,* 81 (December 1987), 1303–1319. Phase II of the CCC model posits several intervening variables—the regime's long-term performance and changes in social structure and mass alignments—as distinct from independent variables such as socioeconomic change. A reviewer of an earlier draft of this book has contended that such a distinction is untenable in practice, and I agree. My Phase II framework is, therefore, a streamlined version of the CCC model.

43. For one such study, see Keith Jaggers, "The Farewell Party: A Rational Choice Approach to Democratization," paper presented at the Annual Meeting of the Midwest Political Science Association, Chicago, April 15–17, 1993.

44. Huntington, *The Third Wave;* Francis Fukuyama, *The End of History and the Last Man.* New York: Free Press, 1992.

45. Przeworski, *Democracy and the Market.*

46. The why-necessary–how-possible dichotomy is taken from Little, *Varieties of Social Explanation,* p. 4. The triviality of social science laws was most persuasively argued by Karl Popper, *The Open Society and Its Enemies.* Princeton: Princeton University Press, 1950.

47. Andrew Abbott, "What Do Cases Do? Some Notes on Activity in Sociological Analysis," in Charles C. Ragin and Howard S. Becker (eds.), *What Is a Case? Exploring the Foundations of Social Inquiry.* Cambridge: Cambridge University Press, 1992, p. 65.

48. Charles Ragin, *The Comparative Method.* Berkeley: University of California Press, 1987, p. 83.

49. Charles C. Ragin, *Constructing Social Research.* Thousand Oaks, CA: Pine Forge Press, 1994, p. 92.

50. This was a favorite criticism of Aaron Wildavsky.

51. Gabriel A. Almond, Scott C. Flanagan, and Robert J. Mundt, "*Crisis, Choice, and Change* in Retrospect," *Government and Opposition,* 27, no. 3 (Summer 1992), 366.

52. Ragin, *Constructing Social Research,* p. 91.

53. The origins of transitology lie in Guillermo O'Donnell, Philippe Schmitter, and Laurence Whitehead (eds.), *Transitions from Authoritarian Rule,* 4 vols. Baltimore: Johns Hopkins University Press, 1986. On more recent transitology, see Terry Lynn Karl and Philippe C. Schmitter, "Modes of Transition in Latin America, Southern and Eastern Europe," *International Social Science Journal,* 128 (1991), 269–284.

1

Historic Discontinuities: Dynasties, Republics, Partitions

Early in the nineteenth century, the Russian poet Alexander Pushkin remarked that the history of Poland was and ought to be a disaster. In 1939, Russia's Foreign Minister Vyacheslav Molotov contemptuously referred to Poland as the bastard offspring of the Versailles Treaty. Both observations came at a time when Poland had been dismantled as an independent state. After Pushkin's death, Poland was not to reappear on the map of Europe until 1918. Polish historians today debate whether the country did not also disappear from the political map of Europe during the Soviet-imposed communist period.

A nation's history does not end when it has lost its statehood and independence. Historical revindications often serve as a powerful force of national mobilization in contemporary movements. The cynical eighteenth-century partitions of Poland, just like the forcible mid-twentieth-century incorporation of Poland into the Soviet political bloc, remain points of reference for many Poles and color their world outlook.

Relations with Russia and attitudes toward socialism have certainly affected Poland's political development in this century, but the nation's efforts at establishing constitutional rule, checking the power of its leaders, and reacting to foreign threats also need to be examined if we are to make sense of the character of the postwar communism regime, its prolonged crisis and sudden collapse, and the system that came to take its place—the so-called Third Republic. Before examining the Phase I antecedent communist regime, this chapter sets out to describe the many other regimes—monarchies, republics, and foreign occupations—that Poland has experienced in its long history.

Dynastic Poland

The Polish language belongs to the western group of Slavic languages that includes Czech and Slovak. Poles form part of an even wider Slavic world that encompasses an eastern linguistic group—composed of Russian, Belarus, and Ukrainian—and a southern group—Serbo-Croatian, Slovene, and Bulgarian. Much historical evidence suggests that the original home of all the Slavs was territory that came to be ruled by Polish kings between the fourteenth and eighteenth centuries.

The ancestors of the Poles were drawn from such different ethnographic groups as the Polanie (literally, "dwellers of the plain"), Pomeranians ("coast dwellers"), Mazovians, and Silesians. The conditions initially promoting physical security for these tribes also retarded the establishment of a unified state. As the historian Oskar Halecki writes, "Dwelling in the center of the Slav world, removed from the routes of the great migrations and even from the great trade routes, the tribes which were to form the Polish nation only experienced later the grave difficulties and dangers that beset their neighbors."[1] But when the Germanic danger became acute, the various tribes accepted the leadership of the Polanie, and this name was soon employed to designate all of these groups. Relative security together with the geographical dispersion of the tribes delayed the founding of a Polish state until the second half of the tenth century—about a century after Slavic states had emerged in Carinthia (in what is now Austria), Moravia, Kievan Rus, and Bulgaria.

Polish history is generally considered to have begun in 966, the year Mieszko I of the Piast dynasty converted to Christianity and became the nation's first king. External relations during Mieszko's twenty-six-year reign—he died in 992—prefigured much of Polish history. His conversion was designed to strengthen Poland's alliance with Bohemia in the face of a Germanic threat, yet it was a Rus invasion in 981 that stripped the country of much of its land. Mieszko then turned to the Apostolic See for protection and obtained its recognition of Poland as an independent church province and separate kingdom. But it was his son Bolesław Chrobry (967–1025) who did most to consolidate Piast rule over the Polish tribes, symbolized in his coronation on Easter Day 1025. Accordingly, Poland's first chronicler, Gallus Anonymus, described Bolesław as "the father of these lands, defender, lord."[2]

The last ruler of the Piast dynasty, Kazimierz the Great (1310–1370), helped usher in Poland's Golden Age. Kazimierz's achievements included the establishment of Central Europe's second university in Kraków in 1364 (a university had been established in Prague in 1348), the first codification of Polish law, the promotion of trade and commerce between Polish cities, the settlement of previously uninhabited regions, increased protection for oppressed peoples (such as Jews fleeing persecution in Western Europe and peasants threatened with famine), the construction of fortified castles along Polish borders, and the creation of a permanent force of mercenaries to defend these borders. Kazimierz also confronted the Order of the Teutonic Knights at the height of its power and was able to conclude a favorable peace treaty that restored Pomerania to Poland and gave the country access to the Baltic Sea. The Polish saying that Kazimierz inherited a Poland built of wood and bequeathed to posterity a Poland made of stone is more than just figuratively true.

After Kazimierz's death, the crown of the Piasts was offered to the Hungarian dynasty. A twelve-year-old Hungarian princess, Jadwiga, was given in marriage to the favorite of the Polish nobility, Jagiełło, Grand Duke of Lithuania. This union was profoundly to shape the subsequent political development of the Polish state. The creation of the Polish-Lithuanian union transformed the ethnically homogeneous state of the Piasts into a multinational one. The political union created new frontiers that extended from the Baltic to the Black Sea. Large populations of Ukrainians and Belarus were incorporated into the state. The structure of power within the new kingdom was also dramatically changed. Just as Jagiełło had been chosen by the nobility, so in future the Polish throne was to be subject to elective confirmation by this class. In 1386 Jagiełło was formally elected king, baptized into Catholicism, married to the initially disconsolate Jadwiga, and given an elaborate coronation ceremony. The dynastic transfer consummated in that year produced major territorial, ethnic, and structural shifts in the Polish state. It also made possible one of the most glorious military victories in Polish and Lithuanian history—the final defeat of the Teutonic Order at the battle of Grunwald in 1410.

In the second half of the fifteenth century, Poland's internal politics shifted toward a type of democracy exercised by and for the nobility. At this time, regional assemblies (*sejmiki*) began to assert influence in central affairs, thereby increasing gentry encroachment on the power of the wealthy magnates. Although the nobility, or *szlachta*, had generally accepted the legal equality of everyone in its ranks regardless of individual wealth or power, this did not preclude political conflict between groups within this class. By 1493 the Sejm (or national parliament) had been divided into an upper chamber, or Senate, consisting of bishops and high-ranking magnates and a lower Chamber of Deputies representing the lesser gentry. This latter group made up close to 10 percent of the population and represented the largest enfranchised class in Europe (compared with 2 percent enfranchised in Russia and 1 percent in France). The Chamber also included token representation for the burgher class, drawn exclusively from Kraków. Conflict between the two chambers and the strata they represented became a regular feature of Polish politics.

The Polish nobility was a remarkably heterogeneous class at this time. As one Polish historian observed, "In it were the great lords, holders of the highest positions in the state, owners of substantial landed estates, possessors of considerable wealth. . . . At the other end of the spectrum were the poor gentry, descendants of medieval knights, warriors or courtiers, entitled to noble rank and privileges but frequently possessing little or no land."[3] Members of the first group, the magnates, disposed of exceptional power as a result of wealth and office. Accordingly, they "acted as the focus of political activity, as the center around which factions formed; they were the bridges between the central government and the provincial nobility. . . . In many spheres of activity they simply replaced the functions of the royal court and the central government."[4] Not surprisingly, the monarchy often sought out the lower nobility as allies to check the power of the magnates, but the royal pursuit of *absolutum dominium* was irreconcilable with the self-interest of the *szlachta*.

In the mid-fifteenth century, the country's ruling gentry became conscious of Poland's role as *antemurale christianitatis*—Roman Catholicism's easternmost bulwark. Over the next centuries, this Polish version of manifest destiny or mission came to be interpreted in secular, political terms. Poland was viewed as the outpost of European civilization beyond which Russian and Asiatic culture began. As a country at the crossroads of Western and Eastern civilizations, Poland had to face threats both from the Teutonic Order and from the Mongols, Tatars, and Turks to the east. A philosophy emerged that became known as Sarmatianism. This name was derived from the ancient tribe that had lived on the banks of the Dneister River seven centuries before Christ. Jan Długosz, a historian of Poland writing in the fifteenth century, made this myth more credible as he described how these inhabitants of proto-Slavonic lands had conquered local tribes and come to be the ruling elite. The Sarmatian ideology claimed a special mission for Poland—a shield protecting Christianity from paganism. The crowning glory of this historic mission occurred in 1683, when King Jan Sobieski defeated the Turkish armies outside of Vienna, thereby saving Christian Europe from Islam.

The gentry in the Commonwealth of Poland invoked its supposed Sarmatian origins in assuming all the obligations associated with Poland's manifest destiny. The Sarmatian was a heroic knight and a defender of the faith and the fatherland. The myth of the *szlachta*'s common ancestry contributed to the integration of otherwise diverse ranks of the nobility and made other differentiating factors such as language spoken, religion practiced, or wealth accumulated less important. Furthermore, the Sarmatian myth promoted cultural homogeneity within the Commonwealth and led to widespread Polonization of the gentry of Lithuania and Ruthenia (Ukraine).

Two largely unintended consequences followed from the Sarmatian myth. First, Polish burghers and peasants were not treated as integral parts of the nation because their ancestry was considered different. As with Athenian democracy, the exclusion of certain people from the community and the denial to them of political rights were not seen as in contradiction with the notion of democracy. So long as all noblemen enjoyed equal privileges and responsibilities, the crucial test of *szlachta* democracy was passed. But *not* utilizing common ethnicity as the basis for nationhood was eventually to produce mixed foci of identity, divided loyalties, and political tensions within the Polish state.

The second by-product of Sarmatianism was, paradoxically, the "'easternization' of Polish national consciousness," as the historian Andrzej Walicki has contended. Collaboration between the Polish elite and the Polonized elites of Lithuania and Ukraine was pursued at the expense of contacts with the West. Moreover, according to Walicki,

> The Sarmatian ideology developed the concept of a cultural uniqueness of "Sarmatia," its fundamental difference from everything Western. The traditional view of Poland as

the "bulwark of Christianity" ceased to be identical with perceiving Poland as a part and parcel of the West. On the contrary: the ideologists of Sarmatianism constantly warned their compatriots against Western royalism and moral corruption.[5]

Whereas republicanism seemed to locate Poland squarely in the Western European tradition, Sarmatianism pulled the country in the opposite direction. These countervailing tendencies have marked Polish society through to the present century.

Up to the time of the partitions in the late eighteenth century, Poland remained a kingdom, which would appear to be at odds with the idea of republican government. But the king's role was severely constricted by the powers held by the gentry, and in some ways he was limited to functions not unlike those performed by a modern ceremonial head of state. The Polish nobility was convinced of the superiority of its democratic, representative, republican-style system, and the country became identified with *szlachta* democracy rather than monarchy. And despite the *antemurale christianitatis* myth, this form of democratic order also limited the influence of the Catholic church in state matters. As one scholar put it, "*Szlachta* democracy of the federalist republic of nobles frustrated both centralized absolutism and the identification of church and state. Early modern Poland became a haven for dissenting faiths fleeing generalized religious warfare in Europe."[6]

When compared with some of the absolutist, monarchical, and theocratic systems found elsewhere in Europe at the time, Poland's political system seemed exceptional indeed. The Latin term *res publica* (in Polish, *rzeczpospolita*) was used by nobles to indicate this political system's direct descent from the Roman Republic, much in the way that Thomas Jefferson associated fledgling American democracy with Roman origins.

The historic controversy over the Sarmatian myth and the notion of *antemurale christianitatis* has a contemporary resonance. Poland's postcommunist political and intellectual leaders have been engaged in a debate about what the country's status in Europe should be. Although they couch it in different language, advocates of Poland's speedy admission into organizations such as the European Union (EU) and the North Atlantic Treaty Organization (NATO) have in mind Poland's role as a bulwark of Western civilization against the less civilized East. Those who advocate regional cooperation and integration stress common Slavic bonds—though few leaders in Poland today would go so far as to advocate some form of pan-Slavism. In urging Poland to rely on traditional Central European alliance structures the regionalists are, consciously or not, returning to central elements of Sarmatian ideology.

In light of Poland's mixed success so far in becoming a full participant in European politics, the controversy over Sarmatianism has intensified. The historian Janusz Tazbir, for example, asks rhetorically how long the West expects Poles to continue to serve as an eastern bulwark of Western civilization. He questions whether Western Europe ever treated Poland as a full-fledged European country.[7] He notes that in the fifteenth and sixteenth centuries Polish kings eagerly waged

wars against the Turks and in the seventeenth century Poland drove back successive invasions by Turks and Tatars. Yet the only recognition of these historic exploits by an ungrateful and cynical Western Europe was peripheral status providing little real satisfaction to Polish leaders.

Poles' sense of marginalization from Europe increased with the final partition
of the country and, later, the failure of the 1831 insurrection. Many were especially
bitter toward France for lack of tangible support and considered French foreign
policy shortsighted. Some expected France to be revisited soon by the "Cossacks"—pejorative for Russians—as had occurred in 1815, when Alexander I pa-
raded down the Champs Elysée in triumph after his victories over Napoleon. Predictably, the negative heroine of the Romantic poet Adam Mickiewicz's *Books of
the Polish Nation and Polish Pilgrimage* (*Księgach narodu polskiego i pielgrzymstwa
polskiego*)—sometimes branded as a sourcebook for xenophobia—was not Russia
but France.

According to Tazbir, the West's indifference to Poland's fate continued into the
twentieth century. Pleas directed toward France, England, and other Western
powers to send troops to defend and, if need be, die for Gdańsk in 1939, for Wilno
and Lwów in 1944–1945, and for a truly independent Poland in 1944–1947 went
unheeded. Early help for Poland might, he argues, have reduced the numbers of
Western soldiers who subsequently had to die fighting for their own countries but
against the same enemies—Hitler, Stalin, and other communist leaders. Not without irony, the Polish historian remarks that no matter how well Poles spoke
French or English, they seemed never to be able to make themselves understood
by these nations' leaders.

Finally, Tazbir sounds a warning about Poland's future. He points to the historical view that the period of *szlachta* democracy had put a definitive end to anarchy
in the country. But this same *szlachta* also was convinced that Europe would never
permit Poland to be divided. In fact, of course, Europe both permitted and confirmed Poland's dismemberment. Whether the Western type of liberal democracy
adopted in Poland late in the twentieth century would prove more adept at eliminating anarchy and ensuring the country's territorial integrity remains unclear to
Tazbir as to many Poles.

The Republican Commonwealth
and Its Political Principles

The sixteenth-century Reformation in Poland, even though encompassing a small
minority of the population, appears to have nudged the country toward greater
liberalism. It seemed naturally to complement Poland's developing democratic
features. Steps toward greater tolerance were taken when legal recognition was extended to Protestantism in 1555 and the Confederation of Warsaw proclaimed the
principles of religious toleration and religious equality in 1573. The sixteenth cen-

tury also marked the Golden Age of Polish culture, which was contemporaneous with the Polish Renaissance. The country's capital, Kraków, and its royal court, seated in nearby Wawel Castle, became a cosmopolitan center for the arts—this at a time when Ivan the Terrible ruled Russia. This was the age of the astronomer Nicolaus Copernicus, the lyric poet Jan Kochanowski, and the prose writer regarded as the father of Polish literature, Mikołaj Rey.

But even as Polish society was apparently becoming more liberal, confrontation with Muscovy cast a shadow over the country's politics. The Polish-Lithuanian kingdom had been anchored in a union personified by the king, but more durable foundations were needed to fend off Muscovite ambitions in the Baltic region. In 1569 the Union of Lublin sought to institutionalize the relationship by requiring that the separate parliaments of Poland and Lithuania meet jointly to enact legislation. The site of the meetings was to be Warsaw, a town roughly equidistant from the two capitals, Kraków and Vilnius. In 1596, Warsaw officially became the new capital of the kingdom.

The Union of Lublin soon proved to be of exceptional significance when Zygmunt II died in 1572 without leaving an heir, thereby putting an end to the Jagiellon dynasty. The gentry assembled to select a successor and decided to adopt a radical new principle, "one nobleman, one vote," as the method for electing the Polish monarch. This device became the political cornerstone of the post-Jagiellonian Republican Commonwealth, more accurately, the democratic kingdom. Power was now formally vested in the *szlachta*.

Accordingly, in 1573, some 50,000 members representing all ranks of the nobility convened in Warsaw and elected a Frenchman, Henri de Valois, to be king. This first democratic election did not produce a wise choice, for within a year Henri had become disappointed with *szlachta* democracy. It seemed to him to produce little but strife, and he fled to France, where a more secure throne awaited him. In 1575 another convocation was held, and after a bitter dispute over rival candidates the *szlachta* again looked to Hungary and again was not disappointed. The Transylvanian prince Stefan Batory was chosen, and though he ruled Poland for only ten years he became legendary for his exploits in wars with Russia. Under Batory's rule the Commonwealth's eastern territories were consolidated as never before or after.

Heartened by victories over Russia, the rulers of the Commonwealth hatched elaborate schemes designed to extend Polish influence into the tsarist court itself. The figure of False Dimitri, an obscure Russian who had arrived in Poland with claims to the throne of Muscovy, served as a convenient pretext for the ambitious Polish king Zygmunt III Vasa to mount a campaign against Russia. Zygmunt wanted nothing less than the incorporation of Russia into the Commonwealth and the conversion of its heathen people to Catholicism. His successes were as impressive as they were short-lived: Smolensk was captured and Moscow briefly held. Zygmunt's son Władysław was even elected tsar for a brief time. When this arrangement proved untenable, False Dimitri was named tsar and his Polish wife,

Marina Mniszech, tsarina. They held their thrones in the Kremlin for all of ten days. The Polish garrison was then driven out of Moscow, and the Russian boyars chose Michael Romanov to lead the country out of its time of troubles. The Romanovs ruled over an ever-expanding Russian Empire until 1917.

By the mid-seventeenth century, the Republic was more expansive than ever but, inevitably, more vulnerable to enemies surrounding it. To make matters worse, the composition of Poland's ruling elite was less multiethnic than it had been under the Jagiellonian state, and this strengthened centrifugal tendencies among non-Polish nations. The country seemed to fall prey to the perils of imperial overstretch: It had overextended its rule and lacked the economic and military capacity to keep order in the multiethnic state.

A worsening military balance of power was crucial in sealing Poland's ultimate fate, but the country's political structure contributed immensely to its instability and the Commonwealth's eventual collapse. On the one hand, constitutional laws that incorporated the ideas of liberty, equality, and government based on the consent of a significant part of the nation appeared to enshrine the important principle of the rule of law *non Rex sed lex regnat.* The gentry's interests were best served by a system that asserted libertarian, republican values. On the other hand, such political arrangements, though arguably ahead of their time, contributed to a general breakdown of authority and to a popular belief that *Polska nierządem stoi* ("Poland is governed by unrule"). Indeed, foreign adversaries were to use the argument that Poland was ungovernable to justify its dismemberment.

The procedure for electing kings, whether to confirm them in office as under the Jagiellon dynasty or to choose them from a slate of candidates as after 1572, produced intrigues and infighting, and the system compelled the monarch to earn power and prestige rather than to assume them ex officio. Another destabilizing mechanism was the *pacta conventa,* which identified the king's personal obligations to the country in the pivotal areas of foreign policy and finance. Even before his coronation, he had to pledge that he would abide by the terms set by the lower chamber. The related Henrician Articles, promulgated by Henri de Valois in 1573, further obliged the monarch to convene the Sejm regularly and obtain the advice of its permanent council at all times. Failure to comply with the articles freed the gentry from its oath of allegiance and officially sanctioned opposition to the king (*de non praestanda obedientia*). As if these were not sufficient controls on royal power, in 1430 the king recognized the principle of *neminem captivabimus nisi iure victum,* which granted all noblemen personal immunity from arrest until a court could pass sentence and prohibited the confiscation of their land without a court order. In this way, a monarch faced considerable legal obstacles in trying to eliminate political opponents.

There were other institutional arrangements that promoted *szlachta* democracy. At the beginning of the sixteenth century the Sejm passed the act of *incompatibilitas,* which prohibited any individual from holding more than one high state office. Furthermore, lands formally belonging to the crown were to be managed by the Sejm, not by the king. Already in 1505 the famous principle of *nihil novi* found expression in Polish jurisprudence; it meant that "nothing new" in the way of legislation could be enacted by the king unless it received the consent of both chambers. Finally, the sixteenth-century execution-of-law movement insisted that high state officials be held accountable to the gentry. This elaborate checks-and-balances system limiting the prerogatives of the monarch made the Polish state more democratic—and certainly more prone to anarchy—than any European state of the time.

Another insidious political principle that undermined the Commonwealth was *confederatio*, first employed at the beginning of the fourteenth century but possibly having even earlier origins. It sanctioned the mobilization of groups of citizens, specifically the nobles and burghers, for the redress of grievances. A group could also declare itself a confederation in order to advance its special interests; all that was required was a majority vote among those attending the assembly. In sum, "confederation was a legal procedure. It was undertaken in the name of the common good, by citizens acting in defense of the law, and conscious of its protection."[8] But by 1606 confederation had grown into something more, *rokosz,* "a legalized insurrection whereby the nation in arms could even impeach the king."[9] In that year Zygmunt III Vasa, a monarch brought from Sweden and accustomed to much broader royal authority than the Polish nobility allowed, was threatened with deportation for failing to pay adequate attention to the caprices of the gentry. Although this episode was subsequently considered to be a regrettable misunderstanding that had produced unnecessary bloodshed between royalist forces and rebels, fear of absolute government had become so acute among the nobility that it led to the enshrinement of the most famous principle of the Polish Commonwealth, the liberum veto.

The crucial feature of this mechanism was the ability of one member of the Sejm to veto any act under consideration by it. For some time, resort to liberum veto was unnecessary because agreements were carefully worked out prior to Sejm sessions in order to secure unanimity. In 1580, however, the power of the Sejm to impose taxation was quashed when a disgruntled representative invoked this principle. Worse was to come: In 1652 all legislation enacted during a session of the Sejm was nullified when one nobleman cast a veto. Six years later the liberum veto was employed before the session had even begun, thereby paralyzing the actions of central government. Under August III (1733–1763) only one session of the Sejm was able to pass any legislation at all. As one historian reconstructed the *szlachta*'s reasoning in support of this principle, "The *liberum veto* would defend the sovereignty of the individual. God and Europe would defend that of the *Rzecz-pospolita.*"[10] As we shall see, this reasoning proved flawed.

The sheer number of procedures designed as checks on autocracy inevitably engendered the opposite—political chaos and disorder. Some strata of the nobility began to interpret the principles of *de non praestanda obedientia, rokosz,* and liberum veto in conjunction. Taken together, they seemed to spell *liberum conspiro*—"the right to conspire against authority." The so-called Golden Freedom of the Polish nobility was increasingly perceived by leaders of other countries, in particular the Russian tsars, as a way to keep the Polish Republic weak, disorganized, and divided. Members of the Polish nobility were played off against each other, a number of prominent nobles came to serve the interests of the Romanovs, and inherent centrifugal forces in the system of government were exacerbated. Although the Polish state had devised an ingenious system of checks and balances meant to preserve the democracy of the gentry, this system also generated self-destructive tendencies, especially when skillfully exploited by Poland's foes.

The Destruction of the Republic

The political principles of the Republic exacerbated internal instability, but it was a series of armed insurrections and invasions that led directly to the final disintegration of the state. The revolt of the Ukrainian Cossacks in 1648 triggered "the Deluge": In quick succession Tatars, Turks, Russians, and Swedes went to war against Poland. The Swedish army swiftly overran the country and only the miraculous, last-ditch defense of the monastery at Częstochowa in 1655—attributed by devout Poles to the intercession of the Blessed Virgin whose icon, the Black Madonna, is kept there—turned the tide of war. Collaboration by some Polish magnates with foreign armies also produced a short but bitter civil war in 1665–1666.

The last of the Vasa kings, Jan Kazimierz, recognized the urgent need for political reforms and moved toward centralizing power and emancipating the serfs, but the nobility blocked these projects. In this period the Sarmatian myth was rekindled. Once again, the *szlachta* identified itself as the descendants of the ancient Sarmatians and invoked a kind of divine right of the nobility to govern. Jan Kazimierz's designs were frustrated and, like his French predecessor of a century earlier, the embattled monarch abdicated and left for France.

Jan Sobieski, the vanquisher of the Turks at Vienna in 1683, temporarily halted the erosion of the Republic but still failed to introduce a stronger, dynastic form of monarchy. He was bogged down in wars for seventeen years, and paradoxically, his successes ultimately promoted the resurgence of the Habsburg Empire more than they did that of his own country. Moreover, his lack of interest in the eastern borderlands cost Poland dearly. As the historian Norman Davies has written, "In 1686, at the whim of one wayward ambassador, the entire Ukraine, provisionally assigned to Muscovy since the truce of 1667, was needlessly abandoned. This one step . . . marked the transformation of little Muscovy into 'great Russia' and tipped the scales of power in Eastern Europe in Moscow's favor."[11]

The Saxon kings who reigned between 1697 and 1763 were generally absent from and uninterested in the country, and this accelerated the process of political degeneration. The Saxon period was marked by double elections, rival candidacies, and even dethronements and further weakened Poland's place in Europe. Even as unprecedented peace reigned in the country, Poland was becoming a pawn in the strategy of the northern system—the coalition made up of Catherine the Great of Russia and Frederick II of Prussia.

In looking for reasons for Poland's collapse, we should not overlook social and ethnic factors in addition to political ones. Approximately 7 percent of the Polish population in 1791 was made up of burghers. Together with the clergy, who accounted for another 0.5 percent, they enjoyed considerable autonomy from the nobility and possessed legal status protected by royal charters, but played little part in central government (with the inevitable exception of the bishops). Moreover, though a few wealthy burghers could buy their way into *szlachta* ranks, social mobility between the estates—from peasant to burgher to nobleman—was negligible in the seventeenth and eighteenth centuries. In addition, peasant rebellions, particularly among the Cossacks, occurred early in the seventeenth century and should have served as a warning about spreading discontent among the rural population. But *szlachta* democracy stubbornly refused to alter the rigid system of social stratification right up to the death throes of the Republic.

The ethnic makeup of Poland also, obviously, contributed to the erosion of national unity. Although the gentry was almost completely Polonized by the late eighteer.th century, about half of the peasantry was non-Polish, consisting of Ukrainians, Belarus, and Lithuanians. Primarily Polish until the sixteenth century, many towns became ethnically mixed after an influx of German burghers, Dutch Mennonites, Silesian Protestants, and Jewish and Armenian merchants. Large Jewish communities located in urban areas (in addition to rural shtetls) were particularly noteworthy in this period. Seeking a haven from the persecution they were suffering in Western Europe, Jews increasingly migrated to Polish towns. Their proportion of the urban population grew from approximately 10 percent in the early sixteenth century to as much as 80 percent in certain towns in eastern Poland by the eighteenth century. Given such change in social and ethnic structures, it is not surprising that the survival of the Polish state, identified as it had been almost exclusively with the *szlachta*, came under challenge.

Poland's last king was Stanisław August Poniatowski (1764–1795), whose reign corresponded with tsarist Russia's protectorate over Poland. It was Poniatowski's fate to preside over the series of partitions that eliminated the Polish state from the European map. Historians disagree whether he was merely a "creature"—in addition to being a lover—of Catherine the Great or independent and patriotic. From the outset of his reign, he had to contend not only with the powerful Russian empress and with Frederick of Prussia but with his own incorrigible *szlachta*. The Sejm of 1767–1768 demonstrated its intransigence, for example, when it reaffirmed that the Polish state was based on five "eternal and invariable" principles: (1) the free election of kings, (2) the principle of liberum veto, (3) the nobility's right to renounce allegiance to the king, (4) the nobility's exclusive right to hold office, and (5) the nobility's dominion over the peasantry.[12] Unfortunately, within a few decades, it became clear that neither these principles nor the state they governed were eternal and invariable.

Some of these principles were put into practice one last time when the Confederation of Bar rose up against the Polish king. Although quickly crushed with the help of outside Russian troops in 1771, the confederation had extraordinary political significance. It represented a final attempt by the *szlachta* to safeguard its privileged status. More important, it constituted the beginnings of modern Polish nationalism. The uprising by the confederation revealed the military genius of Kazimierz Pułaski, who became an important figure in the American Revolutionary War. It served as the pretext for the first partition undertaken by Russia, Prussia, and Austria of what had become known as the Republic of Anarchy. Finally, the confederation elicited a mixed assessment from the French political philosopher Jean-Jacques Rousseau, who was commissioned to report on the country. In *The Government of Poland,* Rousseau reached this understated conclusion: "It is hard to understand how a state so oddly constituted can have survived for so long." But sensing imminent disaster for the Republic, Rousseau urged: "Establish the republic in the Poles' own hearts, so that it will live on in them despite anything your oppressors may do."[13] This was precisely what Poles had to do for the next century and a half.

The specific plans for annexing various parts of Poland were drawn up by Frederick II as early as 1768, but it was only in 1772 that a formal treaty specifying the lands to be partitioned was concluded. A year later, under duress, Poniatowski and the Sejm formally consented to the partition. The ostensible reason for the first partition was given in the preamble to the treaty:

> In the Name of the Most Holy Trinity! The spirit of faction, the troubles and internecine war which had shaken the Kingdom of Poland for so many years, and the Anarchy which acquires new strength every day . . . give just apprehension for expecting the total decomposition of the state. . . . At the same time, the Powers neighboring on the Republic are burdened with rights and claims which are as ancient as they are legitimate.[14]

The more the government of what remained of Poland tried to reform the country over the next two decades, the more determined were the partitioning powers to have done with Poland as quickly and completely as possible. The Sejm that had been compelled to sanction the partition soon afterward established the first Ministry of Education in Europe—the Commission of National Education. The Four-Year Sejm from 1788 to 1792 introduced unprecedented taxes on revenue from land and on ecclesiastical property. Local government was modernized, and a standing army was established. The famous constitution of May 3, 1791, inspired by the emancipatory ideas of the French Revolution, granted burghers access to public office and representation in the Sejm. And although serfdom was not abolished, peasants were now extended "the protection of the law and the government." Poland was transformed from a nation of gentry to a nation of proprietors.

Reformed in this way, Poland might have been able to foil the ambitions of the partitioning powers. The anarchy and decomposition of the state, cited in 1772 as justification for partition, would undoubtedly have been checked by this remarkable constitutional document. Fearing a revitalized Poland, Russian military forces confronted the new Polish standing army within a year. The threat of full-scale war led to several Polish magnates' signing an act of confederation at Targowica in 1792. This disreputable confederation condemned the May 3 constitution and asked Russian troops to help put down what was viewed as rebellion. Poniatowski cast his lot in with the Targowica confederation. Although perhaps intended only as a political maneuver justified in terms of *raison d'état*, Poniatowski's action was to go down in Polish history as treasonous.

The second partition concluded between Russia and Prussia in 1793 reduced Poland to a rump state. Tadeusz Kościuszko's national insurrection of 1794 foundered and led to bloody reprisals by Russian troops. The spiral of dismemberment continued when the third partition was signed by Russia, Prussia, and Austria in October 1795. All remaining Polish lands were divided up, the king was forced to abdicate, and, by agreement of the three powers, the name Poland was supposed to disappear from international law forever.

The Struggle for Independence

For the next 125 years, the Polish nation was able to survive where the Polish state had not. Still, national survival was by no means a certainty under the partitions.[15] A systematic Germanization process was pursued in the lands occupied by Prussia and, to a lesser extent, Austria. In turn, the Polish population living in lands administered by the tsarist empire was sporadically subjected to violent repression by Russia's rulers. Not surprisingly, Poles organized to confront the occupying powers: "Six times during the years between 1793 and 1864 the Poles rose up to fight for independence and social change. The uprisings disrupted economic development and destroyed hundreds of thousands of the most patriotic families whose properties were confiscated by the partitioning powers."[16]

Some institutional vestiges of the dismembered Polish state remained in the nineteenth century. So long as Napoleon posed a threat to the partitioning powers, Poles felt that a national resurrection was possible. The Duchy of Warsaw, which Napoleon carved out from Prussian-occupied lands, seemed a partial realization of these hopes. But the French emperor's attitude toward his Polish supporters was cynical at best: He used them to buttress his forces in Lombardy, Spain, and even distant Haiti, engaged them in fighting Austria, and marshaled them for his disastrous campaign against Russia in 1812. Napoleon took a Polish mistress, Maria Walewska, who sought favors from him on behalf of her compatriots. Yet he made no firm commitment to help Poles in their struggle for independence, and his defeats at Borodino and Waterloo put an end to even the Duchy of Warsaw's existence. At the Congress of Vienna in 1815, Polish territories were redistributed for a fifth time, among Austria, Prussia, and Russia. One insignificant concession to

Polish nationalism was the creation of a small Congress Kingdom of Poland, with Tsar Alexander I as its king.

Congress Poland symbolized both the expansion of the Russian empire westward and the implicit acknowledgment by the tsar of the Poles' right to limited autonomy. Polish anger over both these developments was expressed in an uprising launched in late November 1830 but crushed by Russian forces by September 1831. A period of bitter repression and forced Russification followed. The Congress constitution was abolished by Tsar Nicholas, state lands were confiscated and deeds transferred to Russian generals and government officials, and the cultural vanguard of Polish society was driven into exile.

But the nationalist movement had not been completely destroyed by repression and emigration. In quick succession other insurrections flared up. In 1846 there was an uprising in Austrian-occupied Galicia, but Austrian leaders played on the ingrained conservatism of the local peasantry and persuaded it to massacre much of the Kraków nobility that had issued the call to arms. Two years later, during the "springtime of nations," revolts were staged in various parts of Poland, extending from Poznań to Lwów. Prince Metternich, the Austrian chancellor, reached this embittered conclusion:

> Polonism is only a formula, the sound of a word underneath which hides a revolution in its most glaring form; it is not a small part of a revolution, but revolution itself. Polonism does not declare war on the monarchies which possess Polish territory, it declares war on all existing institutions and proclaims the destruction of all the common foundations which form the basis of society.

Poles were viewed as conspirators, revolutionaries, anarchists, and even barbarians, inhabiting "swamps, woods and marshes on which wolves and bears swarm in packs and endanger the roads."[17]

In January 1863 Polish insurgents launched one more desperate attack on Russian garrisons. In May a national government was established that received moral support from such Western European states as France, England, the Vatican, and even Austria. Unfortunately, the Polish leadership was fragmented into rival factions. The "reds," or radicals, stressed the indispensability of insurrection to attain independence and the centrality of a peasant revolt to such an insurrection. By contrast, the "whites," led by members of the nobility, sought, initially at least, to reach an accommodation with Russia. Even setting aside internal differences, the uprising was doomed without outside help. By October 1863 it had been brutally suppressed and a number of its leaders hanged. In 1864 Congress Poland was abolished and its territory incorporated into Russia as one of its provinces. The reign of terror instigated by Russian officials was designed to eradicate Polish nationalism once and for all.

Sensing advantages for Germany in Russian repression, Bismarck instituted his own *Kulturkampf* in Prussian-occupied lands. It, too, sought to eliminate all manifestations of Polish language and culture. In stark contrast, following its 1867 *Ausgleich* (compromise) with Hungary, Austria granted virtual autonomy to Galicia in southern Poland. The differential treatment meted out by the partitioning powers left enduring marks on Poland's regional political cultures.

The series of nineteenth-century insurrections left the Poles exhausted and forlorn. Following an analogy drawn by their national poet Mickiewicz, many now believed that Poland, like Christ, was destined to suffer in order to redeem the sins of other nations so that they, too, would become worthy of liberty. In the second half of the nineteenth century Poles came to believe that this cross should be borne heroically and stoically. Catholic messianism helped reinforce the identity of a threatened people, but the role of the church hierarchy has to be treated with circumspection. One historian has pointed out that "the fusion of the Polish national and Catholic identities took place even in the face of reactionary Vatican policies that consistently supported the conservative monarchies and condemned the Polish risings."[18] The emergence late in the nineteenth century of Catholic social doctrine expressing a concern for the plight of workers and peasants exploited by ruthless capitalists gave the church a renewed appeal.

Disillusionment with romantic nationalism coupled with the beginnings of industrialization led to a shift in the secular value system espoused by intellectuals at the end of the nineteenth century. The new intellectual currency was positivism— the belief that reason and intelligence determine the pace and direction of progress. A corollary of positivism was "organic work"—a spirit of industriousness intended to raise the social, economic, and cultural level of the nation and, in this way, make Poland strong again.

Exhaustion with the insurrectionary tradition coupled with continued dour life under the partitions led many Poles to work at developing their own civil society separate from alien state structures. Most generally, civil society signifies living in a collective entity that exists independently from the state. As sociologist Adam Seligman has written, "the sense of a shared public is constitutive of civil society." But, further, "civil society is, most essentially, that realm where the concrete person—that particular individual, subject to his or her own wants, caprices, and physical necessities—seeks the attainment of these 'selfish' aims. It is that arena where the 'burgher' as private person seeks to fulfill his or her own interests."[19] Seligman makes clear the particular relevance of the notion of civil society to Poland: "Poland never had an autonomous State in modern times. The idea of civil society thus provided the only ideological alternative to foreign domination."[20] Late nineteenth-century positivism was a manifestation of Poles' seeking to forge a civil society—fusing the individual's private and public spheres all the while remaining outside the reach of alien state structures. The task of constructing an independent civil society was resumed almost a century later, when Poles found no other way to confront externally imposed communist rule.

Polonia Reconstituta

At the turn of the twentieth century, economic development led in Poland, as in many other European nations, to the rise of mass political movements, in particular those of the left. In 1893 a Polish Socialist Party (Polska Partia Socjalistyczna—PPS) was secretly formed that emphasized the primacy of national independence over proletarian internationalism. It argued that socialization of the means of production could be achieved only if national oppression were removed and capitalism allowed to flourish. This would lead, in turn, to the eventual overthrow of the capitalist order by socialist forces. PPS leaders such as Józef Piłsudski were reluctant to subordinate the Polish socialist movement to a Russian one, which would have reproduced Poland's inferior status in socialist institutions. By contrast, the Social Democratic Party of the Kingdom of Poland and Lithuania (SDKPiL), founded in 1894, was more internationalist, and its best-known leader, Rosa Luxemburg, held that the struggle for national independence was anachronistic. In the case of Poland, regaining independence would produce a poor capitalist state unprepared for a socialist revolution.

On the right, the movement known as National Democracy (ND) was formed in 1887. Led by Roman Dmowski, it was extremely nationalist. It did not advocate Polish independence by any means possible but, rather, stressed the need to give a homogeneous, all-Polish character to any new state. For Dmowski, Poland's past failures were related to its religious toleration, ethnic equality, and humanitarianism. In particular, the sizable Jewish and Ukrainian minorities had weakened the social fabric of Poland and made it an "effeminate nation." Minorities had to be fully assimilated if a strong Polish nation was to come into being. Dmowski remained equivocal about the desirability of national independence but underscored the importance of collaboration with the Russian autocracy, which he justified in terms of Neo-Slavism.

In sum, on the eve of World War I Polish political leaders envisaged very different alliances that could lead to the reemergence of a strong state. Dmowski's scenario assumed that only a pro-Russian policy could provide the opportunity for statehood, while Piłsudski's conception was predicated on the total collapse of the Russian Empire. The fortunes of war were to prove the latter's views correct.

But Piłsudski was not one to let history run its course. Five days after the war began he led a company of riflemen—a precursor of his famous legions—against Russian troops. His decisiveness and determination in this military engagement meshed well with popular anti-Russian sentiments and went a long way toward making him the obvious candidate to become independent Poland's first strongman.[21]

During the war years offers were made by the various combatants to enlist Poland on their side. As Davies has noted, "In 1914–16, the Tsar, the Kaiser, and the Emperor-King proposed mounting degrees of autonomy. By 1917, the President of the United States, the Provisional government in Petrograd, and even the leader of the Bolsheviks declared themselves in favor of Polish independence. In 1918, they were copied by France, Italy, Japan, and, last of all, Great Britain."[22] But the reemergence of a Polish state was ultimately contingent on the outcome of the war, in particular on the weakening of the partitioning powers. The Bolshevik

Revolution of October 1917 represented a step in this direction. Russia withdrew from the war, signed an unfavorable peace treaty with Germany, and annulled tsarist partition agreements. The approaching collapse of the central powers, in turn, presaged a weakened Germany and a collapse of the Habsburg Empire.

On January 8, 1918, President Woodrow Wilson put forward his general plan for peace in the Fourteen Points. The thirteenth point foresaw a "united, independent and autonomous Poland with free unrestricted access to the sea" and situated on "territories inhabited by an indubitably Polish population." On November 7 of that year, just prior to the armistice, a provisional government was set up. Four days later Piłsudski officially became head of state as well as supreme commander of the army. The Polish state had finally been reconstituted.

The interwar Second Polish Republic did not emerge, therefore, in the manner envisaged either by the nineteenth-century romantic or positivist theorists or by most socialist thinkers. Instead, a fortuitous combination of external actors and events provided the necessary conditions for reclaiming Polish statehood.

The formative years of the interwar republic also did not generate universal enthusiasm among Poles, contrary to what might be expected given the 150-year interval since the first partition. The constitutional system was modeled on the French Third Republic and reproduced all of its shortcomings: a weak president, a powerful legislature, a profusion of political parties (in 1925 there were ninety-two registered parties and thirty-two actually represented in the Sejm), and rapid turnover of governments. The premier of the first national government was Ignacy Paderewski, more famous as a concert pianist than as a founding father of the Second Republic. Its first president, Gabriel Narutowicz, was assassinated in 1922, two days after he was sworn in. No Polish king had suffered such a fate. The first elections, held in January 1919, demonstrated deep political divisions between Poles who had lived under the different partitioning powers. In the former Kingdom of Poland the right-wing National Democrats scored a clear victory, while in Galicia the centrist Piast faction of the Polish Peasant Party (Polskie Stronnictwo Ludowe—PSL), led by the indomitable self-educated peasant Wincenty Witos (who thrice became premier in the interwar years), was the winner. The 1922 elections proved to be the last genuinely free elections of the interwar republic, for Piłsudski's coup in May 1926 put an end to just eight years of fledgling democracy.

What is more, between 1918 and 1921 Poland became embroiled in no fewer than six conflicts, all brought on by border disputes. The Poles took on the Ukrainians regarding eastern Galicia; the Germans twice threatened Poland concerning Poznania and Silesia, where three national uprisings broke in these years; the Lithuanians wanted the return of their capital, Vilnius; the Czechs disputed the border in the Cieszyn region; and, most important, Soviet leaders questioned Poland's historic right to western Ukraine.

In the "forgotten war" between Poland and Russia of 1920–1921, Piłsudski's troops, which were not connected with the White Armies fighting the Bolsheviks, captured Kiev in May 1920. A Russian counteroffensive drove them back to Warsaw itself by August, and Lenin established a Provisional Polish Revolutionary Committee at Białystok, headed by Polish communist leader Julian Marchlewski. Throughout this war Lenin seemed more intent on creating a "red" Poland than in annexing lands for Russia as the tsars had done. Ultimately his hopes were frustrated by Piłsudski's military genius: In the "miracle on the Vistula," the Polish commander turned the imminent capture of Warsaw into a rout of the Russian army, advanced eastward rapidly, and contemplated striking at Moscow itself. In the end Piłsudski agreed to a favorable peace treaty with the Bolsheviks, signed in Riga in March 1921. By this treaty Poland was awarded more land than the British intermediary, Foreign Secretary Lord Curzon, had proposed in July 1920. In addition to Piłsudski, another key figure in Poland's victory over the Bolsheviks in 1920 was the PSL's Witos, who rallied the countryside against the Russian invaders.

Later, the Ribbentrop-Molotov pact, concluded on the eve of World War II, more than offset Russia's 1920–1921 losses. The pact's secret protocol gave the Soviet Union all of eastern Poland, that is, western Ukraine and parts of Belarus. Soviet Foreign Minister Molotov asserted that this was the fate that the illegitimate offspring of the Versailles Treaty deserved.

Interwar Poland turned out to be ethnically more heterogeneous than Wilson had anticipated. In 1921 about 70 percent of the population was ethnically Polish and the rest minorities. The latter included approximately 5–6 million Ukrainians, 3 million Jews, 1.5 million Belarus and more than 1 million Germans. Deprived of statehood for so long, the new leaders of independent Poland were concerned more with asserting their national goals than with regulating the status of minorities. Thus, although anti-Semitism never became official government policy, neither was it opposed with much energy by Piłsudski's governments. Furthermore, from the perspective of another minority group in the country—the Lithuanians—General Łucjan Żeligowski's capture of Vilnius in October 1920 and the incorporation of the entire region around the city into Poland two years later smacked of Polish imperialism. Clearly, the Second Republic's policies toward minorities were not a model of toleration.

Poland's interwar class structure seemed archaic when compared with that of many Western societies. The peasantry constituted the most numerous class—in the early 1920s, approximately three-quarters of the population was engaged in agriculture—but was, on the whole, impoverished. Also on the land was the landed aristocracy, which included those with extraordinary wealth and prestige, those whose estates were rapidly shrinking, and those whose politics were, paradoxically, of the radical left. Although the size and political influence of this latter group were very limited, some of its members became prominent leaders. Thus Aleksander Gella observes that "socially Piłsudski was a typical representative of the revolutionary intelligentsia of noble origin, he was hated by the nationalistically-oriented bourgeoisie as a leftist but loved by his soldiers, who originated from all social classes."[23] Another son of the surviving interwar landed nobility—

Wojciech Jaruzelski—went on to make his mark in politics in the communist period.

In contrast to the nobility, the working class was expanding, growing from 22 percent to 25 percent of the population in the 1920s alone and increasing in political visibility, though not enough yet to make a difference. In turn, the bourgeoisie, or capitalist class, accounted for a minuscule 2 percent of the population and constituted only a small sector of the middle class.

For Garrison Walters, the most important group in interwar Poland was the middle class, broadly defined. The middle class—including its small capitalist sector—accounted for about 11 percent of the population. Walters disaggregates the middle class into small-scale capitalists and the intelligentsia and draws attention to Polish society's peculiar makeup:

> In the 1920s and 1930s the typical representative of the American middle class would have been a small businessman, someone with at best a high school education but making a good income. In contrast, the typical member of the Polish (or East European) intelligentsia would have been a government employee, probably no more than a glorified clerk, possessed of a university education and perhaps an advanced degree, but making a very small salary and with little hope of ever having any financial independence.[24]

The peculiar status of the intelligentsia was historically conditioned. For Gella, "the growth of the intelligentsia is attributable in part to the efforts of the imperial courts in Moscow, Berlin, and Vienna to 'denobilize' the Polish nobility."[25] Even though it ranked high in prestige, the intelligentsia lacked the commercial and entrepreneurial skills needed to bring the socioeconomic change that middle classes elsewhere were able to engineer. Without a group capable of displaying risk taking, dynamism, and innovation, Poland was to fall farther behind other European countries in economic development.

The parliamentary system was weakened by a number of inconclusive elections and vacillating governments between 1922 and 1926. In the end Piłsudski lost patience and launched a coup in May 1926. The new regime strengthened the power of the executive—Piłsudski was even prevailed upon to become premier for several years—but for the most part his dictatorship was camouflaged in parliamentary guise. Parliamentary support was drummed up by forming a Nonparty Bloc for Cooperation with the Government (Bezpartyjny Blok Współpracy z Rządem—BBWR) in 1928, in which the conventional procedure of a cabinet's emerging from an elected legislature was reversed. Increasingly rigged elections, harassment and even internment of opposition officials, and more widespread censorship brought the anticorruption program of Piłsudski's misnamed *sanacja* ("purification") regime into question.

When Piłsudski died in 1935, a colonels' regime, buttressed by a realigned parliamentary group calling itself the Camp of National Unity, was set up.[26] Its major failure was in foreign policy, although in some ways it was only following

Piłsudski's lead. The marshal had resisted overtures to align Poland with one of its great neighbors, Russia or Germany, though nonaggression pacts were concluded with each in 1932 and 1934 respectively. In particular, Piłsudski seemed unconcerned by the rise of the Nazis in Germany and described them as "nothing but windbags." Poland's foreign minister from 1932 to 1939, Colonel Józef Beck, had greater illusions. Great-power status for his country would be attained, he imagined, through the creation of a Third Europe that included the small Central European states, under the leadership of Poland, of course. Even after the 1938 Munich Agreement dismembering Czechoslovakia, the Polish government appeared oblivious to external threats and did little to prepare for the impending European war.[27]

The Ribbentrop-Molotov pact was concluded by the Third Reich and the Soviet Union on August 23, 1939, and a provisional partition line for Poland was agreed upon. Nine days later the Germans invaded Poland, and on September 17 the Russians marched in from the east, claiming their spoils. Polish resistance on both fronts was quickly crushed. Although partition was nothing new to Poland, World War II posed a threat to the very existence of the Polish nation.

The war proved a holocaust for Polish Jews, 3 million (or 90 percent) of whom were killed. Some 3 million other Poles also lost their lives, only a small proportion (10 percent) of them as military casualties. Total battle deaths were about 660,000, approximating the number suffered by British and U.S. forces combined. Civilian populations were transported to extermination camps in Auschwitz-Birkenau (where 4 million people, mostly Jews from various countries of Eastern Europe, were slaughtered), Treblinka, and Majdanek. Summary mass killing took place on city streets and in small villages throughout the country, and many died of starvation and in labor camps in Poland and the Reich. The Nazis found very few willing collaborators in the country (nor did they particularly search for them) and met valiant resistance. It took a month of bitter fighting for the German forces to liquidate the Jewish ghetto of Warsaw in April–May 1943: Close to 60,000 Polish Jews were killed in the uneven struggle. In the sixty-three days of fighting between August and October 1944 that marked the Warsaw uprising, nearly 200,000 Poles lost their lives. The 800,000 survivors were forcibly removed from the capital, and the city was methodically razed to the ground.

In sum, 20 percent of Poland's prewar population, or more than 6 million people, were killed between 1939 and 1945, the highest attrition rate of any nation in the war. Only 50,000 Polish Jews survived the holocaust. Whereas Hitler's genocidal policies were well known, Russian occupation of eastern Poland added terribly to the nation's suffering. If we accept the conclusion reached by the eminent historian Jan Gross, Soviet wartime occupation of the eastern part of the interwar republic may have been worse than Nazi administration of the remainder of Poland. The Soviets sent about 1.25 million Polish citizens into forcible exile, compared with the forced resettlement of 2.5 million Poles by the Germans. However, 13 million Polish citizens were under Soviet jurisdiction, compared with 23 million under Nazi administration. Furthermore, of those deported by the latter, about 1.5 million were transferred from western Poland, formally annexed by the Reich, to central Poland, administered as a *Generalgubernat*. Soviet deportation points were distant Siberia, Kazakhstan, and other parts of Asiatic Russia.

Moreover, up to the time that the Nazis began the systematic extermination of Jews in Poland, in late fall 1941, Soviet mass executions matched German atrocities. The story of the 15,000 Polish officers executed by Stalin's security forces, the NKVD, in 1940, many in the forest of Katyn, is now well documented.[28] But a further 100,000 Soviet-held prisoners may have been killed by the NKVD in June–July 1941 during the evacuation of prisons. By contrast, Germans executed some 120,000 people in the first two years of their occupation of Poland. On the basis of a rough comparison of Nazi and Soviet occupations, Gross concluded that "if we measure the victimization of Polish citizens in terms of loss of life, of sufferings inflicted by forced resettlement, and of material losses through confiscation and fiscal measures, the Soviet actions, relatively speaking, would prove far more injurious than those of the Nazis."[29] Although eastern Poland was characterized by great ethnic heterogeneity—Ukrainians, Belarus, and Jews outnumbered Poles—"all nationalities were victimized during the Sovietization of the Western Ukraine and Western Belorussia."[30]

Given the atrocities committed by foreign powers, the historian R. F. Leslie has argued, "Poles were perhaps more united under foreign occupation than they were under governments of their own election."[31] Yet some of the divisions that were permanently to mark politics under the communist regime could already be discerned in the wartime resistance movements. By 1942 two separate resistance organizations had emerged, the larger linked to the London government in exile, the smaller to the Soviet Union. The Home Army (Armia Krajowa—AK) numbered some 200,000 by 1944 and was united behind General Władysław Sikorski until his death in 1943. After that, the army split into two groups. The first, represented by the new premier and PSL leader Stanisław Mikołajczyk, sought accommodation with the USSR; the second, linked to the commander in chief of Polish forces Kazimierz Sosnkowski, was virulently anti-Soviet. Yet a third approach emerged later when resistance leaders in Warsaw, such as Tadeusz Bór-Komorowski, advanced the strategy that Poles should fight the Germans militarily but had to fight the communists politically. These divisions within the army proved fatal when the ill-conceived Warsaw uprising was launched in August 1944. It was not coordinated beforehand with either the Western Allies or the Soviet Union or even with the London government in exile. The only forces in a position to offer assistance to the besieged insurrectionists were troops of the Red Army, who made only a feeble attempt to help.

In spite of such political divisions, the Polish resistance movement was arguably the most effective of any established in a Nazi-occupied country.[32] Some 150,000 Germans, including top SS officials, were killed in Poland. Well-planned attacks on particularly brutal leaders and elaborate ambushes of military transport, payroll vehicles, and the like became commonplace as the occupation continued.

The other resistance force was the People's Guard (Gwardia Ludowa—GL), whose membership numbered, at most, 50,000 in 1944. This communist organization was less divided than the pro-Western resistance and quickly became aware of the need to work closely with Moscow. With Stalin's approval the Polish Workers' Party (Polska Partia Robotnicza—PPR) was created in January 1942. It gave birth, in turn, to the National Council of the Homeland (Krajowa Rada Narodowa—KRN) in December 1943, which took on the appearance of a rival provisional government to the London one. In July 1944 the council was transformed into the Polish Committee of National Liberation (Polski Komitet Wyzwolenia Narodowego—PKWN), and at the end of the year it officially proclaimed itself the country's provisional government. On January 5, 1945, the USSR officially recognized this government, and twelve days later the Red Army entered Warsaw. Poland's political configuration for the next forty-four years was effectively determined by these two events.

Political realists have argued that no other solution was possible. Western sensitivity to Russia's interests during wartime was dictated by the imperative of maintaining the alliance against Hitler. Already at the Anglo-American conference held in Québec City in August 1943, the foreign ministers of the two countries cryptically expressed readiness "to contemplate a substantial measure of satisfaction on what we understand Soviet territorial claims to be."[33] Satisfying these claims signified accepting the old Curzon line, proposed in 1920 in order to end the Polish-Russian war, as the border between Poland and the USSR. It would have transferred western Ukraine and Belarus from Polish to Soviet jurisdiction. The Québec meeting also resulted in the joint Anglo-American decision not to assist the Home Army in its struggle against German occupation.

In Teheran in November 1943 Churchill, Roosevelt, and Stalin duly affirmed the Curzon line as Poland's eastern border and the Oder and Neisse Rivers as its western one. In this way, "like soldiers taking two steps 'left close,'" as Churchill put it, Poland was transposed 250 miles westward. With German forces driven out of Poland by spring 1945, the British prime minister reaffirmed Polish absorption of the western territories: "by taking over and holding firmly the present German territories up to the Oder, they [the Poles] will be rendering a service to Europe as a whole." Churchill recognized that, as a result, Germany would effectively be divided into five zones of occupation.[34]

After the Teheran meeting, Mikołajczyk spurned an offer to serve as premier of the provisional government because of the reconfiguration of the eastern border that ceded Polish lands to the USSR and the distribution of ministerial portfolios in the government—fourteen PKWN members, four London members. Churchill retorted that he was not prepared "to wreck the peace of Europe because of quarrels between Poles."[35] But the bargaining power of the government-in-exile was whittled away as the Red Army marched into Warsaw in January 1945 and pushed forward to other Polish cities. At the Yalta Conference held the following month, Britain, the United States, and the Soviet Union reached an agreement on an in-

terim government of national unity for Poland. It would be composed of representatives from the two Polish governments, and Churchill was persuaded that the
"free and unfettered elections" called for by the Yalta accord would be enough to
entice Mikołajczyk to return to Poland and take an active part in governing the
country.[36] When he did return in June 1945, the composition of the provisional
government was even more stacked against his party than previously. In addition,
instead of getting the premiership, he had to be satisfied with filling the posts of
vice-premier and minister of agriculture. A month after Mikołajczyk's acceptance
of these secondary positions, the United States and Britain extended diplomatic
recognition to the new Polish government.

The last year of the war had provided a new generation of Poles with a refresher
course in history. Once again Poles were taught that insurrections (such as the
Warsaw uprising) did not lead to national independence. Agreements concluded
among the great powers usually determined how independent Poland could be. In
the early 1990s Poles had reason to reflect again whether even successful movements against outside political domination—as in the case of Solidarity's effective
challenge to the communist regime—could ensure that the country would escape
the vise that geopolitics had imposed on it.

Notes

1. Oskar Halecki, *A History of Poland.* New York: Barnes and Noble, 1993, p. 5.

2. Tadeusz Manteuffel, *The Formation of the Polish State: The Period of Ducal Rule,
963–1194.* Detroit: Wayne State University Press, 1982, pp. 75–76.

3. Andrzej Wyczański, "The Problem of Authority in Sixteenth Century Poland: An
Essay in Reinterpretation," in J. K. Fedorowicz (ed.), *A Republic of Nobles.* Cambridge:
Cambridge University Press, 1982, p. 91.

4. Antoni Mączak, "The Structure of Power in the Commonwealth in the Sixteenth and
Seventeenth Centuries," in Federowicz, *A Republic of Nobles,* pp. 111–112.

5. Andrzej Walicki, "Polish Nationalism in Comparative Perspective," paper presented
at the Conference on European Nationalisms, Tulane University, March 25–27, 1994,
p. 17.

6. José Casanova, "Church, State, Nation, and Civil Society in Spain and Poland," in
Said Amir Arjomand (ed.), *The Political Dimensions of Religion.* Albany, NY: State University of New York Press, 1993, p. 119.

7. Janusz Tazbir, "Serce z zachodniej strony," *Gazeta Wyborcza,* January 22–23, 1994.

8. Norman Davies, *God's Playground,* vol. 1. New York: Columbia University Press,
1984, p. 340.

9. W. F. Reddaway et al. (eds.), *The Cambridge History of Poland,* vol. 1. Cambridge:
Cambridge University Press, 1950, p. 439.

10. Jerzy Lukowski, *Liberty's Folly: The Polish-Lithuanian Commonwealth in the Eighteenth Century, 1697–1795.* London: Routledge, 1991, p. 25.

11. Davies, *God's Playground,* vol. 1, p. 487.

12. Aleksander Gieysztor et al., *History of Poland.* Warsaw: Polish Scientific Publishers,
1968, p. 323.

13. Jean-Jacques Rousseau, *The Government of Poland*. New York: Bobbs-Merrill, 1972, pp. 2, 10.

14. Quoted in Davies, *God's Playground*, vol. 1, pp. 521, 523.

15. For an incisive history, see Piotr S. Wandycz, *The Lands of Partitioned Poland, 1795–1918*. Seattle: University of Washington Press, 1974.

16. Aleksander Gella, *Development of Class Structure in Eastern Europe: Poland and Her Southern Neighbors*. Albany NY: State University of New York Press, 1989, p. 20. The six insurrections included the 1794 Kościuszko uprising, the 1806 rebellion in Poznań province, the 1830 November uprising, the 1846 revolt in western Galicia, the 1848 rebellion in western Poland (Wielkopolska), and the 1863 January insurrection. The 1794, 1830, and 1863 cases involved nationwide revolt.

17. Quoted in Reddaway et al. *The Cambridge History of Poland*, vol. 2, p. 338.

18. Casanova, "Church, State, Nation, and Civil Society," p. 120.

19. Adam B. Seligman, *The Idea of Civil Society*. New York: Free Press, 1992, p. 5.

20. Seligman, *The Idea of Civil Society*, p. 8.

21. For an illuminating biography, see Wacław Jędrzejewicz, *Piłsudski: A Life for Poland*. New York: Hippocrene Books, 1982.

22. Davies, *God's Playground*, vol. 2, p. 378.

23. Gella, *Development of Class Structure*, pp. 23–24.

24. E. Garrison Walters, *The Other Europe: Eastern Europe to 1945*. New York: Dorset Press, 1990, p. 180.

25. Gella, *Development of Class Structure*, p. 21.

26. The best English-language history of the period is Edward D. Wynot Jr., *Polish Politics in Transition: The Camp of National Unity and the Struggle for Power 1935–1939*. Athens, GA: University of Georgia Press, 1974.

27. On foreign policy in this period, see Anna M. Cienciala, *Poland and the Western Powers 1938–1939: A Study in the Interdependence of Eastern and Western Europe*. London: Routledge and Kegan Paul, 1968.

28. The classic study of Katyn is Janusz Zawodny, *Death in the Forest: The Story of the Katyn Forest Massacre*. South Bend, IN: University of Notre Dame Press, 1962.

29. Jan T. Gross, *Revolution from Abroad: The Soviet Conquest of Poland's Western Ukraine and Western Belorussia*. Princeton: Princeton University Press, 1988, p. 226.

30. Gross, *Revolution from Abroad*, p. 225.

31. R. F. Leslie (ed.), *The History of Poland since 1863*. Cambridge: Cambridge University Press, 1983, p. 221.

32. One classic study is Stefan Korboński, *Fighting Warsaw: The Story of the Polish Underground State 1939–1945*. New York: Minerva Press, 1968.

33. Quoted in John Coutouvidis and Jaime Reynolds, *Poland 1939–1947*. Leicester: Leicester University Press, 1986, p. 92.

34. Winston S. Churchill, *Closing the Ring: The Second World War*, vol. 5. Boston: Houghton Mifflin, 1951, pp. 450–451. The other zones were British, French, Soviet, and U.S.

35. *Documents on Polish-Soviet Relations, 1939–1945*, vol. 2 (1967), no. 239, pp. 416–422. Quoted in Coutouvidis and Reynolds, *Poland 1939–1947*, p. 106.

36. On Mikołajczyk and the London Poles' disputes with the PKWN, see Winston S. Churchill, *Triumph and Tragedy: The Second World War*, vol. 6. Boston: Houghton Mifflin, 1953, pp. 331–337, 365–387, 418–439.

2

The Functioning of
the Communist Regime

The first phase of the CCC model uses system functionalism to describe the antecedent authoritarian regime and its basis of power and authority. Six structural factors are examined here:

1. The socioeconomic structure—the nature of the economy and social structure during the Phase I period, establishing the country's level of development and capacity for growth.

2. The international environment—pressures for authoritarianism or democratization stemming from the international system, dependency on another country or political-military bloc for security and economic well-being.

3. The political culture—the subjective political competence of citizens and the bases of popular support for the regime (levels of trust or disaffection, historical origins of mass affective orientations toward political authorities and institutions).

4. Political groups and alignments—the extent to which cleavages based on religion, ethnicity, region, or class exist and are politicized and the ways in which the major political groups and patterns of alignment among them reflect such cleavages.

5. The political structure and performance of the regime—its degree of authoritarianism, capacity for adaptive change, and performance in terms of economic growth and living standards.

6. The ruling coalition—its composition, its leaders' styles, and beliefs among elites hindering its adaptation to changing conditions.

In retrospect, it is clear that the character and functioning of these structural factors were dysfunctional for the communist regime and served as sources for subsequent crises. To this list we can add dysfunctional ideological structures, which have spawned a separate literature.[1] Phase I analysis is limited to a *description* of the main structural features of the communist system and the purposes they were to serve. Phase II analysis, presented in Chapter 3, converts these structural factors into *explanatory* macro-level variables that help identify the sources of political crises and, ultimately, of regime collapse. Before we begin a factor-by-factor analysis, let us consider the more general political and economic conditions faced by the postwar Polish communist regime.

Structural Ambivalence in the Soviet Model

When we combine the Bolsheviks' seizure of power in Russia in 1917 with Poland's fateful geopolitical position, it is fairly obvious that historical determinism played an overwhelming role in Poland's becoming a Soviet satellite after World War II. Had Western armies liberated the country from German occupation in 1945, it is highly probable that Poland would have been spared some forty-five years of communist rule. But precisely because Western forces were never in a position—or wanted to put themselves in a position—to beat the Red Army to Warsaw and most other Eastern European capitals, an iron curtain descended on Europe at war's end.

As a result, between 1944 and 1948 Stalin carried out a step-by-step program of Sovietizing Poland, skillfully exploiting Polish hopes that full-scale Sovietization could be avoided while discreetly (and sometimes not so discreetly) implementing it. As we saw in the first chapter, a representative of Poland's government-in-exile in London, the PSL leader Mikołajczyk, was persuaded to take part in a communist-dominated coalition government. Very quickly he recognized that the influence of the London Poles would be negligible compared with that of Polish communists, and he resigned and fled the country in 1948. On the left of the political spectrum, the PPS had a long tradition of supporting a democratic road to socialism, and for a while after the war it seemed destined to play a pivotal role in the formation of a new political order. Communists themselves were divided between those sensitive to national conditions prevailing in Poland and those willing to espouse the Soviet model. Even the latter group was not composed exclusively of Stalinists.

Despite geopolitical realities, then, the nature of Poland's postwar regime was not altogether clear even as the Red Army marched across the country in the early months of 1945. What degree of political autonomy would be left Polish leaders remained an open question. As much an authority as the historian Joseph Rothschild was not convinced that Poland was earmarked for Sovietization: "it is difficult to decide whether Stalin and the Polish communists never intended to allow free elections in Poland."[2]

By the end of 1945 some signs had appeared that the orthodox Stalinist model would not be forced upon all of Eastern Europe. Soviet troops had liberated neighboring Czechoslovakia but had then departed for home. Competitive parliamentary elections in Hungary had led to a defeat for the communist party. Yugoslavia had charted out a national road to socialism that Stalin seemed unable to halt. Nothing like the Comintern—the Communist International set up after the Bolshevik Revolution to dictate Soviet policy to communists throughout the world—seemed likely to be established again. The 1947 conference in Szklarska Poręba that created the Cominform revealed dissension among Soviet and East European communist leaders about the desirability and scope of a new communist international. Władysław Gomułka was particularly outspoken about this organization. Arguably, the communist regime that was poised to rule Poland at war's end could have included pluralist, democratic, and nationalist features. Furthermore, its commitment to a centrally planned economy and forced industrialization was predicated on the belief that Poland, with its backward, largely agrarian-based economy, needed to be brought to the point of economic takeoff. What were the conditions, then, that sidetracked Poland from a moderate, measured developmental path?

Of all these expectations about a diluted Stalinist system for Poland, it was easiest to forecast that no communist system would countenance political pluralism. The elections called for by the Yalta and Potsdam accords were never likely to be wholly free. Marxist-Leninist ideology posited a transitional period of proletarian dictatorship in order to ensure that the capitalist class would be swiftly liquidated and a classless society created. Both the transitional dictatorship and the ensuing classless society were to be governed by the most valuable economic group in society, manual workers, who alone, classical Marxists held, created wealth in the labor process. One political party was all the workers needed to protect their interests. Any additional parties would prove either schismatic, distracting workers from their real interests, or counterrevolutionary, aggregating the interests of historically doomed classes such as factory owners, entrepreneurs, financiers, and property owners.

Communist ideology could justify the need for a one-party state, but other factors contributed to the inevitability of communist hegemony. From Stalin to Chernenko, Soviet leaders were of one mind concerning the threat posed by any form of pluralism, whether it be autonomy for trade unions, the existence of dissident organizations, or the prospects of a full-fledged multiparty system. When threatened by the emergence of pluralism in a satellite state, Soviet leaders did not shy away from staging palace coups, using covert measures, or sending in tanks to liquidate independent political forces. Such paranoia on the part of Kremlin rulers seems justified in hindsight: When Gorbachev failed to crack down on pluralist tendencies in his empire, it quickly crumbled.

To be sure, in crafting the communist regime in Poland an effort was made to maintain some semblance of pluralism. In particular, given the role played by

Catholicism in the everyday lives of Poles, communist leaders sought to elicit the support of church groups. Two Catholic groups, Znak and Pax, were even provided with representation in the Sejm. But after the events associated with the 1956 Polish October failed to secure genuine political competition, it became clear that communism and pluralism were mutually exclusive. That year, following workers' protests about deteriorating living standards, a self-styled national communist, Władysław Gomułka, was returned to power. Even though he hinted at greater political liberalization, his adoption in the 1960s of the same neo-Stalinist methods of which he had been a victim after the war made Poles cynical about "well-intentioned" communists from then on. The Polish People's Republic was, in short, structurally incapable of accepting pluralism.

Without political competition there can be no democracy, but were minimalist expectations that democratic processes could at least be institutionalized within the ruling communist party in any way fulfilled? Here again, Bolshevik practice was emulated by Polish comrades. Factional activity pitting liberal against hardline communists and national against Muscovite communists occurred at regular intervals in the Polish party. Because it was played out behind closed doors, without allowing a larger public to adjudicate the desirability of particular policy programs, this factional conflict was often ruthless. In 1948 the Stalinist leader Bolesław Bierut was a supporter of Gomułka one day but accused him of a serious rightist-nationalist deviation—cause for Gomułka's subsequent expulsion from the party, imprisonment, and torture—the next. In 1970, Gomułka's opponents in the party set him up for his fall from grace by having him announce food-price increases two weeks before Christmas, thereby triggering massive demonstrations in coastal cities. Edward Gierek was kept around just long enough to sign accords with Solidarity leaders in August 1980, making it possible for his party opponents to unite and accuse him of *both* allowing a counterrevolutionary organization to come into being *and* not recognizing popular discontent early enough. Without open democracy in the communist party, all of society was affected by intrigues hatched by rival communist factions.

Poland's communists have been accused by historians as well as, more recently, by legal theorists of having betrayed the country's national interests during their years in power. The argument is made that, in turn, Bierut, Gomułka, Gierek, and Wojciech Jaruzelski served as mere surrogates of Soviet leaders. There is little question that the Soviet-type policies pursued by Polish leaders were alien to Polish society, whose political preferences seldom overlapped with those of communist policymakers. The policy areas in question and the extent to which Kremlin rulers imposed their views changed over time. Indeed, if Polish leaders were admonished in the 1950s and 1960s for not always being sufficiently internationalist (that is, not following Moscow's imperatives), the memoirs of the Russians who formulated Soviet policy toward Poland in the 1970s and 1980s suggest that it was the Kremlin that urged Polish communist rulers to take fuller responsibility for domestic matters.[3] In sum, like Mickiewicz's famous character Konrad Wallenrod, some Polish communists were persuaded that cooperation with Moscow could be used to advance the national interest. But Poland could never be Poland as long as Polish communist leaders refused to submit themselves to the verdict of the electorate.

These are some of the conditions existing between 1944 and 1989 that precluded the communist regime from engaging in competitive democratic practices and vigorously promoting Poland's national interest. In the following sections, I shall take a closer look at the antecedent regime, beginning with its general economic structure and its functioning and go on to review socioeconomic development in People's Poland, the international environment within which the socialist state operated, the country's political culture, its main political groups, the political structure and performance of the regime, and, finally, its changing leadership. All of these aspects of Poland's "real existing socialism"—a term used by scholars in the 1980s to highlight the pathologies of the communist system—can be treated as factors that caused or contributed to the succession of postwar crises in the country. In the end, these factors drove the communist rulers themselves to seek extrication from this inefficiently functioning system.

The Socialist Economic Blueprint

If socialist democracy was conceptually an oxymoron and practically a system dysfunction, what can be said about the developmental prospects offered by the switch to a centrally planned economy that accompanied the installation of a communist regime? No better critic of the inherently flawed centrally planned economy can be found than the Austrian economist Friedrich A. Hayek, and I shall draw from his analysis.

For Hayek, socialism is flawed at a basic philosophical level; the assumptions that the Marxist economists make about human morality and motivation are inaccurate. The extended order of human cooperation is promoted by capitalism and individualism, not planning and collectivism. The key philosophical ideas espoused by Hayek, which thoroughly shape his economic thought, are found in a chapter of *The Fatal Conceit* entitled "Was Socialism a Mistake?" Underlying his thinking is a less than full understanding of why rules of conduct that have never been formally constructed by individuals but instead emerged from property and market relations function so successfully:

> To understand our civilisation, one must appreciate that the extended order resulted not from human design or intention but spontaneously: it arose from unintentionally conforming to certain traditional and largely *moral* practices, many of which men tend to dislike, whose significance they usually fail to understand, whose validity they cannot prove, and which have nonetheless fairly rapidly spread by means of an evolutionary selection—the comparative increase of population and wealth—of those groups that happened to follow them.[4]

Thus Hayek is drawn to a functional explanation of progress: "What are chiefly responsible for having generated this extraordinary order, and the existence of mankind in its present size and structure, are the rules of human conduct that gradually evolved (especially those dealing with several property, honesty, contract, exchange, trade, competition, gain, and privacy)." Such rules, as we shall see, were noticeably missing from the socialist order, and there was an evolutionary explanation for their absence: "These rules are handed on by tradition, teaching and imitation, rather than by instinct, and largely consist of prohibitions ('shall not's') that designate adjustable domains for individual decisions."[5]

In other words, efficiency-driven rules of conduct cannot be planned, let alone planned rationally. Crucial to Hayek is the "fatal conceit"—"the idea that the ability to acquire skills stems from reason. For it is the other way around: our reason is as much the result of an evolutionary selection process as is our morality."[6] The belief undergirding much of what Hayek terms "constructivist rationalism"[7] and an assumption also embedded in the socialist project—"that anything produced by evolution could have been done better by the use of human ingenuity"—is spurious.[8] The presumption of reason informing many ideologies has a long history and can already be discovered in an Aristotle ignorant of pre-Socratic distinctions between a spontaneous order, or *kosmos,* and an arranged order, or *taxis.* Instead Aristotle asserts that the order of all human activities was *taxis*—the product of a deliberate organization of individual action by an ordering mind.[9] For Hayek, when socialist economic thinkers extend this Aristotelian notion to all of society and reify the role of reason, they destroy any hope for efficient economic performance. It is the presumption of reason by a naive, unscientific, and obsolete methodology such as Marxism that accounts for the rationalist conceit.

Hayek also addresses the often-cited proposition that cooperation is generally better than competition. "Cooperation, like solidarity, presupposes a large measure of agreement on ends as well as on methods employed in their pursuit." Although feasible in a small group, cooperation is less probable in an extended order; further, cooperation cannot by itself ensure effective coordination of efforts with unknown circumstances, as in the economy. By contrast, Hayek describes competition as "a procedure of discovery . . . that led man unwittingly to respond to novel situations; and through further competition, not through agreement, we gradually increase our efficiency."[10] Hayek thereby demolishes one further cornerstone of socialist economic thought.

What are the specific aspects of the Hayekian critique of planning and a state-controlled economy that are relevant to postwar Poland? For starters, he holds that "the whole idea of 'central control' is confused. There is not, and never could be, a single directing mind at work."[11] It follows, then, that state-fixed prices neither represent real central control nor reflect scarcity values determined by the market. Central planners are dependent upon the quality of reporting from the production frontiers, and this reporting is usually shoddy and incomplete.

In addition, the centralized system of allocation of resources is flawed in several ways. Hayek argues that the totality of resources is simply not knowable by anyone. Further, it is impossible under socialism to place value on resources: "Value is not an attribute or physical property possessed by things themselves, irrespective of their relations to men, but solely an aspect of these relations that enables men to take account . . . of the better opportunities others might have for their use."[12] Socialist planners' understanding of value has little regard for the human purposes that services and commodities serve. At the level of the individual enterprise, managers are given incentives to skew reporting: They tend to overstate shortages of inputs in order to be allocated greater inputs in future and to understate the amount of outputs to prevent production targets from being raised subsequently. It follows that it is a rational choice for managers to understate any surplus of inputs, labor, and plant capacity.

Above all, central planning is incapable of performing the task assigned to it—coordinating production across many sectors of the economy. Whereas for Hayek the free market is virtually defined as an information-gathering institution, information about changes in scarcity values under socialism would have to be communicated to central planners instantaneously—a logistical impossibility—for planners to adjust prices in accordance with value rather than material terms. Even in the rare circumstances in which such information is objectively and quickly presented to central planners, it still only aggregates time- and place-specific data that may put planners off track in determining nationwide price structures. Hayek again criticizes the basic assumptions of a centralized information system: The creation of wealth is determined "by the separate, differing information of millions, which is precipitated in prices that serve to guide further decisions." By contrast, "'macro-economic' knowledge of aggregate quantities available of different things is neither available nor needed, nor would it even be useful."[13] Not least of the problems caused by a command economy is that anything that might disrupt the production cycle, such as technological innovation or research and feasibility studies, is discouraged.

Central planners themselves often operate under political directives more constraining than economic ones and therefore make many myopic policy decisions. Unbalanced investment and growth of heavy industry at the expense of light industry, the consumer sector, and agriculture result in political fallout. Together with incompetent and corrupt management, capricious wage policies, a retail price system having no connection with market values, an alienated, unproductive workforce, inefficient use of raw materials, and environmental degradation, the economic system produces a deteriorating quality of life for much of society. Economic failings are the unavoidable consequences of entrusting the making of economic policy to unelected and unaccountable party apparatchiks. Whether an earlier shift toward a mixed economy such as market socialism—which a first wave of Polish reform economists such as Włodzimierz Brus, Michał Kalecki, and Oskar Lange had urged—could have prevented economic disaster is arguable.[14]

The Socioeconomic Structure

Both the introduction and the collapse of a centrally planned economy were drawn out over a number of years. If, with hindsight, a deterministic logic appears to have been at work, producing an almost ideal-type command economy followed by an almost ideal-type reversion to a market-driven one, the devil is in the details of each form. Nationalization of the country's larger factories was carried out shortly after the war, but the struggle to eradicate the private retail sector continued into the early 1950s and, to some degree, was never completed. Similarly, a policy of market-determined prices was pushed by Zbigniew Messner's government in the second half of the 1980s, but it was only with the appointment of a noncommunist prime minister in 1989 that sweeping market reform and privatization were introduced.

In the interim, the centrally planned economy lurched from one set of priorities to another. After the war the first task, mapped out in the 1947–1949 three-year plan, was to rebuild the country's infrastructure and feed its population. The 1950–1955 six-year plan emphasized rapid industrialization almost exclusively. After that Gomułka only tinkered with central planning and insisted on the virtues of austerity. Following him, Gierek thought in strategic terms and envisaged large socialist corporations doing business with their capitalist counterparts in the West. What actually happened was the rapid growth of a second economy— the black market—that provided a genuine if expensive free market in consumer goods. Jaruzelski's martial-law regime sought legitimacy by enacting laws against speculators (as black marketeers were euphemistically termed). Jaruzelski was still strongman when market forces were liberated at the end of the 1980s.

The more durable features of the postwar command economy included (1) an extensive central planning bureaucracy, (2) command rather than indicative planning, which limited plan flexibility and generally blocked input and information from lower economic units, (3) state-owned and state-managed corporations, factories, commercial and financial firms, and retail trade, (4) a state monopoly over the labor market, (5) disproportionately greater investment in the industrial as compared with the consumer and agricultural sectors, and (6) tight controls on prices and wages to check inflationary pressures.

There was an ideological rationale for such a command economy: that social justice could be achieved only if the communist state micromanaged economic affairs. The communist telos of an egalitarian society was never approached in postwar Poland, but it is generally true that in the first two decades of the regime opportunities for lower social groups to become upwardly mobile were increased. According to data contained in the first statistical yearbook published after the fall of the communist regime (thereby increasing their credibility), the proportion of the population employed in agriculture was cut exactly in half, from 54 percent in 1950 to 27 percent in 1990. The percentage of women making up the workforce grew in this period from 31 percent to 47 percent. At the same time, the number of college graduates increased from 3,900 in 1946 to 52,300 in 1990.[15]

In terms of socio-occupational mobility, peasants were recruited into the labor force and became unskilled or semiskilled workers or, at worst, peasant-workers who commuted from farmland to factory. Blue-collar workers moved up the social ladder to administrative and management posts. Women were increasingly recruited into "pink-collar" administrative positions that had been closed to them before as well as into more traditional feminized occupational sectors such as light industry, health care, and the education system. Generally, in the Stalinist period that ended with the 1956 Polish October, key political and economic appointments were made on the basis of individuals' class backgrounds and party credentials rather than formal qualifications. Experience and skills in a particular occupation were a secondary consideration.

Socio-occupational mobility was not confined solely to the party bureaucracy, local administration, and the industrial sector. Central government ministries were soon filled with trusted cadres drawn from the working class and, to a lesser extent, the peasantry. By contrast, individuals of white-collar or intelligentsia background faced discrimination in getting into universities, securing administrative positions, and obtaining professional advancement. The inefficiency, incompetence, and corruption of the Polish communist system owed much to this first wave of party-sponsored *awans społeczny* (social promotion). Communist leaders' notion of affirmative action was extreme in permitting so many poorly prepared persons to be catapulted into positions of political and economic responsibility. Gierek's slogan in the early 1970s of filling the right job with the right person was rooted in an effort to undo the misguided personnel policy of the past.

If upward social mobility was a double-edged sword, it did reduce the rigid stratification in Polish society that had occurred in the interwar period and was partly modeled on *szlachta* democracy. In economic terms, less rigid stratification meant that coalface miners became the best-paid occupational category at the turn of the 1980s. For example, in 1983 they were paid 50 percent more than factory directors, three times more than doctors, and five times more than teachers.[16] In terms of social prestige, only the intelligentsia ranked ahead of skilled workers; private employers and white-collar workers followed.[17] In the 1980s, economic stagnation affected social classes in different ways. Whereas all of Polish society suffered *absolute* deprivation, the greatest *relative* deprivation was experienced by peasants and unskilled workers and the least by professionals and private entrepreneurs. If in 1982 13 percent of peasant households were poor, 40 percent were classified as such only six years later. By comparison, the proportion of households of professionals and entrepreneurs that became poor between 1982 and 1988 went from only 1 percent to 10 percent. Though it was hardly reassuring news for the latter categories, there was an important counterfactual: The number of professional households ranked as wealthy actually increased, from 22 percent to 28 percent.[18] The shift away from a socioeconomic structure favoring workers and peasants and the economic rehabilitation of educated and entrepreneurial groups predated, then, the fall of communism.

In the communist period, inverse snobbery, best exemplified by language use, accompanied the egalitarian drive. Where the traditional Polish form of addressing an unfamiliar person is *Pan* (corresponding to *Usted* in Spanish or, roughly, *vous* in French), communists substituted "comrade." Employing the term "comrade" was intended to project a person's position of power in interpersonal relations.

By the late 1970s, after Poland's economic mini-boom had fizzled, a more ossi-fied class structure had come into being. Socioeconomic mobility was intraclass rather than interclass, and opportunities for occupational advancement were dis-appearing. At the same time, the infamous "new class" of communist officialdom was becoming entrenched. Frequently referred to as the *nomenklatura*, it sought to perpetuate itself by passing on its privileges to its children and raised the entry costs for new recruits by exacting bribes and servility. This engendered a "new" new class of arrivistes who were usually not party members but were connected to the *nomenklatura* through social and economic networking. In this way an exten-sive patron-client nexus was established.

In the pivotal 1970s, a generally well-paid but increasingly radicalized indus-trial proletariat stood guard over its own interests, not least the provision of inex-pensive, government-subsidized foodstuffs. A marginalized but large stratum of farmers kept out of politics in return for extension of the welfare state into this largely private sector. Stalin's collectivization policy was resisted by Gomułka in 1948 and was not forcefully pursued by any of his successors. In the mid-1970s, Gierek granted health care coverage to this group while making it clear how ex-ceptional private farming was in the context of an otherwise collectivized Soviet bloc.[19] Under Gierek, then, class, status, and power in People's Poland were clearly delineated. Significant changes to the socioeconomic structure could now only re-sult from purposive collective action rather than elite-organized social mobility.

The International Environment

International systems theory holds that the constraints on an individual state seeking to build international alliances are greater when the international system is marked by bipolarity, as was the case in the Cold War era, than under multipo-larity, as in the interwar period, when small- and medium-sized powers shifted fluidly from one alliance system to another. It is true that under bipolarity small and medium-sized powers can play off one superpower against the other, but in reality few countries possess assets valuable enough to allow them to exploit such opportunities. For a medium-sized country bordering on a superpower such as Poland, the likelihood of entering into any form of alliance system other than one acceptable to the dominant state is very slim. Poland's political and economic dependency on the USSR was, therefore, virtually inescapable under the conditions of the Cold War.

The Cold War narrative is well known and does not need elaboration here. International systems theory emphasizes that, even if bipolarity restricts the coalition-building strategies of individual states, it nevertheless provides a fundamentally stable international environment. But, equally, any change in the bipolar system, such as the emergence of new international actors (new industrializing countries, the Pacific Rim states, multinational corporations), the growth of international regimes (as in nuclear energy), increasing global economic interdependence, or, simply, the emergent superiority of one bloc, meant that any individual state would be affected considerably by such system change. Indeed, the end of bipolarity in the early 1990s signified profound regime change throughout the Soviet bloc, independent of the measure of domestic struggle to overthrow communism. Poland and Hungary—which staged popular insurrections against their communist regimes—were also quickest to seize the opportunities offered by the emergent less bipolar, more flexible international system. By contrast, in the Balkan countries, the domino or contagion theory—linking democratic changes to international changes—explains the dismantling of the communist party-state more convincingly than the concept of political mobilization.

From its creation in July 1944, the very legitimacy of People's Poland and the international acceptance of the revised postwar boundaries were areas of concern to the communist leadership. If the country had been the bastard child of Versailles during the interwar period, how much truer was it to claim that postwar communist Poland was the illegitimate offspring of the Yalta agreement? Indeed, whereas the Yalta accord was repeatedly invoked by Western powers in the first two decades after the war to criticize the undemocratic nature of the Polish regime, by the 1970s it was communist leaders who invoked Yalta to criticize Western meddling in the region. Yalta had become a euphemism for Realpolitik and mutually recognized spheres of influence.

With regard to the country's borders, Poland's western, or "recovered," territories were recognized as Polish by the Federal Republic of Germany only in 1970.[20] Even after German reunification two decades later, the legal status of Pomerania, East Prussia, and Silesia remained of concern to Polish leaders. The process of German reunification, termed "two plus two" to signal involvement by the two Germanies, the United States, and the USSR, was, under Polish diplomatic pressure, transformed into "two plus two plus one" to indicate Poland's participation whenever the German-Polish border issue came up. Throughout the lifetime of the People's Republic, Polish touchiness about the border question played into the hands of the Soviet Union and helped account for Poland's transformation into its obsequious satellite.

Poland was also economically exploited by the USSR during the first decade of the communist regime. The country delivered millions of tons of coal to its huge neighbor at about 10 percent of world prices. This "trade agreement" was terminated after the Polish October. At the same time, if we were to accept Paul Marer's findings about the balance of Soviet extractions and Soviet aid to Eastern Europe between 1945 and 1960, we would have to recognize that Poland had a net gain in economic relations with the USSR over this period of some US$200 million—by far the most profitable relationship recorded by an East European state.[21] Critics of Soviet imperialism would point, of course, to the loss to the USSR of prewar Polish territories that had both tangible and intangible value. Apologists for Soviet imperialism would respond that, by exchanging agrarian territories inhabited largely by non-Poles in the east for the Silesian industrial and coal basins and the Pomeranian coastal region in the west, Poland lost net territory but gained net resources.

The Polish government was required to contribute to the costs of the Warsaw Pact military alliance. In the peak years of the pact, throughout the 1970s and early 1980s, annual military expenditures in Poland represented close to 10 percent of the total national budget; CIA estimates of Polish military expenditures were considerably higher, at 15 percent to 25 percent. The official 1982 defense budget amounted to approximately US$2.3 billion.[22] By contrast, the 1993 defense budget of US$1.8 billion also represented 10 percent of the total national budget.[23] Democratic Poland therefore spent US$500 million less annually on its defense than People's Poland; the cutback was probably much greater given inflation over this eleven-year period. Much of the savings was accounted for by a reduction in troop strength, from 317,000 in 1982 to 287,000 in the operational forces in 1993. In short, by my estimate Poland's excess military burden to the Soviet-bloc pact amounted to over US$500 million annually.[24] Burden sharing in the defense of the Soviet empire was a form of extraction, then, and much of Polish society was aware that it was helping foot the bill whenever the Kremlin embarked on a new foreign adventure.

In its international politics, Poland was firmly integrated into the various institutions created by the Soviet Union. The most important of these was the Warsaw Pact, though we should not overlook the pact's consultative political committee, which sometimes synchronized foreign policy. Thus, Poland was required to offer "fraternal assistance" to Czechoslovakia in 1968 by joining in the Warsaw Pact invasion of that country. A year earlier, East European states had followed Soviet cues and condemned "Israeli Zionist imperialism" following the Six-Day War in the Middle East. Poland regularly had to express its solidarity with national liberation fronts emerging in what for Poles were exotic Third World nations and to extend diplomatic and material support to socialist dictators who had seized power. The hidden costs of such diplomatic commitments are impossible to gauge.

The Council for Mutual Economic Assistance (CMEA) was an East European version of the Common Market and the European Free Trade Association (EFTA). Poland was part of the more general division of labor within the CMEA and accordingly had to specialize in certain sectors (everything from cosmetics to textiles) while renouncing the development of others (for example, optical products and pharmaceuticals). Although it undoubtedly accrued some advantages from trade within the Soviet bloc, Poland's economy was shattered when markets in the bloc collapsed at the end of the 1980s.

The Cold War environment also had a profound impact on domestic politics. Polish leaders had little choice but to use force to manage political crises. The alternative to repression instigated by Polish communists was military intervention by the Soviet Union. Although some observers described the relatively benign crackdown on Solidarity in the early 1980s as martial law with a Polish face, it remained repression nonetheless.

In sum, the Polish communist regime was firmly in the Second World camp throughout the Cold War era. Polish initiatives such as Foreign Minister Adam Rapacki's 1957 plan for a nuclear-free Central Europe or Gierek's attempt to turn to the West for increased trade and credits invariably advanced a political agenda earlier endorsed by Soviet leaders. These initiatives were therefore never particularly Polish.[25] It is true that postwar Soviet policy toward Poland included some zigzags; indeed, the trend appeared to augur a gradual increase in the nation's autonomy. However, of overriding salience to Polish rulers from Bierut to Jaruzelski was that all departures from the *prevailing* Soviet model required negotiation and, ultimately, approbation from Moscow. The French political scientist Hélène Carrère d'Encausse has referred evocatively to "the shadow of the Kremlin" that hung over East European leaders.[26] This reality shaped what it was possible to do in People's Poland, and it was this reality that had to be changed if, as the popular song of the 1981 Solidarity period had it, Poland was really to become Poland. Thus, the postwar experience could be reduced to "the paradox of a communist state presiding over a nation that is in the Soviet orbit of power and yet not of it."[27]

Political Culture

The study of political culture focuses on the attitudes, values, and knowledge of citizens as they relate to political issues. From the beginning of communist rule, the regime's prescriptive political culture, heavily influenced by the writings of Marx and Lenin, clashed with the modal, existing political culture of Polish society. Indeed, more generally, the utopian thrust of communist ideology appeared to be at odds with human nature. The essayist George Steiner attributed to one of his characters the following end goal of this ideology: "Communism means taking the errata out of history. Out of man."[28] Out of Poland's political culture, too, we could add. These were objectives impossible to attain. In addition, the general cultural context of the ideology and its main sponsor, Russia, served to inhibit the effective exercise of communist power in Poland. Traditional Polish suspicions of Russia made even the most attractive ideology in its hands a hard sell.

The real question is, then, whether the breach between prescriptive and modal cultures was narrowed in the forty-five-year era of Polish communism. Arguably, the two cultures—posited and real—were farther apart on the eve of communism's collapse than in the years after the war. What were the values that seemed irreconcilable in the Marxist-Leninist normative framework and the ingrained attitudes of Polish society?

First, communism required a political culture at once compliant and engagé: Citizens were expected to take an active part in the construction of the socialist order while, at the same time, never meaningfully participating in the political process. In a sense, communist leaders were never sure whether, in Gabriel Almond's typology, a parochial (uninformed), subject (deferential), or participant (assertive) political culture was preferable, given the enormous transformative task at hand. After an initial burst of enthusiasm for rebuilding the war-devastated country, average Poles quickly caught on to the paradox: Their role was limited to serving as hewers of wood and drawers of water. A subject political culture was to be created even while ideology advocated a participatory one.

Polish society was urged to support regime efforts to fashion new relations of production, new economic priorities, and new ways of thinking. Two major difficulties with these campaigns were, to begin with, that not many Poles ever shared the ultimate objectives—state ownership, industrialization, and socialist education—and, second, that the "campaign managers" entrusted with eliciting support for the objectives were plagued with credibility problems of their own. Neither ends nor means were taken seriously by broad sections of Polish society.

The communist regime did not have the luxury of dealing with a normative tabula rasa. As we have seen, over the centuries Polish culture had developed individualistic, antiauthoritarian traditions. Only on rare occasions in history did Poles give their unconditional obedience to rulers, foreign-born or not. The communist regime learned that it would be difficult to overcome society's distrust of government, an orientation that had been nurtured over centuries. The modal political culture was, therefore, an obstacle to building a new order. And while it is possible to exaggerate the importance of historical conditioning, it would be a greater mistake to neglect altogether the impact of ideas associated with *szlachta* democracy and the romantic insurrectionary ideas dating from the period of the partitions on contemporary political beliefs.[29]

In a country that historically had more experience of political anarchy than of authoritarianism or democracy, then, the cyclical revolts against communist rulers came as no surprise. But other dimensions of the value system posited by Marxism and the one internalized by Polish society came into conflict. The atheist world outlook espoused by communism was alien to a nation whose historians had been describing it as the *antemurale christianitatis*. Dialectical materialism as an explanation for human progress left Poles incredulous. Their history had demonstrated the centrality of human agency in bringing about change and, within this framework, the mobilizing potential of patriotism, not class solidarity. For Marx and many Soviet ideologues, work had an instrumental value—to bring about human emancipation and self-fulfillment—as well as constituting a goal in itself. In a nation sometimes stereotyped as lacking a work ethic altogether, such a prescriptive political culture was unlikely to take root quickly.

Nevertheless, on several counts Polish political culture was amenable to transformation. Under the communist regime more egalitarian values began to emerge, though they began to be called into question again during the 1980s, the decade of economic crisis. With the same caveat, there was growing acknowledgment of the advantages of the welfare state and also of state ownership of the larger factories and plants rather than ownership by unscrupulous local or foreign capitalists. Finally, workers and, after them, other sections of society increasingly felt that they were empowered to govern their own spheres of life. The emergence in the 1970s of a civil society managing more and more of its own affairs was not unrelated to the persistent calls of communist leaders for people to become engaged in the major developmental tasks of the nation. Of course, civil society redefined these tasks in ways incompatible with the socialist system. The next chapter examines the shift in the value system in greater detail.

Political Groups

One defining characteristic of a Leninist regime is prohibition of any type of subsystem autonomy, that is, freedom in any area of political life from the influence of the hegemonic communist party. In Poland as elsewhere in the Soviet bloc, the communist regime ruthlessly quashed autonomous group activity during the Stalinist period. Although by the early 1970s some Western scholars, notably Gordon Skilling, detected the emergence of special-interest groups in these communist systems, they were invariably embedded in institutional structures (thus, for example, an education lobby might emerge out of the Ministry of Education).[30] The authorities did, however, create support organizations and groups intended to serve as transmission belts, or mediating structures, between themselves and the public.

If we exclude the political parties and proregime lay Catholic groups given representation in the Sejm, the largest political organization was the Polish Socialist Youth Union (Związek Socjalistycznej Młodzieży Polskiej—ZSMP), which in 1985 had 1.5 million members.[31] While it was not quite the Polish equivalent of the Young Communist League of the USSR—ideological indoctrination was not its principal activity—the ZSMP's national and local officers served as unofficial representatives of the party and at times they doubled as party officials. The national head of the ZSMP was generally a member of the Central Committee and, at times, even of the Politburo or the Secretariat.

The largest formally nonpolitical organization was the Central Council of Trade Unions (Centralna Rada Związków Zawodowych—CRZZ), which had 12 million members dispersed across various branch unions at the beginning of 1980. The CRZZ was stacked with party appointees even though the bulk of the rank and file was not affiliated with the communist party. It represented the interests of the workers in a highly circumscribed way. Although it could not negotiate wage claims with state enterprises, it had influence on decisions concerning bonuses, fringe benefits, and occupational safety standards. Like most mass associations, it seemed particularly preoccupied with providing leisure time activities for its members. Trade unions were also effective in protecting workers from being fired, for example, for unproductivity or absenteeism. They were powerless, however, to halt government reprisals against workers who participated in strikes or engaged in clandestine political activity, as occurred in 1976. The fact that by fall 1980 Solidarity had been created and soon had 10 million members was clear evidence of the failure of the CRZZ to represent workers' concerns.

In addition to the ZSMP and the CRZZ, a third mass organization that was nominally independent of the party and was intended to protect special group interests was the Patriotic Movement for National Rebirth (Patriotyczny Ruch Odrodzenia Narodowego—PRON), set up in 1982 in the aftermath of Solidarity's delegalization. Intended as an umbrella group that could serve as a forum for concerned citizens not in the party to express their views about reform, the PRON attracted little interest in the years of martial law even though it was enshrined in the constitution in 1983. The head of the PRON's national council and three-quarters of the members of its executive body did not belong to the party, but it was enough that several high party officials and many rank-and-file members were active in the PRON for the organization to be discredited. In 1986 its membership peaked at 1.2 million, of whom two-thirds were in the party. Yet, in a strange way, the PRON may have taught the communist leadership that there should be a permanent place in politics for disaffected intellectuals and that a loyal opposition might be preferable to no legal opposition at all. In other words, the PRON helped ease the transition for the Jaruzelski administration from symbolic or manipulated participation at the start of the 1980s to a meaningful kind by the end of the decade.

Other organizations included the Polish Red Cross (3.8 million members), the Polish-Soviet Friendship Society (2.5 million), and the Polish Scout Union, the National Defense League, and the Agricultural Circles (each with close to 2 million). The Veterans' Association, with 800,000 members, was as nationalist an organization as could exist under the socialist system. The Women's League, with 500,000, was as far removed from a feminist movement committed to women's advancement as one could imagine. The volunteer militia reserve was a particularly sinister group that informed on citizens, enforced bylaws and regulations, and, when necessary, roughed up citizens. Ethnic and regional differences were minimal and did not serve as a primary source of organizational activity. Indeed, the authorities suppressed associations that might represent minority groups such as Belarus, Germans, Jews, or Ukrainians. In their place were cultural organizations that highlighted folklore.

In 1956 the first independent workers' organizations were set up in factories. These worker councils were intended to be the cornerstone of workplace democracy in socialist Poland. Because of their democratic and independent character, Gomułka acted swiftly to emasculate them. In 1956, too, the cultural intelligentsia organized around brash new periodicals such as *Po Prostu* and seemed poised to carve out autonomous political space. But the party leadership cracked down on them, and all organized political activity outside the party's reach was banned. Independent political organization had to wait another twenty years before it could have an impact on the system. How political mobilization succeeded in creating independent political groups, above all Solidarity in 1980, is treated in Chapter 3.

Political Structure and
Regime Performance

The organizational framework of the Polish communist regime was modeled on that of the Soviet Union. The most distinctive feature of the model was the idea of separation of powers not, as we might anticipate, of the executive and legislative branches as in many Western states but of the communist party and the institutions of government. The party was to formulate overall policy for the country; the government's job was to implement that policy. The slogan launched in the 1970s—the party directs and the government governs—may not have resolved the many ambiguities stemming from the existence of two massive parallel institutions, but it captured the general division of labor between the two. As the source of policymaking, the communist party was concerned above all with politics. As the implementer of the party's policies, the government performed primarily administrative functions. And if the head of the communist party was the most powerful politician in the country, the government head, or prime minister, was in many ways the country's economic overlord.

Before examining the formal organization of the communist political system, we should recognize that this organization was in large measure a facade for arbitrary rule by an oligarchy propped up by Soviet power. The sociologist Jacek Kurczewski has exposed the charade of legality: "This is exactly the essence of the revolutionary doctrine and practice of Communism: to create an order in which any arbitrary decision by authority is legal, while any reference made to law that runs contrary to the authorities' wish is illegal."[32]

In theory, then, the government and the party had their own legislative and executive structures. Every four or five years, elections were held; 460 deputies were elected to the Sejm in the last communist elections in October 1985. Although all adult Polish citizens had the right to vote, they were presented with a list of candidates approved by the Polish United Workers' Party (Polska Zjednoczona Partia Robotnicza—PZPR). A minority of candidates belonged to satellite parties of the

PZPR or to approved Catholic lay groups or were not party members but had earned the trust of the party. The formula devised by the PZPR that prevailed, with little change, for Sejm elections between 1957 and 1985 was 261 seats for the PZPR, 113 for the United Peasants' Party (Zjednoczone Stronnictwo Ludowe— ZSL), 37 for the Democratic Party (Stronnictwo Demokratyczne—SD), and the remainder for two Catholic lay groups—Pax and Znak—and a nonparty bloc. Given that membership in the PZPR peaked in 1980 at 3 million whereas the ZSL's membership was never more than 500,000 and the SD's barely 100,000, the PZPR formula for distributing parliamentary seats was indeed "generous" to these minor parties.

In the years of crisis following Solidarity's delegalization, the Jaruzelski leadership sought greater legitimacy and, for the 1985 elections, changed the distribution formula: The guaranteed PZPR share was reduced to 245, still giving it a comfortable majority in the 460-seat chamber, while nonparty representation was increased from 49 to 75. Throughout the communist period, then, there were symbolic parliamentary elections but never electoral competition. An even more basic question was whether the Sejm, however elected, had any real say in governing Poland. Generally, the legislative work it performed was symbolic, for all important policy decisions had been taken earlier and elsewhere.

Ostensibly, as in the Westminster model, a government or cabinet was created from the ranks of the Sejm and was answerable to it. In Poland the government was called the Council of Ministers and was headed by the prime minister. Only between 1952 and 1954 (Bierut) and between 1981 and 1985 (Jaruzelski) were the prime ministers leaders of the party as well. Prime ministers were high-ranking party officials and at times may have disagreed with the party head but were never invested with the power of the latter. Poland also had a head of state, formally termed president of the Council of State. Although this was not really a presidency, in his bid to make Poland resemble a Western democracy Jaruzelski appointed himself to this position in 1985 and raised its stature. He remained the country's most powerful figure, however, not because he was president of the Council of State—still primarily a ceremonial position—but because he continued to be leader of the party. Transforming the institution of the presidency was to become a central issue at the roundtable talks.

The PZPR had its party convention, the Congress, generally held every five years. In practice, this convention drafted party programs, identified political and economic priorities, and selected a Central Committee that would represent it over the ensuing five years. Up to 2,000 rank-and-file party members from throughout the country were chosen as delegates to the Congress—their one limited opportunity to interact with the party elite. The Central Committee of about 200 members convened several times a year to debate issues brought before it by the party leadership. As the deliberative body and quasiparliament of the party, it occasionally played a key role in deciding disputes between members of the party oligarchy. For example, it selected Stanisław Kania to succeed Gierek as party leader after the emergence of Solidarity in summer 1980. Later it was the Central Committee that replaced Kania with Jaruzelski in October 1981 to prepare for the imposition of martial law. Again, it was a seriously divided Central Committee that reluctantly agreed to hold roundtable talks with the political opposition in 1989 after Jaruzelski threatened to resign as party leader.

In answer to a common question of Western political science—who governs?—in communist Poland most citizens would have named the executive body of the party—the Politburo—or its head, the first secretary. The Politburo consisted of the twelve or so most powerful men in the country (only one woman served on the Politburo in the communist period), and the party head presided over its weekly meetings. Politburo members and the party leader were officially elected by the Central Committee, but in practice shifting majoritarian coalitions on the Politburo usually persuaded the Central Committee to choose like-minded men of the majority. Even in the Stalinist period, the most important matters of state were discussed and decided upon within this body, giving communist rule in Poland an oligarchical rather than a dictatorial character.

Alongside the Politburo stood another executive body, the Secretariat, which tended to be somewhat smaller. Its primary function was to oversee the party bureaucracy. Thus, the various administrative departments dealing with such core subjects as ideology, internal security, and international affairs and staffed with top-of-the-line apparatchiks answered to individual members (secretaries) of the Secretariat. The Secretariat was chaired by a first secretary, who was the party leader. In this way the role of presiding over the Secretariat lent the party leader his official title, first secretary.

These elaborate structures of government and the communist party were replicated at all levels of administration. From town and rural districts to the provincial level, the government structure included popularly elected councils and appointed chief executives. The party convened annual general meetings of its rank-and-file membership, but these were in practice run by powerful local party bosses. The system bred many problems: duplication of functions, the inevitable unclear lines of demarcation, cumulation of posts by leaders, at times intense rivalry between incumbents of party and government positions, general incompetence, corruption, irresponsibility, and lack of accountability to the public. A persuasive case can be made that communism's collapse was occasioned by such institutional determinism.

Although the structures we have identified did not change in any fundamental way throughout the communist period, the political styles of individual leaders varied and produced differing consequences. Regime performance varied, too. What the Marxists had said of capitalism proved increasingly to be an accurate description of communist regime performance: It tended to deteriorate more frequently and more profoundly over time. Initial developmental breakthroughs were generated by the needs to reconstruct the infrastructure of a war-devastated country and to modernize social and economic relations inherited from the interwar period. The coming to power in 1956 of a perceived nationalist communist—Gomułka—briefly raised expectations about regime performance but did not improve the performance itself. As Gomułka's ascetic lifestyle and value system were converted into nationwide austerity during the "little stabilization" of the 1960s, economic growth rates fell in nearly all sectors, from industrial and agricultural production to living standards and real wages.

The halcyon days of regime performance were the mid-1970s, engineered by the self-styled Silesian technocrat Gierek, through heavy borrowing from the West. Societal quiescence was exchanged for material benefits, which the Gierek regime was able to expand because its economic capacity temporarily increased with the inflow of Western capital. The "social compact"[33] between the party and society seemed to hold for a time, but the disturbing 1976 protests by workers in Radom and Ursus indicated that it was largely contingent on continued improvements in regime performance. When this began to decline rapidly after 1979, Solidarity arose to put forward an agenda of political reform viewed as indispensable to making economic reform effective. Martial law, imposed in December 1981 to ban Solidarity, proved both a political and an economic cataclysm to the system from which it never recovered. Further stripped of its economic capacity by U.S. sanctions and Soviet recession, the Jaruzelski regime began to move steadily to a form of market socialism. Half-measures did nothing to improve economic performance, however, and in 1988 the political authorities searched for ways of sharing economic responsibilities with the opposition while limiting costs to the regime. This led to formal roundtable talks and the semifree elections of early 1989. It seems self-evident that had it not been for rapid economic decline, the communists would never have consented to a transfer of power to the political opposition. Notwithstanding the many sophistic and metaphysical interpretations of the communist collapse—moral bankruptcy, psychological loss of nerve, creation of a civil society—in the end society judged the regime by its performance and decided to have done with it. Marx had been correct that, in the last instance, economic relations determined the political superstructure. He probably would have had no quarrel with the verdict rendered by working people on their incompetent regimes.

Ruling Coalitions and Leadership Style

An anecdote attributed to President Jimmy Carter's national security adviser, Zbigniew Brzezinski, sums up the changes in leadership style of successive Soviet rulers: Under Lenin the USSR was run like a church, under Stalin it was run like an enormous prison camp, under Khrushchev it was run like a circus, and under Brezhnev it was run like the U.S. Post Office. Polish communist rulers were not as diversified a group as their Soviet counterparts, and one particular leadership style dominated for all but ten years of the regime: ascetism. Bierut was probably not an ascetic by choice but was required to follow the "simple" lifestyle actively encouraged by the supreme leader, Stalin himself. By contrast, Gomułka and Jaruzelski were true believers in the socialist project and pursued personal virtue as defined by the Marxist value system. They were no less demanding of themselves and their comrades than of the society they sought to remodel. Their long working hours, reclusiveness, and personal distaste for items of luxury and leisure (cars for Gomułka, alcohol for Jaruzelski) made them difficult for even other communist leaders to relate to. Jaruzelski was tormented more than Gomułka had been by the transparent failures of the regime, and he distanced himself from the crude Stalinist methods used to control society. Of all the Polish communists who rose to leadership posts between 1945 and 1989, few could match Gomułka and Jaruzelski for their concern with pursuing their own sometimes simplistic ideals of egalitarianism and social justice.

In the coalitions forged by these leaders, however, differences were apparent. Bierut had been forced into a coalition with the nativist Gomułka in 1944 and then was compelled to purge him from the coalition in 1948. Crucial to his tenure as party leader were effective working relationships with the security and defense establishments, both controlled at this juncture by Soviet officials appointed to Polish posts. Gomułka's ruling coalition primarily co-opted party officials linked neither to the liberal (Puławska) nor to the hard-line (Natolin) faction. Jaruzelski adopted a "clipping of wings" policy that, in terms of appearance, followed that of Gomułka: Liberals and conservatives were regularly purged from top party posts in equal numbers. By the late 1980s, however, his coalition was dependent on support from party reformers, who supplied it with the political resources needed to approach the Solidarity opposition and set up roundtable talks.

The accession of Gierek to the position of party first secretary in 1970 produced a distinctive leadership style for the next decade. Nominally a technocrat, Gierek adopted a noblesse oblige approach that opened up the party to anyone interested in joining it—Catholics, Marxist heretics, the ideologically indifferent, careerists. As a Silesian, Gierek was more "Westernized" than previous communist leaders. He had been baptized, had lived during the war in the West (as a coal miner in Belgium), spoke French, and developed a sycophantic relationship with French President Valery Giscard d'Estaing that included highly publicized hunting trips. It was Gierek who set about making available to Poles a "people's car"—the Polski Fiat 126p—the ultimate symbol of the pretentious communist consumer society. Family members and friends of Gierek took advantage of their connections to acquire riches and status. Gierek began the transformation of Poland from a seminary to a shopping mall.

Turning the party into a catchall institution had consequences for the inner leadership. It became a looser, less disciplined coalition. Gierek became an "imperial party secretary," more imperious than authoritarian. His prime minister, Piotr Jaroszewicz, was a contrast in style to Gierek: He had lived in Russia, spoke Russian, and was solicitous of the Kremlin's views. In Carl Linden's term, the prime minister set up a "second antagonistic axis" to the party leadership and at times seemed to have more de facto power than Gierek.[34] Other ambitious politicians were no longer frightened to challenge the first secretary's authority in this period, and both the security head Franciszek Szlachcic and Economic Minister Edward Babiuch made bids to replace him.

The ruling coalition of the 1970s was, in short, a more precariously divided group than earlier ones. Cracks within the Politburo appeared at the same time that the political opposition began to organize. The coexistence of a shaky ruling coalition and a more determined opposition provided Solidarity with the opportunity to organize in 1980. Several days after Solidarity was legalized, Gierek's coalition came apart, and he was removed as party head.

Two paradoxes appear in this account of leadership style and coalition making. Whereas Gierek adopted a co-optive rather than a repressive style toward an increasingly antagonistic society, it backfired and led to both better organized opposition groups and factional intrigues within the elite. In turn, Jaruzelski as a true believer internalized a far more constraining belief system that might have been expected to militate against his quickly adjusting to the changing political and economic conditions of the 1980s. Yet he proved to be remarkably adaptable and was able to create the opening to the opposition that ended Marxism's rule in Poland.

In this chapter we have examined the socioeconomic structure of the communist regime, the international environment within which it operated, Poland's political culture, and the political actors dependent upon the communist party. We have analyzed systemic features including the structure of power, leadership coalitions, and style of governing. We now turn to the causes of regime crisis.

Notes

1. I have made an effort to demonstrate the dissonance in applied Marxism in Ray Taras, *Ideology in a Socialist State: Poland 1956–1983.* Cambridge: Cambridge University Press, 1984. I have also sought to highlight how Marxism as critique served to undermine Marxism as state ideology in Ray Taras (ed.), *The Road to Disillusion: From Critical Marxism to Postcommunism.* Armonk, NY: M. E. Sharpe, 1992. In retrospect, it is clear that I attached too much significance to ideological dysfunction and not enough to the nuts-and-bolts structural factors central to the CCC model.

2. Joseph Rothschild, *Return to Diversity: A Political History of East Central Europe Since World War II.* New York: Oxford University Press, 1993, p. 84.

3. See Piotr Kostikow and Bohdan Roliński, *Widziane z Kremla: Moskwa-Warszawa, Gra o Polskę.* Warsaw: BGW, 1992.

4. F. A. Hayek, *The Fatal Conceit: The Errors of Socialism.* Edited by W. W. Bartley III. Chicago: University of Chicago Press, 1991, p. 6.

5. Hayek, *The Fatal Conceit,* p. 12.

6. Hayek, *The Fatal Conceit,* p. 21.

7. F. A. Hayek, *Law, Legislation, and Liberty,* vol. 1, *Rules and Order.* London: Routledge and Kegan Paul, 1973.

8. Hayek, *The Fatal Conceit,* p. 83.

9. Hayek, *The Fatal Conceit,* p. 45.

10. Hayek, *The Fatal Conceit,* p. 19.

11. Hayek, *The Fatal Conceit,* p. 87.

12. Hayek, *The Fatal Conceit,* p. 95.

13. Hayek, *The Fatal Conceit,* p. 99.

14. See especially N. Scott Arnold, *Marx's Radical Critique of Capitalist Society.* New York: Oxford University Press, 1990, chap. 10.

15. Główny Urząd Statystyczny, *Rocznik statystyczny 1991.* Warsaw: GUS, 1991, pp. xxiv–xxvi, xxxvi–xxxviii.

16. Główny Urząd Statystyczny, *Rocznik statystyczny 1984.* Warsaw: GUS, 1984, pp. 156–163.

17. Włodzimierz Wesołowski, *Class, Strata, and Power.* London: Routledge and Kegan Paul, 1979, p. 118.

18. Edmund Wnuk-Lipiński, "Nierówność, deprywacje i przywileje jako podłoże konfliktu społecznego," in *Polacy '88: Dynamika konfliktu a szanse reform.* Warsaw: Uniwersytet Warszawski, 1989. A poor household was understood as one having less than 50 percent of average income per capita; a wealthy one had more than 150 percent of the average.

19. Of the many illuminating sociological studies carried out by both Western and Polish sociologists on changing social structure, two introductory works summarizing developments for different time periods are George Kolankiewicz and David Lane (eds.), *Social Groups in Polish Society.* London: Macmillan, 1973; George Kolankiewicz and Paul Lewis, *Poland: Politics, Economics, Society.* London: Pinter, 1988.

20. For detailed analysis, see W. W. Kulski, *Germany and Poland: From War to Peaceful Relations.* Syracuse, NY: Syracuse University Press, 1976.

21. Paul Marer, "Soviet Economic Policy in Eastern Europe," in U.S. Congress, Joint Economic Committee, *Reorientation and Commercial Relations of the Economies of Eastern Europe.* Washington, DC: U.S. Government Printing Office, 1974, pp. 161–162.

22. The defense budget was 183 billion złoty at a time when the base exchange rate was 80 złoty to US$1.

23. The 1993 defense budget was 37,487 billion złoty. The rate for most of 1993 approximated 20,000 złoty to US$1 (1 billion złoty = US$50,000). The education budget was just slightly higher, at 39,700 billion złoty.

24. Of course, the combination of the ending of the Cold War and severe economic crisis at home necessitated major cuts in defense expenditures. Still, spending levels in the 1990s generally reflected what was needed to maintain a credible defense posture.

25. Two overviews of Poland's international position are Arthur Rachwald, *Poland Between the Superpowers.* Boulder: Westview Press, 1983; Sarah Meiklejohn Terry, *Poland's Place in Europe.* Princeton: Princeton University Press, 1983.

26. Hélène Carrère d'Encausse, *Big Brother: The Soviet Union and Soviet Europe.* New York: Holmes and Meier, 1987, p. 268.

27. John Rensenbrink, *Poland Challenges a Divided World.* Baton Rouge, LA: Louisiana State University Press, 1988, p. 1.

28. George Steiner, *Proofs.* London: Granta Books, 1992, p. 51.

29. On the clash of romantic and realist value systems, see Adam Bromke, *Poland's Politics: Idealism vs. Realism.* Cambridge, MA: Harvard University Press, 1967.

30. H. Gordon Skilling, *Interest Groups and Communist Politics.* Boston: Little, Brown, 1971.

31. All membership figures for 1985 are taken from Główny Urząd Statystyczny, *Mały rocznik statystyczny 1986*. Warsaw: GUS, 1986, p. 23.

32. Jacek Kurczewski, *The Resurrection of Rights in Poland*. Oxford: Clarendon Press, 1993, p. 46.

33. Alex Pravda, "Political Attitudes and Activity," in Jan Triska and Charles Gati (eds.), *Blue-Collar Workers in Eastern Europe*. Boston: Allen and Unwin, 1981, p. 47.

34. Carl Linden, "Opposition and Faction in Communist Party Leaderships," in Frank Belloni and Dennis Beller (eds.), *Faction Politics: Political Parties and Factionalism in Comparative Perspective*. Santa Barbara, CA: ABC-Clio, 1978, p. 379.

3

Crises of the Communist System

Writers striving to explain the crisis of communism have identified numerous factors as sources of popular dissatisfaction and political mobilization against the regime. The list—by no means exhaustive—includes (1) regime performance, (2) relative deprivation and rising expectations, (3) cultural transformations and changing value systems, (4) shifting social cleavages and mass alignments, and (5) rising participatory demands stimulated by the arrival of new groups with new resources and new agendas. All of these factors need to be examined if we are to account for the sudden breakdown of an authoritarian system that had a record of employing force whenever its survival was threatened. Of particular importance is the association among these factors. Although ordering them into a causal chain would seem heuristically contrived, establishing no relationships among them would be an abdication of social science's responsibility to advance explanatory models for historical events.

Phase II of the CCC framework focuses on long-term processes pushing for regime change. Economic development, changes in the social structure, and evolution in the international system—described in the previous chapter as structural features—now become explanatory variables.[1] The outcome variables on which this chapter focuses include value change, cognitive mobilization, political disaffection, and mobilization of opposition forces. All of these variables become, in turn, the factors that increase pressure for a democratic breakthrough. This phase of the analysis, then, describes the long-term processes that remodel the political culture, undermine the legitimacy of authoritarian institutions, and mobilize democratizing political forces. I begin with the macro-level factors that triggered political change.

The Explanatory Variables

Phase II analysis measures the amount of *socioeconomic change* that took place from the Phase I preexisting system to the Phase III democratic breakthrough. It also looks at the influence of developments in the *international system* that produce an unblocking of democratic forces.

Socioeconomic Change

It is important to recognize that East European economies had lagged considerably behind their Western counterparts even before communist systems were established. The political scientist Andrew Janos traces Eastern Europe's backwardness: Around 1800 the ratio of the aggregate national product per capita between Eastern and Western Europe was on the order of 80:100. By 1910, the per capita income gap between six East European and six West European nations had widened to about 48:100. Averaging out the 1926–1934 period produced a further deterioration in the ratio, to 37:100 (for Poland 35:100). Janos makes two separate calculations for level of economic development in the communist period up to 1980 and concludes that "whatever methodological assumptions we make, Communist economies were drifting downward from the relative position their countries had held in the world economy prior to the Second World War."[2] He estimates the 1980 per capita income ratio at 33:100. For Poland it was 34:100, that is, almost unchanged from the 1926–1934 period. The Polish economy seemed, therefore, to be holding its own under communism, at least until 1980. Of course, the economic crisis of the 1980s devastated Eastern Europe further, and the hardship of economic transformation in 1990–1992 reduced gross domestic products (GDPs) by about 26 percent (for Poland 18 percent). Janos's final estimate is a 25:100 ratio, a historic low, between Eastern and Western Europe by the end of 1992. He concludes: "The sad fact is that Eastern Europe has never been more economically backward or underdeveloped compared to the West than it is today."[3]

We need to disaggregate Poland's economic performance under communism to see where successes may have occurred and failures were particularly serious. Statistical data make clear that, despite the ultimate economic failures that were attributable to the communist system, the modernization of social and economic life was undeniable. The proportion of the labor force employed in the agricultural sector was halved, from 54 percent in 1950 to 27 percent in 1990. If we take into account that, according to the last prewar census carried out in 1931, some 73 percent of the population was rural, with 60 percent making their livelihood from agriculture, this transformation of economic life is even more dramatic.[4]

It can be argued, of course, that rapid urbanization would have occurred regardless of communist policy; it may have been an inescapable feature of the modernization that affected most of Europe after the war. Still, the Stalinist fetish with extensive growth encompassing diverse industrial sectors, forced industrialization that channeled virtually all the state's accumulation of revenue and savings into investment earmarked for heavy industry, and production of producer goods so that, for example, massive steel mills were constructed in order to expand the infrastructure for industry shaped the kind of social modernization that resulted.

Thus, employment in agriculture had been halved by 1990 and now ranked behind both industrial and service sectors, but each of these sectors employed about 36 percent of the active workforce. Poland's service sector remained, therefore, about half the size of its counterparts in the West, such as those of the United States and Holland, where about 70 percent of the labor force was employed. The communist modernization model was different from the capitalist one and had distinct consequences.

Table 3.1 presents longitudinal aggregate data indicating the degree of change that occurred in the following areas: gross domestic product (GDP) per capita, percent of the work force employed outside the agricultural sector, urbanization, educational attainment (number of students enrolled in primary, secondary, and higher education), and media diffusion (circulation of newspapers and number of radio and television sets). The data draw our attention to an increasingly better-educated and better-informed population. Steady growth was recorded in the absolute number and proportion of the population enrolled at all levels of the educational system. The falloff in the number of high school and college graduates observed in the 1980s was largely the result of demographic factors and not a sign of educational regression; it was strongly correlated with the decline in primary school enrollment of the preceding decade. A more curious phenomenon was the drop in newspaper and magazine sales by the end of the 1980s. On the surface, it could be associated primarily with the precipitous decline in people's disposable income, combined with an inflationary spiral when prices were freed from state control. Indeed, similar declines are recorded after 1987 in other cultural arenas such as book buying, moviegoing, and attendance at concerts and theaters. At the same time, fewer people were visiting public libraries and borrowing books from them. It appears that the way in which people made use of free time began to change in the last years of communist rule.

When we consider areas not included in Table 3.1, the achievements of the communist regime appear substantial. Real income nearly tripled between 1955 and 1981, the peak year. Material living standards improved: Between 1946 and 1990 meat consumption—historically a reliable indicator of living standards—quadrupled while consumption of potatoes was halved. But again, no improvements were recorded between 1986 and 1990. Furthermore, finding meat in the state stores was a perennial problem. A 1975 survey revealed that 61 percent of respondents regarded the provision of meat as poor or very poor.[5] Not surprisingly, the February 1981 government decision to ration meat was supported by both Solidarity and the public.

It was the country's disastrous economic performance in the 1980s, then, that produced widespread dissatisfaction and caused political mobilization that led to the removal of the regime. Economic decline was precipitated by a conjunction of factors—political instability throughout the decade, the effect of U.S. sanctions imposed after martial law, the beginnings of a worldwide recession, and, of course, the ineffective command economy. But, as Hayek and North have explained, getting

TABLE 3.1 Indices of Economic and Social Change, 1946–1990

Measure	1946	1950	1960	1970	1980	1990
Gross Domestic Product ($US)[a]	—	271	564	955	1,676 4,276[a]	4,099[a]
Urban population (percent)	33	37	48	52	58	62
Workforce outside of agriculture (percent)	—	46	57	66	70	74
Students in primary schools (000s)	3,322	3,360	4,963	5,389	4,260	5,301
High school graduates (000s)	10	29	41	33	121	100
College graduates (000s)	4	15	21	47	84	52
Newspaper & magazine sales (per 1,000 people)	—	73	62	90	98	74
Registered radios (per 1,000 people)	20	59	176	174	243	287
Registered TVs (per 1,000 people)	—	—	14	129	223	260
Telephones (per 1,000 people)	5	8	18	33	54	86
Cars (per 1,000 people)	1	2	4	15	67	138

[a]Until 1992, Polish economic statistics were expressed in terms of Net Material Product (NMP) rather than, as in the West, Gross Domestic Product (GDP). I have provided GDP figures for 1980 and 1990 using the Purchasing Power Parity (PPP) measure. I have also calculated NMP, expressed in US$, for 1950 to 1980. If the ratio of GDP to NMP for 1980 (2.5:1) held good for earlier years, it might suggest, for example, that 1950 GDP per capita was $678. These are notional figures, then.

Source: Główny Urząd Statystyczny, *Mały Rocznik Statystyczny 1994.* Warsaw: GUS, 1994, pp. 402–403, 418–419.

the economic institutions right was the key variable in moving to economic recovery, and this a centrally planned economy was incapable of doing.

Real income fell by one-third between 1981 and 1990—perhaps the ultimate explanation for the communist leadership's allowing the "shadow" Solidarity leadership that had been tracking communist failures for a decade to assume responsibility.[6] Table 3.2 provides more detailed data underscoring the deterioration of living standards between 1982 and 1988 for specific socio-occupational groups. Although there were more poor people in all social groups by 1988, the numbers grew especially quickly within the ranks of unskilled workers and peasants. By contrast, the three groups whose proportion of above-average wealthy people actually increased—if only slightly—in this interval were professionals, intermediate nonmanuals, and skilled workers. In the last years of communism, income distribution began to shift in the direction of the pattern obtaining in capitalist countries. Arguably, the economic expectations of middle-class Poles (professionals and nonmanuals) were growing in this decade, turning this social category (which was not officially recognized as such by communist statisticians) into a political actor ready to coalesce with longer-standing opposition groups in society.

In summary, when assessing the amount of socioeconomic change that occurred under the communist system, we can focus on a time-series analysis and come away impressed by what the system was able to accomplish in a country that

TABLE 3.2   Poverty and Wealth as Measured by Per Capita Income According to Socio-Occupational Group, 1982 and 1988 (percentages)

Socio-occupational Group	Year	Low Income	High Income
Professionals	1982	0.6	21.6
	1988	10.7	27.7
Intermediate nonmanuals	1982	4.3	8.5
	1988	15.1	18.7
Skilled workers	1982	9.0	8.1
	1988	23.5	10.1
Unskilled workers	1982	9.6	6.3
	1988	31.7	2.9
Private farmers	1982	12.8	15.3
	1988	40.2	11.7
Other owners	1982	1.6	31.1
	1988	10.1	30.4

Low income = less than 50 percent of average household per capita income
High income = more than 150 percent of average household per capita income

Source: Edmund Wnuk–Lipiński, "Nierówność, deprywacje i przywileje jako podłoże konfliktu społecznego," in *Polacy '88: Dynamika konfliktu a szanse reform.* Warsaw: IFiS PAN, 1989.

was generally underdeveloped by European standards. This is an argument made by excommunists in Poland today, who contend that current historiography gives the previous system no credit for some of its clear achievements. But if we adopt a comparative framework we find that the communist system may not have advanced Poland's modernization to the fullest. To have expanded the telephone system nearly twentyfold between 1946 and 1990 was a hollow success when it still left Poland close to the bottom of the list of European countries in the size of its telephone grid. Similarly, the number of car owners increased from 23,000 in 1946 to 5.3 million in 1990—interestingly, continuing to rise steadily even in the recession years of the 1980s, which tells us something about both consumer preferences and a rapidly emerging middle class. But the majority of the cars on the road were small Polish Fiats, only marginally better than the notorious East German Trabant and far below the standards of West European auto manufacturers.

Did Poles think in terms of relative deprivation, then, rather than of absolute gains? In order for a nation to feel relatively deprived, comparisons with other societies are necessary. Regime policy toward foreign travel was always more liberal in Poland than in any other Soviet-bloc country, so many citizens had indeed had occasion to visit Soviet-bloc countries regularly but also Western ones. In 1980 nearly 9 million Poles traveled abroad, and by 1990 the number had reached 22 million. Unfortunately, these numbers aggregate everything from one-day visits to neighboring countries such as Czechoslovakia and East Germany to working holidays of several months in Western states so as to return home with hard currency. In general, we can say that comparing Poland with other countries became a natural reaction of many Poles. Furthermore, between 1976 and 1990 an average of more than 25,000 Poles per year emigrated to the West, mostly to Western Europe and North America, and the number would have been even larger if the immigration policies of the host countries had been more liberal. Naturally, the families of emigrants were kept regularly informed of the improving fortunes of their relatives abroad. A significant number of new emigrants even returned to visit their native country in subsequent years as fear of political reprisals faded. Whether it was through direct or indirect learning about the West, therefore, Polish citizens became acutely aware that their country lagged behind the West in many areas of social and economic—not to mention political—life. The sense of relative deprivation began to overshadow the absolute gains recorded under the communist system. When even these gains disappeared in the 1980s and socioeconomic change took on a negative character, the structural crisis of communism became obvious to all.

Regardless of how Polish citizens evaluated socioeconomic change in the communist period, democratization theorists would hold that the fact that change was recorded at all translated into pressure for political reform. In correlating economic development with third-wave democratization, for example, Huntington reports that three-quarters of countries that were nondemocratic in 1974 and had per capita GNPs of between US$1,000 and US$3,000 in 1976 had democratized significantly by 1989. With a per capita GNP of over US$2,000, Poland was already high in the "transition zone" in the mid-1970s. Comparing other countries in this zone (Spain, Portugal, and Czechoslovakia), Huntington concludes: "In the less constrained Iberian environment, political development caught up with economic development in the mid-1970s; in Eastern Europe that did not happen until Soviet controls were removed fifteen years later."[7] He alludes, however, to an additional factor, apart from Soviet domination, that triggered change: "In the third wave, the combination of substantial levels of economic development and short-term economic crisis or failure was the economic formula most favorable to the transition from authoritarian to democratic government."[8] Data from Table 3.1 clearly indicate the disjuncture between overall socioeconomic development under communism and the regression of the 1980s.

Changes in the International Environment

Both the seesaw struggle of the Cold War and the beginnings of a new world order also contributed to the crisis of communism. In the previous chapter we considered the deteriorating correlation of forces between the Soviet bloc and the Western liberal democracies.[9] The USSR seems to have fallen into the trap of imperial overstretch, making it more difficult for Kremlin leaders to enforce the same degree of control over their far-flung satellite states as the Stalinist dictatorship had been able to maintain over its still limited external empire, centered in Eastern Europe. In addition to such strategic considerations, in what other ways did the international environment change to put pressure on the authoritarian regime to democratize?

Of recent theorizing about the reasons for the conversion of many authoritarian regimes throughout the world to democracy in the 1970s and 1980s, the most celebrated analyses are those of Huntington and Francis Fukuyama. Poland presents an illuminating case for testing their contrasting explanations empirically.

In his provocative *The End of History and the Last Man*, Fukuyama is concerned with establishing the connection between democracy and the international environment. Although he intends to stress democracy as influence on rather than product of this environment, at times just the reverse cause-and-effect chain is perceptible. Charting the growth of liberal democracies worldwide, he argues that "there is a fundamental process at work that dictates a common evolutionary pattern for *all* human societies—in short, something like a Universal History of mankind in the direction of liberal democracy." Fukuyama sees this outcome as the end point, rather than a transition moment, in political evolution: "Of the different types of regimes that have emerged in the course of human history . . . , the only form of government that has survived intact to the end of the twentieth century has been liberal democracy."[10] The reason is that it most fully incorporates human ideas about what a just political order should look like. Modern natural science, which provides knowledge about the physical universe, is what Fukuyama identifies as "the Mechanism" that gives history its directionality. Traditionally, Marxists had been suspicious of science because of its purported nonideological or ideologically neutral character. But, citing perestroika as evidence, Fukuyama claims that Gorbachev was driven by the twin needs of military competition and economic development to accept modern technological civilization. The Mechanism is, in essence, then, the modernization imperative that Gorbachev fully recognized.

For Fukuyama, there are no "barbarians at the gate" left to propagate an anti-technological philosophy. He sees nationalism as the greatest threat to modernization in the contemporary world and quotes from Friedrich Nietzsche's *Thus Spoke Zarathustra* for effect: "State is the name of the coldest of all cold monsters." But he does not regard nationalism as sufficiently powerful to pursue an antitechnological thrust. He questions the historical significance of the wave of nationalism that has swept across the newly liberated states of the former Soviet external and internal empires: "It is curious why people believe that a phenomenon of such recent historical provenance as nationalism will henceforth be so permanent a feature of the human social landscape." Instead he stresses "the transitional nature of the new nationalist struggles now occurring in Eastern Europe" and claims that, paradoxically, it is a prerequisite for the spread of liberal democracy in the region: "Nationalism in these cases is a necessary concomitant to spreading democratization, as national and ethnic groups long denied a voice express themselves in favor of sovereignty and independent existence."[11]

Fukuyama's optimism about nationalism's historical contingency and the liberating power of the Mechanism is circumscribed by his reluctant recognition of the decisiveness of human agency. He concludes his book in this way: "It would seem that the chief threat to democracy would be our own confusion about what is really at stake. For while modern societies have evolved toward democracy, modern thought has arrived at an impasse, unable to come to a consensus on what constitutes man and his specific dignity, and consequently unable to define the rights of man."[12] What he has in mind is vacillation within the Western "posthistorical" world, but to varying degrees Poland and the other new democracies of the region have also questioned the nature and scope of rights while rather painlessly establishing procedural democracies. Fukuyama's analysis of democratization, then, highlights the working of universal forces as opposed to that of structural factors.

Like Fukuyama, Huntington is careful to contextualize recent change within a broad historical framework. Accordingly, he identifies two earlier waves of democratization. The first lasted a century, from 1828 to 1926, and consisted primarily of consolidating democratic institutions in Western states. Of paramount importance here were economic development, social modernization, and an intellectual ethos shaped by the ideas of social-contract theorists and of the French Revolution. The second wave subsumed the period from 1943 to 1962 and occurred in countries on the losing side of World War II and later in countries granted independence after colonial rule. Thus, military and political factors underlay it. According to this political scientist, however, reverse antidemocratic waves followed in each case: The interwar years brought dictators to power in Europe, while in the 1960s and early 1970s military governments in Africa, Asia, and Latin America produced praetorian or bureaucratic authoritarianism.

The third wave began in 1974 in southern Europe and by 1990 had led to democratic regimes' replacing authoritarian ones in some thirty countries. Instead of highlighting some universal source of this change, as Fukuyama does, Huntington stresses the varied background of these states. Some had alternated between democratic and authoritarian governments (Southern Cone countries), others were making their second try at democracy (Poland is included here), others had resumed democratic practices after an interruption (Chile), some were making a direct transition (Romania), while a last few were the product of decolonization (Papua New Guinea). Despite their differing starting points, Huntington inquires whether there is some overriding single cause for third-wave democratization, whether there is convergence produced by parallel development (as in GNP levels), whether a demonstration or domino effect (contagion) is at work or, finally, whether a prevailing nostrum or Zeitgeist has come into being.[13]

We have already seen the importance that Huntington attaches to economic development as a domestic source of democratization pressure. He puts little store either in the monocausal or the Zeitgeist theory of democratization. With regard to external influences, he identifies Eastern Europe as the region in which the most dramatic "snowballing," or demonstration effect, has taken place. In particular, changes in the lead country—for him, Poland is this lead country in Eastern Europe—"helped stimulate demands for comparable changes in neighboring and culturally similar countries."[14]

New policies of external actors were also decisive in third-wave democratization. The changing relationship between the superpowers was the basis of such change and has received the attention it deserves.[15] Other outside actors, including international regimes, further contributed to the third wave. The 1975 Helsinki Agreement, concluded by thirty-five European and North American states, pledged signatories to respect human rights and fundamental freedoms. Both the European Community (EC) and the Vatican were especially supportive of democratization. As a model of successful integration and economic growth, the credibility and influence of the EC increased, and it provided tangible incentives for democratization in Poland and the rest of the Soviet bloc. In addition, "Rome delegitimated authoritarian regimes in Catholic countries."[16] Already in the 1970s the Catholic church had become a force for democratic change in Latin America, and after John Paul II's accession in 1978 it became very influential in effecting similar change in the Catholic countries of Eastern Europe, as we have seen.

To summarize the influence attributed by scholars to the international environment as an explanatory variable of democratization, we have assessments that range from Fukuyama's quasi-determinist approach, imputing overriding power to natural science and its political culmination, liberal democracy, to Huntington's disaggregated, discrete analysis ascribing differing weights to different variables in different states. It would be ex post facto rationalization to claim that, in the case of Poland, liberalism had attracted numerous converts by the 1980s and, *qua* ideology, served as the galvanizing force for democratization. Fukuyama is correct to assert that as with nineteenth-century national-unity struggles in Germany and Italy—and, I would add, the nineteenth-century struggle for Polish independence—"nationalism and liberalism were also associated in Poland's drive for national rebirth in the 1980s."[17] But the association between nationalism and liberalism was largely an artifact of communist power, which both philosophical movements opposed. The distinct political identities behind nationalism and liberalism became clearer once the communist regime was dismantled.

More persuasive is Fukuyama's argument that the Mechanism—science—served as an invisible hand. It forced states to adopt the political order—liberal democracy—that could make the most of the modernizing potential of technological civilization. Further, Huntington's more particularist argument that incremental economic development, when followed by deteriorating domestic structures and demonstrably superior external structures, would cause a regime to reevaluate its policies and seek extrication from crisis is borne out by evidence presented in the Polish case. The obvious conclusion, then, is that the international environment, in both its strategic and its often-overlooked metaphysical form, contributed to democratization. The latter implanted a liberal, technocratic ethos in Poland and elsewhere in Eastern Europe. Poland's democracy was both the product of a global phenomenon and, in turn, a source of contagion for other countries in the region.

A discussion of the impact of the international environment in creating pressure for regime change in Poland would be incomplete without consideration of processes unfolding in the international political economy. In an increasingly interdependent world economy, any regime's capacity to maintain growth is in great measure affected by external international processes and actors. Global economic cycles of recession or boom, expansion of world trade, and increasing amounts of aid from international organizations or of loans and credits from foreign governments and commercial banks can augment regime capacity and help it meet rising expectations and increasing citizen demands on government. By contrast, trade barriers and economic sanctions can shrink regime capacity and lead to social explosions.

Between 1971 and 1980 the Gierek administration secured close to US$40 billion in credits from nonsocialist countries, thereby making Poland's economy more dependent on capitalist markets but also more vulnerable to economic cycles in the West. The purpose of obtaining Western investment, licenses, technology, and consumer goods on credit was to generate export-led growth that would in turn be directed to Western states. As Ben Slay writes, "By modernizing the country's industrial and agricultural base and improving the supply of consumer goods and thus work incentives, these imports were to generate increases in Polish hard-currency exports and thus provide the foreign exchange to pay off the credits."[18]

But a combination of factors—many but not all of the communist regime's own making—made this strategy backfire. Deteriorating terms of trade for Poland's agricultural and energy (coal) products, brought about by a glut in world markets by the late 1970s, were exacerbated by a rising interest burden fueled by double-digit inflation in Western states. Thus, although foreign capital flooded Poland for a time, trade with the West did not take off: The proportion of Polish exports going to the EC, for example, increased very slowly, from 17 percent in 1970 to 23 percent in 1985; the increase in imports from EC countries was nearly identical over this period. The collapse of trade with the West took on dramatic proportions between 1979 and 1983, when the volume of Western imports, upon which the economy had become dependent, was cut by 50 percent. It was caused both by Poland's external indebtedness and, therefore, inability to purchase Western goods and by economic sanctions imposed by the United States following the declaration of martial law. Government spokesman Jerzy Urban claimed at the time that sanctions had cost Poland billions of dollars' worth of exports. Trade with the West began to burgeon only in the period 1985–1991, when exports to the EC rose from 23 percent to 59 percent and imports from 21 percent to 53 percent.

In short, the regime's economic capacity was adversely affected by economic dependence on the West. Under a command economy Polish products remained uncompetitive in world markets. Given the increases in the early 1980s in the price of Soviet energy imports and cutbacks in Soviet deliveries, which forced Poland to look to the hard-currency energy markets of the Middle East, it is easy to understand the importance of shrinking regime capacity to regime stability.

Cognitive Mobilization as Outcome Variable

So far we have seen that, under the communist system, Poland underwent considerable socioeconomic change in the postwar period but a decline in regime performance by the 1980s produced new forms of political alignment expressing dissatisfaction with systemic failures. Macro-level change both helped engender micro-level change in the domain of values, causing a culture shift, and reshaped the society's political behavior.

There are two general outcome variables, then, in Phase II of the CCC model. One is value change and the cognitive mobilization it produces, that is, the recognition of the inherent problems of the socialist system. The other is behavioral change and the political mobilization it leads to. Both these outcome variables become explanatory factors for the democratic breakthrough and regime change discussed in Phase III of the analysis.

Attitudinal Change

It is widely accepted that regime performance produced value change, most clearly by stimulating discontent as a result of economic failures. More elusive an issue is the level of cognitive mobilization within society. Such mobilization, based on greater awareness of the sources of the country's crises and the range of alternatives available to resolve them, serves as an indicator of increasing political competence in society. The construction and expansion of civil society could be achieved only if such political competence replaced a subject political culture in which a sense of political inefficacy had been pervasive. The international environment could influence the rate of value change through the diffusion of ideas and culture promoting democratic attitudes. Given macro-level developmental changes, then, was there a shift within Polish society from acquiescent, authoritarian to participatory, democratic political values?

The first data to be considered are the perceptions of communist rulers themselves about cognitive mobilization and attitudes toward the political system. The communist authorities seemed convinced that the macro-level change they had engineered had proved functional for the system. Successful literacy and educational campaigns were largely interpreted as successful political socialization work by the party. Although party theoreticians occasionally reported on the political socialization work still to be done, it was generally not regarded as a serious problem. The modus vivendi achieved with the only institution possessing a viable competing ideology, the Catholic church, reassured party ideologues that anticommunist attitudes had been neutralized. As we have seen, membership in the communist party (the PZPR) had surpassed 3 million in 1980. Another 500,000 belonged to the satellite party, the ZSL, and just over 100,000 small-scale entrepreneurs, white-collar workers, schoolteachers, and the like to the SD. Millions of other Poles were registered in communist-organized trade unions and professional associations and in women's, student, and youth movements. Even if such mass membership largely represented a spurious participation, the numbers were impressive enough for the authorities to deduce that the system could depend on large-scale participatory support. Only when autonomous social mobilization began in the second half of the 1970s did they confront incontrovertible counterfactuals exposing the shallowness of the political socialization activity of earlier decades. Under Gierek, even this evidence was patronizingly dismissed as of secondary importance.

If the party leadership was under the impression that cognitive mobilization was working, on the whole, in their favor, did the results of survey research on popular attitudes toward the regime over time concur? Attitudinal change is not as easily quantifiable as macro-level change, and, because it is ephemeral and cumulative in nature, it is especially hard to measure longitudinally. The reliability of public opinion research in the West has been questioned because of the volatility of public attitudes and their dependence on changing circumstances. As David Mason has observed, "The difficulties are multiplied with such research in communist countries."[19] Respondents were more easily intimidated by interviewers or unwilling in any case to take the chance of giving candid opinions. Samples were unrepresentative and interview teams unreliable. Direct political questions, including approval ratings for party leaders or the system as a whole, were rarely asked. This was at a time when the ruling elite stood to learn much about an enigmatic, elusive, and ambiguous body of public opinion. Usually survey results were not released at all, and when they were it was often as a contribution to the regime's "propaganda of success." Under communist rule, data on societal attitudes were as subject to censure as reporting on natural or economic disasters.

Not surprisingly, writers developed other approaches and coined other terms, such as "silent revolution," "moral insurrection," or "the power of the powerless," to capture imperceptible change in the collective mentality of societies under totalitarian control.[20] But very soon survey data were to become more plentiful, and Mason found that "the problems of reliability and validity of such research were greatly reduced after August 1980."[21] The problem of comparability of earlier survey data (when they can be tracked down in party archives) with results compiled in the 1980s remains, however. Earlier surveys were often intended for the purpose of regime control and were reported exclusively to top party officials, ideologues, and the security apparatus. How accurately they reflected broad popular attitudes at particular points and over time is unclear.

We can reconstruct attitudinal change by assembling the results of disparate studies conducted at different points in time and then relating them to a dichotomous conceptualization of Polish society. The political scientist Scott Flanagan has proposed an authoritarian-to-libertarian (A-L) value-change model that he regards as an inevitable consequence of the industrialization process.[22] Together with Aie-Rie Lee, he suggests that the change is most likely to occur when a society's per capita annual GNP level reaches the US $1,000–US$3,000 range (that is, similar to Huntington's economic prerequisite), when about 50–60 percent of the population has moved out of agriculture into urban areas and entered postelementary education.[23] Libertarian values—Flanagan's term for Western liberal-democratic ideas—are associated with a decline in parochialism in a society, its increasing psychological involvement in politics, declining trust in social and political institutions, and rising levels of partisanship and protest potential. Educational mobility is an indicator of cognitive mobilization and produces higher levels of psychological involvement in politics, conventional and nonconventional participation in the political process, and subjective political competence (a sense of political efficacy).

Table 3.1 has provided data indicating a rising level of educational achievement in Polish society. What evidence is there to suggest that cognitive mobilization was accompanied by a shift to more libertarian values? I shall review survey data, especially from the 1980s, when political mobilization was gathering momentum, to discover whether, even under the authoritarian communist system, Poles were becoming more libertarian in the way depicted by Flanagan.

Attitudes Toward Socialism. Although conducted by different researchers at different points in time among different samples and employing different survey instruments, polls generally inquired about attitudes toward socialism. In 1958 only

13 percent of Warsaw students identified themselves as Marxists; twenty years later the number had increased only insignificantly, to 18 percent.[24] In 1974 61 percent of Kraków students believed that Poland's future was linked with socialism and in 1977 69 percent of secondary school pupils agreed that the good of Poland was tied to the fate of socialism. But in a 1973 survey asking young people what Poles could be proud of, the socialist social order was ranked next-to-last of thirteen characteristics. Barely 9 percent of the 1974 Kraków student respondents admitted being very proud of the social system called socialism.[25] Support for the socialist project was no greater a decade later. In a 1984 survey of Polish industrial workers, Marek Ziółkowski found that only 16 percent of respondents thought that the world should be developing toward the form of socialism existing in Poland; 65 percent opposed such a trend. Opponents of any form of socialism— Polish, Yugoslav, Western, democratic—accounted for 18 percent of this sample of the industrial working class.[26]

Other 1980s surveys confirmed the limited public support for the communist party and the socialist project. Findings of the *Polacy* surveys of the 1980s pointed to at most 25 percent of the population reporting proregime attitudes.[27] Beginning in 1981, another series of polls, replicated at regular intervals, asked the public about its degree of confidence in various institutions—official (the government, the communist party) and unofficial (Solidarity, the church). Here the party always ranked as one of the institutions in which the public had least trust. Even a 1988 study of persons employed in large Warsaw enterprises—seemingly the communists' natural constituency—recorded a minuscule 7 percent of respondents asserting confidence in the party, "probably less than the total number of party members in those enterprises!" as Mason suggestively concludes.[28]

Opposition to the authorities was not limited to unfavorable attitudes. Surveys revealed that a large proportion of the population engaged in activities in protest of martial law. Thus, two-thirds of respondents said that they were responding to underground Solidarity's call not to purchase newspapers on Wednesdays, and 43 percent claimed to be turning off house lights on the thirteenth of each month to commemorate the anniversary of the imposition of martial law.[29] Although this represented very limited political "activism" that was only to fall off further with time, it did reveal that value change was not merely epiphenomenal.

Finally, Edmund Mokrzycki points to government-sponsored survey data showing that young people's attitudes to socialism were extraordinarily volatile in the second half of the 1980s. In answer to the question "Is it worthwhile to continue socialism in our country?" 60 percent of respondents answered no and 29 percent yes in 1986. In both 1987 and 1988 respondents reversed their views: Close to 60 percent wished to continue with socialism and over a quarter still opposed it. In 1989, those opposed to the continuation of socialism (46 percent) barely outnumbered advocates of its continuation (43 percent). Even allowing for government plunking, this attitudinal turnaround needs explaining. Mokrzycki tries to make sense of the pattern of responses as follows: "the reactions to the various ideas usually associated with socialism depend on the context in which they are presented," in particular, how closely they echo "recently still-valid ideological cliches."[30] It seems important, then, to disaggregate the socialist normative structure in order to identify which of its values were supported and which rejected by Polish society.

Political Desiderata. In the early 1970s the sociologist Stefan Nowak found that Poles associated the notion of a good social system more with the view that "it provides equal chances for everybody" (80 percent of survey respondents) than with any other assertion. Ranked next (60 percent) was that "it provides good living conditions for all citizens." Such political values as "freedom of speech" and "having influence on government" ranked only third and fourth, respectively, each mentioned by less than half of the respondents.[31] But after the Solidarity interlude, the perceived components of a good social system had become more directly political. In Ziółkowski's research "polycentric" responses dominated the vision of an ideal social system. Three-quarters of respondents chose freedom of speech as an absolutely necessary condition for a good social system; the next-most-common answers were influence over government decisions (64 percent) and a competitive party system (62 percent). A study completed four years later by Ziółkowski and Jadwiga Koralewicz yielded similar results. More than 70 percent of respondents identified freedom of speech as an essential characteristic of a good social system.[32] The importance of such a "libertarian" value as freedom of speech clearly rose in the fifteen years between these surveys.

We have seen that quintessentially political issues such as freedom of speech and influence on government did not always rank at the top of Poles' list of normative priorities. But Lena Kolarska-Bobińska captured the source of the steady politicization of the value system when she noted that "the prosperity of a household, family happiness (for many people, consumption prosperity), and material values occupy a leading place in the system of values of the Polish society."[33] It was the growing disparity between such material aspirations and the possibility of achieving them that led to the rise of a more political set of values. Further, since this disparity was "usually accompanied by a blockage of political and social aspirations of many groups,"[34] it was inevitable that a postmaterialist value such as political participation would come to have greater meaning for respondents.

By the 1980s perceptions of conflict had also become politically polarized. A comparative survey of oppositional consciousness carried out in 1984 and 1988 by Krzysztof Jasiewicz and Władysław Adamski revealed that "the great majority of those who perceive conflict define it as between the authorities and society." These researchers also found that respect for law was a highly regarded civic value but that respondents were split on whether political conformity ("obedience to the government, whether you approve of it or not") should follow from it: In 1988

43 percent agreed that the authorities should be obeyed (in contrast to 48 percent four years earlier) while 39 percent disagreed (compared with 30 percent in 1984).[35]

One dissenting view questioned whether Poles had a profound respect for the legal order. Although they provided no empirical evidence to support their proposition, the sociologists Piotr Łukasiewicz and Andrzej Siciński claimed "not only that attitudes toward property are ambivalent but that general esteem for the law, for any rules in public life, is rather low." In addition to property and law, attitudes embracing a "primitive egalitarianism" were also part of the socialist "ballast." So, too, was a "claiming attitude," that is, "the expectation and demand that a caring state is obliged to satisfy all the needs of its citizens."[36] These researchers implicitly credited communism with having successfully socialized the public in such key issue areas. They took the criticism occasionally voiced after 1989, summed up in the phrase "nothing has changed," as further impressionistic evidence that the communist normative system had a hold on the public. They concluded: "It is difficult for us to realize to what extent our habits and customs, our thinking and feeling, our imagination and aspirations, and our whole perception of the world is still distorted by the communist system and Weltanschauung."[37] Their general critique of society's attitudes is reminiscent of the logic that says, "The government is good but the people are not; we need only to change the people."

Why Poles appeared to be obedient to a political system they did not like was a research topic examined by Andrzej Rychard and Jacek Szymanderski. In 1984 the most commonly perceived sources of obedience were fear of repression, the demands of everyday life, and acceptance of the legality of the authorities. All three of these were, in the researchers' view, disconnected from trust in political institutions. Whereas fearing punishment and facilitating one's daily life obviously did not rule out distrust of institutions, the third source—legality—apparently did. The researchers' contention was, however, that "one can consider authority as legal without trusting any of its main institutions."[38] Developing the logic further, Rychard and Szymanderski claimed that "an important element of legitimacy in real socialism is the fact that it remained in power. This legality is not a condition of obedience, but rather obedience a condition of legality."[39]

Examining causes of disobedience, the same 1984 survey found that by far the most common reason identified by respondents was lack of trust in the authorities stemming from unfulfilled promises (51 percent). The authorities' incompetence and pursuit of their own interests (16 percent), their undemocratic and repressive nature (6 percent), and the national character of Poles (7 percent) ranked well behind.[40] In general, then, respondents cited pragmatic reasons tied to regime performance rather than ideological ones grounded in the fundamental principles of a worldview such as liberalism for obeying or disobeying political authority.

Sources of Conflict. Not all Polish writers agree, of course, about the scale of attitudinal change within the communist period or even between the communist and postcommunist periods. Communist ideologues have argued both sides of the case: Some claimed that not enough political socialization work had been done; others argued that inculcating socialist values was one of the few achievements of the communist regime. Up to now, I have been suggesting that the anticommunist opposition took heart from surveys showing weak and declining support for the regime. But we should also recognize the line of argument taken by some Solidarity leaders after 1989, which underscored that the communist legacy was deeply entrenched, socialist attitudes resilient, and the timeline for normative transformation a lengthy one.

The existence of the perception that "nothing has changed" is partially substantiated and partially disproved by empirical research. Surveys of Warsaw eighth-graders asking for assessments of the competence, objectives, and honesty of the government tell us about the extent of attitudinal change in an adolescent population living in the crucial decade that led from Solidarity to Solidarity—the 1980s. Assessment of the government's honesty was, perhaps surprisingly, both positive and consistent over time. In late 1981 37 percent gave a positive evaluation of the government that had legalized Solidarity and 30 percent a negative one. In 1986 the respective figures about the reform-committed Jaruzelski government were 36 percent and 28 percent. In 1992 the breakdown for opinions about the honesty of three years of Solidarity governments was 38 percent positive and 36 percent negative.

At the same time, throughout this dramatic period government competence was continually given low marks. Thus, positive evaluations were only 9 percent in 1981, 15 percent in 1986, and 10 percent in 1992. High school students' views about government *intentions* were more positive (64 percent) in 1981—on the eve of the martial-law crackdown!—than in 1986 or 1992 (each with 59 percent).[41] Although this youthful sample is obviously unrepresentative of the rest of society, one conclusion from the findings is very significant. There seems to have been a general respect for the political intentions of those in power. This respect was tempered by perceptions that they were incompetent—and this regardless whether the government was communist or democratic. Rather than reducing this to a "nothing has changed" attitude, I prefer to see it as further evidence that the communist authorities, like the noncommunist ones that followed, were being judged primarily by performance criteria and not by ideological orientations. This realistic orientation can also help explain why, as Mason concludes, "antipathy toward the party did not, through much of the 1980s, translate into a desire fundamentally to transform the system."[42] Judging the ruling party inept was not to be equated with declaring it ideologically bankrupt. Without this caveat, we may fail to understand the bases for both the 1989 *and* the 1993 election outcomes.

Seeking to escape Manichaean explanations for attitudinal change, the political scientist Edmund Wnuk-Lipiński links societal attitudes with change in the salience of matters considered important by citizens. He argues that by 1989 conflicts over values—freedom, equality, independence, dignity, tolerance—had been replaced by conflicts over interests between social groups and classes. This represented an important departure from the previous communist system: Given that "attitudes are determined above all by values, whereas behavior by interests," it was not surprising that "in the sphere of attitudes, the system had been called into question, but in the sphere of behavior, the system had sufficient social consent to enable it to run."[43] But individual and household needs, too, determined behavior. Comparing 1984 and 1990 data on self-reported need satisfaction, Wnuk-Lipiński identifies two areas in which a dramatic change for the worse had occurred—job security and public safety. By contrast, the two significant areas of improvement were freedom of speech and access to reliable information. His conclusion is that "the transformation has unblocked the channels of interest articulation, but at the same time has considerably reduced the feeling of security and curtailed the possibility of fulfilling basic needs." One constant remains, however: "The structures of power (old and new) are, in the popular mind, connected with high incomes which are seen as a form of injustice, given widespread financial hardship."[44]

Egalitarian Attitudes. A research topic that is particularly important in describing value change in a socialist society is the degree of adherence by the public to a set of egalitarian attitudes. In contrast to initial impressions recorded in the early 1970s that Poles were in great measure internalizing values stressing social and economic equality,[45] Mason asserts categorically that "Poles exhibit a dramatic move away from egalitarianism during the 1980s." The clearest evidence comes from surveys in the *Polacy* series, where, he summarizes, "from 1980 to 1988 there is a dramatic decline in those 'decisively' favoring limiting the highest earnings (from 70.6 percent to 27.5 percent)."[46] Jasiewicz went farther, pointing to the "slow but steady shift in societal preferences from 'equality' . . . to 'freedom'—an acceptance of various forms of economic, social and political activity and the differing consequences of that activity."[47] What is the extent of change on this integral component of the socialist value-orientation scale?

On the basis of opinion research, Kolarska-Bobińska concluded that egalitarian attitudes had begun to wane in the 1980s[48] and even 1970s surveys attesting to a high degree of egalitarianism had to be approached with caution. She invoked the classic distinction between equality of opportunity and equality of benefits (or outcomes) to argue that in Poland's communist system egalitarian attitudes primarily reflected support for the former. For her "the principle of equal benefits . . . does not reflect a widely preferred model of social order. Instead, it is a mechanism guaranteeing protection of interests of those groups which do not participate in the governing system, groups which cannot influence the distribution of desired goods."[49] Put another way, given their socialist ideology communist leaders may have found reassurance in survey results pointing to widespread support for egalitarianism in Polish society. Yet paradoxically, these egalitarian attitudes were actually targeted *against* communist rulers, since egalitarianism served for outsiders as a defense mechanism normatively restraining any inordinate buildup of privilege and benefits by the ruling elite. Egalitarian demands were an expression of concern over privilege.

In his 1984 survey of industrial workers, Ziółkowski found greater support for a nonegalitarian, efficiency model of economic order than for an egalitarian one. Nine of ten respondents supported differentials in earnings based on qualifications, and eight of ten accepted dismissal of inefficient workers. Egalitarian values were secondary in respondents' vision of a good socioeconomic system. The necessary precondition of such a system most frequently identified was wages determined by labor input (76 percent), followed by a planned economy and social ownership of the means of production (each with 57 percent). Economic competition (40 percent) also ranked ahead of egalitarian attitudes about wages to be determined by need (18 percent). Ziółkowski concluded that a large majority of Polish workers in 1984 supported both democratic practices and an economically flexible and efficient form of socialism.[50]

Kolarska-Bobińska examined the falloff of support for egalitarianism in the 1980s more closely. Support for an upper limit on wages declined dramatically in the brief Solidarity period, from 90 percent in 1980 to 79 percent in 1981. By 1984 it had dipped farther, to 57 percent, where it stabilized for the rest of the decade (Table 3.3). Support for greater wage differentiation based on qualifications increased from 54 percent in 1980 to a high of 83 percent in 1988. In the 1988 study Kolarska-Bobińska also found that only 28 percent still decidedly favored limiting the highest earnings. Despite the remarkable changes occurring over the next two years, little attitudinal change on these subjects was recorded. In 1990 1 percent fewer than in 1988 said that wage differentials were too great; 1 percent more said that they were still too small.

Attitudes over time about employment policy were less volatile. A full-employment policy was supported by 77 percent in 1980 and 67 percent in 1990, and support for dismissing inefficient employees was 91 percent in 1980 and 86 percent in 1990. In both cases strong attitudes were more common in 1980. Defining egalitarians as those who supported both ceilings on the earnings and full employment and inegalitarians as those who supported neither, Kolarska-Bobińska concluded that by 1990 about 40 percent of Poles were egalitarian and just over 10% were inegalitarian, with half the population exhibiting mixed attitudes. Predictably, attitudinal differences were shaped more by socio-occupational criteria at the end of the decade than at the beginning, with professionals and technicians welcoming more merit-based inequalities and unskilled workers more than ever supporting a full-employment policy. The fact that in 1990 two-thirds of respondents continued to support state control of prices and 62 percent were still committed to workers' self-management suggests that socialist values die hard. Further, support for a market economy remained at the 1984 level of 82 percent. Referring to further data compiled by the Center for Public Opinion Research (Centrum Badań Opinii Społecznej—CBOS), Kolarska-Bobińska pointed to "the nature of the changes at the macro level and those at the micro level." Summarizing CBOS

TABLE 3.3　　Attitudes About Egalitarianism, 1980–1990 (Percentages)

Task	Year	Decidedly Yes	Rather Yes	Rather No	Decidedly No	Hard to Say
Limits on	1980	71	19	5	3	2
earnings of	1981	51	28	9	5	7
the wealthiest	1984	30	27	23	13	9
	1988	28	29	20	13	10
	1990	27	28	22	12	11
Highly	1980	26	28	25	14	7
differentiated	1981	30	32	21	6	11
incomes	1984	44	37	11	3	5
dependent on	1988	40	43	8	2	6
qualifications	1990	37	41	11	2	9
Full employment	1980	50	27	10	5	7
policy	1981	30	24	22	11	12
	1984	25	28	23	11	12
	1988	25	35	16	7	17
	1990	34	33	15	5	13
Dismissal of	1980	69	22	5	1	3
inefficient	1981	59	27	6	2	5
employees	1984	48	34	10	3	5
	1988	45	36	7	4	9
	1990	48	38	5	1	8

Source: Lena Kolarska–Bobińska, "An Economic System and Group Interests," in Władysław Adamski (ed.), *Societal Conflict and Systemic Change: The Case of Poland, 1980–1992.* Warsaw: IFiS PAN, 1993, pp. 96–97. Because of rounding, percentages do not always add to 100 percent.

surveys of 1990–1991, she noted that "respondents think that the greatest changes are in the spheres of life most remote from their own experience (e.g., international relations and politics). . . . the least changed and assessed the least favorably are those spheres with which they have direct personal contact: the place of residence, the workplace, and the family."[51]

We have noted that Jasiewicz interpreted these data as indicating "a slow but steady shift in societal preferences from 'equality' . . . to freedom." The changed preferences were reflected in survey data on public confidence in political institutions and political leaders (Table 3.4). Those representing equality—the communist institutions—fell from grace, while those symbolizing freedom—such as Solidarity—regained stature. In 1984, shortly after martial law had been revoked, popular attitudes toward the protagonists of the conflict were negative. Both the party and

TABLE 3.4   Coefficients of Confidence in Selected Political Leaders and Institutions, 1984–1990

Leader or Institution	1984	1985	1987	Spring 1988	Spring 1989	Fall 1989	Summer 1990
Jaruzelski	0.21	0.51	0.39	0.39	−0.01	0.25	−0.09
Wałęsa	0.04	−0.03	−0.09	−0.01	0.68	0.67	0.49
Church	0.65	0.72	0.65	0.74	0.66	0.58	0.59
Sejm	0.31	0.49	0.45	0.37	0.13	0.58	0.45
Army	0.39	0.46	0.42	0.44	0.19	0.16	0.41
Government	0.17	0.39	0.26	0.26	−0.12	0.61	0.47
PZPR	−0.08	0.12	−0.08	−0.17	−0.48	−0.76	—
Solidarity	−0.52	−0.55	−0.23	−0.46	0.58	0.61	0.45

Note: Variation in the coefficients of confidence is from −1 to +1.

Source: Krzysztof Jasiewicz, "Polish Elections of 1990," in Walter D. Connor and Piotr Płoszajski (eds.), *The Polish Road from Socialism.* Armonk, NY: M. E. Sharpe, 1992, pp. 184–185.

underground Solidarity were distrusted, as were communist trade unions and the police. The Catholic church was, inevitably, the most trusted institution, but moderate levels of confidence in the army and the Sejm were also recorded. Jasiewicz explained such trust "by the character of these institutions as in some sense outside the monocentric order and as symbols of the Polish state."[52] By the time of the democratic breakthrough in summer 1989, Solidarity and its newly created government had joined the church as the most trusted institutions.

Jasiewicz cautioned against taking the view that Polish society was espousing ever more democratic attitudes. Seventy-eight percent of respondents in the 1988 survey agreed that Poland needed "a strong leader who would bring order"— 5 percent more than those agreeing that voters should be able to choose among candidates of various political views. As the 1989 transformation neared, he described a polarized political culture encompassing two contradictory syndromes of values: populist-authoritarian (regime supporters) and democratic-liberal (regime opponents).[53]

Authoritarian Attitudes. In constructing a scale of authoritarian attitudes, Jadwiga Koralewicz found that somewhat fewer people supported authoritarian attitudes in 1984 than in 1978. Interestingly, in interpreting the decline (about 10 percent) in authoritarianism, she pointed out that it was most marked among people with lower levels of education, a social category often regarded as the principal agent of authoritarianism. Part of the explanation she offered for this paradox was that working-class participation in the Solidarity movement in 1980–1981 had socialized the less educated into democratic practices: participating in decision making, assuming responsibility, becoming better-informed. Those with average education also exhibited less authoritarian attitudes in the six-year interval between surveys. Unexpectedly, it was the better-educated who became more authoritarian. Rephrasing this result, Koralewicz reported that "the 'relative increase' of authoritarianism among the intelligentsia is even greater than the 'relative decrease' of authoritarianism among workers." The explanation for this lay in widespread feelings of anxiety, depression, and helplessness among the intelligentsia stemming from its perception of an unjust social order. Neurotic reactions leading to a growth of authoritarianism followed. Koralewicz stressed the uniqueness of this development: "Already in 1978, the Polish intelligentsia was marked by a higher level of anxiety and a lower level of self-confidence than workers. It seems that we were one of the few countries, if not the only one, with a negative correlation between the level of education and self-confidence."[54] Other, more predictable findings of the survey included the greater degree of authoritarian attitudes among members of the communist party, the procommunist trade unions, and rural residents.

Koralewicz also inquired about the relationship between authoritarian attitudes and confidence in particular political leaders. Not surprisingly, in 1984 the correlation between authoritarian attitudes and confidence in state and party leaders such as Jaruzelski and Mieczysław Rakowski was strong. Supporters of Solidarity leaders such as Wałęsa and Zbigniew Bujak were, conversely, not as authoritarian. Religious leaders such as Pope John Paul II and Cardinal Glemp had the confidence of respondents exhibiting various degrees of authoritarianism. Regarding institutions, Koralewicz found that "while a high level of authoritarianism is related to more confidence in official political institutions, confidence in underground Solidarity correlates with a low level of authoritarianism."[55] Finally, from the answers to questions regarding the desired form of social and political life in Poland she drew the disquieting conclusion that in 1984 both the highly authoritarian and the less authoritarian were dissatisfied with the country's current sociopolitical system: "For the former it is not authoritarian enough, while for the latter, it is too authoritarian."[56]

In a different study of attitudes related to authoritarianism conducted at the end of the decade, Andrzej Rychard found growing support for strong leadership of a noncommunist kind. Between 1988 and 1990 the proportion of respondents decidedly agreeing that "A strong leader is needed to establish order" rose from 49 percent to 64 percent (and from 77 percent to 87 percent overall).[57] Although Rychard dismissed the interpretation that such a value change in any way represented nostalgia for the former authoritarian communist system, it remained unclear whether the residue of authoritarian attitudes created under the communist system accounted for the support for strong leadership.

Attitudes Toward Other Nations. Popular attitudes about international politics also tell us about value change in Polish society. The list of countries that are admired or feared, considered to offer assistance or to pose a threat, reveals the degree to which Poles accept or reject such "myths" as Sarmatianism (manifest destiny in the Slavic world), geopolitical reality (the notion of two natural enemies as neighbors), and the common European heritage (traditional friendship with France, Britain, and other Western states).

When we examine Polish respondents' perceptions of other nations, we observe considerable changes in ranking in the period between 1975 and December 1989. Americans went from fifth to first place in this interval in terms of the confidence of Poles; essentially they exchanged places with Russians in these years. The greatest single change, however, was in Poles' confidence in Germans; placing twenty-first in 1975 and maintaining this rank in 1987, Germans became Poles' fourth-most-trusted nation in 1989 (after Americans, Italians, and Hungarians). As Renata Siemieńska, author of the study, concludes, "The results of the Polish research confirm the hypothesis formulated elsewhere that above all trust is extended to nations that have achieved economic successes."[58]

A different data set tells us more about likes and dislikes of Poles. In 1991 68 percent of respondents said that they liked Americans and only 1 percent that they disliked them. The scores, in descending order, for other nations were French, 61 percent and 2 percent; Italians, 59 percent and 1 percent; English, 50 percent and 3 percent; and Hungarians, 44 percent and 4 percent. The most disliked were Gypsies, 9 percent and 47 percent; Ukrainians, 9 percent and 38 percent; Arabs, 7 percent and 32 percent; Russians, 16 percent and 32 percent; Romanians, 17 percent and 29 percent; and Germans, 23 percent and 34 percent (a marked contrast to Siemieńska's 1989 finding). Attitudes toward Jews were mixed, 17 percent and 19 percent. Aleksandra Jasińska-Kania correlates these preferences with the reasons given for them, observing that "the wealth of a nation, Catholicism, and wartime allies exerted the strongest relative influence on Poles' likes when other factors were controlled." Her factor analysis reveals internally consistent sets of attitudes toward four ethnic and nationality groups: (1) advanced capitalist economies and liberal democracies (such as the United States, England, and France), which received the highest scores; (2) those most different from Poles from an ethnic viewpoint (Chinese, Gypsies, Arabs, and, to a lesser degree, Jews), which received mixed evaluations; (3) the postcommunist countries (such as Russia, Belarus, Lithuania, and Slovakia), which were generally negatively assessed; and (4) two neighbors with which historical conflict remained imprinted in people's minds (Germany and Ukraine), which were very negatively assessed.[59]

The value of such surveys is in observing how the cultural makeup of other nations is evaluated by respondents, thereby revealing something about their own sense of national identity.[60] The trivial but inescapable conclusion deriving from both data sets presented here seems to be that Poles want very much to be like Americans and to avoid resembling Russians, Ukrainians, Gypsies, and, in varying measures, other Slavic and East European nations. This is a bizarre, self-deprecating self-image that may haunt Poland's political leaders once citizens recognize that little progress is being made toward becoming an American-type society (or, for that matter, a second Japan, as Wałęsa once promised). These data also suggest that such a national value system may dampen prospects for effective regional cooperation.

A survey question closely related to attitudes toward other nations is one identifying countries perceived as potential threats to Polish independence. Survey results revealed dramatic changes between 1980 and 1990. Half of the respondents in 1980 identified the USSR as the most serious threat, with the Federal Republic of Germany a distant second with 15 percent. Despite many years of communist propaganda discrediting them, capitalist countries, including NATO and the United States, were seen as threatening by only 10 percent of respondents. By 1990, however, perhaps by default, Germany was named most often (41 percent) as threatening, and the USSR was down to 17 percent and Russia to 4 percent. When questions were posed more generally, Adamski found that 59 percent of respondents decidedly agreed and 87 percent overall agreed with the statement that "The East has always exploited us." The corresponding figures for Western exploitation were less than half this—16 percent decidedly, 40 percent overall. By contrast, the West was ranked not far behind the East (46 percent to 66 percent) in being regarded as having a moral obligation to lend assistance to Poland. Still, more than three-quarters of respondents agreed with the assertions "Nobody will help us, we can rely only on ourselves" and "Poles expect too much from other countries." Adamski reconciled this apparently dissonant set of attitudes in the following way: "It seems that Poles are realistic. The belief in the moral obligations of other nations does not interfere with a belief that Poles should depend mainly on themselves."[61]

From Authoritarian to Liberal Values?

To conclude this section on the culture shift of the communist period, I turn to a qualitative account offered by the psychologist Janusz Reykowski. In his view it is inaccurate to view the communist period as a single continuous struggle between totalitarian rulers and opposition freedom fighters. "Both positions are ahistorical," Rejkowski contends, for "they are based upon an assumption that over decades the same forces were fighting for the same issues."[62]

Synthesizing survey data from 1988, Reykowski identifies three normative sociopolitical orientations. The democratic orientation (DO) focused on various forms of participation and was therefore a source of political support for the opposition. The social harmony orientation (SHO) accepted limited political goals in the interest of maintaining consensus and generally fostered acquiescent attitudes toward the regime. The social rights orientation (SRO) was a "swing" category that could shift the political equilibrium within the system. This category expected the system to provide economic and material benefits to the public. Citizens subscribing to this orientation were most likely to alter their overall assessment of the political system depending upon whether it was delivering the goods or not. Reykowski concludes, then, that "while the DO is likely to generate negative attitudes of a 'non-reversible' character toward the system, the SRO allows for the reversal of such attitudes if living conditions improve and the system is able to satisfy basic needs." He adds, "All this taken together seems to put into question the widely accepted notion that the entire Polish society (or at least its overwhelming majority) espoused the same sociopolitical values, was inimical toward the system over the entire forty-five-year period, and just waited for a convenient opportunity to topple it."[63]

Available data on attitudes for the late 1950s, the 1960s, and the early 1970s concur that the communist system/socialism/the party first secretary received mixed evaluations. Radio Free Europe surveys of Polish citizens visiting the West indicated in the 1970s that the majority of respondents would have voted for the communist party and, next, for a social democratic party if elections had been free.[64] The regularly replicated and publicly reported survey research carried out in the 1980s on citizens' evaluations of the nation's and their own fortunes in the previous year ("Was 1989 a good year for Poland? for you?") tell us of societal shifts from pessimism to optimism and back. Similarly, regarding changing attitudes toward socioeconomic issues with high political salience, Kolarska-Bobińska found that tolerance of inequalities and of unemployment increased throughout the 1980s but then seemed to decline; views differed from one group to another—blue-collar workers versus managers, for example—depending on their instrumental values.[65]

It is a difficult task, then, to develop a longitudinal scale measuring culture shift along such continua as materialist/postmaterialist (of questionable relevance to a former Second World country as materially deprived as Poland)[66] or authoritarian/libertarian. To be sure, the notion of self-actualization that is central to the libertarian value system has been implicit in the construction of a civil society so much heralded by Western scholars.[67] Predictably, their emphasis has been on the social domain (freedom from tyranny) rather than on the psychological (freedom from a closed belief system) or the physical (freedom from material limitations). Yet, given the macro-level socioeconomic data presented earlier in this chapter, it is the physical domain that was most significant: The Polish struggle against communism can be depicted as a libertarian drive for freedom from the material impoverishment that communist economics produced.

As important as the scope of authoritarian-libertarian shift for cognitive mobilization[68] was the timing of the politicization of the A-L cleavage, which took place in the late 1970s and early 1980s. The conditions for this politicization—sufficient levels of industrialization, cognition, egalitarianism, and welfarism—were all in place when the political crisis occurred.[69] The linkage between culture shift and democratic breakthrough, here ascribed to an Asian state, is recognizable to the Polish specialist:

without the growing levels of democratic values, autonomous participation, and anti-establishment orientations that had spread throughout substantial proportions of the population by 1986, the timing of the democratic breakthrough in Taiwan would be hard to explain. . . . In the end, it was the recognition of the altered political realities created by this culture shift that galvanized the opposition forces into action and forced Chiang's hand.[70]

Political Mobilization as Outcome Variable

In addition to culture shift, the second general consequence of macro-level developmental change is for the political behavior of citizens. Political behavior is affected by new social cleavages and mass alignments originating in a transformed social structure. The size, salience, and resources of the principal social groups and classes are determined by their changed place in the social hierarchy. In particular, groups disaffected by social change are likely to turn to political mobilization. From the mid-1970s in Poland, many of the disaffected began to organize, and very soon a variety of newly formed dissident groups was active in politics. One of the objectives of these groups was to create a civil society free from the nefarious influence of the communist party-state. Political mobilization joined diverse social groups together, but it was not accomplished without spadework.

Catholic Groups

From the inception of communist rule, the Polish Catholic church was more than a mere political grouping. Although Cardinal Stefan Wyszyński, primate of the church, was imprisoned from September 1953 to October 1956, Catholicism remained both an institutional and a philosophical force that the communist regime had to reckon with. Moreover, it was the institutional and philosophical *pluralism* within Polish Catholicism that presented the communist authorities in the Stalinist period with a serious challenge to its hegemonic aspirations.

Znak. One Catholic group that seemed willing to cooperate with the new regime was the Znak movement. Its origins lay in the publication by lay Catholics of the newspaper *Tygodnik Powszechny* ("Universal Weekly") in 1945 and then, a year later, of the monthly *Znak* ("Sign"). In 1957 a group of independent Catholic deputies elected to the Sejm with the party's approval became known as Znak as well.

The Znak movement was characterized by a sense of political realism that could be traced back to the political philosophy of the early twentieth-century National Democratic leader Roman Dmowski. Arguing that Poland was forever trapped between West and East, Dmowski advocated cooperation with Russia, if only because in the long term Russia seemed less capable than Germany of maintaining control over Poland. Dmowski had little time for the romantic messianic views expressed a century earlier by Polish patriots. The postwar lay Catholics associated with Znak accepted this logic: they too "denied the value of military struggle" against the widening Soviet presence in the country and were persuaded that "the major danger to Poland came from Germany."[71]

But Znak leaders were not about to accept the Soviet-backed communist seizure of power in Poland as a fait accompli and as a turning point that justified the elimination of political opposition. They insisted on advancing a worldview different from that of the Marxists. Some Znak members, such as Jerzy Turowicz, *Tygodnik's* editor for four decades, emphasized both the moral solidarity of Catholic doctrine and the practical imperative of questioning communist authority. Writing in 1985, he argued that the Catholic church "has a right and a duty to react to events and situations, to accuse and condemn injustice and violence, to defend the wronged and the oppressed, to demand justice and respect for dignity and the rights of man and, particularly, the right to be a self-governing subject, to determine one's own fate."[72]

Within Znak, Stefan Kisielewski advanced an even more liberal view, calling for pluralism and competition of ideas within both church and state, giving priority to the rights of the individual over the abstract notion of the good of humanity, and in many ways establishing a closer dialogue between lay Catholics and liberal-minded communists. Znak's influence began to diminish in the 1970s when it was superseded by the lay left, organized in the Workers' Defense Committee (Komitet Obrony Robotników—KOR). But up to then we can agree with Norbert Zmijewski's conclusion that "initially minimalist and apolitical, Znak's Catholicism gave rise to the use of Catholic morality for political purposes, a morality uniting people and nations fighting against unbidden regimes."[73]

Pax. A Catholic group frequently accused of full collaboration with the communist regime was Pax. In contrast to Znak, Pax was inextricably linked with the philosophy of one person, Bolesław Piasecki. A supporter of totalitarian ideologies since the 1930s, when he led the Polish Falanga, Piasecki was, according to Zmijewski, "convinced that Catholicism could not coexist with liberalism and democracy but could cooperate well with any order which had a plan for the future shape of society, strictly defined moral code and hierarchy of aims."[74] In spite of such Falangist ideas, Piasecki proved at times to be an original thinker. He thought that by joining Catholicism with Marxism Poland would be better prepared to take on the advanced capitalist countries of Western Europe. His sophistry led him to contend that Marxist atheism was directed not against God but against the social role that religion played in contemporary societies. He also, like liberation theologians two decades later, adopted Marxist social philosophy to identify the tasks of a Christian: salvation through work, justice through liberation. By the late 1960s Piasecki's group was more Stalinist than the communist party Politburo, and, not surprisingly, it lost influence within both Catholic and Marxist circles.

Więź. In time many Catholic intellectuals who had initially been attracted to Pax came to reject Piasecki's political program. In 1956 the Clubs of the Catholic Intelligentsia (Kluby Intelligentsii Polskiej—KIK) had been established within the movement, and two years later the periodical *Więź* ("Link") had appeared. In the Więź worldview, Catholics were expected to be maximally engaged in the new social order, and the Polish October was viewed as the point of departure for liberal reform of the country. The leader of Więź was Tadeusz Mazowiecki, later to become the first noncommunist prime minister of postwar Poland. Janusz Zabłocki shared many of Mazowiecki's views but stressed the need for the patriotic engagement of Catholics. By the late 1960s Więź leaders had proposed a division of labor with the communist authorities that anticipated the spirit of the roundtable agreements two decades later. The movement

> saw the resolution of the conflict between Marxism and Catholicism in terms of a division of influence: Catholicism, which had adopted the best ideas of Marxism and developed a universal personalist philosophy, would take over exclusive control of the ideological sphere, while Marxism would be responsible for the economy, allowing external control of the Party's activities while respecting human rights and social pluralism.[75]

Wyszyński. All of these Catholic groups put together did not have the political influence that Cardinal Wyszyński, head of the ecclesiastical hierarchy, enjoyed in the 1960s and 1970s. His prison notebooks from the 1950s reveal a clear understanding of the logic of communist rule.[76] By the time of the Great Novena in 1966, celebrating the millennium of Christianity in Poland, the primate had become an outspoken critic of the Gomułka regime, but he was willing to accept a modus vivendi with Gierek, Gomułka's pragmatic successor, in the 1970s. He met regularly with the party leader, in this way further increasing the church's authority and visibility in the political sphere while personally playing the political role of *interrex*, a ruler between dynasties. Not surprisingly, when embryonic political groups such as independent trade unions or the Workers' Defense Committee began to organize, they turned to the church for shelter.

Cardinal Wyszyński died in May 1981, shortly after participating in two momentous events: the election of fellow Polish Cardinal Karol Wojtyła as pope in 1978 and the legalization of the Solidarity movement in August–September 1980. In referring to Wyszyński as "Primate of the Millennium"—arguably the greatest Polish church figure in ten centuries—Pope John Paul II acknowledged his debt to Wyszyński as he took over steering an extraordinarily subtle course with regard to the communist world that contributed greatly to communist rulers' eventual crisis of identity and loss of will.[77] Wyszyński's role in consolidating the Solidarity movement is more controversial. His appeal to Wałęsa and other trade unionists for reason and realism in confronting communist authorities during the turbulent summer of 1980 seemed to reflect a lack of resolve out of step with the times. At the same time, the communist rulers must have felt that the primate's moderating influence made Solidarity a legitimate partner in the new political reality and contributed to its official registration. Few former communist leaders would today question the enormous political skills possessed by Cardinals Wyszyński and Woytyła in making Marxism an increasingly untenable system of control over individuals' lives.

John Clark and Aaron Wildavsky conclude from all this that "the failure of communism is due to its moral defects." Going farther, they assert that "if one does not organize society morally, one is unlikely to succeed in organizing it materially."[78] It was the Catholic church and Catholic lay groups that, over the decades, constantly challenged the moral bases of communist rule.

The communist rulers must have been conscious of their moral defects and regularly sought legitimation through concessions to the ecclesiastical hierarchy and lay groups. In tandem with the Polish primate and the Polish pope, groups such as Znak and Więź whittled away at Marxist influence: "The rational arguments of Catholics contrasted with the Marxist belief in a religion of humanity where will rather than reason was supposed to change the world."[79] In the late 1960s "the image of the Church as a symbol of national self-identification grew as Gomułka's popularity declined."[80] Whereas Wyszyński invoked nationalist symbols, lay groups appealed to reason and intellect, thereby establishing dialogue with liberal Marxists in the party and strengthening their intraparty influence. Zmijewski comes to a provocative but insightful conclusion:

> In Poland Catholicism . . . fostered internal critique not only because it was well established in Polish culture but also because it did not legitimate any radical opposition to the Soviet-backed regime. Catholics sought for a definition of realist policy, i.e., a policy which would not jeopardize the existence of nation and state. The policy of forcing evolutionary change by increasing social pressure owes a great deal to the involvement of Catholics in politics.[81]

The December 1981 decree on martial law was signed by all members of the Council of State except the Pax leader Ryszard Reiff, who not much later was removed from the body. Catholic priests were active in decrying martial law from the pulpit, harboring underground leaders on the run, and distributing food and clothes to families whose breadwinners had been interned by the martial-law authorities. But in seeking to prevent bloodshed under conditions of martial law, Wyszyński's successor, Cardinal Józef Glemp, called for national reconciliation and soon distanced himself from underground Solidarity. In return, the episcopate received permission from the state to embark upon an unprecedented expansion of church building. Many radical priests continued actively to support Solidarity, however, the best-known being Father Jerzy Popiełuszko of Warsaw. As one writer summarized the activity of radical parish priests, "By recreating sacramentally, in the Durkheimian sense, the collective effervescence of the original experience of Solidarity, they were helping to maintain alive the movement as well as its norms and values."[82] When Popiełuszko was murdered by agents of the security police in October 1984, the Catholic faithful and not the hierarchy turned him into a political and religious martyr. Indeed, the very slow process of erosion of the church's prestige with average citizens began with the Popiełuszko tragedy.

Workers' Organizations: Solidarity

Apart from Catholicism, the other major area of political self-organization not controlled by the party was workers' groups. The political importance of the industrial working class in Poland resulted from two countervailing processes: its rapid expansion in the first two decades of communism and the blocked avenues for its further upward mobility by the mid-1970s. Economic and, increasingly, political mobilization of workers in the 1970s challenged the system to respond to their distributive and participatory demands. Roman Laba has drawn a concise comparison of the demands made by workers on the Baltic coast in 1970, 1971, and 1980 and argued that workers were as politicized in 1970 as they became in 1980 (thereby calling into question the KOR's alleged inspiration of the later Solidarity agenda).[83] These demands were based on perceptions usually quite distinct from those of other social groups. For example, a 1984 research project developed an eleven-level scale to measure respondents' satisfaction with such factors as incomes, housing, food supply, and leisure time. The study found that values of satisfaction with life were below the mean for skilled and unskilled workers and above the mean for white-collar workers and peasants. The same 1984 survey sought to identify the perceived causes of such "social degradation" and categorized thirteen specific factors into two general groups: shortcomings of society (for example, laziness, indifference, indiscipline, alcoholism) and problems linked to political authorities (stifling of criticism, abuse of power, autocracy, corruption, cliquishness, economic mismanagement). Whereas two-thirds of unskilled workers and peasants mentioned alcoholism and laziness as being at the root of Poland's crisis, skilled workers tended to blame the authorities as often as they did society. By contrast, the intelligentsia (those with higher education) most frequently cited economic mismanagement and autocracy as causes of the crisis.[84]

It is hardly surprising, then, that workers and intelligentsia found common ground to organize politically. Sharing understandings of the reasons for the crisis of communism, mass political alignment reflected social cleavages that separated both skilled workers and the better-educated from the *nomenklatura*—party officials and the party-appointed managerial class—and from the peasantry. Within this alignment, workers appeared to be the vanguard group. A comparative Polish-French sociological study conducted in spring 1989 found that "Polish workers perceive themselves as the main actors of change more often than other groups and more often than French workers."[85] The paramount importance of Polish workers as political agents was underscored with the establishment of the independent trade union Solidarity in summer 1980.

In underscoring the indispensability of worker activism and the evolution of the Solidarity movement, we should not lose sight of the fact that a consensus was crystallizing across all groups in society concerning the crisis of communism. In an open-ended question in the *Polacy '84* survey, 81 percent of respondents agreed that dishonesty and theft by those in power were causes of the crisis. In time, the salience of such specific complaints was superseded by the salience of more general criticism such as that the authorities were not concerned with the interests of ordinary people or that channels of interest articulation were blocked. The role of issue salience in building pressure for change lay, then, in the shift from particularist to universalist grievances.

The historian Lawrence Goodwyn and the political scientist Roman Laba have provided extended analyses of working-class activism from the Polish October to the late 1980s. Whereas the establishment of the KOR in 1976 was a milestone in self-organization, both Goodwyn's and Laba's studies trace earlier efforts undertaken by workers to engage in political action. Both question the contribution really made by intellectual groups. Thus Goodwyn concludes: "The mystique created around KOR had the effect of concealing the much more instructive worker dynamics that actually undergirded the remarkable mobilization of civil society."[86] The evolution of a militant working class is a complex subject that cannot be fully covered here. Let us, instead, focus on two important features of the Solidarity experience: its emergence as the most important product of working class consciousness and its self-organization, indicating that as a political group it intended to be governed by democratic principles.

A considerable literature on the origins and evolution of Solidarity has emerged, and controversy has arisen whether the trade union remained an *ouvrieriste* movement or was taken over by dissident intellectuals.[87] Of more importance to our discussion than the exact balance of power between workers and intellectuals in Solidarity is that both social classes saw reason to create a single movement to challenge the hegemony of the communist party. The metamorphosis of Polish society produced by the independent trade union in 1980–1981 was in many ways as profound and sweeping as the events of 1989. Of the political groups of the communist period, the largest and most powerful turned out to be Solidarity.

Its leader in 1980 was a union activist in the Lenin shipyards in Gdańsk, Lech Wałęsa, a courageous if at times self-contradictory and bungling figure who had stood up to the Politburo members sent to Gdańsk to restore industrial peace. Wałęsa and other union leaders set forth visionary goals out of keeping with the harshness of real socialism. Their inability to deal with such mundane political challenges as the provocatively timed increases in the price of cigarettes and vodka of 1980 conveyed the impression that they were more comfortable espousing lofty goals than handling practical matters. Arguably, it was the combination of vision and naïveté that helped Solidarity survive the many challenges issued by the communist regime, and it began to attract followers from diverse social backgrounds.

By the time its membership had reached nearly 10 million in 1981, Solidarity was a broad social movement that included in its ranks workers and white-collar employees, intellectuals and entrepreneurs, Catholics and communists. David Ost argues that "the experience of autonomous public activity was in and of itself a major goal of the movement."[88] It proved to be a critical experiment in political alignment and mobilization that charted the path for the democratic breakthrough later in the decade.

The internal organization of Solidarity developed in response to the broadening of the movement and the idiosyncratic preferences of Wałęsa as well as to the functional imperatives confronting any organization. Ost conceptualizes the symbiosis of these elements as organizational ambiguity and decisive indecisiveness. Solidarity's survival rested on such a strategy, Ost contends, and its organizational ambiguity was therefore intentional. Indeed, it is easy to document many instances of ambiguity in Solidarity and Wałęsa himself. Double-speak punctuated the transcript of the Gdańsk meeting that established Solidarity: Wałęsa concluded that "here in Gdańsk there is a central power except it is not a central body."[89] Earlier he asserted that "everyone can adopt our [Gdańsk] statute," but just as quickly he conceded that chapters could "re-do it any way they like."[90] He continued, "We aren't going to be building chapels in our unions" but added, "As long as I am here, a cross will always be on the wall and a representative of the Primate will be with us."[91] In summer 1981 he officially endorsed strikes during his travels to affected regions, but once back in Gdańsk, made efforts to stop them.

How much of this inconsistency was part of Wałęsa's overall strategy and how much due to his own irresoluteness, vacillation, susceptibility to the influence of his environment, and response to government actions is difficult to say. But we can agree with Ost that Solidarity's survival ability was enhanced in this paradoxical way: "Only an ambiguous authority structure, where the union could appear sometimes to control a unified national movement, and at other times to have control over no one at all, had a chance of allowing Solidarity to succeed."[92]

In considering ambiguity as an organizational weapon, we have to ask why it sputtered when martial law was declared in December 1981. For Ost, Solidarity's ambiguity broke down as effective strategy by July 1981, when the communist authorities embarked on an equally ingenious policy of doing nothing.[93] Why Solidarity was weakened when the authorities did nothing but was destroyed when the authorities did something—impose martial law—is a logical dilemma left unresolved by Ost's analysis. If, however, ambiguity had been intentionally cultivated, it would help explain why Solidarity could survive first under the conspiratorial conditions created by martial law and second during the period of disillusionment and cynicism of the mid-1980s, when societal support for the movement dwindled.

For Jack Bielasiak and Barbara Hicks, the basis of Solidarity's challenge to the political authorities lay in its legitimating formula: "its own internal functioning exemplified a principle of legitimate political authority that contradicted the party-state's primary rationale of legitimacy."[94] The conflict between the independent trade-union movement and the established political authorities could, accordingly, be viewed as one between two forms of rationality. Solidarity's was based on redefining political rules and procedures in Poland, the regime's on the substantive claim of guaranteeing welfarism and delivering material goods to society, in line with the society of plenty that communist ideology promised. Less pressing than overhauling the central political system for Solidarity was, at this juncture, changing the form of government at the subsystemic level. The establishment of self-government in all spheres of society could lead to a self-governing republic, an objective contained in the program adopted at Solidarity's first congress. The organization of Solidarity itself was to be exemplary in this regard: "its principle of democratic, territorially-based organization, which penetrated the party, formed the core of its challenge to the legitimacy of the party-state based on substantive rationality. The organizational weapon was indeed one of Solidarity's strongest."[95]

Jadwiga Staniszkis argued that this revolutionary form of self-government would have proved a "self-limiting revolution" because these self-governing organizations were not interested in taking over or sharing government responsibility.[96] The "conflict of rationalities" argument advanced by Bielasiak and Hicks underscores the irrelevance of this notion. Given the contrasting legitimating formulae employed by the two political forces, a collision was inevitable regardless of Solidarity's efforts to confine its political ambitions.

Jacek Kurczewski has pointed to seeming contradictions in the functions that Solidarity wanted to perform. It aimed to unify society but instead polarized it by forcing citizens to take a stand on its goals. It wanted to civilize the political system (for example, by relaxing censorship laws) but ended up barbarizing the adversary. It pursued political power but found it a burden as rival camps sought to gain control of it. It stood for political egalitarianism vis-à-vis the communist party but promoted inegalitarianism in its own economic policies. Finally, it wanted to institutionalize the social revolution it had launched, but institutions invariably displace idealistic goals.[97]

A clearer understanding of the movement may be reached by examining its notion of self-government. Regional leaders had considerable influence within its national coordinating commission, and, in turn, regional union affiliates enjoyed a large degree of autonomy. In other words, a federal-type structure was adopted that was designed to highlight the coalition of social forces making up the movement. If such structures had been replicated at all levels of government, the result might have been a centrifugal, quasi-anarchic form of democracy justifying the old idea that "Polska nierządem stoi" (Poland is governed by unrule). Structures that made sense for political coalition building, then, were ill-suited to governing. But at times union structures did affect governing. The chaos that reigned in Poland in the second half of 1981 may have been primarily the result of the government's rather than Solidarity's going on strike: Police were kept off the streets, distribution of goods to shops slowed, and administration came to a standstill.

But wildcat strikes organized by regional unions played an important part as well in engendering chaos. The ideals of decentralized democracy propounded by union magnates seemed to be taking hold.

Solidarity's governance of itself was, therefore, a crucial aspect of its general politics. The new, highly skilled working class and the traditional one combined to provide a model of democratic activity consistent with its espoused social democratic ideology. Workers' innate common sense turned out to be a sturdier base for alternative government than the intellectual contortions of some Solidarity experts. As Laba argued, it was precisely the worker roots of Solidarity that gave the movement its nobility.[98] The Solidarity organizational experience thus invites a reformulation of Roberto Michels's iron law of oligarchy as "who says organization says oligarchy, but not always."[99]

During 1980–1981 Solidarity's leaders were confronted with a variety of tactics employed by the communist authorities to split and weaken the movement. Seven institutional relationships that were key to Solidarity's survival were deliberately sabotaged. By casting doubt on Solidarity's ability to develop working relationships with six major political actors and by exaggerating the likelihood of collaboration with the seventh, the regime sought to undermine the rationally based legitimacy that Solidarity claimed to have appropriated in presenting itself as the embodiment of the genuine interests of Polish society. The inability of Solidarity chiefs to identify trustworthy partners was to undermine its alliance-building strategy.

1. Solidarity could not depend on maintaining a lasting working relationship with the ruling *communist party*. Although some leaders, such as the party chief Stanisław Kania, Jaruzelski, and the union negotiator Mieczysław Rakowski appeared trustworthy, the party always seemed a hairbreadth away from being taken over by hard-liners, as the sinister Bydgoszcz affair of March 1981 (when security agents beat up local Solidarity activists) indicated. Hard-liners would then destroy Solidarity. This depiction of the party was actively fostered by the ruling elite so that Solidarity could never be certain that negotiations with it would prove useful or durable.

2. Solidarity could not count on the *government* as a reliable partner in negotiations. When even a minister as supposedly well-disposed toward the union as Rakowski walked out on talks with Wałęsa in August 1981, cooperation with the government seemed bound to prove ephemeral, unpredictable, or irrelevant. Solidarity leaders were kept guessing whether the August accords reached with the government meant anything.

3. The *Soviet Union* was the wild card in the political events that even Polish communists stressed they could not control. The senile Brezhnev, his aging Politburo, and his World War II generals were impatient with the Polish communist party's tolerance of Solidarity. If a few Solidarity activists engaged in bravado verbal attacks on the USSR, it served only to heighten the threat posed by the regional hegemon.

4. Other *trade unions* enjoying communist support were being established to challenge Solidarity. These included branch unions running across an economic

sector and autonomous unions with some independence. To complicate matters for Solidarity, some local union chapters previously part of the communist structure applied to join Solidarity, and it was not always clear whether they were acting in good faith. Even rural Solidarity, set up in 1981 as a farmers' organization, was suspect given its better rapport with the authorities.

5. The actions of the *Catholic church* did not inspire full confidence. First Cardinal Wyszyński, then Cardinal Glemp expressed only lukewarm support for the free trade-union movement. The church was self-interested, its primary constituency was the countryside, and it was unwilling to risk its privileged position in Polish society to defend a workers' movement.

6. Some *social groups* were not proving reliable supporters of Solidarity. In summer 1981 large numbers of Poles of different social backgrounds—doctors and carpenters, technicians and peasants—were leaving the Poland of Solidarity for the refugee camps of Austria. By fall 1981 some groups had grown sufficiently disenchanted with Solidarity that they ceased to participate in demonstrations and strikes called by the movement's leadership.

7. To believe the regime, Solidarity *could* trust the Polish *army*. Military goodwill missions in fall 1991 to the countryside (to distribute fertilizers, repair tractors, harvest crops) and to the cities (to fix potholes, bring order to long queues, and root out corrupt practices) were intended to demonstrate that the army was on the side of society. Official opinion polls reflected the popularity that followed from its cultivated image of being equally intolerant of government's and Solidarity's mishandling of politics. The army was presented as the one institution capable of putting right the ills of Polish society—as naturally sharing Solidarity's cause but being more efficient at advancing it.

It was the military that imposed and enforced martial law, and it was Jaruzelski's military regime that by fall 1982 had declared Solidarity illegal. Even now that extensive archival collections have been opened up, there is very little evidence that Solidarity leaders appreciated the danger of this. Instead, during 1981 they seemed to be fixated by the first two relationships just identified, with the party and the government. To be sure, Wałęsa and his colleagues had good reason to be suspicious of the intentions of Kania, his Politburo, and the communist government. If Solidarity was characterized by organizational ambiguity, the communist regime was distinguished by normative ambiguity: Some leaders seemed to offer authentic partnership for the social movement while others were surrogates for the Soviet Politburo. But even if the regime was to some degree successful in misrepresenting Solidarity's institutional allies, in the long term the social movement achieved in the realm of social consciousness what it may have failed to achieve in the area of alignment politics.

Dissident Intellectuals: The KOR

We have been discussing how Poland's transformed social structure contributed to the rise of Solidarity and how Solidarity as a political group came to represent a

broad-based social movement whose strength and weakness were both determined by political alignments. In addition, the *issues* considered to be of common
concern to social groups affected the pattern of mass alignment. The political
salience of different kinds of issues—such as the belief that without the participation and input of average citizens the authorities would continue to mismanage
the economy—played a direct role in the rise of Solidarity.

Although Solidarity was the culmination of organized opposition to the communist authorities in the 1970s, the creation of the KOR in 1976 was crucial in a
number of ways. First, its membership included many well-known dissidents who
had served an apprenticeship in the opposition: Jacek Kuroń, Jan Józef Lipski,
Adam Michnik, Karol Modzelewski. Second, it quickly proved more than a mere
discussion group, becoming an important source of support for the workers and
their families in Radom and Ursus who had been persecuted for their role in the
June 1976 protests. When interfactory strike committees were set up in summer
1980, the KOR became a critical channel for communication across the country.
Third, its establishment gave other groups the confidence to organize as well.
Within three years, a Committee for the Defense of Human and Civil Rights
(Ruch Obrony Praw Człowieka i Obywatela—ROPCiO), a "Flying University" offering occasional lectures to students by dissidents, a nationalist Confederation
for an Independent Poland (Konfederacja Polski Niepodległej—KPN), and the
Free Trade Unions of the Coast, which included Wałęsa in its leadership, had come
into being. Fourth, the program and strategy developed by the KOR proved to be
very effective in the context of the late 1970s. In particular, the call for the construction of a civil society that would, in time, expand in number of participants
as well as in scope of action and the forging of informal ties with Catholic groups
proved extremely successful initiatives.[100] Although the KOR's leadership recognized the limits of the group's usefulness and disbanded in 1981, its individual
members went on to play key roles during the roundtable talks in 1989 and in the
politics of the Third Republic. If only by representing the prototype of an opposition group in a communist regime, the KOR ensured itself a place in Poland's
history.

To highlight the role of the KOR as much more than a support group for politically repressed workers, let us avail ourselves of the term used by Neil Ascherson
to capture political opposition in the late communist period—"forum politics."
Although "forum" was not a term used in the Polish oppositional context, its
counterpart in other socialist states (for example, Civic Forum in Czechoslovakia)
often preferred the word to "movement," "association," or "league." Ascherson lists
the shared characteristics of forum politics, of which the KOR was Poland's primary example: 1) an emphasis on human rights, (2) nonviolent methods, (3) the
vision of a self-managing civil society functioning independently of the state, (4)
belief that such a civil society could be constructed even before the communist
system was replaced, (5) stress on the importance of cross-national activity in the
development of civil society, (6) advocacy of social liberalism, thereby distin-

guishing forum politics from positions held by the Catholic church, (7) the frequent Marxist pedigree of practitioners, who were either the offspring of communists or had themselves been critical Marxists, and (8) third-way ideals that made forum politics often skeptical of Western capitalist models.[101] Ascherson was convinced that "the Forum people were to lead the revolutionary movements of 1989 throughout central and north-eastern Europe, and to form the first post-revolutionary governments."[102] Yet for a variety of reasons they quickly lost influence in the emergent democratic systems, as we shall see in Chapters 4 and 5.

In sum, political group alignment had a profound effect on the political process in communist Poland. Through trial and error, the repeated efforts undertaken to merge Catholic, worker, and intellectual movements ultimately proved successful, gave rise to Solidarity, and by the late 1980s posed a renewed threat to the political authorities.

Conclusion

We can now summarize our findings concerning the consequences of macro-level variables for cognitive and political mobilization. In this Phase II analysis, we have examined change in political attitudes and behavior as a result of macro-level change in People's Poland. We have traced the evolution of mass alignments and the mobilization of opposition forces that followed from socioeconomic development. Cleavages based on ethnicity or religion, which usually inhibit uniform democratic mobilization, were largely absent in Poland. Economic-functional cleavages, such as class differences that focus attention on hierarchical arrangements, tend to promote democratic mobilization. Yet in Poland the class alliance—rather than schism—between workers and intellectuals was crucial to success in the democratic drive. What we have learned in this chapter is that, in terms of both political attitudes and behavior, the operative distinction was between rulers and ruled, communists and civil society, authoritarians and liberals. The next chapter describes what happened when these two forces were pulled toward each other.

Notes

1. These same issues are central to the analysis of the breakdown of communist systems offered by Paul G. Lewis, *Central Europe Since 1945*. London: Longman, 1994, chaps. 5 and 6.

2. Andrew Janos, "Continuity and Change in Eastern Europe: Strategies of Post-Communist Politics," *East European Politics and Societies*, 8, no. 1 (Winter 1994), 3–4.

3. Janos, "Continuity and Change in Eastern Europe," p. 5.

4. Data reported in Irving Kaplan, "The Society and its Environment," in Harold D. Nelson (ed.), *Poland: A Country Study*. Washington, DC: U.S. Government Printing Office, 1984, p. 107.

5. Zbigniew Sufin, *Społeczeństwo polskie w drugiej połowie lat siedemdziesiątych.* Warsaw, 1981, p. 33.

6. Główny Urząd Statystyczny, *Rocznik statystyczny 1991.* Warsaw: GUS, 1991, pp. xxiv–xxvi, xxxvi–xxxviii.

7. Samuel P. Huntington, *The Third Wave: Democratization in the Late Twentieth Century.* Norman: University of Oklahoma Press, 1991, p. 63.

8. Huntington, *The Third Wave,* p. 72.

9. For recent studies of the Cold War outcome, see Michael J. Hogan (ed.), *The End of the Cold War: Its Meaning and Implications.* Cambridge: Cambridge University Press, 1992; William Hyland, *The Cold War Is Over.* New York: Times Books, 1990; Allen Lynch, *The Cold War is Over—Again.* Boulder: Westview Press, 1992.

10. Francis Fukuyama, *The End of History and the Last Man.* New York: Avon Books, 1993, pp. 45, 48.

11. Fukuyama, *The End of History and the Last Man,* pp. 211, 272, 274.

12. Fukuyama, *The End of History and the Last Man,* p. 337.

13. Huntington, *The Third Wave,* pp. 31–34.

14. Huntington, *The Third Wave,* p. 105.

15. See the sources listed in n. 9.

16. Huntington, *The Third Wave,* p. 86.

17. Fukuyama, *The End of History and the Last Man,* p. 215.

18. Ben Slay, "Poland and the International Economy in the 1980s: The Failure of Reforming Socialist Foreign Trade and Prospects for the Future," in Walter D. Connor and Piotr Płoszajski (eds.), *The Polish Road from Socialism.* Armonk, NY: M. E. Sharpe, 1992, p. 42.

19. David S. Mason, *Public Opinion and Political Change in Poland, 1980–1982.* Cambridge: Cambridge University Press, 1985, p. 9.

20. On collective mentality, see Ray Taras, "When Fatalists Rebelled: Cultural Theory, Conflicting Ways of Life under Socialism, and Counterrevolution in Eastern Europe," *Cultural Dynamics,* 4, no. 1 (1991), 55–89.

21. Mason, *Public Opinion and Political Change in Poland,* pp. 9–10.

22. Scott Flanagan, "Value Change in Industrial Societies," *American Political Science Review,* 81, no. 4 (December 1987), 1303–1319.

23. Scott C. Flanagan and Aie-Rie Lee, "Economic Development and the Emergence of the Authoritarian-Libertarian Value Cleavage," unpublished paper, July 1992.

24. Aleksandra Jasińska-Kania, "National Identity and Images of World Society: The Polish Case," *International Social Science Journal,* 34 (1982), 93–112.

25. The survey results are reported by Mason, *Public Opinion and Political Change in Poland,* pp. 74–75.

26. Marek Ziółkowski, "Individuals and the Social System: Values, Perceptions, and Behavioral Strategies," *Social Research,* 55, nos. 1–2 (Spring/Summer 1988), 151–154.

27. Krzysztof Jasiewicz, "Kultura polityczna Polaków: Między jednością a podziałem," *Aneks,* 48 (1988), 70.

28. David S. Mason, "Public Opinion in Poland's Transition to Market Democracy," in Connor and Płoszajski, *The Polish Road from Socialism,* p. 158. He cites the research examining seven Warsaw enterprises carried out by Bogdan Cichomski and Witold Morawski, "The Perception of Justice in Poland," paper presented at the Annual Meeting of the International Studies Association, London, March 1989.

Crises of the Communist System 109

29. Mason, *Public Opinion and Political Change in Poland*, p. 215.

30. Edmund Mokrzycki, "The Legacy of Real Socialism, Group Interests, and the Search for a New Utopia," in Connor and Płoszajski, *The Polish Road from Socialism*, p. 277.

31. Stefan Nowak, "Ciągłość i zmiana tradycji kulturowej," unpublished manuscript, University of Warsaw, 1974. A summary of Nowak's findings was published in *Polityka*, no. 14, April 10, 1976.

32. Jadwiga Koralewicz and Marek Ziółkowski, *Mentalność polaków: Sposoby myślenia o polityce, gospodarce i życiu społecznym w końcu lat osiemdziesiątych*. Poznań: Nakom, forthcoming. Cited by Janusz Reykowski, "Psychological Dimensions of a Sociopolitical Change," in Connor and Płoszajski, *The Polish Road from Socialism*, p. 224.

33. Lena Kolarska-Bobińska, "Social Interests, Egalitarian Attitudes, and the Change of Economic Order," *Social Research*, 55, nos. 1-2 (Spring/Summer 1988), 116. The ethos of consumption was documented by Jadwiga Koralewicz-Zębik, *Przemiany systemu wartości i więzi społecznej w Polsce*. Warsaw: Polish Academy of Sciences, IFiS, 1984.

34. Kolarska-Bobińska, "Social Interests, Egalitarian Attitudes, and the Change of Economic Order," p. 116.

35. Krzysztof Jasiewicz and Władysław Adamski, "Evolution of the Oppositional Consciousness," in Władysław Adamski (ed.), *Societal Conflict and Systemic Change: The Case of Poland, 1980–1992*. Warsaw: IFiS, 1993, p. 50.

36. Piotr Łukasiewicz and Andrzej Siciński, "Attitudes on Everyday Life in the Emerging Postsocialist Society," in Connor and Płoszajski, *The Polish Road from Socialism*, pp. 117–118. In their methodological postscript, the authors acknowledge that their research is based primarily on qualitative studies of lifestyles, including "such nontypical materials as jokes and rumors passed around in Poland in recent years" (126).

37. Łukasiewicz and Siciński, "Attitudes on Everyday Life in the Emerging Postsocialist Society," p. 116.

38. Andrzej Rychard and Jacek Szymanderski, "Crisis and Conflict with Respect to Legitimacy," in Adamski, *Societal Conflict and Systemic Change*, p. 199.

39. Rychard and Szymanderski, "Crisis and Conflict with Respect to Legitimacy," p. 205.

40. Rychard and Szymanderski, "Crisis and Conflict with Respect to Legitimacy," p. 206.

41. Barbara Frączak-Rudnicka, "Political Socialization in Poland: Changes in Warsaw's Adolescents' Political Attitudes, 1981–1986–1992," in Jerzy J. Wiatr (ed.), *The Politics of Democratic Transformation: Poland After 1989*. Warsaw: Scholar Agency, 1993, p. 54.

42. Mason, "Public Opinion in Poland's Transition to Market Democracy," p. 158.

43. Wnuk-Lipiński, "Economic Deprivations and Social Transformation," in Adamski, *Societal Conflict and Systemic Change*, p. 74.

44. Wnuk-Lipiński, "Economic Deprivations and Social Transformation," pp. 87, 91.

45. George Kolankiewicz and Ray Taras, "Socialism for Everyman?" in Archie Brown and Jack Gray (eds.), *Political Culture and Political Change in Communist States*. New York: Holmes and Meier, 1977, pp. 101–130.

46. Mason, "Public Opinion in Poland's Transition to Market Democracy," p. 159.

47. Krzysztof Jasiewicz, "Dynamika przemian postaw politycznych w latach osiemdziesiątych," unpublished manuscript, 1989. Cited by Mason, "Public Opinion in Poland's Transition to Market Democracy," p. 159.

48. This account is taken from Lena Kolarska-Bobińska, "Economic System and Group Interests," in Adamski, *Societal Conflict and Systemic Change*, pp. 93–114. See also her other works: Lena Kolarska, "Niereformowalna władza czy spółeczeństwo?" in Witold Morawski and Wiesława Kozek (eds.), *Załamanie porządku etatystycznego*. Warsaw: Uniwersytet Warszawski, 1988; "Poczucie niesprawiedliwości, konfliktu, i preferowny ład w gospodarce," in *Polacy '88: Dynamika konfliktu a szanse reform*. Warsaw: Uniwersytet Warszawski, 1989, pp. 81–159.

49. Kolarska-Bobińska, "Social Interests, Egalitarian Attitudes, and the Change of Economic Order," p. 122.

50. Ziółkowski, "Individuals and the Social System," pp. 154–155.

51. Kolarska-Bobińska, "Economic System and Group Interests," p. 105.

52. Krzysztof Jasiewicz, "From Protest and Repression to the Free Elections," in Adamski, *Societal Conflict and Systemic Change*, p. 129.

53. Krzysztof Jasiewicz, "Kultura polityczna polaków: między jednością a podziałem," *Aneks*, 48 (1988), 95.

54. Jadwiga Koralewicz, "Authoritarianism and Confidence in Political Leaders," in Adamski, *Societal Conflict and Systemic Change*, p. 174. The five-point scale was based on questions related to parental obedience, respect for authority, reliance on leaders, tough leadership, obedience to superiors, respect for women having no sexual relations before marriage, and conformity with tradition.

55. Koralewicz, "Authoritarianism and Confidence in Political Leaders," p. 183.

56. Koralewicz, "Authoritarianism and Confidence in Political Leaders," p. 185.

57. Andrzej Rychard, "Old and New Institutions of Public Life," in Adamski, *Societal Conflict and Systemic Change*, p. 215.

58. Renata Siemieńska, "Zaufanie Polaków do innych narodów w okresie politycznych i ekonomicznych przemian," in Aleksandra Jasińska-Kania (ed.), *Bliscy i dalecy*, vol. 2. Warsaw: Uniwersytet Warszawski, Instytut Socjologii, 1992, pp. 208–209, my translation.

59. Aleksandra Jasińska-Kania, "Zmiany postaw Polaków wobec różnych narodów i państw," in Jasińska-Kania, *Bliscy i dalecy*, vol. 2, pp. 220, 231–232. This volume contains additional chapters on Poles' attitudes toward Russians, Germans, and Jews.

60. On this, see Peter Weinreich, "National and Ethnic Identities: Theoretical Concepts in Practice," *Innovation in Social Science Research*, 4, no. 1 (1991).

61. Władysław Adamski, "Poles between East and West," in Adamski, *Societal Conflict and Systemic Change*, pp. 160, 164.

62. Reykowski, "Psychological Dimensions of a Sociopolitical Change," p. 218.

63. Reykowski, "Psychological Dimensions of a Sociopolitical Change," pp. 225–226.

64. Random sampling was, of course, impossible. One interesting point is that temporary visitors to the West were usually those who enjoyed the party's confidence and would, accordingly, have been more inclined to support the party. Yet the former prime minister and last party first secretary Mieczysław Rakowski noted that the first shocking results the party received in the 1989 parliamentary elections were from Poland's embassies and offices abroad. Though largely party appointees, the majority of these officials nonetheless cast their votes against the ruling communists. See Mieczysław Rakowski, *Jak to się stało*. Warsaw: BGW, 1991. The most informative single work on opinion polling in Poland is Mason, *Public Opinion and Political Change in Poland*.

65. Kolarska-Bobińska, "Social Interests, Egalitarian Attitudes, and the Change of Economic Interests," pp. 111–139; see also her "Poczucie niesprawiedliwości, konfliktu i preferowany ład w gospodarce."

66. One Polish sociologist, Renata Siemieńska, collaborated with Ronald Inglehart on the study of postmaterialist values in Poland, but I am unaware of any resulting publication.

67. On self-actualization and, specifically, self-governing, see Jadwiga Staniszkis, *Poland's Self-Limiting Revolution.* Princeton: Princeton University Press, 1984.

68. I have considered the importance of culture shift in Poland using a different model (Aaron Wildavsky's cultural theory) in "When Fatalists Rebelled."

69. On these conditions, see Flanagan and Lee, "Economic Development and the Emergence of the Authoritarian-Libertarian Value Cleavage."

70. Scott C. Flanagan and Huo-yan Shyu, "Culture Shift and the Transition to Democracy: The Case of Taiwan," paper presented at the Annual Meeting of the American Political Science Association, Chicago, September 1992, p. 31.

71. Adam Bromke, *Poland's Politics: Idealism vs. Realism.* Cambridge, MA: Harvard University Press, 1967, pp. 239–241.

72. Jerzy Turowicz, "Kościół i polityka," *Tygodnik Powszechny,* no. 12 (1985). Quoted by Norbert A. Zmijewski, *The Catholic-Marxist Ideological Dialogue in Poland, 1945–1980.* Aldershot, England: Dartmouth, 1991, p. 25.

73. Zmijewski, *The Catholic-Marxist Ideological Dialogue in Poland,* p. 39.

74. Zmijewski, *The Catholic-Marxist Ideological Dialogue in Poland,* p. 55.

75. Zmijewski, *The Catholic-Marxist Ideological Dialogue in Poland,* p. 87.

76. Stefan Wyszyński, *Zapiski więzienne.* Paris: Editions du Dialogue, 1982.

77. On the inability of the communist rulers to stir up rivalry between Cardinals Wyszyński and Woytyła, see Andrzej Micewski, *Cardinal Wyszynski.* San Diego: Harcourt Brace Jovanovich, 1984.

78. John Clark and Aaron Wildavsky, *The Moral Collapse of Communism: Poland as a Cautionary Tale.* San Francisco: Institute for Contemporary Studies Press, 1990, p. 345.

79. Zmijewski, *The Catholic-Marxist Ideological Dialogue in Poland,* p. 138.

80. Zmijewski, *The Catholic-Marxist Ideological Dialogue in Poland,* pp. 141–142.

81. Zmijewski, *The Catholic-Marxist Ideological Dialogue in Poland,* p. 146.

82. José Casanova, "Church, State, Nation, and Civil Society in Spain and Poland," in Said Amir Arjomand (ed.), *The Political Dimensions of Religion.* Albany, NY: State University of New York Press, 1993, p. 135.

83. Roman Laba, "Worker Roots of Solidarity," *Problems of Communism* 35 (July-August 1986), 47–67. On conflicting public discourses between the organized opposition (including Solidarity), the Catholic church, and the party-state, see Jan Kubik, *The Power of Symbols Against the Symbols of Power: The Rise of Solidarity and the Fall of State Socialism in Poland.* University Park: Pennsylvania State University Press, 1994.

84. Reported in Adam Sarapata, "Society and Bureaucracy," in Connor and Płoszajski, *The Polish Road from Socialism,* pp. 98–103.

85. Andrzej Rychard, "Participation and Interests: Dilemmas of the Emerging Social and Political Structure in Poland," in Connor and Płoszajski, *The Polish Road from Socialism,* p. 176.

86. Lawrence Goodwyn, *Breaking the Barrier: The Rise of Solidarity in Poland.* New York: Oxford University Press, 1991, pp. 386–387. See also Roman Laba, *The Roots of Solidarity: A Political Sociology of Poland's Working-Class Democratization.* Princeton: Princeton University Press, 1991.

87. Neil Ascherson, *The Polish August.* Harmondsworth, England: Penguin, 1983; Abraham Brumberg (ed.), *Poland: Genesis of a Revolution.* New York: Vintage Books, 1983; Goodwyn, *Breaking the Barrier;* Laba, *The Roots of Solidarity;* David Ost, *Solidarity and the*

Politics of Anti-Politics. Philadelphia: Temple University Press, 1990; George Sanford, *Polish Communism in Crisis.* New York: St. Martin's, 1983.

88. David J. Ost, "Indispensable Ambiguity: Solidarity's Internal Authority Structure," *Studies in Comparative Communism,* 21, no. 2 (Summer 1988), 197. See also his *Solidarity and the Politics of Anti-Politics.*

89. Transcript of the founding conference of national Solidarity, September 17, 1980, p. 66. The English translation of the transcript was made available by David Ost. The Polish version was first published in *Krytyka,* no. 18 (1984).

90. Transcript of the founding conference of national Solidarity, p. 12.

91. Transcript of the founding conference of national Solidarity, p. 48.

92. Ost, "Indispensable Ambiguity," p. 191.

93. Ost, "Indispensable Ambiguity," p. 199.

94. Jack Bielasiak and Barbara Hicks, "Solidarity's Self-Organization: The Crisis of Rationality and Legitimacy in Poland, 1980–81," *East European Politics and Society,* 4, no. 3 (Fall 1990), 489.

95. Bielasiak and Hicks, "Solidarity's Self-Organization," pp. 511–512.

96. Staniszkis, *Poland's Self-Limiting Revolution.*

97. Jacek Kurczewski, *The Resurrection of Rights in Poland.* Oxford: Clarendon Press, 1993, pp. 212–215.

98. Laba, "Worker Roots of Solidarity."

99. Roberto Michels, *Political Parties.* Glencoe, IL: Free Press, 1949.

100. The best account is Jan Józef Lipski, *KOR: A History of the Workers' Defense Committee in Poland.* Berkeley: University of California Press, 1985.

101. Neal Ascherson, "1989 in Eastern Europe: Constitutional Representative Democracy as a 'Return to Normality'?" in John Dunn (ed.), *Democracy: The Unfinished Journey, 508 BC to AD 1993.* New York: Oxford University Press, 1992, pp. 225–226.

102. Ascherson, "1989 in Eastern Europe," p. 224.

4

Coalition Formation and Crisis Resolution

The primary objective of Phase III analysis is to explain how a new ruling coalition, representing a different set of actors and a different set of preferences, is able to coalesce politically and supplant the incumbent regime. Central to such a takeover is a change in the current rules of political competition. The preceding chapters have pointed to the rules established under the communist regime. Following Ken Jowitt, in examining regime transition I disassociate my approach from the transitology literature guilty of "ignoring the Leninist legacy's impact on the range of viable political choices available to leaderships in the Soviet Union and Eastern Europe."[1] Rule changes are shaped by the experience acquired under the previous system; they are sources of contention and may be accompanied by crisis and polarization of the preferences of the contenders for power. The scope for rule change is delimited by a host of factors, including the degree to which the current rules are long-standing and ingrained. Moreover, under conditions of uncertainty—as in a bargaining process characterized by actors having differing resources with shifting utilities and contrasting issue salience—choices about new rules will be contingent. These choices may shape the transition process more than the final institutional outcome.

In Donald Share's terminology, then, incumbents and opposition are faced with the general choice between a conflictual transition through rupture and a consensual transition through transaction.[2] But even a consensual transition may produce a polarization of contender preferences and fundamental regime change. In both cases, a key decision point is reached at which a new ruling coalition begins to be formed. This process is the subject of this chapter.

The Potentially Winning Coalitions

Key factors affecting coalition formation are issue salience, issue distances between actors, and the different kinds of resources held by actors and their relative amount and value. The assumptions are that (1) actors will seek to form the winning coalition that maximizes their share of the spoils and minimizes their issue distance from the other coalition members and (2) the ruling capacity of any potential coalition is enhanced as it gains command of a greater proportion of the available resources and is lessened by internal dissonance and by intense opposition to the potential coalition's objectives.

In this case study of the Polish transition, I examine the three most viable potentially winning coalitions that arose in 1989, gauging the probability of each one's winning and the implications of its winning for the new constitution, policy outcomes, and the transition to democracy. Then I explain why one particular winning coalition emerged (in terms of its mobilization of resources, manipulation of the issues, and so on) and what would have been necessary for a different outcome.

The most likely coalition—and one that had won out in previous postwar crises in Poland—would have been based exclusively on party retrenchment. Communist party hard-liners and reformers would have suspended their internal squabbling in the face of growing opposition, as after October 1956 with Gomułka's appointment, after December 1970 with Gierek's accession to power, and after December 1981 with the imposition of martial law. But political circumstances were different in the late 1980s. By summer 1988, party membership was declining, and the level of internal dissonance in the party had reached unprecedented levels. The resource share—measured in terms of popular legitimacy, performance, and control—of the coalition based on party retrenchment had been declining since martial law. Its policy preferences would have been for cosmetic change only, and the result for the polity would have been muddling through with a high risk of continued unrest. The party coalition failed, then, because of high dissonance, declining resource share, declining issue salience (Marxism), and disagreement over the party's hegemonic role in society.

Just as important in examining weaknesses developing within the party in the late 1980s is to gauge the level of disunity *after* its June 1989 election defeat. As I show in this chapter, the transition was in many ways an effort at the self-transformation of autocracy.[3] The communist party leadership had every reason to expect to continue governing; after all, that had been the purpose of allocating 65 percent of parliamentary seats to it. The swift disintegration of the party after the elections was, arguably, more unexpected and more consequential than the election result. The failure to patch together a viable party coalition before and after the roundtable talks is, therefore, at the heart of the coalitional analysis.

A second coalition alignment that also failed to come about would have consisted of party liberals (endorsed by Jaruzelski), joining with the Catholic episcopate and Solidarity trade-union leaders. KOR activists would have been excluded, as indeed the original roundtable composition proposed by the party envisaged. Internal dissonance here would have been coded as modest, but the resources mobilized by this group, too, would have been at best moderate—given the exclusion of the conservative party apparatus, which was responsible for implementing policies, and the KOR intellectuals, who were needed to draw up the blueprint for a self-governing society. Issue salience would have been high ("government of national unity"), but the consequences for the polity would have been unpredictable because such a coalition would have been a government without experts.

The coalition that did win out was larger than the minimal one necessary to govern. It consisted of party liberals and both radical and moderate Solidarity tendencies, with the church receiving many benefits from its officially nonpartisan position. Here resources were maximized while internal dissonance remained moderate. Policy preferences and intended consequences were designed to resynchronize the prospective ruling coalition with society. Although the probability of this coalition's emerging was initially lower than that of the first or the second scenario described, the learning process for authorities and opposition figures alike at the roundtable talks narrowed ideological differences considerably. In assessing various potential coalitional outcomes, then, by examining the balance of resources and the shifts in issue positions we arrive at a better understanding of why one particular coalition won out. We also can speculate in a more informed way about what would have been necessary for a different outcome.

One parsimonious way of approaching such complex questions is to chart changes in contenders' fortunes during successive stages of the crisis. Figure 4.1 offers an issue-distance and resource-distribution representation for the main actor groups that participated in the democratic breakthrough in Poland. It describes where contenders fell on the left-right policy-preference continuum and how resources were distributed among them. Placement along the horizontal axis is based on a single cross-issue summary; it is a sum of multiple issues with changing salience. The vertical axis gives estimated power ratings on a five-point scale, summarizing the different types of resources available to the contenders. The analysis displays the various possibilities that were available at the onset, management, and resolution stages of the crisis; it illustrates the strategic logic of the situation and helps to identify what had to change in order for one or another outcome to occur.[4]

The principal mode of coalition analysis is a rational-choice perspective seeking to explain how actors established a particular coalition, but nonrational properties are not excluded from the framework. These include leadership style, personalities (for example, risk-averse and risk-taking leaders), leadership skills (such as bargaining and brokerage abilities or ideological and semantic appropriation), and serendipitous events affecting contenders' positions. To summarize, the objective in this chapter is to explain how the democratic breakthrough was achieved by looking at the contenders, their resources and issue preferences, and their actions and responses to others' actions.

Contenders and Their Resources

The contenders, whether incumbents or nonincumbents, are defined as the groups competing for direct participation in and control of decision-making

Figure 4.1   Issue Distance and Resource Distribution in the Polish Crisis, 1988–1989

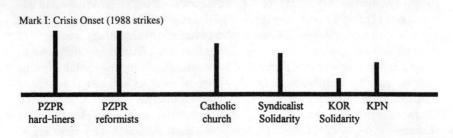

Mark I: Crisis Onset (1988 strikes)

| PZPR | PZPR | Catholic | Syndicalist | KOR | KPN |
| hard-liners | reformists | church | Solidarity | Solidarity | |

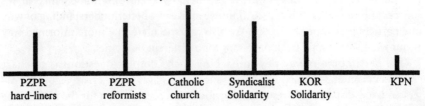

Mark II: Crisis Management (February 1989 start of roundtable talks)

| PZPR | PZPR | Catholic | Syndicalist | KOR | | KPN |
| hard-liners | reformists | church | Solidarity | Solidarity | | |

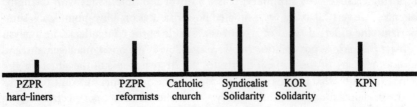

Mark III: Crisis Resolution (September 1989 coalition government)

| PZPR | PZPR | Catholic | Syndicalist | KOR | KPN |
| hard-liners | reformists | church | Solidarity | Solidarity | |

Vertical axes indicate resource distribution; horizontal axes indicate issue distances. Total available resources are considered fixed across the three crisis points; only the distribution pattern changes.

structures. Although contenders can also be defined as individuals, the process of transition from one regime to another is primarily shaped by organized interests, associations, and institutional leadership groupings. The political constituencies of the contenders are generally larger groups in society, such as social classes and mass movements, that do not aspire to direct political power but whose support or acquiescence is vital for maintaining the influence of a group contender.

Contenders for power in Poland included, first of all, the incumbent leadership under Jaruzelski. The dilemma for the long-ruling communist party was how to extend its rule and at the same time extricate itself from crisis.[5] The nonincumbent contenders have generally been grouped into a unitary Solidarity opposition camp. What turned Solidarity into such an umbrella organization was the communist regime. Referring to actors at the roundtable negotiations, government spokesman Jerzy Urban referred mockingly to the monolithic opposition as opposed to the more pluralistic government coalition.[6] As it entered negotiations with the authorities, Solidarity could, notionally, be differentiated into its former KOR advisory team (Jacek Kuroń, Adam Michnik) and its 1980 union leadership (Wałęsa, Marian Jurczyk). Of course, some activists could be classified with either (Zbigniew Bujak). The fact that many other fault lines ran through Solidarity became clear once the communists had been defeated at the polls and this umbrella group began to splinter as it formed successive governments.

Minor contenders that hoped to play roles in coalitional politics included a strongly nationalist and anticommunist dissident party, the KPN. Under its leader, the former communist party member Leszek Moczulski, it had become an ambitious and noisy if not particularly influential contender. At the opposite end of the political spectrum, the communist National Trade Union Accord (Ogólnopolskie Pororzumienie Związków Zawodowych—OPZZ), headed by Alfred Miodowicz, had been gaining adherents, against all odds, in the late 1980s. The OPZZ steadily distanced itself from the communist party even though Miodowicz was a member of its Politburo. It aspired to be a catalyst for party conservatives; by unifying these forces, Miodowicz believed, political and trade-union pluralism could be suppressed. The institution that mediated between communist and Solidarity forces was the Catholic episcopate. If harboring the ambition to be kingmaker—both in the negotiations and in the legislative elections—can be considered as contending for political power, then the church was very much a contender.

The question of resource distribution among contending actors has received considerable, though usually implicit, attention in the political science literature on Poland.[7] At times, resource distribution is treated as an independent variable that affects policy outcomes; for example, Gierek's acceptance of the August 1980 agreements legalizing Solidarity was the outcome of the trade union's newfound power to organize nationwide strikes. At other times, resource distribution is regarded as the dependent variable, linked with macro-level change. Thus, the buildup of Solidarity's resources would be viewed as the natural product of a better-educated, more aware, and better-organized society. The way in which resource distribution was affected by macro-level change may represent the single most important macro-micro-linkage that emerged during Phase II development. Furthermore, resource distribution has traditionally been cast solely in terms of the balance of power between party authorities and opposition groups and has been regarded as a dichotomous variable. This approach needs to be modified if we are to make sense of the willingness of two sides with unequal resources to agree to the desirability of regime transition and to bargain as partners over the mechanics of that transition.

We can distinguish three kinds of resources held by political contenders: (1) incumbency in office (electoral seats held by the PZPR, the ZSL, and the SD and, after June 1989, by Solidarity Citizens' Committees [Komitety Obywatelskie—KO]), (2) nonincumbency resources and influence (control of the bureaucracy, wealth, media access, public opinion), and (3) coercion (the security apparatus disposed of by the party versus the mass-mobilization potential of Solidarity). A common assumption in political science is that the resources of incumbency are invariably much superior to those of outsiders. Incumbents can serve as gatekeepers controlling access to the political sphere as well as enacting public policy that curries favor with the society.[8] Furthermore, the more tangible resources under the control of incumbents, such as their accrued wealth, their interconnectedness with the economic elite (the *nomenklatura* in communist systems), and the support they derive from the military, appear even to be independent of the established political regime. Conversely, even if systemic change occurs, the elite of the ancien régime continues to hold power resources sufficient to undermine the transition and, at the least, to remain an occasional crucial political actor in the new system. In short, even with the final electoral and coalitional outcomes that followed in Poland in 1989, the communists still controlled vital political resources.

Some scholars believe that it is crucial to allow outgoing incumbents a key role in the transition process in order for democratic consolidation to proceed. Terry Karl and Philippe Schmitter see greater prospects for democratic consolidation when old-regime elites and their democratic opponents reach a negotiated transition that demarcates respective spheres of influence in the new system rather than leaving the old-regime elite as a wild card in it.[9] Donald Share and Scott Mainwaring focus on the amount of control exercised by authoritarian elites and recognize that it is precisely this control that allows the democratic process to be initiated. As noted earlier, they term such an elite-controlled democratic breakthrough "transition through transaction."[10] For Michael Burton, Richard Gunther, and John Higley, "the key to the consolidation of new democratic regimes lies in the transformation of political elites from disunity to consensual unity via elite settlements or elite convergences."[11] The terms of the settlement, or pact, are important in that they help promote elite unity—the necessary precondition of democratic consolidation. Karl and Schmitter also anticipate the desirability of extending political shelter to old-regime elites in their inclusion requirement: Any actor having the propensity or resources to play the role of spoiler in the new system must have its interests satisfied in the foundational pact.[12]

To restate the logic of pacts and democratic consolidation, even if the existing elite's resources decline dramatically it is important to provide it with sufficient safeguards in the new system—including opportunities for convergence with the new rulers—rather than risk its becoming discontented and mobilizing the few but dangerous resources it has held onto. Negotiated transitions also contribute to a consensual transition to democracy in that they develop a momentum of their own. Especially where contenders dispose of political resources and little else—as in the case of Solidarity—they will have greater inducements to mobilize such resources in negotiations reshaping the political sphere. Likewise, the loss of exogenous support (Kremlin backing for the Polish communist leadership) inclined the old-regime elite to use its remaining resources in a bargaining environment.

Nonincumbency resources include wealth, media access, public opinion, and the opposition's counterpart to state coercion, civil disobedience and industrial strife. Solidarity's financial resources were not a key factor determining its bargaining position in 1988 and 1989, but the size of its past membership, its extensive networks within the industrial sector, its fusion of intellectual and working-class leaders, and its moral capital (a term employed frequently by the historian and Solidarity activist Bronisław Geremek) were crucial resources that could not be taken lightly. Internal cohesion within this social movement during the all-important period of negotiating, its realistic expectations about bargaining with the authorities (learned from the 1980–1981 experience), its determination to keep negotiations going regardless of temporary deadlocks, and the uncanny political intuition of its leader were resources that had a multiplier effect and took on greater value as talks continued. The access to the media and to a wide and sympathetic public that came from negotiating with incumbents proved to strengthen Solidarity's bargaining position. The party's media monopoly was broken, and Solidarity's popular policies underscoring the need for democracy were now disseminated nationwide. In Urban's caustic view, the protracted roundtable discussions were transformed into an enormous television propaganda campaign for Solidarity.[13]

Finally, public opinion seemed to be clearly on the side of Solidarity from the beginning of the talks. Aware that, as it entered roundtable negotiations, it enjoyed greater public support than the party and government, Solidarity could claim greater popular legitimacy than its adversaries and make use of this resource at critical junctures. Thus, in a January 1989 survey, 54 percent of respondents asserted that Solidarity had more supporters than detractors, while only 25 percent believed that this was the case for the government and a tiny 6 percent that the communist party's supporters outnumbered its opponents.[14] Yet the calculation made by party leaders in opening dialogue with their opponents was that their own public approval rating might improve, especially since some momentum in their favor had already been generated. Thus, Internal Affairs Minister Czesław Kiszczak felt that trust in the party might rise from 30 percent to 40 percent if the roundtable proved successful.[15] Trust in the government, army, and the Sejm might increase from already high levels; in particular, the economic reforms enacted by Prime Minister Rakowski since his appointment in October 1988—such as expanding the private sector and encouraging joint ventures—had already doubled government approval ratings, from 34 percent to 72 percent between August and November 1988.[16] Although the ruling coalition might not record any significant relative gains in public support compared with Solidarity, a successful roundtable could provide important absolute gains. If in addition there were early elections, in which because of their organizational superiority the authorities would be able to capitalize on their recent gains in public support, their prospects might be better than regime performance warranted. So, at least, went the reasoning of party leaders hoping to benefit from the policy of dialogue.

Since the communist authorities initiated talks with the Solidarity opposition, the Polish case appears to reflect an elite-controlled, negotiated transition—the kind that Schmitter and Karl believe enhances the prospects for democratic consolidation.[17] But the buildup of Solidarity resources and the meltdown of regime ones in the course of the negotiations and the ensuing elections suggest that the elite very quickly lost control of the transition process. Especially when we consider the political outcome, it seems doubtful whether there was any carryover of the resources of the communist elite to the new system. At best, because of the negotiated but circumscribed nature of the transition, no obstacles were placed in the way of the old political class in transforming itself into a new economic class, but its political wild-card role was effectively eliminated. In addition, democratic consolidation seems to have been achieved by the Solidarity side's reneging on the original terms of the pact. The elections were more politicized and confrontational than the roundtable accord had anticipated, thereby making the result, in practice, zero-sum. The winner-take-all approach to the 35 percent of Sejm seats contested hastened democratic consolidation.

In addition to the raw resources disposed of by contenders, it is important to indicate the changing value of these resources over time. The relative strengths of the various contenders are determined by dependent variables in Phase II of the analysis—changing value systems and mobilized political forces. But the process of negotiation creates a dynamic of its own. The utility of certain resources is less once the political circumstances have changed. For instance, the resources held by the party were of little (in the case of its control of the bureaucracy) or no (in the case of its staffing of the security apparatus) use within a bargaining forum. Indeed, the coercive apparatus was unusable once a policy of dialogue had been adopted. The resources held by Solidarity (such as moral capital) were both less tangible and more useful. Further, how effectively contenders operationalized their resources was as important as the raw resources themselves. Given the changes occurring in actors' resource levels and resource use during the roundtable talks, it is not surprising that the original set of political rules fashioned under these conditions would prove to be highly contingent and subject to replacement.

In describing contenders and their resources, we also need to consider the logic underlying time-series analysis. Generally, every transition can be conceptualized as having two stages—onset of the crisis and resolution. In such a two-stage treatment, the first stage may represent not the onset of crisis *sensu stricto* but the beginning of a liberalization stage—a major turning point at which decisions are made that set new processes and trends in operation. An intervening stage can be added if there was an important intermediate step in the transition to democracy or a coalition emerged that ruled for a while and brought a temporary resolution only to give way to another. In the Polish case, the roundtable talks represented such an intermediate step. The first stage was the strikes of summer 1988 that raised the specter of a return to August 1980. The second stage was the attempted management of the crisis through the convening of roundtable talks in February 1989. The third stage was the establishment of a noncommunist government in August 1989 in the wake of the June elections. This resolution was not the kind that was intended at the roundtable: instead of simply reducing communist influence in government, as envisaged by the roundtable power-sharing arrangements, it replaced the communist incumbents altogether.

Figure 4.1 displays the contenders' resources and issue distances at these three stages, thereby suggesting the most likely coalitional outcomes over time. These capture the changing logic of strategic rational-choice options for each contender at each stage. Given the array of issue preferences and the resource distribution, the question is how each actor tried to advance from the current *most likely outcome* to a *preferred outcome* by manipulating the issue agenda, reaching compromises, building resources, and working to change their valuation. By looking at different phases of crisis it is possible to indicate the changes that took place during each transition episode. Thus the process can be conceptualized as a series of distinct games with their own ascendant and declining contenders arriving at specific and changing outcomes. The time-series analysis shows that potentially winning coalitions possessing an array of resources at one stage of the transition process did not ultimately win. By comparing the resource distributions at the different stages we arrive at a clearer appreciation of how the coalition that began as an underdog was able in the end to gain power.

Issues and Their Salience

The socioeconomic changes outlined in Chapter 2 and the changes in the normative framework described in Chapter 3 engendered a crisis within the ancien régime and resulted in a reformulation of the issue agenda. Debate over the command economy, which in the 1960s had centered on reform proposals such as decentralization, became focused in the mid-1980s on fundamental principles such as the role of the market in a socialist society. Structural reform of the system became more salient and capital accumulation by the state to finance investment for industrialization became less so. The issue that gave rise to democratizing movements in the Soviet republics in this period—national identity—was never salient in Poland. Nancy Bermeo correctly notes that "the literature that focuses on the last wave of authoritarian transitions says little indeed about the role of ethnicity or national identity as either a stimulus or a barrier to successful democratization."[18] Fortunately, in the case of Poland, the transition can be studied without much reference to ethnic relations or, to a lesser extent, to questions of national identity. In the compressed time span of the negotiated democratic breakthrough

the salience of certain issues increased while the irrelevance of others was underscored; the slogan "Let Poland be Poland" no longer constituted an effective bargaining strategy.

Although democratization can be reduced to a single issue—change in the
form of government from authoritarian to democratic—it does not emerge in a
political vacuum. Rather, it is embedded in a political context replete with salient
issues. Typically, three or four major ones can be identified. At the Polish roundtable, the key issues concerned institutional arrangements: how many legislative
seats would be openly contested, what method would be used to produce a second
chamber (the Senate), and what the powers of a revamped presidency would include. These three questions in turn spawned the controversies over related issues
described below.

In identifying contenders and the issues separating them, I employ traditional
left-right categories, locating actors' positions on issues across the spectrum from
revolutionary through reformist to conservative. Whereas in the postcommunist
era the right often constitutes a mix of hard-line communist and nationalist
forces, the center liberal-democratic parties, and the left social democratic forces,
the ideological and empirical referents used here represent the conventions current at the time of the breakthrough. The typology of players in the Polish transition is straightforward, consisting of reform-minded and intransigent groups
within the camps of both the regime and the opposition. This typology is consistent with those put forward by both O'Donnell and Schmitter[19] and Przeworski.[20]
They, too, identify four typical actors in the transition process: hard-liners and reformers (*duros* and *blandos* in O'Donnell and Schmitter's terminology) among
the incumbent political elites in the pretransition authoritarian system and moderates and radicals (or, for O'Donnell and Schmitter, minimalists and maximal-
ists) in civil society, that is, outside the current political class. The one caveat in the
Polish case is that the Catholic church was officially designated by both camps as
the facilitator for the talks. It seems important to highlight the church's sometimes
partisan and sometimes independent role.

A more complex problem is to arrange the contenders in terms of their distance
from one another at different stages of the negotiations. All the contenders are po-
sitioned on a single left-right axis. Given that multiple issues exist, contenders may
not necessarily line up on each of them in the same left-right relative position, but
estimates of the distance between contiguous contenders are based on a sum of all
the issues involved. The space between contingent actors varies, then, in terms of
the degree of issue agreement. Distance between contiguous actors is determined
by their overall levels of disagreement across the multiplicity of issues identified.
Low disagreement among ideologically contiguous contenders provides a "cordial"
bargaining range and is represented by one unit of distance along the left-right
alignment. Two units denote moderate or substantial disagreement levels that
strain relations, and three units means high or intensely emotional disagreements.

If resources are concentrated in the center, then the existence of extremist contenders makes little difference. In contrast, if resources are monopolized by con-

tenders that are poles apart, the authoritarian regime is in danger of being over-thrown or replaced by the opposition should resource distribution shift. A transition to democracy may occur without crisis if extreme issue polarization produces agreement to negotiate. This is especially clear in the Polish case, where the resources of the incumbent regime declined and the need for new coalition partners became inescapable. At the same time, excluded contenders sought a negotiated settlement with incumbents in order to lessen the risks of confrontation and to make the move to democratic structures less threatening for incumbents.

Contenders and Issues in the Polish Transition

The Communist Party

By 1988 it was clear to insiders (party leaders), outsiders (Solidarity leaders), and external brokers (Gorbachev) alike that the resources of Poland's political opposition had been accruing as it built an independent civil society. The communist leadership felt under pressure to redistribute rewards and values in a manner more reflective of society's preferences. As economic crisis deepened, certain political actors—primarily party reformers—stressed the need to establish larger coalitions in order to secure a broader mandate and to diffuse responsibility for state policy (in 1981 Solidarity was accused of being unwilling to shoulder even partial responsibility). In selecting new coalition partners, insiders were swayed by the size of their constituencies as well as by the need to reduce issue distances between competing groups. Furthermore, the position of the communist political class had turned into a free fall. As Jadwiga Staniszkis writes, members of this political class had become "dependent on the state, unaccustomed to expressing their own position (that in the past did not need justification), and caught in the trap of their own calls for 'reforms.'"[21]

In December 1988 an extraordinary meeting was held in Paris that brought together for the first time some of the communist bloc's leading dissidents. Among them was Wałęsa, making his first foreign trip in many years. At a concluding press conference, the Soviet writer Lev Timofiejev asserted, "There would be no Gorbachev and no Sakharov in Paris if not for Poland's Solidarity." According to the recollections of one of Solidarity's main leaders, Geremek, "For me the year 1989 began really in Paris, in mid-December 1988. There would be no perestroika, no Gorbachev, if not for Poland's Solidarity. In the ensuing months the list of facts which would never have occurred increased dramatically."[22]

Solidarity's brief existence in 1980–1981, with its then pro forma commitment to the socialist system, had another important consequence for the Polish communist party. As Geremek put it, "It took away the party's own legitimacy, which was based on the assumption that it served the national interest and represented it in Moscow. Though it did not wish to recognize it, the suspicion arose, especially in 1989, that the party might in fact be the representative of the Soviet Union's interests in its own country, not the other way around."[23]

What were the pivotal events that led to the party leadership's conversion to the cause of reform in the late 1980s and to the system's total destruction in 1989? According to one Politburo member, the national referendum called by Jaruzelski in fall 1987 to seek approval of a package of political and economic reforms was understood by the party leadership as a pathbreaking step toward the Polish road to socialism so often talked about in the past.[24] In order to obtain public approval of proposed price increases (price rises announced suddenly in both 1970 and 1976 had triggered antigovernment demonstrations), the referendum asked whether voters supported accelerated economic reform even if it might cause temporary hardship. In referring to the referendum the sociologist Jacek Kurczewski has correctly observed that "to vague questions one gets vague answers. To an absurd question one gets an answer which is absurd."[25] Nevertheless, the fact that a referendum was held at all pried open additional political space, as the Politburo had intended, and augured a series of party initiatives. Strikes organized by activists of the still illegal Solidarity movement in May 1988 did not immediately produce any significant political concessions. The symbolic politics pursued by party leaders in postcrisis situations, especially creating a game of musical chairs for political leaders (about which the public had become blasé), this time involved the replacement of the prime minister. Zbigniew Messner, who had presided over limited economic reform, was dumped in favor of the communist party's consummate politician, Rakowski. On the surface, a party liberal was succeeding an unimaginative technocrat. In reality, Alfred Miodowicz, head of the proregime trade unions and regarded as a hard-liner, had been influential in having Messner removed, thereby casting doubt on whether political liberalization was indeed the desired outcome of the change.[26]

In July 1988 Gorbachev visited Poland and embraced the cause of reform, declaring that Poles had the right to determine their own political destiny. Without this personal endorsement from the Kremlin leader it is doubtful whether Jaruzelski could have gone ahead with plans for talks between the ruling party and political dissidents. The urgency of breaking out of a cycle of crises was heightened when Solidarity staged a second wave of strikes in August, but the strikes were only the most dramatic sign of crisis. The government-run polling agency found that the percentage of respondents agreeing that the general economic condition of the country was poor had risen from 64 percent at the end of summer 1987 to 85 percent at the end of summer 1988. More ominous for the authorities, the proportion of respondents agreeing that the *political* situation was bad had nearly doubled, increasing from 21 percent to 41 percent over the same period. According to Public Opinion Survey Center Assistant Director Piotr Kwiatkowski, "The communist party (PZPR) was rapidly losing what remained of its authority: early in 1988 the non-approvers outnumbered the supporters. Starting from 1988, the net support for PZPR was expressed in negative numbers only."[27]

As traditionally happened in crisis situations, the party's Central Committee's Eighth Plenum convened on August 26. On the same day, Interior Minister Kiszczak appeared on television officially to announce the desirability of roundtable talks with representatives of various social and occupational milieux: "I stipulate no preconditions regarding the subject of the talks nor regarding the composition of participants."[28] A round of "talks about talks" began in August 1988 between Politburo member Józef Czyrek and Solidarity leader Andrzej Stelmachowski. It was quickly followed by an informal meeting between Kiszczak, Wałęsa, and their teams of advisers on September 16. Held in Magdalenka, the venue for future full-blown roundtable negotiations, this meeting explored the viability of roundtable negotiations and the scope for compromise between party and opposition positions. The last of these informal Magdalenka talks before the formal roundtable began was held on January 27, 1989.

The first tangible public result of Kiszczak's offer was the appearance on state-owned television of Wałęsa on November 30, 1988, in a debate with the fiery Miodowicz. Wałęsa scored a debating victory, and soon afterward he received a passport to travel to the extraordinary Paris meeting, held December 10–11, where he confirmed his still unblemished international prestige as a Nobel Peace Prize laureate. A week later, on December 18, Solidarity held a major meeting in Warsaw that established the Citizens' Committee advising the Solidarity leader. This proved an important juncture in the late organizational development of Solidarity.

The Eighth Plenum seemed to embrace liberalization but at the same time provided discouraging signs about the likelihood of political change. In this respect it scarcely differed from many preceding Central Committee sessions at times of crisis. It condemned efforts at political destabilization undertaken by the opposition while accepting Kiszczak's initiative for immediate roundtable talks with opposition members. But a more obvious caesura in the formulation of party policy on liberalization was the first session of the Central Committee's Tenth Plenum, held shortly after the Paris conference, in late December 1988 and mid-January 1989. In terms of personnel changes the meeting marked the departure of party conservatives such as General Józef Baryła and their replacement with liberals such as Janusz Reykowski. In substantive terms, it is significant that the first section of the Politburo's theses on party reform was titled "The Polish Road to Socialism Today." According to this document, "In many areas of systemic transformations, Polish approaches are pioneering and blazing new paths." Even the experience of the Stalinist era had shown that "Poland was not a place where distortions occurred on such a scale as are revealed today in other countries. The PZPR also carried out in public the quickest and deepest accounting with them." In addition, the Tenth Plenum theses asserted that "socialism on Polish land grew on national soil." More, the party considered itself nothing less than "the critical inheritors of the entire history of the Polish nation and state" and believed that it had sustained Poland by "defending her national interests, the sovereignty of the country, and the durability of the alliance system originating in the Yalta-Potsdam framework of territorial-political order on our continent."[29] The PZPR was proclaiming, then, that it was the least evil of regional communist parties, that it had largely been faithful to Polish national interests and that, where unpopular international alliances had been forged, they reflected the Realpolitik sanctioned by the West both in wartime and during the Cold War. A scant year after the sophistic theses of the Tenth Plenum had been advanced, the PZPR ceased to exist. To be sure, the theses did refer to a modern type of socialism that in future would fuse a socialist democratic state and a civil society, but they did not entirely abandon the idea of the party's leading role in society or the internal party principle of democratic centralism. Whether sufficient room remained for negotiating constructively with Solidarity seemed doubtful.

On January 16, 1989, however, the Plenum's second session came out squarely in favor of political and trade-union pluralism. This occurred only after heated debate and a divisive vote: 143 members supporting pluralism, 32 against, 14 abstaining. The feasibility of roundtable talks, in abeyance for four months, now became real. Conceding the need to legalize Solidarity, the party sought to steer the required changes. Rakowski made reference to a new, less dominant role for the party in society. His conception was intended to form part of the Tenth Plenum theses but, significantly, was defeated by diehard communist hard-liners. Still, he expressed confidence that as prime minister he had bailed the party out of a crisis: "When I was nominated to be prime minister and started with our early reform program, all the opinion polls predicted our victory" in free elections.[30]

The first of Jaruzelski's threats to resign his posts—as party leader, president of the Council of State, and commander in chief—forced the Plenum to give his leadership and its policy of dialogue a vote of confidence: It was endorsed unanimously, with four abstentions.[31] That Jaruzelski had persuaded his closest associates—Prime Minister Rakowski, Defense Minister Florian Siwicki, and Interior Minister Kiszczak—to threaten to resign, too, made his case unassailable. If, however, any one of these leaders had not gone along with Jaruzelski, had allied himself with the Central Committee conservatives, or had put himself forward as an alternative to Jaruzelski, the final vote at the Tenth Plenum in favor of dialogue might have been different. Although it is difficult to estimate what proportion of the party rank and file supported liberalization, one calculation is that 50–70 percent of party members backed Jaruzelski's initiative.[32]

Shortly thereafter, party notables gathered one final time before the roundtable talks to theorize about the future character of Polish socialism. The party's third national theoretical-ideological conference was held February 2–4 and, as in the case of the first two, provided no new ideological directions. Symbolically, this final confirmation of the PZPR's theoretical sterility was followed two days later, on February 6, by the beginning of the roundtable between the governing coalition and opposition forces. The talks ran till April 5, 1989, and for the first time since the late 1940s effectively displaced the Central Committee as the most important locus of political decision making.

On May 5, the broader party leadership reconstituted itself, this time as the Second National Conference of Delegates to the Tenth Congress.[33] The electoral platform that the party intended to use to contest the competitive elections the following month was the most notable product of this meeting. The party resolved to undertake a major overhaul of party statutes and suggestively noted that the PZPR could not continue as the party it had been since 1948.[34]

To summarize, a series of events seemingly engineered by party leaders seemed to spin out of control for them and affected their resource capabilities. Following the 1987 referendum verdict on economic reform, the Wałęsa-Miodowicz television debate that embarrassed the authorities, and the industrial strife of summer 1988, the Jaruzelski administration could continue to perceive the Solidarity movement as off balance, but it could have no doubt about the political consciousness of most of the key sectors of society—industrial workers and intellectuals—and their resolve to bring about change. By the time the Tenth Plenum opened in December 1988, the party was in disarray. A sizable minority of Central Committee members refused to acquiesce to any declaration espousing political and trade-union pluralism; for them even the relegalization of Solidarity was too bitter a pill to swallow. Others, the party paternalists, believed that the party would do itself credit by charting change and leading the country to democracy; Rakowski represented this viewpoint. Finally, the three generals, Jaruzelski, Kiszczak, and Siwicki, the best-informed and probably most alarmed about the state of Polish society, urged genuine compromise, which they treated as a goal in itself.

Party-Solidarity Interaction

The opposition's strategy preceding the roundtable talks was to stress its utility to the authorities in crisis management. It refrained from threatening to mobilize and organize popular upheaval—at least not immediately. The unproven electoral record of the opposition made reformist party leaders (though as "reformists" they had retained pivotal positions in the martial-law period) additionally tempted to secure Solidarity's co-responsibility at perceived low risk to the party. Survey data available to party leaders at the time suggested that the party could expect to gain no less than 25–30 percent of the vote and Solidarity 20 percent, with the remainder of the electorate uncommitted.[35]

Authorities and opposition shared certain fears: impending economic disaster accompanied by a return to the social anarchy of late 1981, when not even Wałęsa could rein in the wildcat strikes throughout the country. They also shared the same generalized vision with regard to getting out of this impasse: the urgency of profound structural economic change going beyond that attempted by the Messner government of the mid-1980s and the interconnectedness of economic and political reform. By 1988 Jaruzelski needed a partner more influential and dynamic than the embattled reformist wing of the party with which he collaborated had proven to be. The opposition, in turn, was ready to come in from the cold and obtain institutional guarantees and formal influence for itself. The extent to which compromise and a satisficing strategy characterized the opposition at this stage depended upon its perceptions of the authorities' resources. Although in objective terms these remained preponderant, many opposition activists sensed a loss of will and a crisis of confidence within the party leadership, evidenced in its concession to hold Poland's first referendum since 1946 in November 1987. In terms of substance, it was hard to object to the referendum, but because it was proposed by the communists Solidarity called for a boycott. It was the first public test of will between incumbent and opposition camps since martial law had put an end to political contestation. The turnout for the referendum was 67 percent—far from the 98 percent claimed by the communists in pre-1980 elections, about the same as in elections held in the 1980s, but far from the low level intended by the boycott call. About two-thirds of those who voted backed the reform package. Here, too, both government and opposition could claim victory. Although a substantial majority of the electorate turned out at the ballot box and voted for the government proposal, the proposal failed on the technicality that a simple majority of all those eligible to vote had not been obtained.

When the party leadership countenanced the televised Wałęsa-Miodowicz debate, it was regarded less as a sign of liberalization than as evidence of weakness. But the memory of martial law still haunted the dissidents, and they had learned from the mistake of overconfidence committed by Solidarity at that time. Further, the impressive resources they had marshaled by 1988, which could be lost as suddenly as in December 1981, inclined the opposition to dialogue.

In 1988, then, party reformists and the "constructive" opposition were drawn to each other and together could mobilize sufficient power to carry through an anti-monocratic breakthrough. Even though he did not conduct case-study analysis, this was the coalition that struck Adam Przeworski as being most viable. We recall that his four-actor typology includes hard-liners and reformers inside the authoritarian bloc and moderates and radicals in the opposition. If party reformers carry political weight independent of the hard-liners and can expect to receive some support under competitive conditions, Przeworski argues, they should prefer democracy with guarantees over other alternatives. Thus

> Extrication is possible if (1) an agreement can be reached between Reformers and Moderates to establish institutions under which the social forces they represent would have a significant political presence in the democratic system, (2) Reformers can deliver the consent of Hardliners or neutralize them, and (3) Moderates can control Radicals.[36]

Przeworski assigns values to each of the actors based on their pursuit of different alliance strategies that envisage different potential outcomes: (1) the survival of the authoritarian regime unchanged, (2) the survival of the regime with concessions, (3) democracy with no guarantees for the actors, and (4) democracy with guarantees. In the strategic situation existing in Poland in 1989, the latter outcome had the greatest payoff for party reformers and the second greatest pay-off (after democracy without guarantees) for opposition moderates. The alliance forged at the roundtable corresponded to Karl Deutsch's analysis of leadership as being a composite of the most inside of the outsiders and the most outside of the insiders.[37]

Both party reformers and opposition moderates increasingly defined their identity in terms of serving as the prime agents of change. The alternative of confrontation was unrealistic for both sides. Over fifteen years the authorities had done everything in their power, short of a return to the Stalinist police state, to eliminate the opposition; there was nothing left to be tried to reach that objective now. Solidarity had created an alternative society replete with underground "second-circulation" press, books, theater, and postage stamps. Its self-legitimation claims were persuasive, but it remained shut off from institutions of power.

In addition, the co-optation by one side of the other's prominent figures had produced a stalemate. The politics of confrontation pursued by either side could produce no outright winner. A form of national reconciliation, first discussed by Jaruzelski and Wałęsa in November 1981, once again became compelling. At that time two variants were considered: a tripartite agreement among party, church, and Solidarity and a more contrived coalition consisting of the three governing parties, communist and Solidarity trade unions, the church, and Catholic lay groups represented in the Sejm. The party opposed the first variant and Solidarity the second, and martial law quickly followed. By 1988 the authorities were more receptive to the first variant, so much had the balance of resources shifted in seven years. Paradoxically, it was the second variant, rejected in 1981 by Wałęsa, that actually ended communist rule in Poland. In August 1989 the parties traditionally allied with the communists, together with parliamentary Catholic groups, broke off talks with Kiszczak and decided instead to join the winning Solidarity coalition, thus propelling the Soviet bloc's first noncommunist premier, Tadeusz Mazowiecki, to power. Indeed, the Central Committee apparatus had increasing difficulty thereafter in imposing party discipline on its own increasingly autonomous parliamentary club.

In short, there was declining polarization on specific issues (around which roundtable working groups were set up) among eventual coalition partners. Furthermore, the salience of issues tended to converge for these actors (with the exception of party hard-liners, the OPZZ, and the KPN). Party liberals needed coalition partners and were willing to seek a negotiated settlement by reducing issue distance with Solidarity. The latter, in turn, attempted to make the move to democratic structures less threatening for incumbents.

The change in power ratings reflected in the crisis management stage was based on the successes and failures of each contender's negotiating strategy at the roundtable talks. By the resolution stage, the incumbents had lost most of their remaining resources with the elections and the establishment of Mazowiecki's government. Formally they still possessed coercive resources, but the improvised institution of the presidency (given to Jaruzelski) and official control of key ministries (defense and national security, left to two other party generals) were of limited utility to the shrinking party in a Solidarity-dominated coalition government. KOR advisers soon occupied center-right ground, and the church's postelection salience began to decline even as its power grew. An unplotted further stage following Mazowiecki's replacement by Jan Krzysztof Bielecki in 1990 was to see a shift of resources and of issue salience to right-of-center forces sandwiched between Solidarity and the KPN.

The Solidarity Opposition

How were the liberalization moves originally limited to party bodies and orchestrated by the Jaruzelski leadership perceived by the Solidarity leaders? To what extent were Solidarity leaders aware of the growing schisms within the PZPR that would help them calculate their own political strength when the course of political liberalization still seemed reversible? As Geremek summarized the political situation after the summer 1988 strikes, although the authorities discerned an unpredictable partner "the Party wanted legitimacy for its authority, which it could obtain only from a stronger partner that had general societal support."[38] The appointment of Rakowski as prime minister in mid-October was viewed as a bad sign; it seemed to put an end to hopes for the quick legalization of Solidarity, given Rakowski's role in breaking off talks with Wałęsa in August 1981 and his triumphalist speech justifying Solidarity's dissolution on his visit to the Lenin shipyards in 1982. Rakowski reasoned that, because of his close personal contacts with a number of Western European leaders, he could obtain economic assistance to see Poland through its economic crisis while having to accept only limited political liberalization that would keep Solidarity out of the political process. In addition, Miodowicz's uncompromising position on union pluralism caused the first round of "talks about talks" to founder. The Czyrek-Stelmachowski and Kiszczak-Wałęsa meetings in August and September 1988, where the roundtable idea was first put forward, were in danger of going nowhere.

According to Geremek, Rakowski's unsuccessful trip to Austria and West Germany, together with "the dramatic debates and simulated games regarding economic perspectives that were held in the Central Committee, from which a frightening picture emerged," produced PZPR self-doubt. Party authorities began to think in new terms: "Let us do things as we did in 1945; let us return to the situation before mistakes began to be made. Poland is again in ruins. Let us create an opposition party on the PSL [Mikołajczyk] model. This time let that party not make the mistake of turning its back on us, and we won't repeat the mistake of destroying the opposition."[39] The implied sense of magnanimity on the part of the party seemed out of keeping with its imminent irrelevance.

The roundtable talks were, at the time, justifiably viewed by the opposition as a potential trap. Rakowski had submitted to the Central Committee a declaration of the "Rakowski doctrine": bring the opposition into the orbit of the authorities where it could be kept from accumulating political capital, corrupt it, divide it, and compromise its leading figures. Moreover, as we have noted, the party remained divided about talks with the opposition, and only the threat of resignation of the three generals of the former martial-law team forced it to accept the idea. Rakowski may also have threatened to resign.[40] Party hard-liners such as Miodowicz and Warsaw Party Secretary Janusz Kubasiewicz were kept off balance by the political maneuvering of the ruling elite. At the same time, because of their own intransigence toward the opposition they would not be invited to participate in meetings such as the one at Magdalenka, where historic decisions were about to be made.

Roundtable Procedures

Without Jaruzelski's approval there would have been no roundtable talks in spring 1989. How, then, did he see his role in the overture to the political opposition? Geremek cites a remark made by the general: "'Please remember that only General de Gaulle was capable of getting France out of Algeria.'" Geremek drew the obvious conclusion: "This was a portentous statement, because it meant that only General Jaruzelski could get the PZPR out of Poland."[41] Although Jaruzelski was pivotal in the democratic transition, a number of other communist leaders—day-to-day participants of the roundtable talks—seem to have been committed to the success of the negotiations. Among these were, in Solidarity's perception, Kiszczak and Stanisław Ciosek. Other liberals included Politburo members Kazimierz Barcikowski, possibly Czyrek, and Reykowski.[42]

Geremek expanded on the distinctive role at the roundtable played by Kiszczak:

> I believe he was the engine of this whole great political operation which, in the authorities' conviction, was to be the roundtable process. The security apparatus that he headed knew the country's real situation much better than any other apparatus of power. Apart from Jaruzelski, Kiszczak perhaps best recognized what was happening in Poland and because of that best recognized the necessity for reforms. He also had a sense of his own strength that the party apparatus lacked after its painful experience of total uselessness under martial law. Kiszczak believed that he could risk the reforms he considered necessary. When he opened the roundtable talks with an introductory speech in which he said, "We are beginning a Polish experiment," he understood that the experiment was a risk that he could afford. That is why I believe that he had instructions and full power from General Jaruzelski.[43]

Indeed, it was Kiszczak who presided over the opening ceremony of the roundtable on February 6 in the Palace of the Council of Ministers in Warsaw. There was nothing in the constitution that anticipated a forum that, in effect, proved to be an unelected constituent assembly. Then again, the communist party had ruled the country for thirty years before it was thought expedient to enshrine the PZPR's leading role in the constitution. The constitutionality of the martial-law decree and the military council that ruled Poland for the next year were also debatable. Regime transitions such as France's change from the Fourth to the Fifth Republic are grounded more in the constitutional deficiencies of the previous regime than in existing constitutional provisions.

The roundtable had two sides and three major subtables. Representatives of the communist leadership, described as the "coalition-government" side, included the satellite parties (the ZSL and the SD) and the proregime Catholic bloc (Pax). Miodowicz's OPZZ was officially on the coalition side but throughout the talks carved out a position independent of the party leadership. The assertiveness of the OPZZ highlighted the increasing improbability of a conservative-liberal reconciliation within the party and the end of hopes for a patched-up one-party ruling coalition. In turn, the cavalier treatment accorded to representatives of the ZSL and the SD during the roundtable talks by communist party leaders was to boomerang only months later when the issue of forming a new coalition government arose.

The "opposition-Solidarity" side was represented by a delegation from the ad hoc Citizens' Committee of the Chairman of Solidarity. The Catholic episcopate was not officially a side and declared its neutrality. It sent representatives to mediate and facilitate discussions; for example, a bishop and two priests were delegated by the secretariat of the episcopate to the Magdalenka sessions. But participants in the talks concurred that church representatives invariably backed the positions advocated by Solidarity.[44] Party trust in the nonpolitical nature of the church proved overoptimistic both during the negotiations and in the electoral campaign that followed.

The subtables of the talks included one on socioeconomic policy, another on trade-union pluralism, and a third on political reform. These subtables in turn often created working groups to consider specific topics such as wage indexation, workers' self-management, and local government reform. Over six hundred participants had provided input into the roundtable negotiations by the time the talks adjourned two months later. Clearly, the actors and issues involved in the political-reform subtable were most important in determining the transition and the new rules of the game. Narrowing the crux of the negotiation process further, the private talks between top party and Solidarity leaders at a villa in Magdalenka (the site of Wałęsa's earlier meetings with Kiszczak in 1988) were of the utmost importance in arriving at a negotiated transition. Although tentative agreements reached in private had to be approved at the official political-reform subtable, the result of the test of wills between the high-powered delegations attending Magdalenka invariably stood. Wałęsa, for example, participated only in the negotiations conducted with the authorities in Magdalenka (as well as the ceremonial opening and closing sessions of the roundtable). Jaruzelski did not directly participate in talks but was provided with a running account by Kiszczak by telephone during breaks. In addition, he had his own special staff to address roundtable issues, separate from the staffs assembled by government negotiators Kiszczak, Czyrek, and Ireneusz Sekuła (a deputy premier and labor minister who went on to become one of the most prosperous excommunist entrepreneurs). This led at times to serious problems in coordinating the authorities' policy positions.

The secretive nature of the discussions at Magdalenka caused some observers to think that a tacit deal was being worked out between two elite groups. For example, it was regularly alleged over the next few years that in exchange for extricating itself from politics the ruling communist class was to have free rein in appropriating for itself the economic assets previously owned by the state. This idea became known as *uwłaszczenie*, "appropriation." But for the most belligerent anticommunist forces it was the political ties between communists and Solidarity that aroused most suspicion. Even on the fifth anniversary of the roundtable conclusion in 1994, anticommunists charged that the agreement had changed very little in Poland. Suspicions about it were captured by the definition of Magdalenka as "a place where during roundtable talks open communists (Kiszczak, Jaruzelski, Ciosek) reached an understanding with their own agents (see exposure of agents) and crypto-communists (Michnik, Kuroń, Geremek) in order to hold onto power, rob Poland, and cheat true Poles and patriots (Morawiecki, Jurczyk, Gwiazda)."[45]

Roundtable Bargaining

Readiness to fulfill commitments affects the making of commitments, and this was clearly in evidence at the roundtable. The general character of the roundtable discussions was pragmatic, which surprised both sides given their perceptions of each other up to that time. As Geremek recalls them,

> In none of the negotiations did General Kiszczak ever invoke ideological arguments. He never referred to the ideology of the communist movement. They all used pragmatic arguments almost exclusively. The first was the question of power.... The second essential argument was Poland's place in the communist system. This concerned both relations within the bloc of real socialism and dependence on the Soviet Union—our place in the Soviet empire.[46]

Geremek noted how Solidarity negotiators exploited this weakness: "We contended that the Polish leadership was not keeping up with Gorbachev and his reforms."[47] Nevertheless, the party's trump card was its mythical monopoly on good relations with the Soviets.

Expectations about the final outcome differed dramatically from what actually came to pass by summer's end 1989. Both party and Solidarity leaders assumed that they would remain government and opposition for some time to come. There might be limited power sharing, negotiators speculated, but no full power transfer. The diffidence of Solidarity was evidenced in the fact that its negotiating team brought up defense policy only once throughout the bargaining, proposing a 20 percent cut in military and security apparatus budgets. It was enough for the authorities to point to data showing recent decreases in funding for these two institutions for Solidarity to drop the subject.

Early in the talks, party representatives persisted in asking the opposition, "Do you really want socialism, or do you want to overthrow it?" This negotiating tactic was designed to persuade Solidarity representatives that only by agreeing to be co-opted and serve in a communist-majority government could the charge of seeking to overthrow the regime be deflected. Co-optation would, of course, have done little to change the underlying principles of the system, because political competition would have been put aside. In addressing whether Solidarity supported or opposed socialism, Mazowiecki responded, "You talk about socialism, but tell us exactly what socialism you're referring to—Swedish socialism or Pol Pot's socialism?"[48] One Solidarity answer was "Let's say that we are for socialism; later we'll decide what it means."[49] Geremek saw the issue not in terms of what type of socialism was preferable but in terms of "the need to disarm the party." He added, "Instead of legitimating the system we wanted to jump-start the process of democratization." The essential difference for Geremek was between liberalization as proposed by Rakowski and democratization—similar to the distinction between inclusiveness and competition discussed in the introduction. "Liberalization has been tried many times and leads nowhere. Its essence is to restore homeostasis to the system."[50]

Generally, the party leadership was more divided than its piously expressed commitment to succeed at roundtable talks suggested. According to Geremek, "The lack of a clear political identity of the reformist group dominant in the PZPR power structure made its consolidation more difficult and weakened its chances in conflicts with conservative elements."[51]

At a meeting of the heads of the working groups for the round-table on March 17, 1989, Ciosek provided the most alarming assessment of the threat posed by party hard-liners to a successful agreement to the talks. It came in the form of a reply to Michnik's expressed concern about the "rush that the government side is imposing" on the talks and his suggestion that "waiting might be better than a false start." Ciosek's view was that "the machine has been started, and halting it would be a great problem." Furthermore, the quick tempo was necessitated by fear that Politburo members opposed to the contract would gain the upper hand if agreement was not reached soon: "Our will is weakening, I say this openly. It is not that we are opposed to an agreement but that over time we are becoming ever weaker," Ciosek reported. "After a twelve-hour, very difficult discussion, the Politburo agreed that, yes, we are entering into this contract." But referring to "aggressive" comments made by Urban, the government's spokesman, and a hard-line article published in *Trybuna Ludu* by the veteran party journalist Jerzy Majka, Ciosek admitted that "what characterizes our [the government coalition's] dialogue is not chaos but political struggle. This struggle is taking place within the governing party." As a result, Ciosek asserted, "I've been telling you that there isn't just one 'red spider.' There is a plurality of 'red spiders.'"[52]

Invoking the potential militancy of party conservatives as a reason for speeding the talks along was sound bargaining strategy for Ciosek and the authorities. But it had a disadvantage as well, for it became clear to Solidarity delegates at the roundtable that the PZPR was to some degree split and therefore vulnerable. At the same time, in pressing its advantage Solidarity also had to know when to stop, for it never assumed that party disunity would necessarily lead to the crumbling of the entire communist regime. The more cautious and moderate Solidarity leaders, such as Geremek and Mazowiecki, were taken by surprise, then, at the speed of the party's demise in the second half of 1989. They were subsequently criticized for not having been more uncompromising at the roundtable.

At the center of negotiations was, obviously, the issue of how Solidarity was to be represented in politics. Having failed to co-opt it into the government, the party proposed successive formulae to get it into the legislature. Even before the formal roundtable began, it seemed likely that the authorities would be willing to offer Solidarity 30–40 percent of the seats in the Sejm. But this bloc was to be *allocated* to Solidarity, and no direct contests between the party and the opposition were foreseen. Further, both regime and opposition would support a common platform that of necessity consisted of generalities and platitudes.

For Solidarity's leaders, such an arrangement would turn the organization into a satellite party resembling the ZSL or the SD. It also resonated of a private extraconstitutional agreement rather than a formal, legal provision. Consequently, they quickly rejected this proposal. As Lech Kaczyński put it to regime negotiators, "Keep your controlling packet and give the rest not to us but to society."[53] Better that 30 percent of the seats be freely contested, Solidarity reasoned, than that 40 percent be allocated to it without a political fight. Coupled with this requirement was Solidarity's insistence that such a "contract Sejm" be a one-off venture—that future elections be fully democratic. When regime negotiators were reminded that public opinion overwhelmingly favored free elections, the "allocated, uncontested seats" proposal was dropped.[54]

These negotiators held out for the idea of "nonconfrontational" elections, however, and to this end proposed a joint national list of candidates from both sides that would reflect the proportion of seats allotted to each side in the single-member constituencies. The idea of a joint ticket that would blur political differences between government and opposition was, again, rejected by Solidarity. It recommended instead that the national list consist exclusively of candidates nominated by the party, in this way allowing it to secure for itself the legislative majority that both sides agreed was nonnegotiable.

In some respects, the national-list proposal represented a pillar of the future regime envisaged by the communist reformers. Staniszkis describes the logic that persuaded them of the desirability of a transition based on the national-list concept:

> The reformers in the communist party undertook political reforms not with the intention of giving up power, but in order to create a more effective stabilizing mechanism

in conditions of a severe crisis. It was expected that the "national list" would be elected and would still constitute the center of power (and one endowed with a new legitimacy), while the institutions to which the opposition would be admitted would be more or less phony (like the previous ones).[55]

Solidarity's bargaining strategy was, then, to accept the political reality of continued communist rule—locked in through the national list—while maximally exposing the charade of such rule. Many observers believe that, more than the Solidarity sweep of seats in contested Sejm elections in June 1989, it was the unexpected (even for Solidarity) defeat of most candidates on the party's unopposed national list that thwarted the communists' plans for remaining in power. The debacle of the communists on the list had international implications as well: It presaged the defeat of older-generation communists throughout much of the Soviet bloc in 1989.

In addition to efforts to incorporate Solidarity into a party-dominated coalition through a contract Sejm, regime negotiators proposed the restoration of the institution of the presidency that had been abolished in 1952. The assumption was that the president could serve as a stabilizing force and as a symbol of continuity in the transition period. The party's obvious candidate was Jaruzelski, and even much of Solidarity recognized the advantages of having the long-serving Polish leader preside over a protracted transition. Even after the June electoral defeat of the communists, Michnik acknowledged this political desideratum in the formula he proposed on July 4: "your president, our prime minister." Just as at the roundtable, so too with regard to this formula, charges were made of collaboration between two powerful elites. Staniszkis reports that one Senate deputy "charged Michnik and his supporters of 'being tempted with playing the role of an avant-garde' (though the expression Leninism was not spoken, the context of the statement suggested its possibility)."[56]

Notwithstanding such open efforts to share spoils and thereby to stabilize the transition, disagreement between the two sides arose over the regime's idea that the president should be elected by the Sejm, in which the party would continue to hold a majority, and that the term of office should be a lengthy seven years. More contentious than who would occupy the presidency (Jaruzelski was the obvious choice) were the powers to be conferred upon it. The ruling coalition proposed extensive powers that would have created a presidential system. Presidentialism was to compensate for whatever influence communists lost in a multiparty, partially freely elected Sejm.

The opposition accepted the principle that a communist president—even if it were the individual who had imposed martial law in 1981—could provide the regime with the safeguards it needed in a period of transition. In particular, the opposition acknowledged that the presidency should be given responsibility for defense and foreign policy. But it could not accept the full package of a powerful president (which Wałęsa must have rued having opposed once he took office), a Sejm elected noncompetitively, and a joint national list.

Seeking resolution of the political standoff over the regime package, Kiszczak threw in another new idea based on a former institution—the reestablishment of the second chamber, the Senate, that had been abolished after the spurious results of a referendum held in 1948. Kiszczak expected that senators would be appointed by the president rather than elected, though the president would first consult with all parties represented in the Sejm.[57] The initial proposal for a return to an upper house provided Solidarity with no new or added incentive to accept the enlarged package. After deadlock on the issue, the party negotiator Alexander Kwaśniewski, apparently spontaneously, suggested that the senate might be transformed into a freely elected body.[58] The idea of such a senate, in which Solidarity could flex its political muscle, laid the basis for compromise. No better evidence that roundtable negotiations were taking on a momentum of their own and leading in unanticipated directions is available than Kwaśniewski's perhaps inadvertent suggestion. Several days later, after Jaruzelski had considered the implications of this twist in the regime's negotiating position, the proposal was formally put to Solidarity.

Since it was not envisaged that this upper chamber would have much power (even though it would elect the president in joint session with the 460-seat Sejm) and since the original formula of electing two senators from each of forty-nine provinces (later amended to include three each from Warsaw and Katowice provinces, for a total of 100 seats) overrepresented rural Poland, where the party seemed stronger than Solidarity, the risks for the regime seemed worth taking. For Solidarity, completely free elections even to a less important chamber symbolized a dramatic break with the practices of the communist regime. It was desperately anxious to challenge the party in such a head-to-head contest. When Solidarity was able to extract from the regime a general commitment to make the next elections fully democratic—the final roundtable resolution pledged that "the sides will do everything to ensure that the composition of the next parliament will be determined completely by the will of the voters"[59]—the basis for the roundtable agreement had been secured.

Difficult negotiating lay ahead as the party, for a moment, seemed to back away from Senate elections and then suggested a national list for the Senate and sought to expand the president's decree powers. These eleventh-hour revisions were beaten back but other technicalities remained to be worked out. One was an eventual agreement to hold a second, runoff round for Sejm and Senate elections whenever the leading candidate failed to obtain 50 percent of the vote in the first round. As Solidarity had hoped, only the party would present a national list of candidates. No provisions were made for a second round here, because even Solidarity anticipated that since the party candidates were running unopposed they would secure the necessary 50 percent of votes cast. This proved shortsighted when the national-list candidates went down to defeat.

Another outstanding issue was how the Sejm could override a veto cast by the president or the Senate. A compromise was worked out whereby either a presidential or a Senate veto of Sejm legislation could be overturned by a two-thirds majority of the Sejm. This meant that if the party and Solidarity were to sweep all the representation set aside for them, the party bloc of 65 percent of the Sejm would be insufficient to overturn a Solidarity-dominated Senate veto. Conversely, a communist president could veto a bill and find it improbable that it would be overturned by the minority Solidarity group in the Sejm.

One issue that was left unresolved by the roundtable was the independence of the judiciary. The communist delegation, led by Procurator General Łucjan Czubiński, refused to give up party control over the appointment of judges. In turn, Solidarity insisted that judges belong to no political party. While the communist negotiators held out for a procuracy subordinate to no other body, the opposition demanded the subordination of this often abusive body to the Ministry of Justice. In the end, the protocol of the roundtable agreement simply reported the positions of the two sides rather than recommending a solution to the deadlock.[60]

In sum, the key elements of the negotiated transition were, therefore, a contract Sejm with a built-in 65 percent party-controlled majority, a national list of unopposed party candidates that was to make up part of this majority, a hundred-member Senate elected freely, and a president elected jointly by the National Assembly—Sejm and Senate in joint session. After all the careful calculations, expectations, and perceptions of the adversary on both sides, it seemed unlikely that such a checks-and-balances pact could produce a lopsided victory for either side. The meticulously crafted pact was intended to ensure that the transition proceeded at a pace that posed no risks to either the old or the new elite. Shortly after it was signed on April 5, a national survey suggested a different reading of the agreement by the public. Fifty-nine percent of respondents believed that the opposition had gained support through the roundtable process, only 3 percent said the party was the beneficiary, and a surprisingly small 18 percent thought that both sides had increased their support.[61] These first impressions were a foretaste of the election results to come.

The June 1989 Elections

The semifree elections agreed upon at the roundtable left the two principal protagonists with little time to prepare full-fledged electoral campaigns. The communist party had never participated in competitive elections, and the Solidarity opposition was neither legal nor even a political party as late as April 1989. Indeed, in the elections themselves, Solidarity candidates were listed as belonging to Citizens' Committees (KO) rather than to a formal party. Even after the elections, Solidarity deputies were organized into a Citizens' Parliamentary Club rather than a formal party. To support the electoral campaign of this semiorganized political group, Adam Michnik assembled a staff of journalists who had worked for *Tygodnik Mazowsze* ("The Mazowsze Weekly"), Solidarity's Warsaw newspaper, and began publishing a daily, *Gazeta Wyborcza* ("The Electoral Gazette") in May. Introducing KO candidates and their platforms was the initial raison d'être for what was soon to become one of Poland's most widely read dailies.

The uncharted waters affected opinion pollsters as well. According to a Public Opinion Survey Center director, "There were no typical pre-election polls in Poland in 1989. CBOS and OBOP [the two major polling organizations] made an attempt to find out about the pre-election mood of the people, but the final surveys were conducted three weeks prior to the election."[62] Still, these polls did test regional variations, voter interest, and knowledge about individual candidates in some detail.[63] What became clear from the survey results was that the communist party was facing defeat. Although these results were not published at the time and therefore could not have influenced voters, they all pointed to at least a two-to-one ratio of support for Solidarity compared with the communist coalition (Table 4.1).

As we have seen, at the time of the roundtable negotiations some advisers to the communist leadership calculated that the party might obtain at least a quarter of votes cast. It might even win a majority of the openly contested seats to the Senate, since, as we have seen, Senate constituencies overrepresented rural areas and Solidarity's strength lay primarily in the cities. But the results of an opinion poll carried out in mid-May for a French polling organization already indicated that only in about ten provinces was the party in a position to win even one of the two senatorial seats, which meant at best a total of just ten seats in the upper chamber. These provinces were largely agrarian, located in central (Wielkopolska) and north-central Poland.[64]

TABLE 4.1   Voting Intentions of the Electorate, April-May 1989 (percentages)

Poll & Date	Government Coalition	Solidarity Opposition	Undecided
CBOS			
April 10	15	38	47[a]
May 17	14	34	52[b]
OBOP			
May 2	25	45	30
May 16	23	57	20
May 23	24	55	21

[a] The political attitudes of the "undecided" included 8 percent who supported the party, 27 percent Solidarity, and 13 percent neither.
[b] The political attitudes of the "undecided" included 11 percent who supported the party, 28 percent Solidarity, and 13 percent neither.

Source: Piotr Kwiatkowski, "Opinion Research and the Fall of Communism: Poland 1981–1990," *International Journal of Public Opinion Research,* 4, no. 4 (Winter 1992), p. 370.

The final results produced, as expected, a Solidarity sweep of the 35 percent of contested Sejm seats. But even for the 65 percent of the seats set aside for the government coalition, the majority of party-backed candidates failed to receive the 50 percent of votes required to avoid a second round. In terms of the popular vote distribution, earlier party forecasts proved accurate. The government coalition obtained just over a quarter of all valid votes cast (26.8 percent) and Solidarity 69.9 percent (the remainder going to independents).

Turnout for the first round was 62.7 percent of eligible voters—less than anticipated given the historic nature of these elections, and the one important setback Solidarity suffered. A number of reasons can be advanced for the sizable number of nonvoters. One was that the assumption that if elections were democratic the reasons for not voting in the past (boycott, the perceived irrelevance of the ritual, a sense of voter inefficacy, a general lack of interest in politics) would disappear proved unfounded.[65] Another possible reason was that these elections had been worked out by the two establishment parties—the communists and Solidarity—and therefore lacked authenticity. The same suspicions aroused by the talks in Magdalenka—"elites talking to elites," in Staniszkis's encapsulation of the attitude of the populist faction in Solidarity[66]—were now spreading as Poles contemplated whether voting had in fact become meaningful. In addition, registered voters had no way of knowing how "historic" this election was to be. That the party would still control 65 percent of Sejm seats no matter what happened at the polls was a deterrent to voting.

In more closely examining the "two establishments" perception as a possible cause of abstention, Jasiewicz disaggregates nonvoters into three categories: the 23 percent who did not see the importance of politics to their own personal situation, the 10 percent who were unable to get to their polling places even though they wanted to, and the 5 percent who staged a politically motivated boycott.[67] Whatever the exact causes, the relatively low turnout was one of the few results of the elections that heartened the ruling communists. They could continue to question whether Solidarity had really been given a popular mandate to govern.

One particular surprise was Solidarity's capture of all but one of the Senate seats. The one government-coalition winner was an atypical communist candidate—a millionaire who had financed an expensive electoral campaign. The breakdown of the popular vote for the Senate was 20.4 percent for the government and 65.0 percent for Solidarity (again, the remainder going to independents).[68] Significantly, Solidarity had sufficient support even in the most rural Polish provinces to elect its slate, defying the party's calculations.

Solidarity's stubborn refusal to provide candidates for a national list proved to have been a stroke of genius. About 35 percent of voters crossed out the names of *all* the candidates on the uncontested national list. Only two party-backed candidates won the necessary 50 percent majority to avoid participating in a second round. Virtually the entire top party leadership, then, was humiliated by this result (as a presidential aspirant, Jaruzelski did not run for parliament), and not even

Solidarity had anticipated that a second round would be needed. As it happened, a legal invention was required whereby in place of another national list, new seats were created for communists out of existing constituencies. In the interests of political stability, the Catholic Church had to urge voter support for the party list when elections for the new seats were hastily arranged.

The role of the church in the elections was not regarded as benign by the ruling communist coalition. Although the church appealed for national accord and purportedly served as impartial mediator during the electoral campaign, its support at the grassroots level was crucial to Solidarity's success. Thus, once established, the vast majority of Citizens' Committees began their operations in parish halls, and some never left them until after the election. Except for the nationally produced Solidarity campaign materials, many of the flyers and leaflets for local candidates were printed using church-owned presses. Most important, priests were active in many different ways in support of KO candidates. One writer identified thirteen methods employed by the clergy in localities to ensure Solidarity victories, from organizing candidate meetings with voters, protecting Solidarity posters from defacement or removal, and warning KOs of unfavorable publicity to using religious occasions (Mass, Corpus Christi processions) to urge voter support. It was not uncommon for priests to lead prayers for a Solidarity victory.[69] The roundtable agreement foreseeing a nonpartisan role for the church in the elections was clearly not respected. That the communist party, which had reneged on promises for democracy throughout Poland's postwar history, should have been surprised by the partisan activism of the church in the 1989 elections is not without irony.

The election results had a domino effect on other provisions of the roundtable agreement. Recognizing public anger at his imposition of martial law in 1981, Jaruzelski announced that he would not be a candidate for the revamped presidency. He entertained little doubt that Solidarity's 99 Senators and 161 Sejm deputies would vote against him and rob his election to that post of legitimacy. But in July Solidarity leaders still planned to bide their time and remain in the ranks of the opposition. When Wałęsa made clear that he did not intend to stand for the presidency, Jaruzelski reversed his earlier decision and, on July 19, was elected by a bare majority in the two houses—270 to 233, with 34 abstentions. Strategic voting by the KO parliamentary bloc allowed him to take the office but only at the pleasure of Solidarity.

The last issue to be resolved in summer 1989 was the formation of a government. Since the communist bloc held a working majority in the contract Sejm, it had been assumed by both sides all along that it would name a prime minister to form a cabinet. On August 2, Jaruzelski nominated Kiszczak, the congenial head of the party's roundtable negotiating team, to the post. But this would have left both major offices in the hands of leaders of the communist party and, what is more, the chief architects of martial law. Solidarity opposed Kiszczak's nomination. With the surprise defection of the two satellite parties (the ZSL and the SD) from the government camp, Wałęsa announced on August 17 that the Citizens' Parliamentary Club was prepared to form a coalition government with these two small parties. That same day, Acting Prime Minister Kiszczak gave up trying to form a communist government. The next day Wałęsa and the leaders of the ZSL and the SD, Roman Malinowski and Jerzy Jóźwiak, went to the Belvedere Palace, the residence of the president, formally to present him with the coalition-government proposal.

In line with Michnik's July 4 proposal "your president, our prime minister," on August 24 Tadeusz Mazowiecki—Catholic intellectual, editor of the earlier opposition newspaper *Tygodnik Solidarność* ("Solidarity Weekly"), and longtime Wałęsa adviser—was appointed prime minister. With all but the hard-line communists accepting the new political reality, Mazowiecki was given a vote of confidence by the Sejm (378 to 4, with 41 abstentions). On September 12 he submitted his cabinet nominees to the Sejm for approval. Eleven of the twenty-three ministerial posts were taken by Solidarity, only four were given to the PZPR, and the rest went to the ZSL, the SD, and an independent. Although communist ministers were to hold onto the pivotal defense and security portfolios, Mazowiecki's cabinet represented the first noncommunist government in Eastern Europe since the Stalin era. The Sejm vote approving his cabinet now had no opposition: 420 to 0, with 13 abstentions. Few participants at the roundtable talks of a few months earlier could have foreseen this course of events or this outcome.

After the June Elections:
The Party Drops Out as
Political Contender

Even with electoral defeat, party notables felt that the negotiated transition provided the political safeguards that would allow a communist-based government to continue to rule. Prime Minister Rakowski's speech in the Sejm to the parliamentary clubs of the PZPR's satellite parties, the SD and the ZSL, the night after the June election was intended to scare the coalition partners into voting for Kiszczak as prime minister. Geremek described the intent of the speech: "Rakowski equated the departure of the small clubs from the PZPR-led coalition with the outbreak of civil war. Reject Kiszczak tomorrow and the day after tomorrow there will be martial law."[70] By August 14, however, Kiszczak had not been able to form a government but no civil war appeared imminent.

Following the electoral cataclysm of the PZPR, the Thirteenth Plenum was summoned on June 30 and then adjourned to July 28–29. Since Jaruzelski had accepted the office of president, Rakowski was appointed party leader. The Central Committee called for a party congress to decide the future of the PZPR. The Fourteenth Plenum convened on August 19 and was confronted with the defection of the two satellite parties to the Solidarity coalition. Predictably, it condemned the ingratitude these parties were showing the PZPR for it securing them parliamentary seats at all.[71] As Mazowiecki was officially being designated prime minister on that day, the Plenum could not come to terms with the SD's and the ZSL's defection and ominously declared that history would hold them responsible for the dismemberment of the social coalition. Seemingly dismissing the electoral verdict passed on it, the Plenum insisted that the party should be represented in the new government in terms of its "political and state potential."[72] In Skierniewice the next day, Party Secretary Leszek Miller launched the slogan "your government, our program." On October 10 Rakowski, with Warsaw chief Kubasiewicz, flew to Moscow to present their assessments of the political situation to Kremlin leaders. All of these efforts were designed to prevent the disappearance of the PZPR from the Polish political landscape.

At the Central Committee's Fifteenth Plenum on September 18, it was reported that 72 percent of party respondents favored radical change in the party. Two weeks later, on October 3, the second session of the plenum committed the PZPR to holding the Eleventh Congress in January, democratizing its methods of selecting delegates and electing leadership, and changing the party's name, program, and structures.[73] The Politburo report to the Central Committee still cautioned, in characteristically ambiguous and pompous terms, that "the road to such a [transformed] party cannot be just a linear continuation, but neither should it produce self-destruction of the party—building a new one on the ruins of the old."[74]

Ideological Currents in the Party

One significant group within the PZPR in its last year of existence called precisely for building on the ruins. The Eighth of July Initiative (or movement), led by party activists at the University of Warsaw, advocated parliamentary democracy, a free market that would link efficiency with social responsibility (if that was not a contradiction in terms), intraparty democracy in place of democratic centralism, and the rejection of Leninism. A party with such a program would represent democratic socialism, and before the Eleventh Congress the movement formed the Social Democratic Bloc.[75] Its most prominent leaders included Marian Orzechowski and Tadeusz Fiszbach.

According to the political scientist Karol Janowski, there were some two hundred different political programs and platforms in existence in Poland by the end of October 1989. Other than the Eighth of July Initiative, which was committed to "social democratic fundamentalism," Janowski identified another major ideological program filling the PZPR vacuum, "postcommunist doctrinal-leftist fundamentalism."[76] It opposed the return of capitalism to Poland and the selloff of its national resources to private interests while supporting the special status of the working class and the offical trade unions and the general value system of the PZPR. The Socialist Bloc, as it called itself, maintained that the achievements of

Polish socialism should be protected.[77] Rakowski was identified with this ideological current.

Although a third group, the Movement of Working People, associated with Adam Schaff, sought to bridge the gap between the two "fundamentalisms," it was the Social Democratic Bloc whose influence was most apparent in the resolutions passed at the PZPR's Sixteenth Plenum on November 6.[78] In any case, on December 31, 1989, the Sejm changed the country's name and removed the language in the constitution referring to a socialist state, the working masses, and the PZPR's leading role. Political differences within the disintegrating PZPR would, from then on, have no bearing on matters of state.

But political differences continued to plague the Jaruzelski leadership. When an opportunity presented itself to curry favor with the public, it often seemed unable to do so—perhaps a reflex from decades of ignoring popular sentiment, perhaps a sign of hard-line retrenchment within the party. One major opportunity to elicit popularity came well after the June elections, on the day Mazowiecki was named to form a noncommunist government. PZPR leaders received a letter from the Romanian communist party that condemned the Polish party's tolerance and referred obliquely to previous Soviet invasions of Warsaw Pact countries (in 1956 and 1968). But the PZPR leadership (including Rakowski) failed publicly to rebuff the critique. One explanation of this failure may have been effective rearguard action by hard-liners. Further, the Chinese communist party's crackdown on democracy supporters in Tiananmen Square had occurred only months before, and the recourse to force by disaffected elements in the security apparatus (that is, an early Polish version of the August 1991 putsch in the USSR) could not totally be excluded.

At the same time, Gorbachev had refused even to meet with the Romanian emissary carrying the letter of complaint about the Polish communist betrayal—a fact quickly known in Warsaw.[79] Further, another hard-liner, Politburo member Kazimierz Cypryniak, described how Soviet support for the use of force as a conflict-resolution method had disappeared. In his memoirs Geremek recounted Cypryniak's comments: "'All our contacts to date have been severed. There are new people there [in Moscow] now who do not understand our arguments. Up to now we have been talking with a group of people we have known for years. They understood our interests, we understood theirs. Now the situation has changed. They are pragmatists, and we have no access to them.'" Geremek concluded from this that "by 1989 each group within the power structure could articulate its views, and there was no longer an arbiter who could say which position was correct. Until then it was Moscow that had been saying this."[80]

By December 1989 circumstances had changed so drastically that candidates for the leadership of the communist successor party were lining up to meet with Wałęsa so as to broaden their popular support. These included not only his preferred candidate, Fiszbach, but also Rakowski and Miller. The last Central Committee Plenum of the PZPR was the Seventeenth, held January 6, 1990. Ostensibly ratifying documents to be considered by the congress and carrying out a survey for a proposed new name for the party, Barcikowski recalled that this session was "very dramatic" and engaged in a "very probing discussion." The onetime Politburo member added that, "fortunately, the dominant view was that Polish matters were matters for Poland and it was necessary to continue on the road of reform."[81]

The PZPR's last congress began on January 27, 1990, and quickly finished the business of dissolving the party. Over the next three days a new party—Social Democracy of the Polish Republic (Socjaldemokracja Rzeczypospolitej Polskiej—SdRP)—was established that inherited the PZPR's real estate and financial assets. Rakowski nominated Kwaśniewski as head of the SdRP's executive council, and Miller was elected general secretary.[82] Eighty-nine delegates, including twenty-five Sejm deputies, decided to establish a separate party—the Polish Social Democratic Union (originally, Union of Social Democracy)—with Fiszbach as leader. Although both parties expressed a commitment to freedom, equality, social justice, parliamentary democracy, and serving Poland's national interests, the SdRP was more pragmatic and the Union more idealistic in its commitment to the socialist project. Coming full circle, in March 1990 an additional leftist party was formed that designated itself the Union of Communists of the Polish Republic "Proletariat." Polish communism seemed to return to where it had been a century earlier—a marginalized and schismatic ideological current.

Jaruzelski and Change in the Power Structure

Ideological conflict within the PZPR was not the sole axis along which the party disintegrated. A revealing case of institutional confrontation between the traditional party power base, the Central Committee, and an emerging one within the new parliamentary system, the PZPR Parliamentary Club (or Caucus), can be discerned in the last six months of the party's existence. Jaruzelski's part in favoring the parliamentary group was crucial in the demise of the Central Committee and with it, effectively, of the Leninist party.

The "party-savers" who had been so noisy at the August Fourteenth Plenum were suffering from a major disadvantage: Jaruzelski was no longer with them organizationally, and probably not ideologically either. His distancing himself from the PZPR affected the composition of the Mazowiecki government. Initially the party wanted to obtain the posts of deputy premier, television committee head, six ministerial portfolios (finance, communications, transport, foreign affairs, defense, and internal affairs), and the secretaries and undersecretaries of state in all ministries. But Jaruzelski's acceptance of a new coalition government and his own institutional power base as president rather than party leader made him less dependent on the party's goodwill. Moreover, the PZPR Parliamentary Club consisted primarily of managers and party bureaucrats, not blue-collar workers, thereby eliminating "class conflict" from the newly elected Sejm.[83]

Reformed Polish socialism in the variant put forward by Jaruzelski was to be based on the existence of competing noncommunist parties. PZPR members who were Sejm deputies had inherited a more prominent role—to confront the representatives of other parties who made up the coalition government. This implied a changed relationship between the party's parliamentary deputies and the party bodies. Given that the most determined resistance to reform had come from within these party organs and was especially in evidence within the Central Committee, it is not surprising that Jaruzelski saw advantages early on in siding with party deputies in the Sejm. These deputies themselves were intent on increasing their independence and, in so doing, gaining the stature within the party organization that their counterparts in the noncommunist parties enjoyed. In this respect, Carl Linden's "second antagonistic axis" of Leninist systems[84]—the friction between party and state that played so important a role in the Gierek-Jaroszewicz competition in the mid-1970s—was now actively fostered by Jaruzelski so as to outflank the conservative party apparatus.

An important step in diluting the authority of the Central Committee within the PZPR was the convening of the first—in Jaruzelski's term, "historic"—joint plenum of the Central Committee and the Parliamentary Caucus on June 30, 1989. It was at this meeting that Jaruzelski officially proposed Kiszczak as candidate for the presidency. The day before, the Politburo had also debated this nomination. Explaining his own unwillingness at that time to stand, he recognized that he was more often perceived as the instigator of martial law than as a proponent of the "reform line." As with the imposition of martial law, for which Jaruzelski invoked overriding reasons of state, the party leader once again reflected on the highest interest of the state: "If on the road to an agreement and to unifying all social forces an obstacle emerged, even if the obstacle were to be Wojciech Jaruzelski, there would be only one possible solution."[85] In his speech to the joint meeting he made clear that the new president had to be widely recognized as a reformer but also a leader who would "keep his head high." Obviously referring to himself, Jaruzelski remarked that an inappropriate candidate for the office of president would be a person who would be "the object of some kind of charitable gesture."[86]

Despite the overwhelming electoral defeat suffered by the party, Jaruzelski still contextualized political change within the framework of Polish socialism. He interpreted the roundtable agreement as intended to bring about "unity of action in the most important matters serving Poland, the real Poland, a Poland whose construction of socialism develops on the road to democratic reforms that are a great historical experiment, offer us a great opportunity, put us in the avant-garde of the reformist processes occurring in the socialist world."[87]

Sejm Deputy Marek Boral used the joint session to express dismay at meeting the Central Committee under such adverse circumstances: "We were very worried that the road taken by the Central Committee and that taken by the party as a whole would part ways. The experience of the last month, the changes that have occurred, and our role in the group of deputies confirm these fears." In particular, Boral accused the Central Committee of failing to persuade Jaruzelski to accept the presidency. Several other Sejm deputies also expressed their disappointment at the party chief's decision, and Ludwik Bernacki even deduced from this that the Caucus remained powerless within the party: "As deputies we would like to exert influence and join in making decisions on matters important to the party and the state."[88] Deputy Roman Ney was even more critical of what he saw as the insidious role of the Central Committee in discouraging Jaruzelski's candidacy: "Looking at it from the other side, that is, not sitting here in the Central Committee building but outside, the General is systematically being badly served. . . . this is perceptible at each move made in the party; whenever we find ourselves in party organizations it becomes apparent."[89] Central Committee members retorted that they had wanted Jaruzelski to become president but by this stage the Caucus had more influence on him.[90]

One speaker quickly caught the irony of the joint session: "Here I heard that we are meeting for the first time, and, in effect, already our roads are just about going separate ways."[91] Another irony, apparently lost in the Caucus–Central Committee showdown, was that governing in late June 1989 was already out of the hands of party groups, however constituted. This was clearly illustrated in Prime Minister Rakowski's late arrival at the joint meeting to report that the Council of Ministers had just frozen prices and wages. Władysław Baka, party secretary for economic matters, admitted that he and other members were hearing this for the first time but took comfort from this. The Central Committee had earlier agreed, he asserted, that "the matter of a price freeze does not require political consultation." In an understatement, Baka observed that "this is an illustration of relations that are really characterized by the full autonomy of the government, in which the party leadership shows the greatest confidence."[92]

The final irony that emerged from this joint meeting was purely symbolic in nature. At the end of the session Jaruzelski informed the deputies' group that it was the custom at the end of a Central Committee Plenum to sing the International. "I am counting on you deputies—party members—to join in." As power was being transferred from the party administration to party parliamentarians, the party chief was not sure that the latter were well versed in the party ethos or even that they could be counted on to take it up.

The Parliamentary Caucus

The emergence of the Parliamentary Club, with its membership of 173 beleaguered and electorally tainted deputies, did signal the decline of the party ethos and of the International, sung for the last time when the demise of the PZPR was made official.[93] It also pointed to a commitment to a democratic form of socialism. The success of the SdRP in the 1993 elections owed much to the action of the Caucus in rejuvenating the socialist movement in the second half of 1989. This was achieved quietly, while political attention was focused on the early fortunes of the Mazowiecki government. Recognition of the transfer of power took time, however, and required a flurry of deliberately ambivalent policy statements.

Neither the Thirteenth Central Committee Plenum, held in June–July 1989, nor the Fourteenth Plenum, convened the following month, reached any firm conclusions about what the relationship between the Caucus and the Central Committee should be. Additional joint sessions between parliamentary and party bodies were obviously a way to ease the transition, and the most important of these was a meeting between the presidium of the Parliamentary Club and the Politburo of the Central Committee, held September 16, 1989.

Sejm Deputy Józef Oleksy (later to become marshal, or speaker, of the Sejm and then prime minister) presented a lengthy report on the objectives of the Caucus. Acknowledging that "only the Eleventh Congress can ultimately delineate the role of the parliamentary fraction in relation to the party and its leadership," he was clear about how the balance of power had to shift: "We have to be aware that today the vast majority of issues that the party wishes to adopt—impose and regulate— for the state has to pass through the Parliamentary Club. In such a context the Club has to be seen in a new light, very different from that of the past unfavorable, bad practice."[94] Oleksy complained that hardly had the Caucus been formed but "immediately opinions began to circulate about the 'maverick" or 'destructive' work of the Club, about efforts at secession and lack of consciousness and political 'maturity' with regard to the Central Committee." At the heart of such criticisms, he added, lay "the desire to ensure that the Club remained entirely at the disposal of the party leadership."[95] The Club was receiving little help from the party bureaucracy and, indeed, was being portrayed in the party press as a rebellious faction. Yet, as most of its members readily believed, it was now the most important means the party had left of influencing matters of state. The party's official position on the newly formed Mazowiecki government was to lend it support qua government of the Polish state, not the government of Solidarity. But when deputies asked whether party support was to be unconditional, what the party's policy was on changes in property relations, on reprivatization, on trade unions, on constitutional reform, on subsidies, unemployment, and the market, and on the overhaul of the Ministries of Defense and Internal Affairs, Central Committee departments could provide no guidelines whatever. If party representatives in the Sejm appeared cautious, unsure of themselves, less adversarial, the inference was that they could not be otherwise when the party bureaucracy was deserting them. The paradox emerged, therefore, that once the Caucus had freed itself from party discipline in making decisions it was in greater need of the expertise and information base that the party bureaucracy could provide.

The long-standing issue of party unity was addressed in Oleksy's speech to Politburo and Caucus presidium members. It contained a series of contradictory views but thus clearly revealed the agonizing of a party loyalist in the first month of a noncommunist government. On the one hand, he proposed that the Parliamentary Club have the right to produce a supplement to the party daily *Trybuna Ludu*, thereby implying that the club's position was not always accurately reported by the newspaper. On the other hand, he contended that party unity had to be strengthened, that it was unsatisfactory to observe how "today it is the *apparat,* not political conceptions, that cement the party together," and that it would be regrettable if members came to "understand the party as a structure and stopped directing the party at the central level as a political movement."[96] On the one hand, he detected a selective, even capricious attitude toward reformers on the part of the party leadership. On the other, he expressed concern about "the degree of ideological and psychological 'desertion' of party members" and the impact this might have on the creation of a strong leftist party.[97] On the one hand, his vision of the successor party to the PZPR—not an unoriginal one—was of a predominantly parliamentary group that, in place of the ideological erosion that was inevitable, would be transformed into a platform for all leftist forces. On the other, he was disappointed that the term "socialism" had all but disappeared from the political lexicon and continued to be employed only by party chief Jaruzelski.

In an October 1989 Politburo resolution, it appeared that the Caucus–Central Committee relationship was finally to be clarified. The document asserted that "the party can pursue its state policies in the highest organ of state authority, which is the Sejm, through its representatives, that is, deputies." This signified that the role of party deputies within the overall power structure of the PZPR had to be enhanced. They therefore had to "have access to data and documents just like members of the Central Committee." Further, winning a parliamentary seat now was to entitle the deputy to participate in party congresses and national conferences.

In addition, in all parliamentary matters deputies were to be guaranteed access to the party leadership, and in matters affecting the PZPR Parliamentary Caucus deputies could even take part in Central Committee Plenum meetings as a right. It was recommended that regular meetings of the Politburo and the presidium of the Parliamentary Caucus should be held to assess progress in the party's legislative work. A number of other joint activities between the party parliamentary group and party structures (Central Committee administrative departments and commissions and provincial organizations) were suggested. But the revised party principles demonstrated that high-level apparatchiks had not completely abandoned the Leninist concept of democratic centralism. In return for automatic entry of deputies into select party bodies, certain obligations of deputies to the party were made clear. The Parliamentary Caucus was to brief Central Committee departments about bills tabled before the Sejm, including supplying minutes of Sejm and Senate sessions. Further, "the Central Committee of the PZPR, in creating for its deputies the necessary conditions to carry out the mandate of a deputy, expects from them a thorough internalization of the program, policy, and resolutions of the party; these ought to be the source of inspiration for deputies' activities, the goal being implementing them in the Sejm."[98]

The careful delineation of deputies' rights to participate in the deliberations of party bodies suggested a guarded, tradition-bound approach on the part of the 1989 Politburo that ratified these changes. In general, only matters affecting deputies, their caucus, and their parliamentary activities entitled them to take part in party bodies. We could legitimately question whether such "enhanced" participation was in fact a privilege or whether it constituted a newly imposed constraint on the growing and inevitable autonomy of the Sejm. What was left out of the proposed changes was even more important: deputies' input into the selection of the PZPR leadership. There was nothing in the 1989 principles to suggest the PZPR would operate like other political parties, its leaders emerging from the parliamentary group. In these respects, the socialist organizational ethos continued to overshadow the unique Polish experiment in democracy. From the PZPR Politburo's perspective in late 1989, the objective remained to invigorate socialist democracy, including its many pathological features.

The communist equivalent of a backbench rebellion was seen in the reaction of the Parliamentary Caucus to the leadership's initiatives. In January 1990 it issued an appeal to vote for reformists as delegates to the upcoming Eleventh Congress. It urged the election of delegates "who were not afraid to attack conservatives, the old order, the old routine, the trepidation before profound changes." Specifically, "the PZPR Parliamentary Caucus believes that newly elected delegates should themselves immediately plan the Congress." The tradition had been for a specially constituted Central Committee commission to prepare the draft program and select the candidates for delegates to party congresses. Not that it made much difference at this point, but the Caucus's practical concern with overhauling the procedures used to plan party congresses was designed to construct a "credible, modern leftist party" on the ruins of the PZPR.[99]

In the week preceding the Eleventh Congress, the Caucus issued a further policy statement regarding the future of the PZPR. Again, the group's focus was on securing autonomy for itself vis-à-vis the party bureaucracy. The Caucus "recognized the right of delegates to take the final decisions regarding the future of the party." Ensuring the "organizational unity and practical cohesiveness" of the Caucus was therefore seen as "a political value in itself." The call for the PZPR's dissolution was linked to the explicit notion of forging a different Polish road to socialism: "We support the creation of a completely new, pluralist leftist party whose program will reflect the will and aspirations of progressive forces of the Polish nation."[100]

The unexpected confrontation between the two PZPR organizations was perhaps best illustrated in the selection of a leader to head the successor party. Rakowski had actively canvassed support for election throughout the fall of 1989, using Plenum meetings and the party press to advance his position. But the chairman of the PZPR Parliamentary club and onetime ideological secretary, Marian Orzechowski, questioned Rakowski's credentials to lead a new party and suggested that such a party would have changed in "symbols and emblems only."[101]

Jaruzelski Deserts the Party

If Jaruzelski had played a pivotal role in the overture to the political opposition and in the democratic breakthrough, he distanced himself from the internal politics of his party. His vision in summer 1989 was of a presidency that would *replace* the party's leading role and, simultaneously, would not be partisan. But he had to confront a series of political landmarks in this period. When, on August 17, 1989, the formation of a Solidarity-led government seemed inevitable, he remained unsure what the Soviet reaction would be.[102] There was always a possibility that, as in December 1981, Jaruzelski would be asked to serve as proxy for a Soviet-initiated crackdown on the burgeoning opposition. According to Geremek, the most important factor dissuading Jaruzelski from using force at this critical juncture was "the personal stigma, the stamp of December 13, that he carried. Someone else might have been able to take that decision. Not he. In addition, an argument that ultimately also was involved was that a decision to introduce martial law in Poland would be a verdict on Gorbachev. This was also excluded given the unique relationship between Jaruzelski and Gorbachev."[103]

On November 23, 1989, the president met with representatives of the three coalition clubs to consider the draft for a new constitution. It was clear that Article 3, referring to the leading role of the party in society, was outdated and had to be removed. But the deletion of other constitutional principles seemed to trouble Jaruzelski more. As Geremek reported,

> Unexpectedly the general returned to the principle of social justice, which, together with the entire first part of the constitution, was to be deleted. He said, "For forty years I firmly believed that in furthering this principle I was serving Poland. Now we're deleting it, even though it's an important principle." I answered that I too thought it was important but that precisely over those forty years it had been compromised in Poland. He didn't protest. He hadn't said that in order to bargain. He wanted to share with someone a thought that had driven his life and whole career—as he put it, service—that had brought him so much bitterness and disappointment. I felt I was speaking with a person who at seventy was turning his back on his whole life and his whole career path, and preserved for himself only the most important ideals.[104]

Asked whether he believed that real socialism was unreformable in Polish conditions, Jaruzelski answered, "I never reached that conclusion."[105] There was a prescient note to this response.

Not surprisingly, then, the general took heart from the verdict rendered by the electorate in 1993 bringing socialists to power. From the preceding account we have discovered, however, that the PZPR's efforts to reform itself from within failed, and ultimately the party was overhauled from without—perhaps even too successfully from the perspective of Poland's neoliberal forces. Thus, the Fifth Plenum's thesis that changes in the party went together with a party in changed political circumstances was verified—if not exactly in the way the Central Committee had anticipated. Party hegemony throughout society collapsed when reform was attempted. Correspondingly, a more pragmatic party could find little popular support—at least in the immediate aftermath of its dogmatic forty-five-year rule over Polish society. Within four years, however, a revamped party of the left, built on the ruins of the PZPR and co-opting its younger generation of leaders, succeeded in taking power using new rules of the game that had largely been forced upon it.

Competing Explanations for the Polish Transition

The cross-national wave of democratization that reached its high point with the collapse of communist systems across the Soviet empire beginning in 1989 required the development of new explanatory frameworks in the social sciences. The study of transitions quickly developed into an important subfield of comparative politics. Whereas there was consensus on the significance of the phenomenon being studied—transitions from authoritarian rule—there was considerable disagreement on approaches to the examination of their sources, nature, and consequences. There is now a large and divergent literature addressing transition issues. In concluding this chapter, let us review four theoretical contributions made by specialists in Central European politics at the time transitions in the region began.

My approach has been to describe the logic of the coalition game from the perspective of each contender. An emphasis on mutual perceptions and on relative position and power in this third phase of the CCC model shares some characteristics with the interactionist framework used to analyze the Hungarian transition.[106] Bruszt and Stark suggest that the crisis of East European socialism, rather than involving strong states confronting strong societies, is more accurately viewed as the confrontation of weak states with weak societies. In the Polish case this was clearly not the case. The overwhelming power of the Leninist party-state had been unequivocally demonstrated in December 1981 when Jaruzelski declared martial law and crushed the Solidarity movement. The weak-society thesis also does not capture the Polish situation at the end of the 1980s. Although the opposition was weaker than in 1980—this was readily acknowledged by leading dissidents after the Magdalenka agreement—the mobilization potential of a self-conscious civil society had not diminished, as was apparent from the waves of strikes in 1988 and the setting up in December of that year of a Citizens' Committee of the Chairman of Solidarity. This happened at a time when Solidarity was still banned and in the absence of any possible patron group such as the KOR, which had dissolved itself eight years earlier.

Interactive effects with other Soviet-bloc transition processes were very limited in the case of Poland, since it led the bloc in initiating government-opposition dialogue. Obviously Gorbachev's new thinking had a major influence on the strategies of Polish political actors. Opposition forces and party reformists alike welcomed the chance to see what practical policy consequences the new thinking might have for the forging of a new ruling coalition. The only other interactive intrabloc connection—a limited one at that—was the ruling Hungarian Socialist

Workers' Party's purported willingness, expressed in February 1989 at the time the Polish roundtable had begun—to establish a multiparty system under its patronage. In the Polish negotiations, therefore, there was no learning process based on modes of interaction between rulers and dissidents elsewhere in the bloc.

A second explanatory framework has been proposed by Arista Maria Cirtautis and Edmund Mokrzycki, who distinguish between the articulation and the institutionalization phase of political transformation. The first "refers to a process whereby a given group develops a set of values and principles which subsequently provides this group with an ethically founded basis for action."[107] Solidarity in Poland was an example of this process. Its articulation of values and principles held by much of society, as documented in the previous chapter, provided it with a growing constituency. Where "there is a 'formal overlap' between the articulation of values and principles within a group and the socio-cultural and economic conditions external to it, a challenge to the old order is likely to result."[108]

Institutionalization signifies "the creation of formally sanctioned organizations and procedures that orient social behavior to recognizable, stable, and consistent patterns." This phase of the transformation produces splitting within the ranks of a formerly unified opposition: "the formal overlap between the new political leadership and the broader social audience will begin to lose its supportive character as the substantive difference between the new leadership and various social groups becomes clear." This is due to the logic of institutionalization: "The new leadership will seek to create institutions that will impose the way of life internal to the group upon society at large. Social groups threatened by the imposition of a new pattern of sanctions and rewards will mobilize to resist these changes."[109] Thus, if the leadership can no longer sustain the value consensus that had emerged earlier, as under Solidarity, a gap emerges between the new elite and critical social groups. The construction of liberal capitalist institutions by the first Solidarity-rooted governments in Poland produced such cleavages, evidenced by new waves of industrial unrest and peasant self-defense.

For Cirtautas and Mokrzycki, then, "Events in Poland since 1989 have demonstrated the extent to which a successful transition between the articulation and institutionalization phases is neither automatic nor assured."[110] But they also draw attention to an important theoretical problematic. By concentrating attention on politics at the top during transitions, research can neglect the significance of developments at the social base of a polity.

A third framework for examining democratization in the region has been advanced by the Polish political scientist Grzegorz Ekiert. His account seems designed to bring the state back into the equation that determines democracy. Ekiert observes that "East Central European domestic society was never organized by the logic of a market system, but rather by a peculiar blend of etatist economic policies and a household type of production."[111] As are Bruszt and Stark, he is aware of the danger of confrontation between a weak state and a weak society, but, provocatively, he considers this more probable in the transition process itself rather than in the pretransition phase: "The transition to democracy is likely to occur in situations in which the powers of the state and civil society simultaneously expand. In East Central Europe, however, given the immensity of change both in the polity and economy, it is more probable that the power of the state and civil society will simultaneously decline."[112] The key to successful transition becomes, therefore, "a revival of the state through the infusion of a civil culture, democratic institutions, and the consolidation of the new political society, together with economic reforms."[113] Both state and civil society stand to be strengthened by expansion of a sense of citizenship across society, removal of the dichotomy between public and private life, and adherence to the ideals of social justice in the postcommunist phase.

A final analytic framework is one developed by Piotr Sztompka, a Polish sociologist. Naturally, he is more drawn to the problematic of cultural structures than a political scientist might be, but, with Ekiert, he recognizes the impact of the public-private dichotomy on the drive for democratization: "The most fundamental and lasting cultural code organizing thought and action in the conditions of real socialism is the opposition of two spheres of life: private (personal) and public (official)."[114] The "cultural bias" toward the private world was perceived

> as an adaptive "boomerang response" to the totalitarian wish to invade and completely subjugate the private life of the citizens, and partly as a side-effect of the regime's successful attempts to restrict and even eliminate the pluralistic network of voluntary associations, communities, social circles, and political groupings which mark the mediating buffer-zone between the authorities and atomized, isolated citizens.[115]

Sztompka is concerned that the public-private dichotomy might not disappear in the transition to democracy: "By some irony of history, the core opposition of public and private sphere, together with most of its psychological and behavioral expressions, has outlived the communist system, and stands in the way of postcommunist reforms."[116] Among the manifestations of this dichotomy he cites continued political apathy, the "us versus them" attitude of much of society toward the first Solidarity governments, persistent illegal economic practices, and envy and resentment of individuals who are successful in postcommunist economic and political life. In concluding, this sociologist invokes Ralf Dahrendorf's metaphor of the "three clocks": the hour of the economist (who pursues market reform) is short and the hour of the lawyer (who enacts legal and constitutional change) is even shorter when compared with the hour of the citizen. "The rebuilding of the cultural codes, discourses, and underlying social life . . . takes longest and meets the strongest, even if unwitting, resistance."[117]

These diverse analytic frameworks are all concerned in one way or another with the common problem of uneven development, between civil society and the state, articulation and institutionalization of values, public and private spheres, or institutional architecture and cultural codes. As described in the last two chapters, the CCC framework underscores the connection between high politics and culture shift at the base of society. In the next two chapters I will examine the new democratic political system, how it has functioned, and the economic reform that is at its heart. In the process I try to shed light on the degree to which uneven development across spheres has been overcome during the drive for reform.

Notes

1. Ken Jowitt, "Weber, Trotsky, and Holmes on the Study of Leninist Regimes," *Journal of International Affairs,* 45 (Summer 1991), 36. See also his *New World Disorder: The Leninist Extinction.* Berkeley: University of California Press, 1992.

2. Donald Share, *The Making of Spanish Democracy.* New York: Praeger, 1986. See also his "Transitions to Democracy and Transition Through Transaction," *Comparative Political Studies,* 19 (January 1987), 525–548.

3. The term is taken from Philippe C. Schmitter, "Dangers and Dilemmas of Democracy," *Journal of Democracy,* 5, no. 2 (April 1994), 58.

4. This is a departure from the coalition analysis used in the original CCC model, which employed mathematical formulas to model the rational choice of actors in the coalition formation process, but retains the original logic of that analysis.

5. The Polish roundtable was the first case of pacted transition in the Soviet bloc, but it is worth noting that the Esquipulas accords (also known as the Arias peace plan), signed in August 1987 in Guatemala by five Central American presidents, produced talks between the Sandinista government and the contras in Sapoa, Nicaragua, beginning in March 1988. These talks, in turn, opened the way for competitive elections held in February 1990 that resulted in the defeat of the ruling socialists. Although some parallels between the Nicaraguan and Polish cases are obvious, there is no evidence that Polish communists consciously took any cues from the Sandinistas. In particular, the Polish communists initiated talks with the opposition later than the Sandinistas but were defeated by it at the polls earlier than in Nicaragua.

6. See the summary of Jerzy Urban's press conference of February 21, 1989, in *Rzeczpospolita,* February 22, 1989.

7. For a study that considers the fortunes of liberals and conservatives in the party, see M. K. Dziewanowski, *The Communist Party of Poland.* Cambridge, MA: Harvard University Press, 1976. For a study of the best-known opposition group and its increasing resources, see Jan Józef Lipski, *KOR: A History of the Workers' Defense Committee in Poland.* Berkeley: University of California Press, 1985. The extensive Solidarity literature throws further light on resource distribution between the social movement and the party. See, for example, Abraham Brumberg (ed.), *Poland: Genesis of a Revolution.* New York: Vintage Books, 1983.

8. For a careful study of the increasing populism of budgetary allocations by communist regimes after succession and political crises, see Valerie Bunce, *Do New Leaders Make a Difference?* Princeton: Princeton University Press, 1981. Also Bogdan Mieczkowski, "The Relationship Between Changes in Consumption and Politics in Poland," *Soviet Studies,* 30, no. 2 (1978), 262–269.

9. Terry Lynn Karl and Philippe C. Schmitter, "Modes of Transition in Latin America, Southern and Eastern Europe," *International Social Science Journal,* 128 (May 1991), 269–284. Also, Karl and Schmitter, "Democratization Around the Globe: Its Opportunities and Risks," in Michael T. Klare and Dan Thomas (eds.), *World Security: Trends and Challenges at Century's End.* 2nd edn. New York: St. Martin's Press, 1993.

10. Donald Share and Scott Mainwaring, "Transitions Through Transaction: Brazil and Spain," in Wayne A. Selcher (ed.), *Political Liberalization in Brazil.* Boulder: Westview Press, 1986, pp. 175–215.

11. Michael G. Burton, Richard Gunther, and John Higley, "Introduction: Elite Transformations and Democratic Regimes," in John Higley and Richard Gunther (eds.), *Elites and Democratic Consolidation in Latin America and Southern Europe.* Cambridge: Cambridge University Press, 1992, p. 35.

12. Karl and Schmitter, "Modes of Transition in Latin America, Southern and Eastern Europe," p. 281.

13. Jerzy Urban, *Jajakobyly.* Warsaw: BGW, 1992, p. 157.

14. Centrum Badań Opinii Społecznej (CBOS), "Reaktywowanie 'Solidarności'— nadzieje i obawy," BD/34/5/89. Cited by Marjorie Castle, "A Successfully Failed Pact? The Polish Political Transition of 1989," unpublished doctoral dissertation, Stanford University, 1993 draft, chap. 4, p. 18, n. 18.

15. Cited in Wojciech Adamiecki et al. (eds.), *Okrągly stół: kto jest kim.* Warsaw: Myśl, 1989, p. 246.

16. CBOS, "Opinie o rządzie Mieczysława Rakowskiego," BD/329/88 (December 1988). Cited by Castle, "A Successfully Failed Pact?" chap. 4, p. 69. See also Rakowski's own account of opinion polls in Mieczysław Rakowski, *Jak to sięle stało.* Warsaw: BGW, 1991, p. 159.

17. Schmitter and Karl, "Modes of Transition in Latin America, Southern and Eastern Europe." However, they tentatively classify the mode of transition in Eastern Europe as reformist, that is, based on a political initiative coming from the society rather than an elite-controlled breakthrough.

18. Nancy Bermeo, "Surprise, Surprise: Lessons from 1989 and 1991," in Nancy Bermeo (ed.), *Liberalization and Democratization: Change in the Soviet Union and Eastern Europe.* Baltimore: Johns Hopkins University Press, 1992, p. 197.

19. Guillermo O'Donnell and Philippe C. Schmitter, *Transitions from Authoritarian Rule: Tentative Conclusions About Uncertain Democracies.* Baltimore: Johns Hopkins University Press, 1986.

20. Adam Przeworski, *Democracy and the Market.* Cambridge: Cambridge University Press, 1991.

21. Jadwiga Staniszkis, *The Dynamics of the Breakthrough in Eastern Europe: The Polish Experience.* Berkeley: University of California Press, 1991, p. 98.

22. Jacek Żakowski, *Rok 1989: Geremek opowiada, Żakowski pyta.* Warsaw: Plejada, 1990, p. 29, my translation.

23. Żakowski, *Rok 1989,* p. 131, my translation.

24. Interview with Janusz Reykowski, Stanford, May 22, 1991.

25. Jacek Kurczewski, *The Resurrection of Rights in Poland.* Oxford: Clarendon Press, 1993, p. 349.

26. See Miodowicz's speech at the Eighth Plenum, reported in *Trybuna Ludu,* August 29, 1988.

27. Piotr Kwiatkowski, "Opinion Research and the Fall of Communism: Poland 1981–1990," *International Journal of Public Opinion Research,* 4, no. 4 (Winter 1992), 364.

28. *Życie Warszawy,* August 27–28, 1988. Kiszczak added that those who rejected the constitutional order of the Polish People's Republic could not participate.

29. X Plenum KC PZPR. *Podstawowe dokumenty i materiały: 20–21 grudnia 1988 r., 16–18 stycznia 1989 r.* Warsaw: Książka i Wiedza, 1989, pp. 16, 21, 24, my translation.

30. "The Geoffrey Stern Interview: Mieczysław Rakowski," *LSE Magazine,* (Summer 1991), 14.

31. Karol B. Janowski, "PZPR—od monolitu i monopolu do agonii (analiza przypadku)," unpublished paper, Warsaw, April 1990, p. 21.

32. This is Castle's calculation, based on confidential sources and interviews with leaders. "A Successfully Failed Pact?" chap. 4, p. 24.

33. On the political regression that occurred at the Tenth Congress, see Karol B. Janowski, *Demokracja socjalistczna w koncepcjach polityczno-programowych PZPR.* Warsaw: Państwowe Wydawnictwo Naukowe, 1989, p. 390.

34. *Trybuna Ludu,* May 8, 1989.

35. Cited in Rakowski, *Jak to się stało,* pp. 214, 224.

36. Przeworski, *Democracy and the Market,* p. 68.

37. George Breslauer called my attention to this idea of Deutsch's; unfortunately, neither of us can locate the publication in which Deutsch advanced these notions.

38. Żakowski, *Rok 1989,* p. 14, my translation.

39. Żakowski, *Rok 1989,* p. 16, my translation.

40. Żakowski, *Rok 1989,* p. 54.

41. Żakowski, *Rok 1989,* p. 214, my translation.

42. Żakowski, *Rok 1989,* pp. 46, 54.

43. Żakowski, *Rok 1989,* p. 53, my translation.

44. See, for example, notes taken by Krzysztof Dubiński and published as *Magdalenka: Transakcja epoki.* Warsaw: Sylwa, 1990, pp. 88–92.

45. "Mały słownik III Rzeczypospolitej," *Wprost,* no. 27 (July 4, 1993), p. 38, my translation.

46. Żakowski, *Rok 1989,* p. 113, my translation.

47. Żakowski, *Rok 1989,* p. 131, my translation.

48. Żakowski, *Rok 1989,* p. 114, my translation.

49. Żakowski, *Rok 1989,* p. 71, my translation.

50. Żakowski, *Rok 1989,* pp. 71, 78, 74, my translation.

51. Żakowski, *Rok 1989,* p. 112, my translation.

52. Quoted in Dubiński, *Magdalenka: Transakcja epoki,* pp. 129, 131, my translation.

53. Quoted in Dubiński, *Magdalenka: Transakcja epoki,* p. 53, my translation.

54. The parliamentary scholar Stanisław Gebethner provided the political reform subtable on February 10 with data showing that 88 percent of Poles in 1988 wanted free elections. This crucial intervention is noted by Castle, "A Successfully Failed Pact?" chap. 5, p. 22.

55. Staniszkis, *The Dynamics of the Breakthrough in Eastern Europe,* p. 80. For further discussion of the national list and the electoral system, see Paul Lewis, "Non-Competitive Elections and Regime Change: Poland 1989," *Parliamentary Affairs,* 43, no. 1 (January 1990), 90–107. Also, David M. Olson, "Compartmentalized Competition: The Managed Transitional Election System of Poland," *Journal of Politics,* 55, no. 1 (February 1993), 415–441. For the party leadership's view, see S. Perzkowski (ed.), *Tajne dokumenty Biura Politycznego i Sekretariatu Komitetu Centralnego: Ostatni rok władzy, 1988–1989.* London: Aneks, 1994, pp. 399–402. Also, Żakowski, *Rok 1989,* pp. 195–201.

56. Staniszkis, *The Dynamics of the Breakthrough in Eastern Europe,* p. 160.

57. A senate so conceived—as an institution for patronage by the political leader—is not as extraordinary as Kiszczak's proposal appeared. Appointment to the Canadian Senate is used to reward longtime friends of the prime minister's party.

58. Rakowski, *Jak to siłe stało*, p. 203. From an interview with him Castle concluded that Kwaśniewski's proposal was a "sudden impulse" on his part. "A Successfully Failed Pact?" chap. 5, p. 48. Since participants in the roundtable were encouraged to brainstorm, especially when an impasse was reached, this sudden impulse is not as unlikely as it may seem.

59. *Porozumienie okrągłego stołu.* Warsaw: NSZZ Solidarność, Region Warmińsko-Mazurski, 1989, p. 7, my translation.

60. Other than the appointment of judges and the status of the procuracy, a third legal issue left unresolved by the roundtable was capital punishment, which Solidarity sought to end. See Jacek Kurczewski, *The Resurrection of Rights in Poland.* Oxford: Clarendon Press, 1993, pp. 88–92.

61. CBOS, "Okrągły stół: Opinie o przebiegu i politycznych rezultatach rozmów," BD/95/16/89 (April 1989). Cited by Castle, "A Successfully Failed Pact?" chap. 5, pp. 78–79.

62. Kwiatkowski, "Opinion Research and the Fall of Communism: Poland 1981–1990," p. 369.

63. See the section "Przewidywania" in Lena Kolarska-Bobińska, Piotr Łukasiewicz, and Zbigniew Rykowski (eds.), *Wyniki badań, wyniki wyborów: 4 czerwca 1989.* Warsaw: Ośrodek Badań Społecznych, 1990, pp. 13–74.

64. Paweł Kuczyński, "Sondaż przedwyborczy dla 'Le Journal des Elections,'" in Kolarska-Bobińska, Łukasiewicz, and Rykowski, *Wyniki badań, wyniki wyborów: 4 czerwca 1989,* pp. 13–25. The French organizer of the poll was Georges Mink.

65. This is an argument advanced by Jacek Raciborski, "Wzory zachowań wyborczych a dawne modele wyborów," in Kolarska-Bobińska, Łukasiewicz, and Rykowski, *Wyniki badań, wyniki wyborów: 4 czerwca 1989,* pp. 206–207.

66. Staniszkis, *The Dynamics of the Breakthrough in Eastern Europe,* p. 199.

67. Krzysztof Jasiewicz, "Zachowania wyborcze w świetle badań z serii 'Polacy,'" in Kolarska-Bobińska, Łukasiewicz, and Rykowski, *Wyniki badań, wyniki wyborów: 4 czerwcza 1989,* p. 181.

68. Stanisław Gebethner, "Wybory do Sejmu i Senatu 1989 r. (wstępne refleksje)," *Państwo i Prawo* 44, no. 8 (August 1989), 3–14.

69. Krzysztof Kosela, "Rola kościoła katolickiego w kampanii przed wyborami czerwcowymi," in Kolarska-Bobińska, Łukasiewicz, and Rykowski, *Wyniki badań, wyniki wyborów: 4 czerwcza 1989,* pp. 129–135.

70. Żakowski, *Rok 1989,* p. 234, my translation.

71. "Stanowisko w sprawie powołanie rządu i aktualnej sytuacji politycznej przyjęte przez XIV Plenum KC PZPR, 19 sierpnia 1989 r.," *Trybuna Ludu,* August 21, 1989.

72. Żakowski, *Rok 1989,* pp. 252–253.

73. "Stanowisko XV Plenum KC PZPR w sprawie głównych zadań partii w okresie poprzedzającym XI Zjazdu," *Trybuna Ludu,* October 5, 1989.

74. "Referat Biura Politycznego KC PZPR wygłoszony przez L. Millera," *Trybuna Ludu,* October 4, 1989.

75. "Deklaracja 'Ruchu 8 lipca,'" *Trybuna Ludu,* October 13, 1989.

76. Janowski, "PZPR," p. 33. This summary account of the Social Democratic and Socialist Blocs owes much to Janowski's analysis.

77. "Oświadczenie Warszawskiego Robotniczego Forum Zjazdowego," *Trybuna Ludu,* November 20, 1989.

78. "Tezy deklaracji programowej, zasady wyboru delegatów na XI Zjazd PZPR, założenia statutowego modelu partii," *Trybuna Ludu,* November 8–9, 1989.

79. Żakowski, *Rok 1989,* p. 255.

80. Żakowski, *Rok 1989,* pp. 124–125.

81. Maksymilian Berezowski, *Koniec epoki.* Warsaw: Novum, 1991, p. 61, my translation. Berezowski conducted interviews with six major party figures, including Jaruzelski.

82. *Trybuna Kongresowa,* 29–31 January 1990; also, "Podstawowe dokumenty Kongresu założycielskiego Socjaldemokracji Rzeczypospolitej Polskiej," *Sprawy bieżące,* February 4–5, 1990.

83. Żakowski, *Rok 1989,* p. 276.

84. Carl Linden, "Opposition and Faction in Communist Party Leaderships," in Frank P. Belloni and Dennis C. Beller (eds.), *Faction Politics: Political Parties and Factionalism in Comparative Perspective.* Santa Barbara, CA: ABC-Clio, 1978, p. 379.

85. Stenogram z zebrania klubu poselskiego PZPR odbytego dnia 30 czerwca 1989 r. w sali nr 561 gmachu KC PZPR (wspólne z członkami KC PZPR), "Wystąpienie Wojciecha Jaruzelskiego," p. 4, my translation.

86. Stenogram z zebrania klubu poselskiego, 30 czerwca 1989 r., "Wystąpienie Wojciecha Jaruzelskiego," p. 8, my translation.

87. Stenogram z zebrania klubu poselskiego, 30 czerwca 1989 r., "Wystąpienie Wojciecha Jaruzelskiego," p. 6, my translation.

88. Stenogram z zebrania klubu poselskiego, 30 czerwca 1989 r., "Wystąpienie Marka Borala," p. 12; "Wystąpienie Ludwika Bernackiego," p. 19, my translation.

89. Stenogram z zebrania klubu poselskiego, 30 czerwca 1989 r., "Wystąpienie Romana Ney," p. 32, my translation.

90. Stenogram z zebrania klubu poselskiego, 30 czerwca 1989 r., unnamed "Towarzyszka, członek KC PZPR: Wystąpienie," p. 43.

91. Stenogram z zebrania klubu poselskiego, 30 czerwca 1989 r., "Głos z sali," p. 13, my translation.

92. Stenogram z zebrania klubu poselskiego, 30 czerwca 1989 r., "Wystąpienie Władysława Baki," p. 79, my translation.

93. A documentary film, *Ostatki* ("Remainders") captures the poignant but more often comic scenes of the PZPR's last congress in January 1990.

94. "Wystąpienie tow. Józefa Oleksego na wspólnym posiedzeniu Biura Politycznego KC PZPR i Prezydium Klubu Poselskiego PZPR w dniu 16 września b.r.," Informacja Nr II/175/89 (27 September 1989), p. 1, my translation.

95. Informacja II/175/89, "Wystąpienie Józefa Oleksego," p. 2, my translation.

96. Informacja II/175/89, "Wystąpienie Józefa Oleksego," pp. 9–10, my translation.

97. Informacja II/175/89, "Wystąpienie Józefa Oleksego," p. 14, my translation.

98. "Zasady współdziałania Komitetu Centralnego i instancji partyjnych z partyjnymi posłami i Klubem Poselskim PZPR," Zatwierdzone przez Biuro Polityczne KC PZPR, October 24, 1989 r., my translation.

99. Klub Poselski PZPR, "Wezwanie Klubu poselskiego PZPR do członków partii," January 1990, my translation.

100. "Stanowisko klubu poselskiego PZPR przed XI Zjazdem PZPR i Kongresem nowej partii," January 19, 1990, my translation.

101. *Trybuna Ludu,* January 25, 1990, my translation.

102. Żakowski, *Rok 1989,* p. 250.

103. Żakowski, *Rok 1989,* p. 252, my translation.

104. Żakowski, *Rok 1989,* pp. 378–379, my translation.

105. Berezowski, *Koniec epoki,* p. 11, my translation.

106. László Bruszt and David Stark, "Remaking the Political Field in Hungary: From the Politics of Confrontation to the Politics of Competition," in Ivo Banac (ed.), *Eastern Europe in Revolution.* Ithaca, NY: Cornell University Press, 1992, pp. 13–55.

107. Arista Maria Cirtautas and Edmund Mokrzycki, "The Articulation and Institutionalization of Democracy in Poland," in *Social Research,* 60, no. 4 (Winter 1993), 791.

108. Cirtautas and Mokrzycki, "The Articulation and Institutionalization of Democracy in Poland," p. 792.

109. Cirtautas and Mokrzycki, "The Articulation and Institutionalization of Democracy in Poland," pp. 793, 796.

110. Cirtautas and Mokrzycki, "The Articulation and Institutionalization of Democracy in Poland," p. 818.

111. Grzegorz Ekiert, "Democratization Processes in East Central Europe: A Theoretical Reconsideration," *British Journal of Political Science,* 21, pt. 3 (July 1991), 305. His account draws on Ivan Szelenyi, *Socialist Entrepreneurs: Embourgeoisement in Rural Hungary.* Madison, WI: University of Wisconsin Press, 1988.

112. Ekiert, "Democratization Processes in East Central Europe," p. 311.

113. Ekiert, "Democratization Processes in East Central Europe," p. 313.

114. Piotr Sztompka, "The Intangibles and Imponderables of the Transition to Democracy," *Studies in Comparative Communism,* 24, no. 3 (September 1991), 299.

115. Sztompka, "The Intangibles and Imponderables of the Transition to Democracy," p. 300.

116. Sztompka, "The Intangibles and Imponderables of the Transition to Democracy," p. 304.

117. Sztompka, "The Intangibles and Imponderables of the Transition to Democracy," p. 310. The "three clocks" metaphor comes from Ralf Dahrendorf, *Reflections on the Revolution in Europe.* New York: Times Books, 1991, p. 93.

5

Democratic Structures of the Third Republic

Since 1990 the new political system in Poland has come to be known as the Third Republic, suggesting that People's Poland was never really Poland. Although most of the symbols and some of the structures of this Third Republic are derived from the interwar period, the geopolitics and problems of the present regime closely resemble those of People's Poland.

For many Poles, what constitutes Phase IV of our model—the new democratized political system of the Third Republic—has proved anticlimactic, coming after herculean struggles to crack open an ossified monolithic system. The issues of democratic consolidation and economic development are central to Phase IV analysis because they represent the changes triggered by the negotiated transition of Phase III. In some areas, the dimensions and nature of these changes remain unclear more than five years after the roundtable agreements. In other areas, the changes seem complete and irreversible.

Phase IV replicates for the new system the system functionalism applied in Phase I to the antecedent regime. The intricacies of the new system remain unfamiliar to many scholars and students of comparative politics, given its recent origin and its continually changing ground rules. In order to provide a comprehensive system-functional analysis of its features, the last two chapters of this book address distinct subject areas pertinent to Phase IV analysis. I begin in this chapter by examining the new constitutional arrangements and political institutions of the Third Republic, including the important question of executive-legislative relations and the checks-and-balances system. I also look at political parties, political groups (including the electorate), election results, and leadership—all central to the democratized political process. I present data indicating whether attitudinal changes have been of sufficient magnitude that we can speak of the evolution of a different, democratic political culture. If the agenda for this chapter seems ambitious, we should recall the limited time span being analyzed, from the time of the democratic breakthrough in 1989 to mid 1995.

Chapter 6 addresses the interrelated topics of socioeconomic development, the international political economy, and international relations. I weigh the evidence informing us about regime performance in socioeconomic matters since 1989. I examine Poland's distinct capitalist transformation and assess the extent of the crucial linkage between democracy and delivery.[1] I also explore whether Poland's interaction with the post–Cold War international environment has reinforced the new democracy, examining in particular the role of the international political economy in enhancing Poland's democratic and capitalist prospects.

The First Years of Regime Transition: Political Fragmentation

Judging by the early years of the democratic transition, Poland's politics had seemingly little to recommend them. An impression was conveyed of unbounded ambitions pursued by contending political actors and an absence of even minimal solidarity in a movement that was previously united as Solidarity. Institutional disorder and rampant greed seemed the other dominant characteristics of the emergent regime. How accurate were such impressions, and were they passing phenomena or durable features of the postcommunist system?

It is clear that Poland did not establish the institutions crucial to stable democratic practice overnight. The "Little Constitution," the first draft of which was vigorously supported by President Lech Wałęsa, was passed by the Sejm in much-amended form only in November 1992—over three years after the democratic breakthrough.[2] In fall 1994 the Sejm began debate on seven different versions of a new constitution proposed by Wałęsa and the main parties. Only Wałęsa's version proposed a strong presidency. It seemed unlikely that a completely new constitution would be in place in time to shape the powers of the president elected in November 1995. Already in the 1992 constitutional act the powers of the president, the prime minister and the cabinet, and the Sejm were balanced, to the satisfaction of none of them.

Poland had six prime ministers, more than any other European country, in the period 1989–1995. From the inevitable and welcome "positive disintegration"[3] of the catchall Solidarity movement, a surfeit of personal ambitions and a deficit of coalition-building skills produced splintering within large (the Democratic Union [Unia Demokratyczna—UD]) and minor (Polish Beer Lovers' Party [PPPP]) political parties alike (for the major parties of this period, see Table 5.1). There was a widespread negative perception of fragmentation, too. Splits within the Solidarity-derivative political elite produced self-serving and myopic political behavior among breakaway leaders. That politics were highly personalized is best illustrated by the behavior of the president himself. Initially Wałęsa chose to forego a strong presidential party, opting instead for antiparty rhetoric. In the view of many, what made the new elite a political class was its unrestrained self-interest in power and

TABLE 5.1   Political Alliances, Parties, Programs, and Leaders

Alliance or Party	Policy Orientation	Leaders
Alliance of the Democratic Left (Sojusz Lewicy Demokratycznej—SLD)		Alexander Kwaśniewski, Leszek Miller, Józef Oleksy Ewa Spychalska
• Social Democracy of the Polish Republic (Socjaldemocracja Rzeczypospolitej Polskiej—SdRP)	Social democratic, welfarist, secularist, successor to PZPR	
• National Trade Union Accord (Ogólnopolskie Porozumienie Związków Zawodowych—OPZZ)	Radical defender of workers' and pensioners' rights, successor to communist trade union	
• Twenty-five other small parties and organizations		
Polish Peasant Party (Polskie Stronnictwo Ludowe—PSL)	Agrarianist, third-way, interventionist, Christian ethics, successor to PSL	Waldemar Pawlak, Roman Jagieliński
Freedom Union (Unia Wolności—UW) 1994 merger of		Leszek Balcerowicz, Hanna Suchocka, Jacek Kuroń, Tadeusz Mazowiecki
• Democratic Union (Unia Demokratyczna—UD)	Centrist, market-oriented, intellectual, for integration into Europe; *liberal faction:* of KOR origins, interventionist, favoring separation of church and state; *moderate faction:* Christian ethics, antipopulist	
and		Jan Krzysztof Bielecki, Donald Tusk
• Liberal-Democratic Congress (Kongres Liberalno-Demokratyczny—KLD)	Neoliberal, pro-Western; *Janusz Lewandowski faction:* classical laissez-faire; *Lech Mazewski faction:* antistatist, supply-side economics, secular, conservative	

(continues)

TABLE 5.1 (continued)

Alliance or Party	Policy Orientation	Leaders
Union of Labor (Unia Pracy—UP)	Social justice, welfarist, defender of workers' interests, tradition of workers' Solidarity	Rysard Bugaj, Zbigniew Bujak, Alexander Małachowski, Karol Modzelewski
Confederation for an Independent Poland (Konfederacja Polski Niepodległej—KPN)	Piłsudskiite, anticommunist, anti-Russian, nationalist, law-and-order, anticorruption	Leszek Moczulski, Krzysztof Król
Nonparty Bloc for Reform (Bezpartyjny Blok Wspierania Reform—BBWR)	Pro-Wałęsa, Catholic, for presidential system	Jerzy Gwizdza
Alliance for Poland (Przymierze dla Polski) 1994 merger of:		
• Christian National Union (Zjednoczenie Chrześcijańsko Narodowe —ZChN)	Backbone of 1992 Catholic Electoral Action and 1993 Fatherland electoral alliances; right-wing, nationalist, clerical, corporatist, economic interventionist	Ryszard Czarnecki, Marek Jurek, Jan Łopuszański, Stefan Niesiołowski
• Movement for the Republic (Ruch dla Rzeczypospolitej—RdR)	Accelerated decommunization	Romuald Szeremietiew, Jan Olszewski
• Peasant Alliance (Porozumienie Ludowe—PL)	Catholic, for farm subsidies	Gabriel Janowski
• Center Accord (Porozumienie Centrum—PC)	Capitalist, Christian-democratic, anti-Wałęsa	Jarosław Kaczyński, Jacek Maziarski
• Conservative Coalition (Koalicja Konserwatywna—KK)	Conservative	Kazimierz Michał Ujazdowski

November Eleventh Agreement (Porozumienie Jedenastego Listopada)	Laissez-faire, anticommunist, traditional right	
• Conservative Party (Partia Konserwatywna—PK)		Alexander Hall
• Union of Real Politics (Unia Polityki Realnej—UPR)		Janusz Korwin-Mikke
• Christian-Peasant Alliance (Stronnictwo Chrześcijańako Ludowe—SChL)		Henryk Bąk, Józef Slisz, Paweł Łączkowski
• Christian Democratic Party (Partia Chrześcijań-skich Demokratów—PChD)		
Solidarity (Solidarność)	Syndicalist, interventionist, mixed economy	Marian Krzaklewski

its trappings. The British political scientist Frances Millard points out that in the first phase of postcommunist politics politicians were perceived not as "representing people's interests but rather as arrogant, corrupt and self-serving," while political parties were, in turn, "neither clear constituencies of interests nor coherent ideological perspectives . . . patently unable to serve as integrative mechanisms for society or as agents of conflict resolution."[4]

A few comparisons with other states undertaking a democratic transition may indicate whether these Polish developments were unique. In the early years of Brazil's transition, during the 1987–1991 legislature, one of every three members of Congress changed parties. In Poland, however, creating rather than switching parties seems to have been more popular among politicians. As in Brazil, an increasing perception on the part of the public that politics were being forced upon society led to the emergence of symptoms of "civic fatigue"—public disenchantment with the political and electoral process.[5] Intense political competition seemed to outstrip the institutionalization of democracy, which, for political scientist Adam Przeworski, was "the devolution of power from a group of people to a set of rules." If the party system is treated as an integral part of a regime's institutional framework, then its fluidity in Poland until the September 1993 parliamentary elections was a sign of unconsolidated democracy; "democracy is consolidated when compliance—acting within the institutional framework—constitutes the equilibrium of the decentralized strategies of all the relevant political forces."[6] But apart from the party system, the office of the president is subsumed within the institutional framework, and in late 1994 it seemed clear to excommunists and ex-Solidarity leaders alike that Wałęsa was the least compliant of political actors when it came to operating within a fixed institutional system.

It is debatable whether party fragmentation and the associated civic fatigue were inevitable in Poland. Some have argued that a structural determinism was at work that produced both. Thus, Przeworski hints that the nature of the transitional moment was pivotal. In the bid to end authoritarian rule "the struggle for democracy always takes place on two fronts: against the authoritarian regime for democracy and against one's allies for the best place under democracy."[7] The socially heterogeneous character of the postcommunist leadership group in Poland may also help explain why political centrifugalism prevailed. In a number of ways this group was what one writer in a different context has called a "living museum,"[8] consisting of 1950s maverick intellectuals, 1960s student leaders, 1970s trade unionists, 1980s quasilegal entrepreneurs, and 1990s quacks (such as Tyminski). Though not with equal impact, these diverse groups shaped the country's democracy in its first phase and instilled in it certain strengths and flaws.

Poland's political *skansen* (museum) was not as heterogeneous as it might have been had former communists been permitted to play a key role in the first Solidarity governments, but even without them it was remarkably diverse. Career paths alone do not explain the propensity to fragmentation, and James Madison's characterization of human nature, written in 1788 in *The Federalist,* is worth recalling: "So strong is this propensity of mankind to fall into mutual animosities, that where no substantial occasion presents itself, the most frivolous and fanciful distinctions have been sufficient to kindle their unfriendly passions and excite their most violent conflicts."[9]

Noncooperation with other political forces can also be interpreted as a rational strategy in a period of transition. Polish political fragmentation could be viewed through the prism of the prisoners' dilemma that faced political actors in Argentina in the mid-1980s. As William Smith puts it, "In this game of collective action, high levels of uncertainty concerning macroeconomic policy, combined with doubts about the stability of the new democratic regime, structure the expectations of the principal protagonists—state elites, party leaders, business interests, and organized labor—in such a way as to maximize the incentives to pursue strategies of non-cooperation."[10] A rising spiral of political conflict was, then, the product of the prisoners' dilemma. But Smith draws a more optimistic conclusion about Argentina after the democratic breakthrough: "Democratic consolidation will, to a large extent, hinge on the ability of elected politicians and policymakers to defuse the distributional struggle by forging rules, based on consensus, backed up by strong, autonomous social and political institutions." In Argentina, as in Poland, an ideology of neoliberalism served as a mechanism for rule making and institution building. It empowered private capital while limiting the power of the state to regulate the economy. From the breakthrough moment, then, the emerging institutional order in Argentina, as in Poland, seemed likely to become elitist and socially regressive but, at the same time, efficient and growth inducing.

Indeed, postcommunist political fragmentation and the institutions it created could be treated as an indicator of the success of the transition. Competition now occurred over voters, among parties, between leaders. Transition implied a hybrid of oldness and newness in provisional structures despite the obstacles to such "cohabitation." Ancien régime officials decided to forego confrontation when it became rational for them to do so. One of many illuminating analyses of the rational-choice approach is that of a Polish economist who uses a property-rights analysis to highlight the pivotal position of the *nomenklatura* in the transition to a free-market economy.[11] Communist apparatchiks were the principal beneficiaries of rent-seeking activities under the old system and, confronted with the prospects of a transition, asked, "Isn't it possible that the expected benefits within the framework of the new regime, or new structure of property rights, were larger for the major groups of rent-seekers than the rents they could acquire within the existing property rights structure?"[12] One need not subscribe to a conspiracy theory of secret deals at Magdalenka to reach an affirmative answer to this question. So long as we agree that some of the major beneficiary groups of the old system were able now to join the new system as net economic gainers, the transition from communism was a perfectly rational choice for communists themselves to make.

Political Structures

Democratizing the Polish political system required introducing a whole series of new institutions and legal provisions in place of the prevailing ones. A partial list would include (1) completely revamping the Polish constitution of July 22, 1952, and, to enhance constitutional rule, invigorating the appellate Constitutional Tribunal; (2) enacting electoral laws to govern multiparty competition; (3) removing all the official symbols and terms of the previous system (the country's official name, coat of arms, flag, anthem); (4) creating the new institutions of democracy, including the presidency, the Senate, and an overhauled system of local government; (5) passing legislation that would expand private ownership rights and delimit state ownership rights; (6) enshrining principles incorporating civil rights and creating appropriate institutional safeguards for them, for example, the office of the Commissioner for Civil Rights (originally created in 1987); and (7) strengthening the independence of the judicial branch of government, especially giving it control over the procuracy.

Constitutional Change

In order to make good on the promises issued by the communist delegation at the roundtable negotiations, the 1952 constitution had to be amended immediately to provide for the establishment of the presidency, the Senate, and new electoral laws. These institutional changes, enacted on April 7, 1989, did not in themselves signal the end of the ancien régime. After the fast-paced events of the summer, however, the new political reality dictated further constitutional change of a more sweeping nature. Accordingly, on December 29, 1989, the parliament passed legislation formally changing the country's name from Polish People's Republic to the Polish Republic. Furthermore, the first two chapters of the 1952 constitution were replaced by a new chapter entitled "Foundations of the Political and Economic System." According to the constitutional specialist Stanisław Gebethner, the new chapter provided a "radical—even revolutionary—change of the concept of both the political system and the economic system."[13]

The revolutionary changes started with the very first article, which had previously defined Poland as a socialist state. Now it stated that "the Polish Republic is a democratic legal state implementing the principles of social justice."[14] Thus, the very character of the Polish state was redefined with this change. In addition, the former language of Article 1 saying that power was vested in the hands of working people in town and country was deleted. New Article 2 asserted that "supreme power is vested in the nation." Gone, then, was the class nature of communist society. Related to this, whereas former Article 3 identified the leading role of the PZPR in Polish society, it was removed and a new Article 4 outlined the bases of a multiparty system: "Founded on the principles of free will and equality, political parties organize citizens of the Polish Republic with the objective of influencing the policies of the state in a democratic manner."[15]

The December 1989 changes also encompassed the economic system. All references to the special status of socialist forms of ownership (state and cooperative) were removed. Article 6 now read: "The Polish Republic guarantees freedom of economic activities regardless of the form of ownership." Article 7 follows with "The Polish Republic protects ownership and the right to inheritance and guarantees full protection of personal ownership."[16] Furthermore, earlier provisions concerning a centrally planned economy were struck out of the new version.

A third occasion to revise the constitution was on March 8, 1990, and represented an overhaul of local government in preparation for elections to be held two months later. Instead of the administrative principle of democratic centralism, French-style communal assemblies and prefects were to form the basis of the new system. Central budgetary allocations were to be slashed and "self-government" (*samorząd*) was now also to carry with it self-financing responsibility.

A fourth major constitutional revision was enacted on September 27, 1990, and concerned the procedure for electing the president. Article 32 made the election direct, the term of office five years, and the powers of the office distinct from that of the parliament. In general terms, the president was "the supreme representative of the Polish state in internal and external affairs."

The most comprehensive constitutional reform act came with the passage of the so-called Little Constitution on October 17, 1992. It sought to distinguish further between the powers of the president and those of other branches of government. The title of the October act was a reference to Poland's earlier little constitutions, such as the February 20, 1919, act investing Piłsudski with the office of chief executive. As one constitutional specialist explained it, "This description is reserved for an act that regulates the fundamental principles and institutions of the political system, above all, the organization and method of functioning of state authority, for a transitional period."[17] In spite of the important revisions contained in the Little Constitution, parts of the 1952 constitution technically remained in force. For this reason, a completely new constitution rather than an extensive series of amendments to an earlier document remained a legal desideratum, though it inspired a political wrangle that remained unresolved as late as 1995.[18]

Originally drafted by the Sejm in August 1992, the Little Constitution was amended by the Senate and incorporated some of Wałęsa's proposals before being signed into law on November 17, 1992. The final version seemed to formalize the gridlock of Polish politics. The country was to have "a presidential-parliamentary system of government." The president's powers of forming governments were enhanced, and the Sejm was no longer designated as the highest organ of state power. The president could initiate legislation, veto it (subject to an override by a two-thirds majority of the Sejm), dissolve the legislature if it did not pass a budget within a three-month period, and exercise stewardship over defense and national security matters. The government was now empowered to rule by decree, but even here the president had veto power, in which case the matter would go to the Sejm for resolution. Certain subjects were off-limits for decrees: budget matters, constitutional issues, personal freedoms, and (as a concession to left-wing parties) social security measures.

Institutional Reform

Establishing a constitutional framework that sets out the political rules of the game and the institutions that allocate values in society is the most daunting challenge for a new regime. The political science literature on institutionalism can tell us which designs seem most appropriate to a country at a particular stage of economic development with a specific social and ethnic makeup and aiming at the consolidation of its new democracy. But let us begin the analysis of institutional change in Poland by referring to the pioneering work of an economic historian, Douglass North, on the evolution of economic structures.

For North, "institutions exist to reduce the uncertainties involved in human interaction. These uncertainties arise as a consequence of both the complexity of the problems to be solved and the problem-solving software (to use a computer analogy) possessed by the individual. There is nothing in the above statement that implies that the institutions are efficient."[19] North's interest is in understanding why some societies develop efficient, adaptive, growth-promoting institutions and others do not. The answer lies largely in a society's willingness to consider abandoning institutions that do not work: "It is essential to have rules that eliminate not only failed economic organization but failed political organization as well. The effective structure of rules, therefore, not only rewards successes, but also vetoes the survival of maladapted parts of the organizational structure."[20] Further, pursuing Friedrich Hayek's argument, North shows that "the society that permits the maximum generation of trials will be most likely to solve problems through time."[21]

This trial-and-error approach can work only if a degree of continuity and stability is guaranteed. In societies less complex than modern ones, informal constraints grounded primarily in codes of behavior ensured stability even as institutions underwent incremental change. Modern political systems can provide the stable conditions required for institutions to adapt to new exigencies by creating and enforcing formal constraints. According to North, "stability is accomplished by a complex set of constraints that include formal rules nested in a hierarchy, where each level is more costly to change than the previous one."[22] It is here that efficiency-promoting constitutional provisions and institutional designs become so important to the success of a new regime.

With the emergence of many new democracies in the 1980s, political scientists were drawn to the problematic linking democratic consolidation to an array of institutional variables. As two writers already noted in 1984, "political democracy depends not only on economic and social conditions but also on the design of political institutions."[23] Accordingly, the subsequent literature on democracy concentrated on the part played by such factors as presidential and parliamentary systems and party and electoral systems. In general, the consensus was that the rules that placed constraints on political actors had to be devised in such a way that actors found it in their interest to maintain rather than to subvert democracy.

The institutional choices available for consolidating democracies are very limited. Essentially, the question is, as put bluntly by Juan Linz and Arturo Valenzuela, "Presidential or parliamentary democracy: Does it make a difference?"[24] Seeking an answer to this question, Matthew Shugart and John Carey report that the breakdown rate has been 50 percent for presidential regimes and 44 percent for parliamentary systems. This result is largely inconclusive, then. Further, when we factor out Third World cases of chronic instability, parliamentary systems prove more prone to democratic reversal than presidential ones.[25]

Identifying the sources of threats to young democracies may suggest what type of institutional arrangement will prove more stabilizing. Some time ago Seymour Martin Lipset underscored the degree to which newly democratic regimes were judged by their current performance, making them more vulnerable to collapse in the face of economic or social crisis. Citizens in new democracies frequently fail to distinguish between the source of political authority (such as the constitution) and the agent of authority (the current government). The failures of a particular government become equated with flaws in the political system. New democracies cannot counter this presumption because they are, by definition, unable to invoke a record of past successes.[26] To make matters worse, ineffective or simply underachieving governments in new democracies confront the threat of breakdown because of the sudden free flow of information to citizens and their newly acquired rights of association and speech.[27]

The separation of powers is the most obvious way of deflecting public criticism of a particular government. But tensions between executive and legislative branches can impede overall regime efficacy, thereby exacerbating public discontent. Separation of powers between the two branches, together with the simultaneous legitimacy of the president and the legislature, contribute to stalemate when agendas and policies of the two conflict. Stalemate is further exacerbated when the president and the majority in the legislature belong to different political parties. Protection from concentration of power in one branch, as through an elaborate checks-and-balances system or through a semipresidential system in which institutional power sharing is formalized, can have the effect of inhibiting policy formulation and implementation. Key to ensuring both effective and responsible government is attaining an equilibrium state as described by Przeworski:

> To be stable and effective, democratic institutions must not generate governments unresponsive to the changing relations of political forces, governments free from the obligation to consult and concert when they formulate policy, governments unconstrained to obey rules when they implement them. Yet they also must not paralyze decisions and their implementation. All interests must be represented in the making of policy, but none should be able unilaterally to block its formulation and implementation.[28]

Pacts among democratic actors, including those in control of different branches of government, to suppress excessive political competition in the interests of democratic consolidation can prove especially functional for an emergent democracy.

Shugart and Carey list the possible benefits of presidential systems of government. They provide for accountability: Popular election of the president for a fixed term cannot be overridden by shifts in coalitions, as in parliamentary systems, and the president's performance is transparent to voters. They ensure identifiability: Voters have a clearer idea of what alternative governments would do, and therefore they can vote prospectively, in anticipation of contenders' performances. These systems lock in mutual checks between president and legislature, since each has an independent popular mandate; in parliamentary systems, in contrast, the prime minister (and the cabinet) and the parliament have a joint stake in surviving as long as possible and not facing early elections, which can lead to muted opposition. Finally, by virtue of being above partisan politics, the executive in a presidential system can serve as arbiter of political conflict and mediator of legislative disputes.

At the same time, the presidential system, in which the chief executive has an independent mandate from the people, has its disadvantages. The president may be intolerant of legislative opposition to his policies. In attempting to break down immobilism, he may try to bypass the legislature and rule by decree or to force constitutional reform favoring his office. (Both options have been tried in Poland.) But if an "immobilized" president accepts his fate while remaining committed to democracy, the resulting political stalemate and the inability to handle crisis and instability may eventually incline the military to intervene in politics, as in Chile in 1973.[29] Again, evidence of political turmoil in Poland in 1992 indicates that this scenario is not as far-fetched as it may appear.

The threat of stalemate seems to be much more benign in a parliamentary system. A prime minister usually belongs to the same party as the majority in parliament. Should the prime minister lose the support of the legislative majority, institutional measures such as dissolution of parliament, a vote of no confidence in the government, or asking another leader to form a new government minimize the danger of prolonged deadlock. Above all, parliamentary systems ensure wide representation for various groups. Even if a single party wins a parliamentary majority, the largest losing party can assume the role of official opposition while all the other parties begin to work toward increasing their representation next time. Representation is particularly important for new democracies, since all significant political actors learn to have a stake in continuing with the democratic game. Presidentialism is more of a zero-sum game: One group's victory is the other groups' loss, and this for the duration of the president's term in office. Juan Linz concludes, therefore, that "parliamentarism provides a more flexible and adaptable institutional context for the establishment and consolidation of democracy."[30]

However, a parliament characterized by a fragmented party system and shaky coalition governments can engender political instability on its own.[31] The resulting political chaos can mimic the problems of stalemate between president and legislature and may even provoke an antidemocratic coup.[32] The threat of breakdown in this case leads to the inescapable conclusion that a strong party system enhances the prospects for political stability. In particular, a two-party system in which each of the contenders must appeal to a broad section of the citizenry is likely to produce moderation, accommodation, and aggregation of diverse interests.[33] In turn, the number of parties in a political system is a function of the electoral system, that is, whether elections are decided by simple majority in single-member constituencies, by proportional representation in multiple-member districts, or by a combination of the two. As we shall see in the case of Poland, as the probability of a parliamentary rather than a presidential system increased, manipulating electoral rules so as to produce a strong party system became very important in ensuring political stability.

A presidential system characterized by a strong executive is an unlikely outcome of democratic transitions from communist rule. Indeed, the raison d'être for extrication from authoritarianism is the creation of institutional pluralism, wherein many parties and many bodies share power and check one another. Keeping actors committed to democracy means dispersing power widely. But political leadership remains pivotal during transitions. One writer has described how the behavior of political elites could stabilize or undermine democratic government in a pluralist society. Where socioeconomic cleavages are deep and easily converted into political cleavages, adversarial politics within the elite may deepen political fragmentation. Consensual elite behavior can, by contrast, counterbalance societal cleavages and produce consociational democracy.[34] Popular perceptions of leadership in Poland have highlighted adversarial relations, but the daunting task of coalition building to form governments has hinged more on consensual, pragmatic politics.

The balance of power between executive and legislative branches of government has had particular importance in Poland. The powerful personality and broad ambitions of President Wałęsa have commonly been held to be the main reason for concern with the extent of executive power. Cynics in Poland depicted Wałęsa as seeking to establish the dictatorship of the proletariat that the communists had failed to provide (the reference being to Wałęsa's working-class origins).[35] But a sequence of largely ineffectual and unstable government coalitions, together with bickering among the many parties represented in the Sejm and the fact that it is virtually in continuous session, have drawn further attention to the problem of executive-legislative relations even when we discount Wałęsa's role. In May 1992 the president himself described this three-cornered conflict as a "Bermuda triangle" that had drawn in himself, the Sejm, and the government.

In the Polish case, Andrew Michta lists four events as crucial in shaping the hybrid presidential-parliamentary system:[36] (1) the election for president in 1990, (2) the elections for the parliament in 1991, (3) the "war at the top" between Wałęsa and Sejm leaders over the respective powers and responsibilities of the president, the parliament, and the prime minister and the cabinet, and (4) approval of the

Little Constitution by both parliament and president in 1992, resulting in the compromise of a mixed presidential-parliamentary system. One writer has summed up contrasting views of the hybrid constitution: "Some articles in the Polish press denounced the document as creating a 'Sejmocracy,' while others complained that it gives the president too much power." But a Sejm member signaled the main achievement of the Little Constitution: "This bill's greatest advantage is that it can be passed at all."[37]

The Little Constitution dropped wording describing the Sejm as the supreme authority in the country. The president was now given the right to appoint the prime minister and to approve the prime minister's government. If this government failed to win a vote of confidence (by an absolute majority) from the Sejm within fourteen days, it would be the turn of the Sejm to appoint a new government within twenty-one days and obtain the absolute majority (Article 59). If this failed, too, president and Sejm each had one more chance to produce an approved government—this time by only a simple majority. Although the president had many powers—dissolving parliament, initiating legislation, calling a referendum, convening meetings of the Council of Ministers (the government), making judicial appointments, and ratifying ministerial appointments for defense, internal security, and foreign policy—certain presidential decisions required the countersignature of the prime minister or other minister concerned. Furthermore, the government was given decree power in certain domains, and here again, the president had to countersign.

In addition to the presidency and the legislature, many other government institutions have recently been overhauled. Some have been discarded and replaced by new structures. Functional ministries such as defense, foreign affairs, and internal affairs have been remodeled and restaffed. The Supreme Court and the Constitutional Tribunal have been given greater responsibility for the impartial mediation of disputes, though decisions of the latter are still subject to a two-thirds override by the Sejm. A completely new state security agency has replaced the communist security apparatus. Other ancillary institutions inherited from the antecedent regime have, sometimes surprisingly, survived by being reorganized rather than scrapped. These include the Central Office of Planning, the Central Office of Statistics, the National Bank, the Main Control Office, the Ombudsman, and the Office of the Council of Ministers. New institution building has been aimed primarily at expediting economic transformation. It includes the Economic Committee of the Council of Ministers, the Social Committee of the Council of Ministers, the Ministry of Property Transformation, the Ministry of Foreign Economic Cooperation, and the Antimonopoly Office. Local government has been given new responsibilities and revenue bases, while a return to an intermediary level of administration (the *powiat* or county) has been debated at length. Changes in political and administration structures are intended, therefore, to expedite the processes of democratization, decentralization, and de-etatization.

One other important institution set up by the Sejm was the Commission on Constitutional Responsibility. Among its tasks was to examine charges of violations of the constitution leveled against former political leaders. In 1993 it considered whether legal proceedings should be initiated against Jaruzelski and Kiszczak for having destroyed minutes of Politburo meetings held between 1982 and 1989. Jaruzelski had argued that the documents had to be destroyed because the inexperience of some Politburo members had led to their making statements that could prove compromising. More important, according to Jaruzelski, they recorded sensitive negotiations with church and opposition figures who could be harmed by revelation of their bargaining stances. The majority of members of the commission, chaired by SdRP deputy Jerzy Wiatr, decided to recommend to the National Assembly that it suspend the legal proceedings against Jaruzelski and Kiszczak. Earlier, the commission had found charges of economic wrongdoing by members of Hanna Suchocka's government unfounded. Some deputies had felt that her ministers had profited from their position in government. Referring to both cases, Wiatr contended that, in contrast to the same commission in the previous Sejm, his social-democratic-majority one had demonstrated impartiality in judging communists and noncommunists alike.

Ruling Coalition and Leadership Style

Explaining the democratic transition requires us to examine political leadership. A full, systematic analysis of the bargaining skills, political intuition, personality traits, and leadership styles of all the individuals who participated in the pacted transition or in crafting the new democratic order would be impossible here. Furthermore, the factors of luck, timing, sequence of discrete events, and serendipitous processes also affected particular outcomes, as did nonrational and particularistic aspects of decision making and coalition formation. The focus of this section, necessarily selective, is on the "war at the top" in the early years of post-communism. We can learn much about the political style of the Third Republic's first leaders by describing how they engaged each other in a struggle for power while a power vacuum still existed and the rules of the game had not been fixed.

The personal relationships between president and prime ministers (see Table 5.2) have varied. Mazowiecki was originally selected by Wałęsa to serve as prime minister in 1989 because he promised to rein in the Warsaw intelligentsia of which Wałęsa had always been deeply suspicious. Mazowiecki soon proved independent-minded as Wałęsa's stature as national leader began to erode.[38] The schism between Wałęsa and his former Solidarity advisers was formalized when Mazowiecki decided to run for president. Wałęsa's victory over the prime minister and the broader Solidarity camp in presidential elections in December 1990 raised fears that he would create an imperial presidency. Only the president could now claim a direct mandate to govern from the people; the Solidarity government was, after all, an offspring of the tainted contract Sejm.

Wałęsa turned to the Solidarity lawyer Jan Olszewski to form a new government to replace Mazowiecki's, but Olszewski was reluctant to head a cabinet in which

TABLE 5.2   Presidents and Prime Ministers in the Third Republic

Presidents	Elected	Supported by	Left office
Wojciech Jaruzelski	August 1989[a]	postcommunists, Solidarity	December 1990
Lech Wałęsa	December 1990	Solidarity	December 1995

Prime Ministers	Appointed		
Tadeusz Mazowiecki	August 1989	Solidarity	December 1990
Jan Krzysztof Bielecki	December 1990	KLD, PC	December 1991
Jan Olszewski	December 1991	PC, ZChN, PL, PSL	June 1992
Waldemar Pawlak	June 1992[b]	PSL	July 1992
Hanna Suchocka	July 1992	UD, KLD, ZChN, PSL	October 1993[c]
Waldemar Pawlak	October 1993	PSL, SdRP	March 1995
Józef Oleksy	March 1995	SdRP, PSL	to present

[a] By the National Assembly.
[b] Nominated prime minister but unable to form a government.
[c] Lost a vote of confidence on May 28, 1993, but headed a caretaker government until October.

the architect of the reform program known as "shock therapy," Leszek Balcerowicz, remained as finance minister. Unable to persuade Olszewski to drop this precondition, Wałęsa selected Jan Krzysztof Bielecki, a leader of the free-market Liberal-Democratic Congress (KLD), a private businessman, and a supporter of the strict monetarist views espoused by Balcerowicz. Despite the rhetoric of a strict monetarist policy, Bielecki's government ran up an enormous budget deficit. Bielecki concurred with Wałęsa that new elections to the parliament should be held swiftly, but Mazowiecki and the majority of the Sejm felt that the president was manipulating the political process for his own ends and aiming to enhance the powers of the presidency at the cost of parliament. By an overwhelming vote of 314 to 18, with 40 abstentions, the Sejm decided to hold elections only in October 1991.

Following these elections, in which the KLD fared less well than expected, Wałęsa was compelled to appoint a new prime minister. In December, after he had proposed first a continuation of the Bielecki government and then a cabinet headed by Geremek, his long-serving adviser, a center-right coalition in the Sejm forced him to designate Olszewski as prime minister. Wałęsa's defeat on the issue of an early election had already drawn attention to increasing tension between executive and legislative branches. The fact that twenty-nine parties were represented in a fragmented Sejm after the 1991 elections made Wałęsa's task of assembling a coalition sympathetic to him even more difficult. Haggling between Olszewski and Wałęsa over the composition of the cabinet further delayed Olszewski's formally taking power. The new prime minister's apparent determination to abandon the

International Monetary Fund (IMF)–designed austerity program—evidenced earlier in his scepticism about Balcerowicz as finance minister—was vividly depicted in his assertion that the hidden hand of the market often turned out to be the hand of an economic huckster.

Olszewski was committed to enhancing the power of the prime minister, and he quickly replaced Wałęsa's appointee as defense minister—even though the still-operative, much-amended 1952 constitution gave the president broad authority over security and defense policies. The showdown between Olszewski's defense ministry and Wałęsa's national security bureau represented more than a clash of personalities; it brought into question the fundamental question of executive-legislative relations and who was responsible for what policy.

In February 1992, frustrated by what he saw as an obstructionist parliament and a meddling president, Olszewski asked the Sejm for emergency decree powers but was unable to secure them. Then Olszewski's civilian defense minister, Jan Parys, decided to pension off his predecessor, Navy Rear Admiral Piotr Kołodziejczyk, and this led to an attempt at a wider purge of senior military officers supposedly compromised by service under the communists. Parys charged that Wałęsa's own chief of staff, Mieczysław Wachowski, had planned to organize a coup by the army general staff to end the purported anarchy of democracy. Charges and countercharges of coup plotting brought high drama to Polish politics, and the prospects of democratic consolidation seemed bleak.

As if this were not enough, in spring 1992 several sealed envelopes were presented to Wałęsa by Olszewski's interior minister. They contained the names of some sixty persons who, it was alleged, had been collaborators and agents of the communist regime. The "revelations" contained in these documents included copies of Wałęsa's purported loyalty pledges to the communist secret police after the December 1970 political unrest. Olszewski was clearly behind the disclosure of secret police dossiers on prominent officials, though he may have been unaware that some files contained forged documents. In reality, Olszewski's effort to disclose confidential files on political leaders was a strategy to sweep away established political actors and replace them with new ones.

In summary, the inability of prime minister and president to achieve any type of modus vivendi, Olszewski's effort to obtain decree powers, a tug-of-war over who was in charge of the armed forces, charges of a coup attempt, and efforts to embarrass Wałęsa with the collaboration issue, all led to Olszewski's removal in June 1992. Some observers claim that the dismissal of Poland's most anticommunist prime minister was itself a subtle coup by the political elites of the old communist regime.[39]

In June 1992 the PSL leader Waldemar Pawlak was asked by Wałęsa to form a government, but disputes between potential coalition partners over budgetary proposals and the PSL's own suspect past prevented him from obtaining the necessary parliamentary support. We recall that in its earlier incarnation as the ZSL this party had served as an auxiliary of the communist regime. Furthermore,

Pawlak himself was never active in the Solidarity movement. In July, after Wałęsa had threatened "extraordinary measures" (possibly a dissolution of parliament and new elections), a seven-party coalition rallied around the Poznań lawyer and UD member Hanna Suchocka as prime minister. Suchocka's career path was not as tainted as Pawlak's. It is true that before joining the Citizens' Movement for Democratic Action (Ruch Obywatelski Akcja Demokratyczna—ROAD)—the forerunner to the UD—she had belonged to the SD, also a satellite of the communists before 1989. Also widely publicized was the fact that Suchocka had only abstained from rather than voted against the historic martial-law decree, rubber-stamped by the Sejm in 1982 so as to legitimate martial law retroactively. Predictably, while she was prime minister she and the UD were the target of charges of "recommunization." Still, Suchocka had also voted against Solidarity's delegalization in 1982 and been expelled from the SD. As prime minister she kept her distance from the UD's more left-wing faction.

Having survived initial attacks on her character, Suchocka was able to establish a stable parliamentary coalition while maintaining a modus vivendi with the president. After a period of stormy relations between president and three prime ministers, the relationship between Wałęsa and Suchocka became a model of coexistence. Pundits reported that Poland's first woman prime minister brought elegance, tact, and articulateness to political leadership—qualities all missing in the president. The complementarity of the two leaders ended only in September 1993, when Suchocka's party suffered electoral defeat. Not least of Suchocka's accomplishments were her successful visits to European capitals, enhancing Poland's image at a time when the country's young democratic order had come under attack. It was during her term that the Little Constitution, regulating the relationship between president and prime minister, was adopted.

Even during the Suchocka-Wałęsa entente and even with the enactment of a revised constitution, Poland still felt the magnetic pull of the "Bermuda triangle" described by Wałęsa—the three-cornered struggle for power among president, prime minister, and parliament. A pivotal issue was whether the military forces reported to the defense minister or the president—the subject that sparked charges of coup attempts in the Olszewski-Wałęsa "war at the top." The Little Constitution skirted the matter: Article 35 stated that the president was the commander in chief of the armed forces. But with regard to the prime minister's choice of ministers of defense, internal affairs, and foreign affairs, the president had to be consulted (Article 61); it seemed that his formal approval was not required. The matter was still not resolved in June 1994, when the National Defense Committee (Komitet Obrony Kraju) tabled discussion of the issue, and, indeed, took on renewed urgency in November 1994, when Prime Minister Pawlak eventually succumbed to Wałęsa's pressure for the removal of Defense Minister Kołodziejczyk for a second time. Still, Pawlak insisted that he would make the choice of Kołodziejczyk's successor. Eventually the conflict between Pawlak and Wałęsa extended to other cabinet appointments, including foreign minister, as well. Wałęsa also accused the PSL leader of stalling on privatization and refused to ratify the government budget that Pawlak had proposed. The PSL itself was divided on how to react to the president's confrontational tactics, and in March 1995 Pawlak stepped down as prime minister.

The largest party in the ruling coalition, the SdRP, nominated Józef Oleksy, then marshal of the Sejm, as Pawlak's replacement. SdRP leader Alexander Kwaśniewski acquiesced to his deputy's selection as prime minister, preferring to wait himself for the late-1995 presidential contest. Whereas Pawlak had been uncommunicative, the affable Oleksy brought a more colorful style to the office. An economist by training, he had served as a high-level PZPR apparatchik throughout the 1980s until becoming the reform-minded leader of the PZPR's parliamentary caucus in 1989. Wałęsa confirmed Oleksy as prime minister in March 1995 and signed the budget into law after he had secured approval for his own nominees for the defense, foreign affairs, and security portfolios.

Wałęsa's gamble in forcing the excommunists to assume direct power was predicated on their becoming entrapped in a political morass during the months leading up to the presidential elections. Thus, by April Wałęsa was taunting Oleksy for planning to travel to Moscow (as U.S. President Clinton intended to do as well) to attend celebrations commemorating the fiftieth anniversary of the Allies' victory in Europe during World War II. Wałęsa said that he would remain at home on this important occasion for Poles. He added that the constitution gave the president the responsibility for directing foreign policy and therefore Oleksy could not represent the Polish state during his Moscow visit. His gamble in confirming an excommunist as prime minister and then limiting his autonomy was likely to backfire, however, if the SLD skillfully exploited its new power and visibility to enhance the chances of an excommunist's being elected to succeed Wałęsa as president.

It is unclear whether Wałęsa proved to be a strong or a weak president. He lost to the Sejm on the issue of the first electoral law, which legislators had insisted should be hyperproportional. Wałęsa had wanted to set minimal thresholds for Sejm representation, thereby limiting representation for minor parties.[40] When a revised electoral law more in line with his intentions was passed to govern representation to the Sejm elected in fall 1993, the socialist alliance's victory was not what Wałęsa had had in mind when he had first suggested drafting an electoral law that would produce strong parties. He failed to obtain approval from the Sejm for a version of the Little Constitution that would have redefined the powers of the executive. His political style—populist forays into factories and dairy cooperatives—was attacked for bringing the dignity of the presidency into question. His response—that he had no interest in becoming a "champagne-drinking president"—resounded like a statement from a communist leader. His self-description of his leadership style—"I pull, I push, I initiate"—seemed to many citizens crudely manipulative. His expressed concern about the emergence of a "political mafia" prompted him to counter the rise of a strong nonsocialist party in parliament at a time when the excommunists were weak. This strategy boomeranged when the socialist alliance emerged as the strong party. The fear of an emergent hegemonic force or leader was Wałęsa's pretext for dismissing even his closest associates. As he put it in 1992, "That is why I am merciless: My price is losing friends; theirs, losing their posts." But this penchant for waging war at the top with other members of the former Solidarity leadership and regularly purging his close associates, even within his own office, may have meant that he outsmarted only himself in the end.

The six prime ministers who formed governments since Kiszczak's failure to forge a last communist cabinet had contrasting career paths. They included a Catholic intellectual, a private entrepreneur, a Solidarity lawyer, a youthful farmer, a woman who had previously belonged to a communist satellite party, and a Marxist-trained economist. Certainly this complemented the background of the president—an electrician by trade. The diversity of political leaders is suggestive of a decline in the status of intellectuals. As with Polonia Reconstituta in 1918, intellectuals who had struggled alongside other social groups for an independent country seem to have been marginalized once the task was accomplished. Dissident intellectuals were seen as political amateurs, and new leaders, less well-known, needed only a respectable past to launch a political career. But that is not so different from the situation in established democratic systems—an important sign that democratic politics in Poland are normal.

Political Parties and Groups

Democracy is often equated with political pluralism, a multiparty system, and free elections. It is of central importance, therefore, to examine the political groups that give Poland its democratic character—the party system and its evolution since 1989 and the electorate and electoral behavior during this same period.

Political Parties

Since 1989 Polish politics have been rapidly professionalized, and we can identify two major types of political parties. The first, of which the KPN and the Christian National Union [ZChN] are examples, is based on a return to narrow national and religious loyalties. One writer noted before the 1993 parliamentary elections that "the new parties in Polish politics are Catholic, nationalistic, and right wing. They claim for themselves a continuity of resistance against communism, and they reject dissident intellectuals as left wing and cosmopolitan, elitist and alienated."[41] The second type, the most important of which was the UD, is a catchall party seeking to advance broad political programs. All the parties have certain common characteristics, however. As two observers wrote in 1992, today "all perceptions are dominated by a super-sensitivity to Western reactions."[42]

The first six alliances/parties in Table 5.1 are the ones that won seats in the 1993 legislative elections. Other parties that conducted campaigns follow; their importance may have been greater in earlier years of the democratic Sejm. Some of the parties included in the table no longer exist as separate entities and have merged with others. All of them have been torn between the ambition to hold power, wariness about entering into alliances in which they may become junior partners, and, for parties tracing their origins back to Solidarity, fear of being dominated by Wałęsa. At the outset most of the parties were conservative, but they miscalculated in two ways: They competed for ground among themselves, each seemingly wishing to lay claim to a Thatcherite-type pedigree, and most of them moved too quickly to the right, assuming that the electorate's anticommunism had already put it there or that it would soon follow. In another respect, however, the Polish right did reflect the two main variants of political conservatism long found in Western Europe: a traditionalist approach stressing family, God, and the nation, often very populist in form, and a neoconservativism stressing economic individualism and free markets and associated with urban professional groups. In Poland conservative parties have ranged from the tradition-oriented, such as the ZChN and the PSL, to the laissez-faire, such as the KLD or the Union of Political Realism (UPR). A cluster of political orientations distinguishes the conservative parties from others.[43] The dichotomy presented in Table 5.3 is designed to underscore substantive differences between two ideal-type political orientations, but in practice contemporary Polish parties picked-and-chose from both lists, thereby producing the schismatic tendencies observed in the party-formation process after 1989.

Mapping the differences between the constituencies of political parties requires a separate framework, and here the notion of political fields developed by East European specialists can be applied to the Polish case.[44] The liberal field takes in the intellectual elite, especially the technical intelligentsia, and the new entrepreneurial and incipient middle class.[45] This was the political space disputed by the UD and the KLD until their merger in the Freedom Union (UW) in 1994. The Christian-nationalist field is located between the emergent entrepreneurial (capitalist)

TABLE 5.3   Main Political Orientations of the Polish Electorate

Left of Center	*Right of Center*
Western	Nationalist
Secular	Clerical
Urban	Rural
Industrial	Agrarian
Civil rights	Social order
Social liberalism	Conservatism
Political liberalism	Authoritarianism
Meta-communism	Anticommunism
Interdependence	National defense

class and the working (above all, the labor aristocracy) and peasant classes. This center-right field was represented by the ZChN, the Center Accord (PC), and a plethora of peasant parties, but it seems to have had least appeal for the electorate in 1993. The social democratic field pulls together the traditional working class and the intelligentsia. The SdRP is theoretically the major force within this field, but other groups operating in it include the Union of Labor (UP) of Ryszard Bugaj and Zbigniew Bujak, Solidarność '80, and Labor Solidarity (Solidarność Pracy). Figure 5.1 locates some of these parties in terms of three principal axes.

Not only have parties often splintered but also, conversely, they have entered into electoral alliances with other groups to capture votes and win seats, adopted different names during electoral campaigns, and joined forces to form clubs within parliament. For example, the ZChN ran in the 1991 parliamentary elections under the label Catholic Electoral Action (WAK). For the 1993 parliamentary elections, a similar Catholic alliance was called Fatherland. For the 1995 presidential elections, the ZChN became part of the Alliance for Poland. In turn,

Figure 5.1   Parties and Political Space in the 1990s

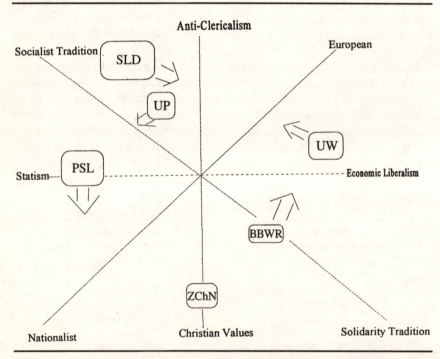

Arrows represent directional tendencies since the September 1993 parliamentary elections.

Source: Adapted from "Jak powstały nasze rysunki?" *Polityka,* no. 28 (July 10, 1993), p. 15.

various offshoots of the former communist system such as the OPZZ trade unions joined with the SdRP to constitute the Alliance of the Democratic Left (SLD). And again, the numerous peasant parties have regularly formed parliamentary blocs as well as electoral alliances. In short, individual parties and party alliances have been fluid in Poland since 1989, and this makes tracking all of them very difficult. The new electoral law for the 1993 elections did, however, put an end to political fragmentation within parliament, bringing about more of a crystallization of the party system.

The strongest electoral showing of any party in 1991 was that of the UD. Its leaders claimed that it had no ideology or program,[46] but its internal divisions were precisely over matters of principle. The UD consisted of a recognizably left-wing ROAD group, centrist Mazowiecki supporters, and, until 1992, a right-wing faction under Aleksander Hall. The latter group was largely fellow-travelers of the KLD and, in October 1992, broke away to form the Polish Convention (Konwencja Polska). Given the diversity of views it contained, the UD held together for a long time by projecting itself as a movement that was liberal on social issues but monetarist on economic ones. The first postcommunist government of Mazowiecki was in practice a UD prototype; the UD was officially founded in December 1990. The government of Suchocka, in power from July 1992 to September 1993, was a carefully crafted coalition based on the UD's alliance with the right-wing nationalist ZChN but also backed by the KLD, the Polish Economic Alliance business lobby, two Solidarity farmers' parties—the Peasant Alliance (PL) and the Christian-Peasant Alliance (SChL)—and the small Christian Democratic Party (PChD). In sum, the often-praised Suchocka government represented a seven-party coalition that commanded two hundred seats in the Sejm—the most successful instance of coalition building in Poland to date. Electoral defeat in September 1993 led the UD to join forces with the KLD to form the UW in 1994.

The KLD served as a critical mass for the Bielecki government, which spanned the period between Mazowiecki's resignation and Olszewski's nomination. It was a neoconservative grouping that aggressively pursued a Thatcherite image and invoked its supposed close organizational ties with the British Conservative Party. It enjoyed particular strength in the Gdańsk region, the origin of its leadership. While in government its leadership was accused of using U.S.-style pork-barrel politics to increase its popularity. In fall 1993 it failed to capture enough votes to be represented in the Sejm and agreed to serve as a junior partner to the UD in the UW.

The right-wing ZChN formed one of the backbones of the Olszewski government. This party, too, suffered internal tensions that eventually resulted in the expulsion of one of its leaders, Antoni Macierewicz. Its head until 1994, Wiesław Chrzanowski, was implicated in secret police work when files were released in June 1992. As with Catholic parties in France and Italy, an important constituency for the ZChN was older women. After its 1993 election debacle, the party joined the conservative Alliance for Poland.

The controversial Olszewski administration was propped up by other parties as well. These included a number of peasant organizations—the PSL, the PL, and the Solidarity Polish Peasant Party (Polskie Stronnictwo Ludowe "Solidarność" or PSL "S"). Most important, Olszewski was backed by the PC, an increasingly nationalist party that at the time still enjoyed "most-favored party" status with Wałęsa.

The strategy of the right-wing KPN was to stay in opposition in the hope of eventually capitalizing on widespread social discontent. It was critical of the IMF-driven government economy policy and opposed the 5 percent ceiling on the 1992 budget deficit. Nationalist in political and economic matters but also etatist, it was the greatest loser in the 1993 elections, receiving some 200,000 votes less than in 1991. Its membership fell at this time to 27,000.

Over time the PSL elbowed out most of the other peasant parties. Given that the rural population in Poland accounts for 37 percent of the electorate, the PSL has become a strategic political actor. The nomination of its leader, Waldemar Pawlak, to form a government in early summer 1992 gave it added visibility even while it was being criticized as an offshoot of the ancien régime. In 1994 the SdRP formed a coalition government with the PSL and consented to the nomination of Pawlak as prime minister.

Until 1993 the SLD was frozen out of all government coalitions because of its roots in the old communist party (PZPR). It played the parliamentary game effectively, however, and gave informal support to the governments headed by Olszewski and Suchocka. Its electoral performance has been more consistent than that of most other parties. It controls traditional socialist bastions such as the light industrial center Łódź, in the center of Poland, and the mining region around Sosnowiec, in Silesia. It is also by far the most disciplined of all parties internally. The SLD was regularly defended from ultrarightist attacks by the UD, which raised the suspicions of those who believed that the Magdalenka process had resulted in an implicit deal between the communist and opposition establishments. When, in November 1994, the SLD and the UD's successor, the UW, reached an agreement on who should be president of Warsaw, some political observers speculated that this marked the beginning of even closer cooperation between the excommunists and the exdissidents of the old Polish People's Republic.

During late 1992, several additional political groups gained widespread attention. The former defense minister Jan Parys set up a new organization, the Movement for the Third Republic (Ruch dla Trzeciej Rzeczyspospolitej—RTR), whose demagogic line was that Poland's democracy, and even its sovereignty were being threatened by Wałęsa's dictatorial, "soft-on-communists" approach. In turn, Olszewski, also upset by Wałęsa, set up the Christian Democratic Forum (Chrześcijańsko-Demokratyczny Forum—ChDF) and received the backing of the former ZChN leader and interior minister Antoni Macierewicz. This led to the formation of a new umbrella organization, the Movement for the Republic (RdR). At the end of 1992 these political figures, all disenchanted with Wałęsa's presidency, campaigned vigorously throughout the country on the platform of eradicating all remaining communist influence. Paradoxically, then, by this stage eliminating communist influence had become a euphemism for attacking Wałęsa as part of the ancien régime.

In summer 1993 Wałęsa seemed partially to embrace the idea of a presidential party that would contest elections and be represented in parliament. The Nonparty Bloc for Reform (BBWR) failed to capture voters' enthusiasm and in the September 1993 elections barely achieved the minimum 5 percent threshold for representation in the Sejm. Yet one of its members, Zbigniew Religa, captured more votes (over a half-million) in winning a Senate seat than any other candidate. A nationally known surgeon specializing in heart transplants for children, Religa became estranged from the BBWR after its electoral failure, and the party leadership was entrusted to Jerzy Gwizdza.

The closest thing to a right-wing national front that Poland has seen is a Farmers' Self-Defense Union (Liga Samoobrony Chłopów). Led by Andrzej Lepper, the movement undertook militant action in 1993, often defied police orders, and engaged in protests intended to defend farmers' interests. The Russian nationalist leader Vladimir Zhirinovsky met with Lepper during his visit to Poland in 1993. A year later, Lepper was jailed and more moderate Union supporters broke away to form a new group headed by Janusz Bryczkowski.

The Electorate

Contrary to the widespread impression that it was communism that had shattered a long-standing commitment to Polish democracy, prior to 1989 there really had only been one genuinely free election in the twentieth century. The first one held after independence, in 1919, was provisional. Those in 1922 proved to be the first and last free elections of the Second Republic. The 1928 and 1930 elections were rigged by the Piłsudskiites. In 1935 and 1938 elections were boycotted by an opposition claiming that they would not be fair. Setting aside electoral support for ethnic minority parties (22 percent of the 1922 vote), voting was fairly evenly divided among right-wing parties (29 percent), center parties (24 percent), and leftist parties (25 percent). Ten political clubs were organized in the Sejm in 1922, the largest being the National Democrats (98 seats of 444). Given that ND leader Dmowski often expressed contempt for the democratic process and that Piłsudski refused to participate in the procedures established by the 1921 constitution, the period 1922–1926, in which Polish democracy supposedly flowered, was dominated by antidemocratic sentiment. The fragmented and ineffective Sejm became an institution fostering popular discontent and alienation. Democratic values came to be cherished only after 1926, and then by the center and left opposition marginalized by Piłsudski's coup. The rightist parties espoused authoritarianism, and the original BBWR (Nonparty Bloc for Cooperation with the Government)—formed originally for the 1928 electoral campaign—became a figleaf for the fact that pluralism no longer existed. In some of these respects, the Third Republic is strikingly similar to its interwar precursor.

Elections in the Third Republic have produced different outcomes, but—what is perhaps easily overlooked—they have also involved different issues. In June 1989 the single issue for the electorate was the division between "us, Solidarity" and "you, communists." But as Solidarity took power it disintegrated into different factions. If the 1989 election triggered the transition to democracy, Solidarity's fragmentation produced the political pluralism that is the cement of a liberal-democratic system.

In the years following the roundtable agreement, the political landscape changed immeasurably. Whereas elite-focused research had its rationale in the communist period and the study of civil society provided many insights into the political system of late communism, the research agenda of the 1990s has naturally shifted to the study of electoral behavior.

It is ironic, therefore, that the largest single bloc of the Polish electorate is comprised of nonvoters—those formally not involved in, identifying with, or contributing to the public sphere at election time. During the 1991 parliamentary elections in Poland, 57 percent of eligible voters did not cast their ballots, about the same level of abstention as in the May 1990 local elections. In the 1993 elections abstention was still 48 percent. Although there may be traditional class explanations for the nonvoting group—that they consist largely of the less educated and poorer sectors of society, in this way resembling nonvoters in Western countries—they are unhelpful in explaining the high rate of abstention during the politically charged transition process. Other explanations may be advanced: A widespread sense of political inefficacy has not been fully dispelled by the transition to democracy;[47] the lack of clear and consistent political orientations and commitments on the part of postcommunist parties has produced ambivalence in voters; many experience difficulty with partisan identification; there is a nagging sense of not having meaningful choices despite the range of parties competing for office; and many citizens are preoccupied with survival in very difficult economic times. Nonvoting may also be a policy-oriented decision. The consensus among parties in favor of a market economy, the accompanying public-sector sell-offs, and austerity measures received only lukewarm support from a substantial proportion of the electorate, and accordingly, abstention was a form of protest for these voters. Variations in levels of abstention in Poland might also be understood in terms of the categories of Western psephology (studies of electoral behavior), such as regional (industrial versus agrarian), generational (older versus younger), and psychological (organization joiners versus nonjoiners). Finally, nonvoting seems to have had a political geography; the highest rates of participation were recorded in Galicia (the area near Kraków that was once under the Habsburgs) and the industrial region of Pomerania (Poznań and its vicinity, once Prussian) and the lowest in the former Russian-administered Congress Poland (the provinces east of Warsaw) and, next-lowest, the recovered territories (formerly German) in Silesia, where massive postwar resettlement had created social problems such as crime and alcoholism.[48]

Among the reasons Poles have voted as they have are motivations also prevalent within Western democratic electorates. Voters are concerned with pocketbook issues and support the party that is perceived to be committed to expanding the benefits available for a specific group. Choice voting behavior, then, seeks to maximize expected utility. Voters' calculations are also based on the individual utility accruing to them from their party's holding power in the legislature. Such solitary benefits may be more important to certain social groups than to others, but it would seem that they would be especially valued in a society making the transition from a command to a market economy. Here opportunities for individual benefits are tempting given the impression that the playing field is now level and a tabula rasa exists. Thus, entrepreneurs, actual and prospective, seek *solitary* benefits more energetically than a social class conscious of its *collective* interests and of the threats to them, such as industrial workers at large plants threatened with closure. Expectations about individual and group benefits from a particular party at a particular time are, therefore, an underlying source of voting preference. For example, members of the intelligentsia largely viewed Mazowiecki as the best guarantor of individual benefits, while workers and peasants saw their class interests as best protected by their respective class-oriented parties (Wałęsa's original Citizens' Committees, still then umbilically linked to Solidarity, and the PSL).

An electoral factor related to expectations is identity. As in Western democracies, voters use elections to affirm self-identity or group identity. In the case of an emergent market economy and liberal democracy, voters seek to create new identities for themselves as prospective entrepreneurs, independent journalists, larger-scale farmers, and so on. The KLD appealed to voters who fantasized about being successful business persons. However, the process of defining new political identities has been slow in developing since the division between "us" (anticommunists) and "them" (communists) became obsolete in the 1990s. Survey data have consistently revealed that approximately two-thirds of Polish respondents do not identify with any particular party and over 90 percent do not belong to a political party. The emerging Polish middle class appears not yet to have become fully aware of its own interests. Generally, it continues to engage in the kind of political and economic behavior it pursued in the communist era—ignoring the state and its institutions. Paradoxically, only ancien-régime groups such as blue-collar workers, economic managers, and bureaucrats in the pay of the state seem to possess well-defined political interests that the SLD has tapped. The crystallization of the party system is likely to help voters better define new political identities for themselves.

Voting may be based on personalist politics, that is, support for or opposition to individual politicians regardless of their party tickets. Without a presidential party of his own, Wałęsa evolved into a leader supported or opposed primarily on personal grounds. More subtle evidence of personalist voting behavior in Poland came from the 1991 Senate elections: Only five of forty-nine constituencies returned members of the same party while forty-four split their tickets, indicating that voters were selecting individuals rather than party lists.

Voting can, of course, be issue-oriented, too. Especially in the formative period of a new regime, this represents a key source of electoral behavior. A plurality of alternative futures exists as voters and leaders select from a menu of choices: the role of government, the fate of the welfare state, changes in social legislation, economic priorities, the status of minority and disadvantaged groups, foreign policy. Despite this inherent potential for issue-driven voting, the party system generally provided little choice. Single-issue voting, whether on privatization, Balcerowicz's shock therapy, or state interventionism, was impossible because parties across the spectrum, from the right-wing KPN to the postcommunist SdRP, concurred on fundamental principles while disagreeing on methods or pace. Nevertheless, issue salience in voting is likely to increase as parties develop specific policy programs and their voting patterns on legislation become more consistent.

Party programs obviously play a role in influencing voting. Today's programs are far removed from the all-encompassing, inflexible set of canons that characterized Marxist ideology. In the 1991 and 1993 parliamentary elections, the most graphic case of partisan voting was the electoral allegiance to the communist successor party on the part of beneficiaries of the ancien régime. The SdRP was still identified enough with Marxist ideology to elicit voting both in its favor and against it. Partisan allegiance in the case of the Solidarity opposition—expressed so clearly in the June 1989 elections—disappeared with the breakup of the Solidarity coalition. Competition between parties to claim the honor of Poland's authentic Christian Democratic movement, which for a time was seen as of immense strategic benefit in its own right, involved ideological tacking as well as a good deal of posturing. The claim to be Poland's most important party serving the interests of medium-sized and small entrepreneurs also had ideological as well as practical dimensions.

Moreover, "stolen rhetoric" has abounded in Poland's new party system. With malleable identities and programs, until not long ago it was relatively easy for one political group to appropriate the arguments of another as its own. For example, the economic liberalism of the UD borrowed from the KLD, the nationalism of the ZChN had earlier been a consistent feature of the KPN, and the concern for a strong presidential system advanced by the PC was previously identified with the first anti-Wałęsa parties. But such stolen rhetoric only confirmed the importance attached by parties to developing electorally appealing identities. By the time of the 1993 elections, voters had become more discerning about the policy platforms of individual parties.

Electoral Behavior

Since the historic but only partially free elections of June 1989 there have been five elections: the local elections of May 1990, the presidential elections of November–December 1990, the parliamentary elections of October 1991, the parliamentary elections of September 1993, and the local elections of June 1994.

May 1990 Local Elections. As with the election to the contract Sejm, the May 1990 local elections produced another victory for a still relatively unified Solidarity camp, campaigning as Solidarity Citizens' Committees (KO). The electoral law provided for proportional representation in cities and large towns (the Saint-Lague method) and simple majority results in all other areas. Turnout was only 42 percent and in some localities dropped below 15 percent.[49] Even with the emerging split between Wałęsa and Mazowiecki in the Solidarity camp, just over two-thirds of voters in large towns supported the KOs, and while this figure was somewhat lower in smaller towns the simple-majority system produced one-sided representation for them. The direct successor of the communist party, the SdRP, obtained only 8.6 percent of votes, and the once procommunist peasant party, renamed the PSL, captured just over 3 percent. It seemed highly improbable at this time that the latter two parties—hampered at the polls by their communist past—would within three years come to power and form a coalition government at the national level. Of new parties campaigning for the first time, only the KPN and the ZChN made inroads, and in fact independents followed KO candidates in total votes polled.[50]

November–December 1990 Presidential Elections. A discernible change in the electorate's mind-set took place in the period between January and November 1990. Approval of the government, Sejm, and Senate fell from 85 to 55 percent, and the proportion of respondents asserting that living standards were low increased from 65 to 80 percent. It was under these conditions that direct presidential elections were held. The Solidarity organization (still known as the KO) and the embryonic PC (the first group to have demanded Jaruzelski's immediate resignation) were the pillars of Wałęsa's campaign for the presidential office. As his campaign strategist he named Jacek Merkel, who was shortly to become a member of the KLD and was able to tap its constituency on Wałęsa's behalf. Finally, a political movement that was quickly growing in strength, the ZChN, also gave its endorsement to Wałęsa from the outset. By contrast, Prime Minister Mazowiecki lacked a prior organizational base for his presidential campaign and depended on his ROAD to create campaign committees spontaneously. The SdRP, postcommunist but with organizations throughout the country and a relatively large membership (about 60,000), selected Włodzimierz Cimoszewicz as its nominee. The largest party (about 400,000) was the PSL, still seeking to shake off its former communist satellite status. Its candidate was Roman Bartoszcze, then a PSL leader (subsequently removed). Longtime KPN head Leszek Moczulski announced his candidacy. There were thirteen candidates in all.[51]

Many surveys asking respondents about preferred candidates were conducted in the run-up to the 1990 elections. Thus, in May 1990, CBOS found that the four major candidates were Mazowiecki (24 percent), Geremek (19 percent), incumbent Jaruzelski (17 percent), and only then Wałęsa (16 percent). Polls conducted in the summer indicated that Wałęsa (24 percent) had moved ahead of

Mazowiecki (17 percent), Jaruzelski (16 percent), and Geremek (11 percent). At this stage Tyminski, who was to take part in the runoff against Wałęsa in December, had not figured at all in preferences.[52] Opinion polls taken during the campaign showed greater public confidence in Wałęsa than in Mazowiecki (by a margin of about two to one) to resolve such issues as improving living standards, reducing unemployment, freezing foreign debt, and securing the country's western border with Germany.

Some 60 percent of the electorate voted in the first round of the presidential contest in November (Table 5.4). Interestingly, the highest turnout was in the southern provinces once part of Austria.[53] Wałęsa topped vote-getters but fell far short of the 50 percent needed to avoid a runoff. The greatest shock provided by the elections was the second-place showing of the outsider Tyminski and the elimination of Mazowiecki.

In first-round voting, the Tyminski constituency was correlated positively with former communist party membership, recent loss of employment, lower educational levels, and the weaker influence of the clergy in a region. Whether it was correlated with small town and rural residence as many observers (especially bitter Mazowiecki supporters) asserted was debatable.[54] In these presidential elections the voting behavior of women was not markedly different from that of men, although SdRP candidate Cimoszewicz benefited somewhat from his pledge to leave the liberal communist abortion law untouched.

The second round of elections in December brought 7 percent fewer voters to the polls, despite the church's exhortations to participate. Indicating the volatility of the

TABLE 5.4   Presidential Election Results, 1990

Candidate & Party	Votes	Percent Votes Cast	Percent Electorate[a]
First Round (November 25)			
Lech Wałęsa (Solidarity KO)	6,569,889	40.0	23.9
Stanisław Tyminski ("X")	3,397,605	23.1	13.8
Tadeusz Mazowiecki (ROAD)	2,973,264	18.1	11.8
Włodzimierz Cimoszewicz (SdRP)	1,514,025	9.2	5.5
Roman Bartoszcze (PSL)	1,176,175	7.2	4.3
Leszek Moczulski (KPN)	411,516	2.5	1.5
Second Round (December 9)			
Lech Wałęsa	10,622,696	74.3	38.7
Stanisław Tyminski	3,683,098	25.7	13.3

[a] Turnout in First Round was 61 percent, in Second Round 53 percent.

Source: Główny Urząd Statystyczny, *Mały Rocznik Statystyczny 1994.* Warsaw: GUS, 1994, pp. 71–72.

electorate, 12 percent of those who cast ballots in the first round did not do so in the second, but 9 percent of voters were taking part for the first time in the second round. Second-round abstainers were primarily Tyminski supporters—and not those of eliminated candidates—embarrassed, perhaps, by his good showing and now heeding calls by all establishment political leaders not to vote for him in the runoff; as many as 34 percent of first-round Tyminski supporters may have abstained in December. The runoff produced the expected result: Wałęsa received 74.35 percent (10,622,696) of votes cast against Tyminski's 25.7 percent (3,683,098).

October 1991 Parliamentary Elections. Following local and presidential elections, it was the voters' turn in October 1991 to elect a parliament again—one that would be completely untainted by compromises reached with the communists. Controversy flared, however, over the change in the electoral law. The legislation governing elections for the Senate was simple compared with that for the Sejm: Voters would choose 2 senators by plurality in each of the country's 47 provinces and 3 each from the densely populated metropolitan areas of Warsaw and Katowice, for a total of 100 seats. For the Sejm elections, 37 constituencies would provide anywhere from 7 to 17 members each, depending on their size, for a total of 391 seats.[55] Sixty-nine other deputies would be elected indirectly. Parties would provide national lists of candidates and would be apportioned seats on the basis of the number of votes they received in the constituencies.[56]

The electoral law was hypersensitive to the electoral support accorded small parties, since no minimum threshold was required to obtain Sejm representation. Although, as we have seen, the party system had been fragmenting anyway, the law institutionalized this fragmentation. Yet it should come as no surprise that such a law was adopted. At least initially, the architects of the new system wished to ensure that no political force went unrepresented and that each could expect greater gains from participating in the electoral process than from pursuing any form of political activity outside of it. At this time groups had more to lose from opting out of democracy than from staying in, and if they fared poorly in one election they were driven by the hope of performing better the next time. The electoral law accomplished the desired effect in the first stage of the democratic transition and was scrapped as soon as it had outlived its usefulness.

We have seen that the Solidarity bloc splintered shortly after taking power and that Wałęsa failed to establish a presidential party based on his former Solidarity supporters. The electoral law both exacerbated and rewarded such internal differences within a political bloc. Differences over economic strategy and attitudes toward the church further divided the Solidarity movement. To some degree, too, competing assessments of the communist legacy affected unity. In the fall 1991 parliamentary elections, new political parties and alliances were created in accordance with their approaches to three major issues: (1) the Balcerowicz plan—neoliberal economic reform through shock therapy, monetarism, and privatization; (2) the church and its role—religious instruction in schools, opposition to abortion; and

(3) the scope and nature of decommunization—the exposure of former communists and whether to include the postcommunist SLD.

A fourth axis along which political groups divided in the early 1990s concerned attitudes toward Poland's historic role. While some groups triumphantly proclaimed the country's return to Europe, others were more concerned about preserving national traditions. A fifth continuum, important to political actors but less so to the electorate at this time, was attitudes toward a strong presidential system. In spring 1991, Jarosław Kaczyński urged Wałęsa to build a presidential party, accelerate decommunization and economic change, and demand greater powers for the president from the contract Sejm. Wałęsa rejected this strategy and ousted Kaczyński from his advisory team. Although the issue of a strong presidency festered and prompted Wałęsa to set up his BBWR for the 1993 campaign, in 1991 it was still not as central in defining political fields as the others.[57]

To summarize, the 1991 elections involved parties with different programs and strategies. The UD and the KLD attracted proponents of liberal democracy and economic neoliberalism. The peasant parties (the PSL and the PL) rejected neoliberalism. The SLD offered a benign assessment of the previous communist regime but also attracted voters because of its anticlericalist policies, while the KPN and the PC had greatest appeal for the radical anticommunists. Finally, Christian democratic and nationalist orientations were propagated by the WAK and, later, Fatherland electoral alliances.

The 1991 election results (Table 5.5) demonstrated how the electorate took advantage of this menu. There was no overwhelming support for any one political field. Prime Minister Olszewski had chosen to go to the electorate with a single issue: a radical decommunization that would claim victims even among dissidents with lengthy anticommunist apprenticeships. His failure to make this the key issue of the campaign was a result of limited grassroots support from an economically battered society and the concerted opposition of Solidarity politicians fearful for their careers.

Between Parliamentary Elections. The September 1993 elections offered voters more consolidated party programs. The UD had established a reputation as liberal in economic policy but status-quo-oriented in social matters. Moreover, consciously following the successful James Carville strategy that had orchestrated Bill Clinton's victory in the 1992 U.S. presidential elections, Prime Minister Suchocka's campaign advanced the slogan "First of all the economy" (*Po pierwsze gospodarka*)—hardly the best one for an incumbent presiding over high inflation and unemployment to adopt. Many disaffected voters increasingly saw the UD as squarely in the neoliberal shock-therapy camp and therefore turned to the SLD as an alternative. Further, there was a general weakening of antipathy in the electorate to the communist past. Joining the "camp of revolt" against the incumbent leadership was the PSL, which fed on the disaffection of the sizable rural population.

TABLE 5.5   Parliamentary Election Results, October 27, 1991

Party	Percentage[a]	Sejm (N=460)	Senate (N=100)
Democratic Union (UD)	12.3	62	21
Alliance of the Democratic Left (SLD)	12.0	60	4
Catholic Electoral Action (WAK)	8.7	49	9
Center Accord (PC)	8.7	44	9
Polish Peasant Party (PSL)	8.7	48	8
Confederation for an Independent Poland (KPN)	7.5	46	4
Liberal Democratic Congress (KLD)	7.5	37	6
Peasant Alliance (PL)	5.5	28	7
Solidarity	5.1	27	12
Polish Beer Lovers' Party (PPPP)	3.3	16	0
Other parties	11.9	43	20

[a] Turnout was 41 percent.

Source: Adapted from Frances Millard, "The Polish Parliamentary Elections of October 1991," *Soviet Studies,* 44, no. 5 (1992), pp. 846–847.

The most vigorous defender of traditional Catholic values was the ZChN. Although its ratings in preelection polls were dismal, it held out hope that, as in the 1991 campaign, when parish priests throughout the country exhorted worshipers to vote for electoral list 17 (WAK), the church would throw its support behind the Catholic party at the last moment. Parties identified above all with uncompromising anticommunism were the KPN, the PC, and Olszewski's RdR. By contrast, Wałęsa's BBWR was designed to attract those who approved of the government's policies since 1990.

Between 1989 and 1993 the center of political gravity—regardless of the proliferation and splitting of parties—was an informal coalition of groups favoring neoliberal economic reform and support for the Catholic church. For the many voters who had been hit hard by the economic program of the coalition, the September 1993 parliamentary elections offered the opportunity to express opposition to neoliberalism and the meddling church. Even the UD's electoral campaign hinted at anticlericalism and proposed an opening to the leftist parties. For a large bloc of voters, supporting the party that was least tainted by the problems that had emerged since 1989 seemed the rational choice. That party was, of course, the ex-communists.

In 1993, therefore, Poland's political structure had begun to crystallize. Two blocs on the right had emerged: the liberal-conservative (the UD and the KLD) and the traditional right (the ZChN and the Conservative Party[PK]).[58] The major difference between the groups involved the role of the church in public life. These parties had, in some shape or form, ruled Poland since the formation of a noncommunist government in 1989. What had happened during their time in government that caused them to be the principal losers in the fall 1993 elections?

Even after shock therapy, the ideology of the right continued to advocate an unmodified laissez-faire version of capitalism. This involved a commitment to the near-total privatization of the economy, the withdrawal of the state from economic regulation, a radical reduction in the state's welfare functions, commercialization of society, disempowerment of trade unions, elimination of worker participation in management bodies, and a strong executive branch—in practice, government by decree with the acquiescence of the president. Referring to the failed effort to achieve a communist utopia, the neoliberal motto was "No more experiments." But unregulated capitalism itself seemed very much like an experiment whose results were, in 1993, mixed at best.

According to Ryszard Bugaj, professor of economics and a leader of the leftwing UP, this new system proved to be a fiasco. He cites the following failures: (1) high unemployment, (2) a tax system favoring the rich, (3) tax evasion by private firms and the growth of corruption and graft, (4) a dramatic decrease in state outlays for health care, education, housing, and culture, (5) forced privatization of enterprises without consideration of economic (value of the company) or social ("the rich get richer") consequences, (6) doctrinaire monetarist policies, (7) regulations that discriminated against state enterprises, (8) undermining of employee participation in management, and (9) a sharp increase in crime.[59]

These phenomena had adversely affected many groups in society. They contributed to overall depoliticization, apathy, and voter abstention, cynicism, retreat into private life, and skepticism that the change of regimes had made much sense. Other than the few groups that profited enormously from the new system, the rest of society had become passive and disconnected from mediating structures such as interest groups. Apathy could lead to the emergence of a power elite, which, in turn, could breed a populist reaction. Signs of a populist undercurrent could be found in some survey data: 80 percent of workers believed that "if the right people were in power, things in Poland could very quickly become much better." About 60 percent also agreed that "if we really got down to business, in a few years we could build an economy like Japan's or Canada's without anyone's help."[60]

The neoliberals argued that only their program could transform Poland into a powerful economy. Yet given Poland's stage of economic development, skepticism arose whether a neoliberal program was appropriate. National income was only about US$4,000 per capita. Neoliberalism assumed that there would be marked inequalities and very limited welfare measures. Its strategy in the Polish context was similar, according to Bugaj, to the break in billiards, driving individual balls far apart. Polish citizens doubted that a "lyrical" form of capitalism could ever evolve in the country. At the same time, they began to perceive the differences between communism and social democracy.

September 1993 Parliamentary Elections. A new electoral law changed the way in which deputies were to be elected to the Sejm. Individual candidates rather than party lists became more central: 391 seats were to be contested in multimember constituencies, and 69 other seats were to be distributed to parties receiving more than 7 percent of the national vote.[61]

Only one electoral alliance (the SLD) cleared the 8 percent threshold needed to send deputies to parliament (Table 5.6). The Catholic alliance Fatherland came up short, with 6 percent of the national vote. In addition, just five parties not running as part of an electoral alliance were able to cross the 5 percent threshold required for a party to be represented in parliament; in the fractious Sejm dissolved by Wałęsa in May 1993 twenty-nine parties were represented. The Solidarity party, which abandoned Wałęsa several months before the election and in turn was abandoned by him, barely failed to reach the threshold. Wałęsa's own creation, the BBWR, just managed to gain the 5 percent needed for representation. A party representing the German minority in Silesia sent four deputies to the Sejm; the electoral law made parties representing Poland's minorities exempt from the 5 percent requirement. (Curiously, no such "affirmative action" provision for minorities obtained in local elections.)

The victory of the left in the 1993 parliamentary elections had been expected for some time before election day, September 19. From summer on, polls had indicated that the SLD would win; what remained in question was the size of its

TABLE 5.6   Parliamentary Election Results, September 19, 1993

Party	Percentage[a]	Sejm (N=460)	Senate (N=100)
Alliance of the Democratic Left (SLD)	20.4	171	37
Polish Peasant Party (PSL)	15.4	131	36
Democratic Union (UD)	10.6	74	4
Union of Labor (UP)	7.3	41	2
Confederation for an Independent Poland (KPN)	5.8	21	0
Nonparty Bloc for Reform (BBWR)	5.4	16	2
German minority	0.6	4	1
Fatherland Alliance (*Ojczyzna*)	6.4	0	0
Solidarność ("S")	4.9	0	10
Center Accord (PC)	4.4	0	0
Liberal Democratic Congress (KLD)	4.0	0	1
Others	14.8	2	7

[a] Turnout was 51 percent.

Source: Główny Urząd Statystyczny, *Mały Rocznik Statystyczny* 1994. Warsaw: GUS, 1994, pp. 67–68.

victory. Turnout for the election was 51 percent, better than the 43 percent for the 1991 elections but, nonetheless, an indicator of voter apathy or exhaustion after the drama of the democratic transition.

If the PSL is considered a postcommunist party, then the proportion of voters supporting the left in September 1993 represented just over one-third of voters. It was outperformed by the post-Solidarity bloc (UD, UP, Fatherland, BBWR, Solidarity "S," PC, KLD, and RdR), which received about 45 percent. Votes going to the democratic right (Fatherland, PC, KLD, and RdR) totaled about 17 percent. This figure might have been higher had those who voted for the UD been sure that they would not have been wasting their votes by casting them for any one of the small conservative parties (because of the 5 percent threshold). Support for the outgoing coalition made up of the UD, Fatherland, and the KLD added up to 21 percent of votes. Adding BBWR votes would bring the total to 26 percent. Thus, were it not for personal rivalries and internal disputes within the Solidarity camp, the election result would not have appeared as a stunning SLD victory.

It is also easy, however, to underestimate voter support for the left. The excommunists had made a remarkable comeback nationwide. In the mining center of Sosnowiec, support for the SLD mushroomed from 3 percent in the 1990 presidential elections to 19 percent in the 1991 parliamentary ones and 34 percent in 1993. In Warsaw, Kwaśniewski placed far ahead of other party leaders in votes received: he obtained 149,000, compared with 87,000 for Bugaj, 57,000 for Geremek, and 54,000 for Bielecki.[62] The fact that, among party leaders, the top three vote-getters in Warsaw were politically on the left underscored the electorate's shift in this direction.

Within the SLD alliance, sixty-one deputies belonged to the OPZZ and made it clear that their support for Kwaśniewski's party was conditional. Led by an articulate and dynamic leader, Ewa Spychalska, who had taken over from Miodowicz in November 1991, the OPZZ was a direct descendent of the ancien régime and suspicious of the "liberals from the SLD." Contrary to popular perception, the largest unions in the OPZZ were not hard-hat ones but those of schoolteachers (565,000 members) and farmworkers (411,000),[63] not usually associated with labor militancy. Another party to the left of the SLD but, in contrast to the OPZZ, with origins in the Solidarity movement of 1980–1981 was the UP. Its Sejm representation rose from five—when we add the UP precursor Labor Solidarity's four seats to the one obtained by Zbigniew Bujak as head of the Democratic-Social Movement— and a combined 2.5 percent of the vote after the 1991 elections to forty-one (and 7.2 percent) after the 1993 elections. Its leadership, made up primarily of radical Solidarity leaders from a decade earlier, felt so uncomfortable with both the current liberal policies and the communist pedigree of the SLD that they refused to take part in the SLD-PSL coalition. Indeed, the UP half-seriously charged the SLD with having stolen the economic program of the neoliberal KLD. Not without justification, shortly after the 1993 elections the UP's Ryszard Bugaj predicted that the SLD in government would go on to steal the program of the UD. The role of a "red Balcerowicz" would be assumed by an SLD finance minister. By contrast, the UP program sought to halt the general privatization process, pass a flexible budget whose deficit would not be pegged to an IMF-preset percentage, and improve social programs. Both the OPZZ and the UP intended, then, to keep the SLD committed to a program as socialist as possible, but otherwise they had little in common.

Outgoing Prime Minister Suchocka expressed confidence that the SLD would not veer from the road to reform: "I am fully convinced that the new government will get Poland in good shape," she said. "Poland is well thought of in the West. I believe the next government will follow the same road." Although during the campaign Suchocka had stressed Poland's projected 4 percent annual growth rate for 1993—one of the highest in Europe—the SLD professed concern for the economically disadvantaged throughout the election campaign. It got more mileage from its slogan "It doesn't have to be like this" (*Tak być nie musi*). As leader of the coalition that won Poland's parliamentary elections, Kwaśniewski provided similar assurances: "We are going to be a good partner for the West," he said. "We are going to continue the reforms." He pointed out that the victorious SdRP had changed: "We are neither communists nor postcommunists." Another SdRP leader, Józef Oleksy, also gave assurances that the West would not be displeased with Polish economic policy once unspecified "minor alterations" had been made. "These changes will not be dangerous for our Western partners." Oleksy cautioned that the SLD had no plans to abandon the rigorous economic reforms of the Solidarity-backed governments of the past four years, and he denied Western reports that the SLD would relax financial discipline and increase the budget deficit, now limited to 5 percent of GDP as agreed upon with the IMF. He said that if there was a need to increase the deficit by even 1 percent the SLD would do so only "after negotiations with the IMF." Such an increase would be considered only to permit an increase in welfare payments for the socially disadvantaged and those on fixed incomes who had been hit hard by unemployment and declining living standards. But he reiterated that "the SLD is for a market economy and is a respecter of democracy."[64]

A sanguine analysis of the 1993 elections was provided by Zbigniew Brzezinski,[65] who suggested that excommunists had now returned to the political process, as distinct from returning to political power. He grudgingly gave credit for their electoral victory to the SLD's better organization, the fact that its leaders had never been fully called to account for their communist past, the suffering many citizens had undergone in the transition to a market economy, the refusal of the Solidarity governments to submit to inflationary policies such as pay increases for public-sector employees, the strict and unpopular antiabortion law, and, related to this, widespread perceptions of the excessive influence of the Catholic church over the government (as evidenced in a bill allowing for religious classes in public schools). In addition, to Brzezinski the neoliberal parties seemed divided and further weakened by Wałęsa's hasty creation of the BBWR. The left alliance was seen by much of the electorate as likely to increase welfare programs, slow down privatization, increase subsidies for farmers and prices of agricultural products, raise taxes on the wealthy, extend state control of the economy, pursue preferential credits for Polish investors, and slow both foreign investment and Polish capital flight. The West's reluctance to open its markets to Polish goods and its lack of significant support for the development of export industry had weakened the Solidarity camp. If the West was committed to stabilizing the political situation in Russia, Brzezinski added, it was crucial to support political and economic stability in countries bordering on Russia such as Poland.

The coalition government formed by the SLD and the PSL was headed by the peasant leader Pawlak. Two deputy prime ministers were from the SLD: Finance Minister Marek Borowski and Justice Minister Włodzimierz Cimoszewicz. A third deputy prime minister, Education Minister Aleksander Łuczak, came from the PSL. Although it was natural for the SLD to appoint one of its leaders, Leszek Miller, to head the Ministry of Labor, less in character for a social democratic party was for it to fill the ministry responsible for property relations (in other words, privatization) with Wiesław Kaczmarek. The three presidential ministries were filled by Wałęsa-approved men: Piotr Kołodziejczyk returned to defense, Andrzej Milczanowski took over internal affairs, and Andrzej Olechowski succeeded Krzysztof Skubiszewski as foreign minister. Oleksy of the SLD was elected by the Sejm as its marshal.

Pawlak's replacement as prime minister by Oleksy in March 1995 led to a cabinet reshuffle, although a number of ministers, for example, Kaczmarek in privatization, stayed on in their posts. Two deputy prime ministers were from the PSL—the holdover Łuczak and the agriculture minister Roman Jagieliński. The third deputy prime minister was the SLD-backed finance minister, Grzegorz Kołodko. The PSL also received the post vacated by Oleksy: Józef Zych became marshal of the Sejm. There was one holdover in the three presidential ministries, with Milczanowski receiving the endorsement of the Oleksy government to remain in internal affairs. The new foreign minister was Władysław Bartoszewski, a joint choice of Oleksy and Wałęsa, whereas the new defense minister was Zbigniew Okoński, Wałęsa's preference. Interestingly, then, the presidential ministries were staffed using the formula of one Wałęsa favorite, one prime-ministerial favorite, and one mutual candidate. Oleksy announced that his government's program would differ little from that of Pawlak's, and a powerful directorate of the two coalition partners, subsuming the top six SLD leaders and the top five PSL ones, was established. Nevertheless, promising honest government, Oleksy dismissed several Pawlak-appointed ministers implicated in financial scandals.

June 1994 Local Elections. The June 1994 local elections went farther in consolidating the country's party system. One out of every three eligible voters cast a ballot in the elections—in line with turnout at the local level in other countries and a respectable figure considering the number of elections Poland had held in recent years. About 20 percent of the vote went to independent candidates—again, similar to the breaking away from national party lines that occurs in local elections in other democracies. Unusual, however, was the fact that Prime Minister Pawlak called the elections, to be based on the 1990 electoral law, over the objections of President Wałęsa, who wanted to postpone them for a year pending amendments to the law.

The official results were not tabulated by party affiliation. Furthermore, given unusual alliances between parties in specific localities, it was very difficult to arrive at a total number of councillors won by particular parties nationwide. But according to one Polish specialist, three blocs emerged with claims to success.[66] The first was the ruling partnership of two postcommunist parties, the SLD and the PSL. The SLD won the largest number of council seats in Warsaw and in thirty of the forty-nine provincial capitals. In the rural communes, the PSL received up to 40 percent of the overall vote and even more seats. The coalition government seemed to be endorsed by the local electorate, then, shortly after sweeping to power nationally. Its major challenger on the left, the UP, had a disappointing performance in these elections.

The second bloc was the UW, testing the electoral waters for the first time. Coalitions led by the UW won the most seats in the remaining big cities—Kraków, Gdańsk, Poznań, and Wrocław. With its success, the UW seemed to be capturing the political center.

The third bloc was the Catholic right, which patched together three alliances each made up of several parties. The largest of these was the Alliance for Poland, based on the flagship ZChN. The November Eleventh Agreement was headed by the former UD leader Aleksander Hall's Conservative Party, and the most notable of the Secretariat of Center-Right Groups was the former defense minister Jan Parys's RTR. These right-wing Catholic alliances did especially well in nine provincial capitals located close to Poland's eastern border, among them Białystok. Whereas the Catholic right carved out a constituency for itself in these elections, the nationalist KPN continued its slide at the polls.

1995 Presidential Elections. The campaign for the 1995 presidential elections unofficially began in 1994. Growing dissatisfaction with Wałęsa, fed largely by his personal unpopularity and decisions out of step with the public mood (such as his veto in September 1994 of a Sejm bill liberalizing abortion), seemed to open the field to new candidates. But polls gave different indications as to the electorate's favorite to replace him. One poll from January 1993 produced the unexpected result that the UP leader and former ombudsman Ewa Łętowska would have received most votes (13 percent) if the presidential election had been held then. Following her was Zbigniew Brzezinski (11 percent), then Prime Minister Suchocka (9 percent), soon-to-be prime minister Pawlak (9 percent), and only after them the incumbent Wałęsa (7 percent).[67] The SLD's Kwaśniewski did not figure in the list. By the end of 1993 polls began to point to Kwaśniewski as front-runner for 1995. By contrast, summer 1994 polls of presidential hopefuls Kwaśniewski,

Suchocka, Kuroń, Pawlak, and Wałęsa indicated that the latter would lose a runoff with any of the other candidates and that Pawlak would win a runoff with any of the others. By spring 1995, after Pawlak's resignation as prime minister, the SLD leader Kwaśniewski again became favorite to top the voting in the first round of the elections, but he was now followed by the UW's recently selected presidential candidate Jacek Kuroń. Trailing behind the candidates of these two powerful parties were Supreme Court head Adam Strzembosz, advocating a right-of-center program, and Wałęsa, whose support only momentarily increased when he forced Pawlak out of office and wrecked Pawlak's presidential bid.

Perhaps more than on popularity among voters, the outcome of the elections depended on the coalition-building strategies of the leading contenders. The elections caused tension in the ranks of the ruling SLD-PSL coalition as the head of each party sought to become president. This opened up the possibility of cooperation in a presidential runoff between the SLD and the UW, which had edged closer to each other in late 1994, as demonstrated in their agreement on a candidate for president of Warsaw. But Wałęsa had always shown himself to be a master of coalition building and dividing his opposition. His prospects of reelection were strengthened if he could make the runoff a contest between himself and a candidate of the left. The rural Catholic constituency coupled with the industrial Solidarity voter bloc that he could mobilize would be hard to defeat. Moreover, as is seen in many other countries, the resources that an incumbent possesses often tip the scale in favor of reelection. It was Wałęsa's personal unpopularity among large sections of the electorate, then, that provided Kwaśniewski and Kuroń with the chance to inflict an unprecedented political defeat on the embattled Solidarity legend.

Other Political Groups

As we have seen, the Catholic church in Poland can play a pivotal role in the political arena. Yet the role of the church in the Third Republic has increasingly been called into question. The unpopular, highly restrictive abortion law, the requirement that public schools provide religious education (though pupils do not have to take it), the principle that Christian values permeate public broadcasting, and the general triumphalism and arrogance of church leaders in the postcommunist period have alienated many lay Catholics.

In attitudinal surveys carried out during fall 1994 and again in spring 1995, 71 percent of respondents asserted that the church had too much influence in public life. The most trusted of all institutions in Poland throughout most of the 1970s and 1980s, the church now ranked behind the army, the police, radio, and television broadcasting in terms of trustworthiness. Compared with 90 percent confidence levels in the church before communism's fall, only about 50 percent of respondents expressed trust in the church by 1994. Kwaśniewski explained the hostility to the church: "We are not going to have a theocratic state in the middle of Europe at the end of the twentieth century."[68] As parliamentary debate focused on a new constitution, the church held out for official recognition of its special role in Polish society, for the rejection of the notion of a secular state, and for a constitutional ban on abortion.

Arguably, however, it is the tentative agreement established between the Polish state and the Vatican, termed the Concordat, that has the most far-reaching implications for the part the church will play in Polish society.

The term "Concordat" has rarely been used by the Vatican. The 1925 Concordat brought even Piłsudski into conflict with the church. Effectively it allowed the church to make property claims that went back to the nineteenth century. The state did not act impartially, being generous with regard to the Catholic church and less so with regard to the Orthodox. The most recent Concordat was signed in late July 1993 between President Wałęsa and Pope John Paul II. Its opponents alleged that many of its provisions were in violation of the EC treaty. The 1993 agreement consisted of twenty-nine articles and began with the assertion that "the Catholic religion is practiced by the majority of the Polish population." A similar clause in the constitution of the Second Republic was a source of particular controversy, since at the time Poland had a few sizable ethnic and religious groups. The Concordat expressed the intention "to eliminate all forms of intolerance and discrimination based on religion," but it formalized Catholic education in schools. Church marriages were to have the same legal status as civil ones, though there were no changes in divorce laws.

Probably the most controversial aspect of the agreement was Article 22, a cryptic clause dealing with restitution of church property. A special church-state commission was to be set up to make changes in legislation that would "take into account the needs of the Church given its mission and the practice hitherto of church life in Poland." Added to this was Article 27: "Matters requiring new or additional treatment will be regulated by new agreements or understandings." Sejm approval of the Concordat would thus provide a carte blanche for future changes. As one writer has put it, "Today anyone who naively believes that church-state conflict was invented by communists and that with their demise this chapter is closed forever is making a major and possibly in the future a costly mistake."[69] Further, given that the agreement was signed while the Sejm was dissolved, it appeared that the church was daring the political parties to stand up to its considerable power in the midst of an electoral campaign.

When the SLD-PSL coalition government took office, it was careful not to antagonize Pope John Paul II and Polish Primate Cardinal Glemp on the question of Concordat ratification. The fact that the mainstay of the PSL constituency—the peasantry—was largely Catholic and conservative on social issues compelled the PSL, in particular, to tread carefully on the issue. During spring 1995, SLD head Kwaśniewski met with church leaders and appeared to hammer out a constitutional formula that would satisfy both Cardinal Glemp and the government. There would be no provision asserting the separation of church and state. Instead, the state and church were declared to be autonomous and independent in their own spheres of activity. In addition, the constitution would make no reference to the state's neutrality on religious matters. Kwaśniewski's own party balked at this agreement, and it appeared likely that the issue of the church's constitutionally defined role would not be settled before the presidential elections.

The Solidarity trade union held its fifth congress in June 1993 and passed the following declaration: "Four years after Solidarity's victory, the hopes of Poles are seriously challenged. The way that power is exercised by the present political elite evokes ever greater opposition, while faith in the usefulness of raising the costs of transforming the state is rapidly deteriorating."[70] Self-criticism was also not lacking. Solidarity was viewed as ineffective in resolving the major problems faced by working people: unemployment, decline in living standards, and marginalization in the privatization process. The union had only 1.6 million paid-up members, down from nearly 10 million in 1981. Former union leader Wałęsa was invited to the congress at the last moment and—not unexpectedly, given that Solidarity had brought Suchocka's government down—refused the invitation, saying, "This is not my Solidarity." But a year later he attended the congress and seemed to give the union, together with its political symbolism, a central role in his 1995 reelection bid. Still, it seemed highly unlikely that any trade union could ever approximate the popularity and influence that Solidarity had achieved in 1980.

Many potentially influential organizations represent Poland's new entrepreneurs. Chief executives have joined, for example, the Business Center Club, the Business Roundtable, the Club of Polish Capital, the Confederation of Polish Employers, the Polish Business Council, and the Polish Convention of Entrepreneurs. Small business has organized locally through enterprise clubs. In October 1994 the first dedicated local business lobbying group, the Polish Federation of Independent Entrepreneurs, was founded.[71] Inevitably, the question has arisen whether Polish employers prefer a unified and centralized organization transmitting its interests to the government, as in France or Germany, or an individualistic, highly decentralized business lobby, as in Britain or the United States. Together with trade unions, various business groups signed the Enterprise Pact in 1992 that aimed at bringing labor peace to the country. Since then an effort has been made to revitalize a national Chamber of Commerce that all firms would be required to join. Still, whether business interests become more confederated or remain atomistic may not ultimately determine how much influence they have on public policy. As in any democracy, more important may be whether a probusiness or a prolabor party is in power.

Political Culture

Inherent in the concept of political culture is the notion that political values, attitudes, and behavior are deeply embedded in a particular nation. Political culture thus inquires into the more enduring political orientations of a country. As the electoral results described above suggest, Poles have been rather fickle in their political preferences since the democratic breakthrough. The results of attitudinal surveys conducted since 1989 reflect a value system different from that of the past, but in the longer term this may not necessarily amount to a culture shift.

An intriguing debate among scholars has focused on the extent to which the prescriptive communist value system took hold in Soviet-bloc countries and whether many of its vestiges are likely to be observable for some time to come. This debate is often grounded in competing historical interpretations. Whereas some writers have highlighted the deferential, subject culture of many Slavic societies, which was reinforced by Soviet-style authoritarianism,[72] others have stressed the variations in national cultures (for example, the Czech embrace of pluralism, the Polish experience of insurrectionism and antiauthoritarianism) and their general incompatibility with the communist normative system.[73] Evidence of a normative shift back to traditional values or, in contrast, of the persistence of communist values after the democratic breakthrough may be found in survey research conducted in the early 1990s. Generally, we should expect to find the emergence of more liberal values and the disappearance of authoritarian ones if a democratic culture is taking root. To be sure, Andrzej Rychard contends that no specific normative model underlying the democratic transition need exist and argues that we should be sensitive to changes on the social, local, level rather than focusing exclusively on changes on the institutional, systemic level.[74]

The Authoritarian-Liberal Cleavage

Given the unclear consequences for citizens' lives of the unprecedented transition to a market economy and democracy, it should not be surprising that public opinion reflected anxiety, uncertainty, and some cognitive dissonance at the beginning of this decade. For example, the evidence on the core value of the socialist normative system—egalitarianism—is inconclusive. A survey conducted in spring 1991 found that whereas 60 percent of respondents in a national sample agreed that it was the government's responsibility to reduce differentials between the highest and lowest earners, only 34 percent of deputies to the Sejm elected on the communist ticket in June 1989 agreed. Among Solidarity deputies the figure was even lower (24 percent). Similar rates of agreement across the three groups of respondents were recorded on the statement that there is one law for the poor and another for the rich. Yet when asked to evaluate the assertion "If someone is poor it's usually his own fault," the national sample concurred more frequently (28 percent) than party (19 percent) or Solidarity (19 percent) deputies.[75] Even with a change of regime, it appears that public attitudes favored a protectionist, regulatory state while still often holding the individual responsible for personal failure.

In addressing the persistence of egalitarian views, one Polish political scientist has called attention to the changed nature of egalitarianism rather than merely its presence or absence: "With regard to our picture of social consciousness, we have perhaps made the evolution from a 'jealous egalitarianism' where we took from others—even when it did not improve the situation of the taker (a phenomenon also known as gratuitous jealousy)—to an 'egalitarian capitalism' (or altruistic capitalism) where something is given to everyone."[76]

Evidence that the outcome Poles had worked so hard since 1980 to achieve—a Solidarity government—could equally be evaluated harshly comes from a survey reported by USIA analysts Mary McIntosh and Martha Abele MacIver. The researchers found that confidence in Solidarity governments fell from 65 percent in spring 1990 to 45 percent in January 1992. Seven of ten Poles asserted that the country's economic situation was worse in January 1992 than under communism.[77] A CBOS poll conducted in July of the same year revealed the remarkable finding that the last communist prime minister had scored the highest approval rating in terms of ensuring citizens a good life, the prime ministership of Rakowski (1988–1989) being cited by 30 percent of respondents, that of Mazowiecki (1989–1990) by 22 percent, that of Bielecki (1991) by 6 percent, and that of Olszewski (1991–1992) by 3 percent.[78] But there was at the same time little nostalgia for the old system. Two-thirds of respondents were certain that the current political system was better than the previous one, and the same proportion agreed that anyone who was able and industrious had a chance now to get ahead.[79]

Less than half of Poles expressed interest in politics in early 1992—a considerably lower proportion than, for example, for U.S. citizens. Poles also continued to demonstrate relatively little sense of political efficacy; only 28 percent of Polish respondents agreed that voting gave people a say about how the government ran things, while 66 percent disagreed.[80] A separate June 1992 CBOS poll found that, in response to the question whether "there are now organizations, associations, or unions in Poland that serve the interest of people like you," 53 percent of respondents answered negatively and only 26 percent affirmatively. From this the researcher drew the ominous conclusion that "frustration leads to attitudes more compatible with authoritarianism than with democracy, at least in the version practised in Poland."[81]

When asked in the USIA-reported survey what was essential to a democracy, only the view of a system of justice that treated everyone equally commanded the support of the majority of respondents. Political and legal equality was a value cherished by the political opposition, of course, though we should note too that economic justice was a value propagated by the former communist regime. Approximately 40 percent cited freedom to criticize the government and the existence of at least two strong political parties as essential to a democratic system. Finally, on the crucial issue of what type of society was preferable, one in which individual interests and responsibility were dominant or one in which the state provided guarantees, Polish respondents displayed a slight preference for the latter: 36 percent favored statism and 30 percent an "individual-opportunities" society, while 29 percent preferred a middle road.[82] In a separate study reported by

Kurczewski, statism seemed a more dominant orientation: 93 percent of respondents in 1988 and 95 percent in 1990 agreed that it was the duty of the state to safeguard a minimum income for everybody's survival.[83] One Polish specialist was led to the following conclusion:

> The "spirit of socialism" was (and is) especially apparent in the widespread acceptance of a collectivist ethic and of a type of egalitarianism aimed at the levelling down of social differences (*urawniłówka*) to ensure not an equal start for all individuals, but an equal outcome. It was accompanied by a preference for mediocrity and "averageness," a dislike of those who rose above their peers, and a kind of "learned helplessness" whereby individuals transferred to the state all responsibility for their well-being.[84]

After correlating these results with commitment to liberal-democratic values, the two USIA authors reporting these survey results conclude that "only in Poland does one's degree of commitment to liberal-democratic values have a relatively strong independent effect on one's choice of society." The more liberal-democratic one's value system, the more a liberal-democratic society is endorsed. The problem is that, as we have seen, only 30 percent of Poles supported an individual-opportunities society. The corollary is, then, "This may indicate that only in Poland does a 'state guarantees' orientation suggest a substantially weaker commitment to the liberal democratic values of competitive elections, freedom to criticize the government, and equal justice under the law."[85] If this inference is correct, then we may add that as of 1992, when the survey was carried out, the value of state paternalism promoted by the communist regime had not been dislodged by the more traditional antistatist orientation found in much of Polish history. The September 1993 legislative elections serve as confirmation of this.

The fact that, despite worsening economic conditions, in mid-1992 twice as many respondents disagreed with the statement "It would be right to establish a strongman government and do away with democracy" than agreed indicates, however, that support for a welfare state was decoupled from support for authoritarianism.[86] I am prompted to conclude, perhaps prosaically, that an admixture of traditional and communist values persists in democratic Poland. Moreover, the authoritarian-liberal cleavage may not be a cleavage at all. Ireneusz Bialecki and Bogdan Mach, the two sociologists who compared attitudes of the public with those of Sejm deputies, also inquired about the socialist normative legacy. On the basis of their 1991 findings they conclude that "in Poland, 'socialism' is not the opposite, other pole from 'liberalism'; rather, for many people various features of a pro- or antiliberal orientation manifest themselves alongside features of a pro- or antisocialist orientation."[87]

One final dimension of a liberal value system is whether society has an inclusive rather than exclusive understanding of citizenship. Pronounced ethnic boundaries and their enforcement reflect a nationalist, less tolerant view of minorities; inclusiveness suggests tolerance and liberalism. In a CBOS survey of fall 1994, respondents were asked who, in their view, was a Pole. The leading answers were

someone who spoke Polish (cited by 96 percent of respondents), whose citizenship was Polish (92 percent), whose parents were Polish (82 percent), or who lived
in Poland (80 percent). Surprisingly, just over half of the sample (57 percent) said
that a Pole was a Catholic. This approach to nationality is considerably more liberal than the data on attitudes toward others reported in Chapter 2, but it is only a
snapshot of a society at a particular point in time and may not reflect enduring
features.

The Communist Legacy

The question of the communist past is more than a mere scholastic inquiry into
enduring political values. A policy of removing from public life communists of the
nomenklatura and political class was vigorously supported by President Wałęsa
and, to varying degrees, by Solidarity-picked prime ministers. In contrast to this
decommunization was a policy of identifying agents of the former security apparatus, which became a major pursuit of the Olszewski government in 1992. What criteria should be employed in this effort became a controversial issue, however. Setting aside the obvious case of full-time employees of the apparatus, were occasional
informers or those who simply signed oaths of loyalty agreeing to abide by the
principles of the socialist constitution in exchange for release from prison to be regarded as agents? A former Wałęsa adviser and leader of the PC, Jarosław Kaczyński, implicated the president as a communist security officer, but Olszewski's efforts
to identify Wałęsa as such and expose the loyalty oaths he had signed backfired. According to a report of the Commission on Security and Cooperation in Europe,
"the government's mishandling of a list of alleged collaborators in the spring of
1992—a list of dubious reliability—heightened fears that efforts to punish former
communists might turn into an indiscriminate witch-hunt." Given that "Poland's
experience under communism was less severe and the thirst for revenge today is
less intense," it was to be expected that "many Poles seem to have concluded that
the government's energy would be better placed in building the future than in rec-
tifying the past."[88] In June 1992 Olszewski was dismissed as prime minister over
this question.

Was the public supportive of the wide-ranging exposure of agents pursued by
Olszewski, or did it favor limited and selective decommunization? Surveys between 1989 and 1992 revealed that decommunization was consistently perceived
as a minor issue by respondents. Moreover, according to one writer, popular attitudes toward communists, although negative, never approached the paranoic
character of those of the U.S. constituency that was spellbound by Joseph Mc-
Carthy in the 1950s, and this despite the fact that Poland had actually been ruled
by communists for nearly fifty years. To be sure, there was widespread support for
exposure and prosecution of officials who had served in the communist security
apparatus, about 25 percent more people supporting this than decommunization.
Even where consensus existed that higher-ranking, national party leaders should

be punished, over time opinion shifted toward a more forgiving approach—from 64 percent backing prosecution of Politburo members in February 1991 to just 36 percent in July 1992. When asked in September 1992 whether well-qualified communists should be prevented from holding public offices and top posts in state administration and state-run enterprises, two-thirds of respondents said no and only 26 percent concurred. According to Jerzy Bartkowski's interpretation of these data, rather than viewing Polish public opinion as "soft on communists," it is more accurate to underscore its legitimate concern with defending the principles of civil rights and equality under the law for all citizens.[89]

In seeking to explain public attitudes toward communists that were less vindictive than might have been expected, several writers have called attention to a sense of guilt that subjects of the communist regime felt for not having opposed it more vigorously. Tony Judt writes that "it was not for any real or imagined crimes that people feel a sort of shame at having lived in and under communism, it is for their daily lies and infinite tiny compromises."[90] Wiktor Osiatynski describes average Poles' struggle for survival under late communism, "accepting rather than rebelling, looking the other way, wheeling and dealing, bribing when needed" and suggests that, not surprisingly, exposure of agents and decommunization "posed a threat to the sense of psychological well-being of a large number of the Poles."[91] Although Freudian explanations in terms of latent collective guilt and remorse are intriguing, in the context of postcommunist reality it is dubious whether troubled conscience, as opposed to rational choice, explained weak support for decommunization.

Another possibility is that after 1989 excommunists worked hard at being responsive to popular preferences. To test this hypothesis it is illuminating to assess the views of communist deputies elected to the contract Sejm. Were these contract deputies sensitive to charges that their election was spurious and, as a result, especially sensitive to the need to represent public opinion well? If they had redoubled their efforts to serve their constituents because of their tainted election, this might help explain both why virulent anticommunist values failed to take root and why excommunists were returned to power in September 1993.

In Białecki and Mach's comparison of the political priorities of the public with those of Sejm deputies, the three most important issues identified by the national sample in spring 1991 were unemployment, inflation, and agriculture (Table 5.7). The next three were poverty, crime, and housing. Given this ranking, the researchers conclude that these results "very clearly express social expectations about a strengthening of state intervention in the economy, widening the state's protectionist role, and society's weariness with the economic drabness of everyday life."[92]

When another poll in September of the same year asked a national sample what the most important political issues were, protecting social benefits was cited by 49 percent, representing the interests of ordinary people by 47 percent, competent government by 43 percent, support for farming by 31 percent, and safeguarding efficient state industry during the privatization process by 29 percent. Setting

TABLE 5.7   Opinions About the Government's Most Important Tasks in 1990 (percentages)

Task	Solidarity Deputies	Contract Deputies	National Sample
Reducing inflation	5	7	15
Limiting unemployment	1	10	21
Fighting crime	0	6	8
Regulating Poland's relations with neighboring states	0	7	2
Getting rid of disorder	20	14	7
Accelerating privatization	21	4	4
Building new housing	2	2	7
Removing Soviet troops from Poland	4	0	2
Improving public services	2	13	1
Spurring industrial production	13	28	4
Attracting foreign capital	7	4	2
Increasing farm subsidies	2	2	11
Bringing Poland closer to the European Community	2	1	2
Trying leading communists	1	0	3
Fighting poverty	0	3	8
Promoting moral renewal	18	5	4

Source: Ireneusz Białecki and Bogdan W. Mach, "Orientacje społeczno-ekonomiczne posłów na tle poglądów społeczenstwa," in Jacek Wasilewski and Włodzimierz Wesołowski (eds.), *Początek parlamentarnej elity: posłowie kontraktowego Sejmu.* Warsaw: Wydawnictwo IFiS PAN, 1992, p. 131.

·aside the farming item (on which the PSL was rated highest), respondents identified the UD more often than any other party as pursuing these objectives. Significantly, the SdRP was identified next-most-often as pursuing the goals of social benefits, representing ordinary people, and protecting state industry. Decommunization was eleventh and last on respondents' list of priorities, mentioned by only 9 percent. Of all parties, it was Solidarity that was most frequently identified as striving toward this objective.[93]

Even though they had been recently elected in competitive elections, Solidarity deputies identified a very different set of political priorities from those of citizens. Privatization, order, and moral renewal were their top three issues, and increasing industrial production and attracting Western investment were close behind. Only one of the ninety-one Solidarity deputies listed the unemployment problem as top priority. The researchers conclude that economic liberalism as well as a variant of authoritarianism ("return to past values") underlay Solidarity deputies' political attitudes. They add: "The attitudes of the Solidarity deputies were the attitudes of a modernizing elite of a postcommunist society—not the attitudes of a postcommunist society."[94]

Finally, contract deputies, that is, reformed communists, discerned yet another set of priorities. By far the greatest challenge for them was to increase industrial production. Because many of these deputies were themselves employed in state-owned industry, this is not surprising. Further priorities were of an "administrative-technical" kind: doing away with disorder and mismanagement and improving public services.

The researchers stress the three contrasting visions of politics found in these survey results. They note that the public and the contract deputies had more in common with each other than with the Solidarity group. But they also contend, in seemingly contradictory fashion, that "the greatest difference between deputies taken together and society . . . is that the majority of deputies are 'antisocialist' while society is 'prosocialist.'"[95]

The Values of Workers

An examination of postcommunist political culture requires that we look separately at the culture of the social class that was able most effectively to organize against the communist regime—the industrial proletariat that established Solidarity. Before it was transformed into a social movement spanning all classes, Solidarity was the trade union of this group, and workers overwhelmingly supported its candidates during the June 1989 elections. In succeeding years, however, worker support for Solidarity began to wane. In elections to local councils in May 1990, there was a sharp falloff in votes cast by workers, though those voting continued to support Solidarity's Citizens' Committees. Abstentions indicated a withdrawal of support for the government's economic program, which affected most workers adversely. In the 1990 presidential elections, approximately one-third of workers—especially younger ones—broke ranks with the Solidarity camp and supported Tyminski over Wałęsa. In the fall 1991 parliamentary elections, the majority of workers did not vote. Those who did preferred the right-wing KPN; 12 percent of worker votes cast were for Moczulski's party, while the Solidarity party received 9 percent. In the September 1993 elections, the majority of workers supported either the postcommunist SLD or the post-Solidarity UP.[96]

Other than through the ballot box, workers have traditionally exercised political influence through strike action. After the wave of strikes in 1988 that brought government and opposition to Magdalenka for roundtable talks, strikes declined in number in 1990. Whereas in 1980 and 1981 millions of workers staged strikes, in 1989 300,000 workers engaged in industrial action, and in 1990 the number was less than 100,000. But the militant political subculture of workers had not receded. By 1992, in response to market reforms that hit lower-paid workers hardest, about 1.5 million workdays were lost to strikes—ten times more than in 1990.

Workers' perceptions of the former communist system have also changed markedly since 1989. Although they were initially less sympathetic to it than other social groups, the proportion of critics began to decline. The trend can be measured in answers to the question whether the former communist leadership should be put on trial. In March 1991, 56 percent of worker respondents were in favor, 25 percent against. In November 1992 workers were almost evenly split, with 37 percent in favor and 38 percent against. By April–May 1993 only 34 percent of workers still supported trials of communists and 47 percent were opposed.[97] Admittedly, the issue had changed in these years from a judgment on all of People's Poland to a specific assessment of decommunization and the exposure of agents. Nonetheless, coupled with the increase in industrial action, it was a sign of workers' dissatisfaction with the transition to capitalism.[98]

Indeed, divided opinion about the communist past was what prevented workers from being categorized as either a liberal, proreformist minority or a critical, nonreformist majority. Nonreformist workers themselves differed over how to interpret the communist past. To a much lesser extent, the nonreformist group included a minority attached to the Catholic church. Otherwise, workers of all political orientations were among the most anticlerical elements in Poland.

Perhaps the most noteworthy political attitude among workers in 1993 was their belief that no one represented their interests anymore. Already in 1992 59 percent of respondents asserted this, but in 1993 the figure was 65 percent. Neither President Wałęsa nor the government nor the Solidarity and OPZZ unions were seen any longer as defending workers' rights. In a May 1993 CBOS poll asking who best represented the interests of workers, 66 percent of respondents said no one, 17 percent Solidarity, 6 percent the OPZZ, 4 percent Wałęsa, and 3 percent the Suchocka government. Although workers employed in private industry were less likely to strike for fear of losing their jobs, they too seemed to be alienated from the new political system.

When asked for their vision of the future economy, workers responded in terms of three principal orientations.[99] Moderate reformers represented about half the respondents and supported a free-market economy in which they could enjoy some job security and relatively good living conditions. For them a free market had become axiomatic, and other values, such as the importance of social justice, were judged by this standard. A second group consisted of traditionalists supporting egalitarian, etatist measures: limits on incomes, more equal salaries and wages, top-down management of enterprises, and a dominant state sector. The number of traditionalists fell by half, from about 25 percent to 12 percent, between spring 1991 and spring 1993, and egalitarian values seemed to be eroding. The third and weakest group (6 percent in 1991, 3 percent in 1993) was made up of liberals, who accepted both the fact of unemployment and the sell-off of state enterprises.

An illuminating question concerned workers' attitudes toward privatization. The proportion of reform-minded workers supporting the growth of Polish capitalism increased to 82 percent in 1993. But much was expected of Polish capitalists: their wealth had to have been earned honestly, not through speculation but through hard work over the years. Simultaneously, workers' fears of foreign exploitation increased as well. In 1993 only 15 percent of workers supported the sale of state firms to foreigners.

In short, the researchers concluded,

> Real socialism as a certain structure, network of institutions, and rules of the game no longer serves as a reference point for workers' aspirations and visions. Polish workers feel no nostalgia for the previous system. They are, however, increasingly critical of the new order that does not fulfill their aspirations. They prefer a market economy that is friendly (rather than hostile) to the "average person" and does not saddle him with the costs of the transformation.[100]

The internal contradictions of the working-class value system and its specific political subculture have to be placed in a broader context if we are to assess how its culture shift impacted the new political system. The veteran sociologist Włodzimierz Wesołowski concludes that "systemic transformation disintegrates older interest structures and creates new ones."[101] Although the "transgressive interest"—that is, one common to all society—reflects a desire for a private, market economy, it is not easily converted to the particularist interests of various groups. With capitalist transformation, workers' interests have been "decomposed" into specific occupations (textile worker, miner) and, further, into particular firms.[102] For Wesołowski, then, it is difficult to speak any more about the interests and values of workers as a class. Instead, new interest structures differentiate particular socio-occupational categories of workers from each other. With changed interest structures, different political subcultures are likely to evolve. The working class may never again be a unified class actor and may, then, neither be solely blamed for nor solely credited with political developments in the Third Republic.[103]

Conclusion

Having examined these data on popular attitudes, can we say whether the political culture of Poland has been transformed? The political knowledge of citizens—one dimension of political culture—has undoubtedly expanded exponentially as previously government-controlled media have been either democratized or privatized. Some sets of attitudes, such as statist ones, are a throwback to the communist system, while others, such as individualist ones, have been slower to emerge. Political influence is now primarily expressed through the ballot box rather than through self-organization. After the level of political knowledge, this seems to be the next greatest dimension of political-culture shift. There is no incontrovertible evidence, however, of an authoritarian-to-liberal value shift. Indeed, data suggest that the authoritarian-liberal cleavage is itself problematic for understanding contemporary Polish democratic politics. Many citizens wish to mix and match communist and liberal values. Neither reformed communists nor new democrats can

TABLE 5.8   Ratings of Political Regimes, Spring 1994 (percentages)

Country	Approve Old Communist Regime	Approve Present Regime	Will Approve of the Regime in Five Years' Time
Poland	38	69	84
Belarus	64	29	56
Bulgaria	51	59	70
Croatia	28	51	74
Czech Republic	23	78	88
Hungary	58	51	76
Romania	33	60	77
Slovakia	50	53	79
Slovenia	33	55	73
Ukraine	55	24	33

Source: Business Central Europe, October 1994, p. 80.

take heart from the contradictory evidence surrounding the transformation of political culture.

Of respondents throughout Central and Eastern Europe, Poles ranked second, behind the Czechs, in approving of the new political regime and expecting to approve of it in five years' time (Table 5.8). The fact that two-thirds of Polish respondents endorsed the Third Republic is, clearly, solid backing for the democratic system. At the same time, over one-third of respondents expressed approval of the old communist system, a proportion considerably higher than in the Czech Republic though not as high as in Hungary, Bulgaria, or the former Soviet republics of Belarus and Ukraine. I am again drawn to the tentative conclusion that while support in Poland for democracy has grown steadily since 1989, a complete psychological break with the past has yet to occur.

Notes

1. I have borrowed the notion of "democracy and delivery" from the South African specialist Ann Bernstein (ed.), *Democracy, Development, and Economic Growth.* Johannesburg: Urban Foundation, 1992.

2. See Andrzej Rapaczyński, "Constitutional Politics in Poland: A Report on the Constitutional Committee of the Polish Parliament," in A. E. Dick Howard (ed.), *Constitution Making in Eastern Europe.* Washington DC: Woodrow Wilson Center Press, 1993, pp. 93–131. Also published in *University of Chicago Law Review,* 58 (1991).

3. This notion is borrowed from the pioneering work of the Polish psychiatrist Kazimierz Dąbrowski. See his *Positive Disintegration.* Boston: Little, Brown, 1964.

4. Frances Millard, *The Anatomy of the New Poland: Post-Communist Politics in Its First Phase.* Aldershot, England: Edward Elgar, 1994, pp. 142–143.

5. See Timothy J. Power, "Politicized Democracy: Competition, Institutions, and 'Civic Fatigue' in Brazil," *Journal of Interamerican Studies and World Affairs*, 33, no. 3 (Fall 1991), 96. Part of the following account is informed by Power's analysis of Brazil under the New Republic.

6. Adam Przeworski, *Democracy and the Market*. Cambridge: Cambridge University Press, 1992, p. 26.

7. Przeworski, *Democracy and the Market*, p. 67.

8. Charles Anderson, *Politics and Economic Change in Latin America*. Princeton: Van Nostrand, 1967.

9. James Madison, "The Size and Variety of the Union as a Check on Faction," *The Federalist*, no. 10 (1788). Reprinted in Alexander Hamilton, James Madison, and John Jay, *The Federalist*, ed. Benjamin F. Wright. Cambridge, MA: Belknap Press, 1966, p. 131.

10. William C. Smith, "State, Market, and Neoliberalism in Post-Transition Argentina: The Menem Experiment," *Journal of Interamerican Studies and World Affairs*, 33, no. 4 (Winter 1991), 51.

11. Jan Winiecki, *Resistance to Change in the Soviet Economic System: A Property Rights Approach*. London: Routledge, 1991. See also extensive self-references in his "The Polish Transition Programme: Underpinnings, Results, Interpretations," *Soviet Studies*, 44, no. 5 (1992), 834–835.

12. László Urbán, "Hungarian Transition from a Public Choice Perspective," in András Bozóki, András Körösényi, and George Schöpflin (eds.), *Post-Communist Transition: Emerging Pluralism in Hungary*. New York: St. Martin's Press, 1992, p. 92. For Urbán, the answer in the Hungarian case was a clear affirmative.

13. Stanisław Gebethner, "Political Institutions in the Process of Transition to a Postsocialist Formation," in Connor and Płoszajski (eds.), *The Polish Road from Socialism*. Armonk, NY: M. E. Sharpe, 1992, p. 241.

14. *Mała konstytucja z komentarzem, czyli Ustawa Konstytucjyjna z dnia 17 października 1992 r.* Warsaw: Wydawnictwo AWA, 1992, p. 38, my translation.

15. *Mała konstytucja*, p. 38. I translate *zrzeszają* as "organize," though a more literal translation would employ "associate."

16. *Mała konstytucja*, pp. 38–39, my translation. Although the word "private" (*prywatne*) is not found in Articles 6 and 7, it can be inferred from use of the term "property" (*własność*).

17. Maria Kruk, "Co to znaczy 'Mała' konstytucja?" in *Mała konstytucja*, p. 4, my translation.

18. Three English-language sources for the constitutional debate in Poland are *East European Constitutional Review*, *East European Case Reporter*, and *Journal of Constitutional Law in Eastern and Central Europe*.

19. Douglass C. North, *Institutions, Institutional Change, and Economic Performance*. Cambridge: Cambridge University Press, 1992, p. 25.

20. North, *Institutions, Institutional Change, and Economic Performance*, p. 81.

21. North, *Institutions, Institutional Change, and Economic Performance*, p. 81.

22. North, *Institutions, Institutional Change, and Economic Performance*, p. 83.

23. James March and Johan Olsen, "The New Institutionalism: Organizational Factors in Political Life," *American Political Science Review*, 78, no. 3 (September 1984), 734–749.

24. Juan Linz and Arturo Valenzuela, *Presidential or Parliamentary Democracy: Does It Make a Difference?* Baltimore: Johns Hopkins University Press, 1992. For a review of

choices available for institutionalizing democracy, see Larry Diamond and Marc F. Plattner (eds.), *The Global Resurgence of Democracy.* Baltimore: Johns Hopkins University Press, 1993, chaps. 8–17.

25. Matthew Shugart and John M. Carey, *Presidents and Assemblies.* Cambridge: Cambridge University Press, 1992.

26. Seymour Martin Lipset, *Political Man: The Social Bases of Politics.* Baltimore: Johns Hopkins University Press, 1981.

27. Juan J. Linz, "Crisis, Breakdown, and Reequilibration," in Juan J. and Alfred Stepan (eds.), *The Breakdown of Democratic Regimes,* vol. 1. Baltimore: Johns Hopkins University Press, 1978, pp. 20–22.

28. Przeworski, *Democracy and the Market,* p. 37.

29. Alfred Stepan and Cindy Skach, "Constitutional Frameworks and Democratic Consolidation," *World Politics,* 46, no. 4 (1993), 19.

30. Juan Linz, "The Perils of Presidentialism," in Arend Lijphart (ed.), *Parliamentary versus Presidential Government.* New York: Oxford University Press, 1992, p. 126.

31. Peter Taylor and Arend Lijphart, "Proportional Tenure versus Proportional Representation," *European Journal of Political Research,* 13 (1985). On Poland's fragmented party system, see Frances Millard, "The Shaping of the Polish Party System, 1989–93," *East European Politics and Societies,* 8, no. 3 (Fall 1994), 467–494. Also, Vojtek Zubek, "The Fragmentation of Poland's Political Party System," *Communist and Post-Communist Studies,* 26, no. 1 (March 1993).

32. André Blais and Stéphane Dion, "Electoral Systems and the Consolidation of New Democracies," in Diane Ethier (ed.), *Democratic Transition and Consolidation in Southern Europe, Latin America, and Southeast Asia.* Basingstoke, England: Macmillan, 1990, p. 259.

33. Larry Diamond, Seymour Martin Lipset, and Juan Linz, "Building and Sustaining Democratic Government in Developing Countries: Some Tentative Findings," *World Affairs,* 50, no. 1 (Summer 1987), 5–19.

34. Arend Lijphart, *Democracy in Plural Societies.* New Haven: Yale University Press, 1977. More recently, the same writer avers that electoral systems that promote two or three strong parties within a parliamentary—as opposed to presidential—democracy make for political stability; Lijphart, *Electoral Systems and Party Systems.* Oxford: Oxford University Press, 1994.

35. See Jarosław Kurski, *Lech Wałęsa: Democrat or Dictator?* Boulder: Westview Press, 1993.

36. Andrew Michta, "The Presidential-Parliamentary System," in Richard F. Staar (ed.), *Transition to Democracy in Poland.* New York: St. Martin's Press, 1993, p. 58.

37. A. E. Dick Howard, "Constitutional Reform," in Staar, *Transition to Democracy in Poland,* pp. 102–103.

38. On the origins of the Mazowiecki government, see Zbigniew Domarańczyk, *100 dni Mazowieckiego.* Warsaw: Andrzej Bonarski, 1990. On the role of the intelligentsia, see Voytek Zubek, "The Rise and Fall of Rule by Poland's Best and Brightest," *Soviet Studies,* 44, no. 4 (1992), 579–608.

39. See Jacek Kurski and Piotr Semka, *Lewy czerwcowy.* Warsaw: Editions Spotkania, 1992.

40. On the law, see Frances Millard, "The Polish Parliamentary Elections of October 1991," *Soviet Studies,* 44, no. 5 (1992), 838–840.

41. Irena Grudzinska Gross, "Post-Communist Resentment, or The Rewriting of Polish History," *East European Politics and Societies,* 6, no. 2 (Spring 1992), 147.

42. Judith Gentleman and Voytek Zubek, "International Integration and Democratic Development: The Cases of Poland and Mexico," *Journal of Interamerican Studies and World Affairs*, 34, no. 1 (Spring 1992), 72.

43. This is adapted from Andras Körösenyi, "Revival of the Past or New Beginning? The Nature of Post-Communist Politics," in Bozóki, Körösenyi, and Schöpflin, *Post-Communist Transition*, p. 117.

44. These fields are adapted from Támás Kolosi, Iván Szelényi, Szonja Szelényi, and Bruce Western, "The Making of Political Fields in Post-Communist Transition," in Bozóki, Körösenyi, and Schöpflin, *Post-Communist Transition*, pp. 134–139. In the framework, peasants are seemingly absorbed into the new petty bourgeoisie and do not constitute a class. This approach fails to explain the proliferation of parties aiming specifically at picking up the peasant vote.

45. On this class, see Krzysztof Jasiewicz, "Czy istnieje polska klasa średnia?" *Więź*, 7-8 (July–August 1991), 16–24.

46. Indeed, an earlier incarnation of the UD had questioned the importance of having a party system in Poland. See Antoni Szwed, "Czy partie polityczne są Polsce potrzebne?" *Tygodnik Powszechny*, 6 (February 10, 1991).

47. When explaining why, in addition to not voting, most Poles did not undertake any other form of individual activism, respondents in one survey claimed that it was because they had no influence on national (91 percent), local (79 percent), or workplace (60 percent) matters. Piotr Gliński, "Aktywność aktorów społecznych w transformacji," in Andrzej Rychard and Michał Federowicz (eds.), *Społeczeństwo w transformacji: Ekspertyzy i studia*. Warsaw: IFiS PAN, 1993, p. 101.

48. Hubert Tworzecki, "The Political Consequences of the Cleavage Structure: The Bases of Party Support in Post-1989 Poland," doctoral dissertation, University of Toronto, 1994, pp. 104–114.

49. For a detailed account of reasons for not voting, see Radosław Markowski, "Milcząca większość: O bierności politycznej społeczeństwa polskiego," in Stanisław Gebethner (ed.), *Polska scena polityczna a wybory*. Warsaw: Wydawnictwo Fundacji Inicjatyw Społecznych, 1993, pp. 57–86.

50. Jacek Raciborski, "Wybory samorządowe 1990," typescript, Zakład Socjologii Polityki, Instytut Socjologii, Uniwersytet Warszawski, 1991.

51. Frivolous candidacies included those of Jerzy Bratoszewski (a lawyer), Edward Mizikowski (a locksmith), W. Trajdos (claiming to be editor of a nonexistent newspaper), and Bolesław Tejkowski (an anti-Semite). Three serious candidates who were unable to obtain 100,000 signatures (0.4 percent of the electorate) to stand included Janusz Korwin-Mikke (Union of Real Politics), Władysław Siła-Nowicki (Party of Labor), and Kornel Morawiecki (Party of Liberty/Fighting Solidarity). Stan Tyminski rose from frivolous candidate to one who obtained sufficient signatures to enter the contest to a runoff candidate against Wałęsa.

52. These data are cited in Stanisław Gebethner, "Geneza i tło polityczno-ustrojowe wyborów prezydenckich 1990 r.," in Stanisław Gebethner and Krzysztof Jasiewicz (eds.), *Dlaczego tak głosowano: Wybory prezydenckie '90*. Warsaw: Instytut Studiów Politycznych PAN, 1993, pp. 36–37. This work is by far the most comprehensive analysis available on the 1990 presidential election.

53. For a detailed statistical analysis of voting behavior, including turnout, during the presidential election, see Jerzy Bartkowski and Jacek Raciborski, "Wybory prezydenta RP: Kampania, wyniki," in Jacek Raciborski (ed.), *Wybory i narodziny demokracji w krajach*

Europy środkowej i wschodniej. Warsaw: Instytut Sociologii, Uniwersytet Warszawski, 1991, pp. 125–167.

54. Raciborski claimed that there was no such correlation; *Wybory i narodziny demo-kracji,* pp. 147–149. Citing official data from the state electoral commission, Jasiewicz contended that there was one; Gebethner and Jasiewicz, *Dlaczego tak głosowano,* p. 106.

55. Each party would receive a certain number of seats for a constituency based on (1) the number of seats available multiplied by votes received and (2) the product divided by total votes cast. Remainders were used to distribute the balance of the seats.

56. To be eligible for national seats, a party had to win seats in at least five separate constituencies or have polled 5 percent of the national vote. Alliances between party lists were permitted.

57. This analysis is taken from Tomasz Żukowski, "Wybory '93: Przed podniesieniem kurtyny," *Polityka,* no. 28 (July 10, 1993).

58. Following their losses in the 1993 parliamentary elections, the two parties making up the liberal bloc joined to form the UW. Similarly, the more numerous parties making up the right-wing bloc began merger talks. See "Odruch zjednoczeniowy: Kalendarium prawicy pozaparlamentarnej," *Polityka,* no. 48 (November 27, 1993), 3.

59. Ryszard Bugaj, "W prawo, w lewo lub donikąd," *Polityka,* no. 28 (July 10, 1993).

60. Tomasz Żukowski, "Taniec trzech słów," *Polityka,* no. 32 (August 7, 1993), my translation.

61. *Ordynacja wyborcza do Sejmu i Senatu Rzeczypospolitej Polskiej.* Gdańsk: Temida, 1993.

62. Data are taken from Janina Paradowska, Mariusz Janicki, and Radosław Markowski, "Krajobraz po wyborach: Mapa mandatów," *Polityka,* no. 40 (October 2, 1993), 14–15. See also Kenneth Ka-Lok Chan, "Poland at the Crossroads: The 1993 General Election," *Europe-Asia Studies,* 47, no. 1 (1995), 123–145.

63. Mariusz Janicki, "OPZZ przetrzymało: W jednym Sejmie," *Polityka,* no. 49 (December 4, 1993), 14. No data on membership have been compiled since 1989.

64. Reported on the Polish-affairs electronic news service *Donosy,* September 20–23, 1993.

65. *MacNeil/Lehrer News Hour,* September 20, 1993. The transcript was carried on Donosy in the days following Brzezinski's interview.

66. See Anna Sabbat-Swidlicka, "Local Elections Redress Political Imbalance in Poland," *RFE/RL Research Report,* 3, no. 27 (July 8, 1994), 1–8.

67. Stanisław Gebethner, "Posłowie pisane w 1993 r.," in Gebethner and Jasiewicz (eds.), *Dlaczego tak głosowano,* p. 240.

68. Tom Hundley, "Catholic Church Losing Clout in Poland," *Chicago Tribune,* November 13, 1994.

69. Stanisław Podemski, "Zadowoleni i niespokojni," *Polityka,* no. 32 (August 7, 1993), my translation.

70. Jagienka Wilczak, "Ostatni wielcy odeszli," *Polityka,* no. 27 (July 3, 1993), my translation.

71. "Business Group Buffet," *Business Central Europe,* November 1994, p. 33.

72. For a discussion of the extent of continuity between historic and Communist authoritarianism, see Archie Brown and Jack Gray (eds.), *Political Culture and Political Change in Communist States.* London: Macmillan, 1978. For support for this thesis, see Stephen White, John Gardner, and George Schöpflin, *Communist Political Systems: an Introduction.* New York: St. Martin's Press, 1987, chap. 2.

73. On the clash of historic and Communist value systems in Czechoslovakia, see H. Gordon Skilling, "Czechoslovak Political Culture: Pluralism in an International Context," in Archie Brown (ed.), *Political Culture and Communist Studies*. London: Macmillan, 1984. For a recent study of two other Central European states, see Janina Frentzel-Zagórska, "Civil Society in Poland and Hungary," *Soviet Studies*, 42, no. 4 (October 1990), 759–777.

74. Andrzej Rychard, "Społeczeństwo w transformacji: Koncepcja i próba syntezy analiz," in Rychard and Federowicz (eds.), *Społeczeństwo w transformacji*, p. 7.

75. Ireneusz Białecki and Bogdan W. Mach, "Orientacje społeczno-ekonomiczne posłów na tle poglądów społeczeństwa," in Jacek Wasilewski and Włodzimierz Wesołowski (eds.), *Początek parlamentarnej elity: Posłowie kontraktowego Sejmu*. Warsaw: Wydawnictwo IFiS PAN, 1992, appendix, pp. 149–156.

76. Rychard, "Społeczeństwo w transformacji," p. 16, my translation.

77. Mary E. McIntosh and Martha Abele MacIver, "Coping with Freedom and Uncertainty: Public Opinion in Hungary, Poland, and Czechoslovakia 1989–1992," *International Journal of Public Opinion Research*, 4, no. 4 (Winter 1992), 377.

78. Jerzy J. Wiatr, "Social Conflicts and Democratic Stability: Poland in Comparative Perspective," in Jerzy J. Wiatr (ed.), *The Politics of Democratic Transformation: Poland After 1989*. Warsaw: Scholar Agency, 1993, p. 12.

79. McIntosh and Abele MacIver, "Coping with Freedom and Uncertainty," p. 377.

80. McIntosh and Abele MacIver, "Coping with Freedom and Uncertainty," p. 381.

81. Wiatr, "Social Conflicts and Democratic Stability," pp. 14–15.

82. McIntosh and Abele MacIver, "Coping with Freedom and Uncertainty," pp. 381–385.

83. Jacek Kurczewski, *The Resurrection of Rights in Poland*. Oxford: Clarendon Press, 1993, p. 426.

84. Tworzecki, "The Political Consequences of the Cleavage Structure," p. 41. On the notion of "learned helplessness" he cited Mirosława Marody, "Antynomie zbiorowej podświadomości," *Studia Socjologiczne*, no. 105 (1987), 94.

85. McIntosh and Abele MacIver, "Coping with Freedom and Uncertainty," p. 387.

86. CBOS survey data are reported by Wiatr, "Social Conflicts and Democratic Stability," p. 16.

87. Białecki and Mach, "Orientacje społeczno-ekonomiczne posłów," pp. 80–81, my translation.

88. Staff of the Commission on Security and Cooperation in Europe, *Human Rights and Democratization in Poland*. Washington DC: CSCE, January 1994, p. 10. For a compelling argument that the Olszewski government's policy of identifying agents was needed and that Olszewski's removal amounted to a putsch by excommunists, see Kurski and Semka, *Lewy czerwcowy*.

89. Jerzy Bartkowski, "Public Opinion and 'Decommunization' in Poland," in Wiatr, *The Politics of Democratic Transformation*, pp. 80–107.

90. Tony Judt, "The Past Is Another Country: Myth and Memory in Postwar Europe," *Daedalus*, Fall 1992, 102.

91. Wiktor Osiatynski, "Decommunization and Recommunization in Poland," *East European Constitutional Review*, 3, nos. 3–4 (Summer–Fall 1994), 38.

92. Białecki and Mach, "Orientacje społeczno-ekonomiczne posłów," pp. 129–131.

93. Krystyna Skarżyńska, "Potoczna percepcja celów partii politycznych a zachowania wyborcze," in Gebethner (ed.), *Polska scena polityczna a wybory*, p. 90. For further analysis of the public's perception of the goals of political parties, see Jacek Dohnalik, "Profile

światopoglądowe elektoratów poszczególnych partii i osób nieuczestniczących w wyborach," in Gebethner (ed.), *Polska scena polityczna a wybory,* pp. 155–168.

94. Białecki and Mach, "Orientacje społeczno-ekonomiczne posłów," p. 82.

95. Białecki and Mach, "Orientacje społeczno-ekonomiczne posłów," p. 81.

96. Juliusz Gardawski and Tomasz Żukowski, "Robotnicy '93: Co powie wielki niemowa," *Polityka,* no. 26 (June 26, 1993).

97. Gardawski and Żukowski, "Robotnicy '93: Co powie wielki niemowa."

98. See Zygmunt Bauman, "The Polish Predicament: A Model in Search of Class Interests," *Telos,* no. 92 (1992), 113–130.

99. Juliusz Gardawski and Tomasz Żukowski, "Robotnicy '93–chcą rynku z ludzką twarzą," *Polityka,* no. 27 (July 3, 1993). Because not all answers could be coded as representing one of the three orientations, the percentages did not add up to 100 percent.

100. Gardawski and Żukowski, "Robotnicy '93–chcą rynku z ludzką twarzą," my translation.

101. Włodzimierz Wesołowski, "Transformacja charakteru i struktury interesów: Aktualne procesy, szanse i zagrożenia," in Rychard and Federowicz, *Społeczeństwo w transformacji,* p. 138, my translation.

102. Wesołowski, "Transformacja charakteru i struktury interesów," p. 133.

103. My thesis is hardly original. For an incisive sociological account of meta-class evolution in the social structure, see Zygmunt Bauman, *Memories of Class: The Pre-history and After-life of Class.* London: Routledge and Kegan Paul, 1982.

6

Socioeconomic Development, Foreign Policy, and the International Political Economy

It is often claimed that a successful capitalist transformation can anchor democracy. In this chapter I assess this linkage in theoretical terms and then investigate such empirical issues as socioeconomic change, growth, employment, income, privatization, banking reform, and capitalist pathologies. I go on to consider whether the post–Cold War environment has served as a facilitator of democratic consolidation in Poland, examining foreign trade, investment, and debt.

Politics and Economics

For a large number of Polish citizens, the transition to a democratic political system was desirable primarily as a catalyst for converting the economic system from a command model to a free market. Democracy delivers, these citizens firmly believed, the assumption being that only a capitalist system can promote economic development beyond the early stages of industrialization. This kind of determinism has been called into question by the mixed record of the Polish economic transformation. Indeed, the distinguished Canadian political scientist Charles Taylor has been a leading skeptic of such determinism: "What should have died along with communism is the belief that modern societies can be run on a single principle, whether that of planning under the general will or that of free-market allocations."[1]

Of the various components of Phase IV analysis—political structures and groups, leadership, political culture—the "bottom line" for many citizens is general socioeconomic performance and individual well-being. Checks and balances between executive and legislative branches, coalition governments, and electoral systems are important less in their own right than as facilitators of economic growth.

Since 1989 many Poles have become increasingly skeptical about the rhetoric that highlights the values of individualism, freedom, and democracy as their living standards have declined. This section examines the empirical evidence indicating whether Poland's conversion to a capitalist economy has paid off. Economic growth contributes to democratic consolidation by legitimating the new system through its efficiency. Uneven economic growth across sectors—manufacturing, extraction, agriculture—or across class lines—workers, farmers, business—can produce selective disaffection. Depending on the size and importance of groups flourishing or languishing under the new economic system, democracy can be reinforced or weakened. For example, a prospering middle class can consolidate democracy; a battered but militant working class can weaken it.[2]

At the outset, it is important to stress the rather obvious point that in a capitalist system *regime performance* and *economic performance* are no longer the same thing. In describing communist regime performance in Chapter 2 I could collapse the two categories; the performance of a state-owned and state-managed economy was isomorphic with regime economic performance. But since 1989 economic growth has occurred precisely outside the public sector. To be sure, the fiscal, monetary, and price-and-income policies that stimulate growth of the private sector can be regarded as the government's economic performance. The extent to which the state has privatized, made more efficient, or closed down public-sector firms can also measure regime performance. In these respects the government can be held responsible by the public for economic growth or decline. But once we recognize that most economic activity no longer occurs under the auspices of the state, we must turn to analysis of the private sector to gauge Poland's general economic performance. This distinction between economic performance by the regime and that by the private sector is not, however, always made by Polish citizens socialized into communist logic, and the state is still often identified as responsible for economic fortunes. This lies behind the electoral volatility in evidence between 1989 and 1993, when no incumbent party was able to do well when forced to submit to popular review.

Regime performance can also be evaluated by the public or by outside institutions such as the IMF. During fall 1993 the majority of Polish citizens had a sufficiently negative view of the government's economic policies to turn to the socialists and its allies at the ballot box. But outside lending institutions and economic intelligence units, by contrast, were giving the new economic system high grades for performance. Clearly, different performance criteria are employed by different interested economic actors.

The question of regime performance has to be supplemented by that of *regime capacity*, also central to Phase I and Phase IV analysis. After the 1989 political transition regime capacity increased as political authorities were imbued with legitimacy following the introduction of representative government. But regime capacity in the economic sphere declined, partly as a result of the transaction costs of transferring responsibility for entrepreneurship to the private sector but partly too because its revenue base fell precipitously as recession set in. The contrasting measures of regime capacity in political and economic spheres raise the general question of the relationship between politics and economics in a new political system.

Much has been written about the interconnectedness of political and economic reforms. Ever since communist governments began in the 1970s to pursue exclusively economic change, conventional wisdom has been that, to be effective, economic reform must be accompanied by democratization so as to confer legitimacy on the incumbents carrying out change. At the same time, an academic literature has emerged that decries efforts at simultaneous economic and political transition. As one article sums up this literature, "There are two versions of this 'transitional incompatibility' thesis, one focusing on democratization's potential to undermine economic reform, and the other contending that the heavy cost of economic reform can turn crucial social actors against democratization."[3]

An approach more often associated with economists than with political scientists is that political change alone may bring a system limited or no economic gains. The architect of the plan for the rapid capitalist transformation of Poland, the economist Leszek Balcerowicz, underscores this approach: "economic progress cannot be achieved by democratic policies alone.... There is no correlation whatsoever between democracy and economic progress, i.e., economic growth. However, there is a marked correlation between the type of economic institutions, such as property rights or whether the economy is open or closed to the outside world, etc., and economic growth."[4] Balcerowicz is here restating the thinking of mainstream economists in questioning the importance of democratic change. But he is attentive to the opportunities for radical change that are available in the brief period of "extraordinary politics" following a great political breakthrough and recognizes that the return to normal politics narrows the menu for economic choice.[5]

In considering linkages between and different impacts of economic and political change, Robert Bellah also emphasizes the primacy of the economic not only in the importance of outcomes but also in the purity of the process:

> Politics suffers in comparison with the market. The legitimacy of the market rests in large part on the belief that it rewards individuals impartially on the basis of fair competition, a legitimacy helped by the fact that economic transactions are widely dispersed and often invisible. By contrast, the politics of negotiation . . . , though it shares the utilitarian attitudes of the market, often exposes a competition among groups in which inequalities of power, influence, and moral probity become highly visible as determinants of the outcome.[6]

Furthermore, the politics of interest that generally favor the strong at the expense of the weak are a necessary evil of the political realm. Bellah's analysis encourages us to place greater faith in the equitable processes of economics than in those of politics.

Two U.S. economists, Stephan Haggard and Robert Kaufman, have explored the relationship between economic and political *crises*. As a corrective to the democratization literature cited throughout this study, let us take note of these writers' qualification:

> Despite the fact that economic crisis overlapped a new wave of democratization in the developing world, recent literature on the transition to democracy has largely eschewed economic variables. Emphasizing the autonomy of the political realm, this analysis has focused rather on factors such as pact-making among political elites, institutional relations between civilian and military authorities, and the way electoral and constitutional rules structured opportunities for the democratic opposition under authoritarian rule.[7]

With regard to the significance of economic factors for triggering political change, Haggard and Kaufman suggest that "first, we should expect an increase in the incidence of regime change during global depressions; second, we should expect regime change to be more likely the greater the intensity of the external shock a country faces."[8] Assessing economic shocks and regime change in the 1980s in Latin America, Africa, and Asia, they find little correlation and, instead, important intervening variables. Thus, "regime survival appeared to depend on the existence of mechanisms of interest representation that channeled, and therefore controlled, group conflict."[9] In addition, whether international shocks resulted in the defection of key actors supporting the regime depended on their impact on major business interests—rather than on the national economy as a whole—and on the existence of a moderate, rather than radical, opposition alternative to the regime.

Haggard and Kaufman also investigate the sequencing of economic and political liberalization (Figure 6.1). In their Sequence I, economic reform is instituted before a political opening. The idea is to suppress opposition to economic reform for a given period, then reopen the political sphere. This was the strategy of Southern Cone bureaucratic-authoritarian regimes in the 1960s and 1970s, of East Asian states in the 1970s, and of China in the 1980s. In some respects it was also the strategy employed in the 1980s by Jaruzelski in Poland and János Kádar in Hungary. Sequence II involves simultaneous economic and political liberalization, most notable being the case of Mexico in the second half of the 1980s. Sequence III involves democracy first and structural adjustment later. Obtaining political legitimacy for a reformist government is seen as the top priority in the transition. Argentina, Brazil, and Peru in the late 1980s and, for Haggard and Kaufman, much of Eastern Europe are examples here. The advantage of democracy-first sequencing is that new governments can fully exploit the ineptitude of their predecessors. The disadvantage is that the new democratic leadership has to adopt stringent structural adjustment measures and pursue macroeconomic stabilization.

Haggard and Kaufman reach the inevitable conclusion that, regardless of sequencing, consolidation of democratic rule ultimately depends on "the extent to which adjustment policies actually result in economic recovery."[10] Poor economic performance can result directly in a collapse of elected governments, but also possible is a "stylized process of political decay" that "while stopping short of formal

Figure 6.1   Sequences of Economic and Political Liberalization

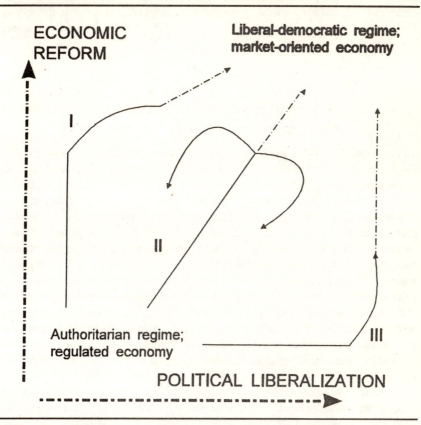

Dashed lines indicate that the sustainability of the path is problematic.

Path I: Economic reform precedes political liberalization (e.g., Chile, Taiwan, Eastern Europe).

Path II: Simultaneous political and economic reform (e.g., Mexico, Nigeria, Russia).

Path III: Political liberalization precedes economic reform (e.g., Argentina, Brazil).

Source: Adapted from Stephan Haggard and Robert R. Kaufman, *The Politics of Economic Adjustment: International Constraints, Distributive Conflicts, and the State.* Princeton, NJ: Princeton University Press, 1992, p. 333. The authors tentatively placed Eastern Europe along Path III, but I suggest it fits better along Path I.

regime change would nonetheless drain constitutional institutions of their democratic content."[11] Sudden *or* gradual economic deterioration can lead to an increase in crime, industrial unrest, riots, civil violence, downward social mobility, and social polarization. They write: "A general erosion of faith in the capacity of democratic government to manage the economy increases the appeal, not only to elites, but to larger publics, of authoritarian solutions to the crisis."[12] This stylized decay, not political fireworks, may represent the most serious threat to democratic consolidation in Poland. It is also a threat to a state's ability to sustain economic reform over time.[13]

Institutions and Culture as
Determinants of Economic Change

To understand an overhaul of the economic system of the proportions of replacing a centrally planned command economy with a largely deregulated, market-based one, it is important to contextualize it within the broader perspective of economic history. For the Nobel Prize–winning economist Douglass North, a prerequisite for improved economic performance is the establishment of institutions that create an incentive structure. As he puts it, "The agent of change is the individual entrepreneur responding to the incentives embodied in the institutional framework." In turn, this presupposes that institutions are both sufficiently stable and sufficiently powerful to enforce rules. The reason for this is, as North makes clear, that "the overall stability of an institutional framework makes complex exchange possible across both time and space."[14] But informal constraints matter as well. These include modification of formal rules, socially sanctioned norms of behavior, and internally enforced standards of conduct. Put concisely, a pervasive work ethic, honesty, and integrity lower transaction costs (which include rule enforcement) and facilitate complex productive exchanges.

Stress on a country's *experience* with institutional adaptation and informal constraint patterns leads North to speak of path dependence. He is careful to distinguish this concept from economic determinism. In any country's history, "at every step along the way there were choices—political and economic—that provided real alternatives. Path dependence is a way to narrow conceptually the choice set and link decision making through time."[15] For example, where institutions initially provided greater incentives for military rule (by granting generals a stake in maintaining existing constraints), for religious fanaticism (by disproportionately rewarding clerics compared with entrepreneurs) or for redistributive policies (by creating disincentives to obtaining economically useful knowledge), the self-reinforcing, path-dependent character of institutions produced poor performance. By contrast, efficiency signifies "a condition where the existing set of constraints will produce economic growth."[16] North sets out what path-dependent growth would look like: "an adaptively efficient path ... allows for a maximum of choices under uncertainty, for the pursuit of various trial methods of undertaking activities, and for an efficient feedback mechanism to identify choices that are relatively inefficient and to eliminate them."[17]

Prospects for economic success improve under capitalism, then, since this system's incentive and constraint structure promotes experimentation and allows decision makers to arrive at the right set of institutions. To be sure, Hayek's admonition about socialism's obsession with designing new rules and institutions should also sound a note of caution about capitalism's capacity to develop efficient institutions. An important assumption inherent in the socialist project was that "since people had been able to *generate* some system of rules coordinating their efforts, they must also be able to *design* an even better and more gratifying system."[18] In some respects, North's effort to escape economic determinism by making allowances for a country's ability to effect discretionary, corrective institutional modification to its inefficient path development conveys the same idealism as advocacy of a planned economy.

The crucial question remains what is required for efficient institutions to come into being. North tells us that "one gets *efficient* institutions by a polity that has built-in incentives to create and enforce efficient property rights."[19] In its many variants, this was the logic underlying regime change in Poland in 1989, and we have examined the rationale of the actors of change in the previous chapters. We need to study economic performance since 1989 to see whether it has improved under a different set of incentives and constraints or whether Poland's path dependence has once again failed to engender efficiency-maximizing institutional arrangements.

In addition to institutions, a second general factor that is usually considered to determine the success of economic change is cultural makeup. Values deeply embedded in society, the logic goes, can either promote or fetter economic development.[20] A pathbreaking recent study of culture and development is Robert Putnam's research on Italy. Examining the civic traditions and economic development of the two major regions of this country, he modifies the analytic framework proposed by North and focuses on social settings as an influence on the operation of institutions. Putnam seeks to account for contrasting levels of development in northern and southern Italy, and he invokes the North's heritage of communal republicanism, itself a result of long experience of civic involvement, social responsibility, and mutual assistance. In the South, by contrast, rule externally imposed a millennium ago promoted vertical ties of dependence and exploitation and, correspondingly, an ethos of mutual distrust and conflict and the destruction of the horizontal ties of solidarity so central to creating social capital. The internal division of Italy into two distinct development zones is parallel to that of Western and Eastern Europe. Finding no correlation in either of the regions between levels of industrial employment in 1901–1911 and those in 1977, Putnam concludes that "a region's chances of achieving socioeconomic development during this century have depended less on its initial socioeconomic endowments than on its civic endowments." Put in terms of causality, "economics does not predict civics, but civics does predict economics, better indeed than economics itself."[21]

Putnam's explication of these results is intended to tell us about the conditions necessary for capitalism to flourish. "Trust lubricates cooperation. The greater the level of trust within a community, the greater the likelihood of cooperation."[22] Trust, along with norms, reciprocity, and networks, helps make up social capital, which is a public good; conventional capital is a private one. For states with little of the latter such as Poland and other countries emerging from communism, it becomes especially crucial to multiply social capital. The alternative to reciprocity/trust is dependence/exploitation. Admittedly, it can also produce a stable social equilibrium, but such an equilibrium will not result in growth. According to Putnam, since it is based on the strategy of "never cooperate" and/or "always defect," it

> may represent the future of much of the world where social capital is limited or nonexistent. For political stability, for government effectiveness, and even for economic progress social capital may be even more important than physical or human capital. Many of the formerly Communist societies had weak civic traditions before the advent of Communism, and totalitarian rule abused even that limited stock of social capital. Without norms of reciprocity and networks of civic engagement, the Hobbesian outcome of the Mezzogiorno—amoral familism, clientelism, lawlessness, ineffective government, and economic stagnation—seems likelier than successful democratization and economic development.[23]

While accepting the importance that should be attached to social capital, Giuseppe di Palma, another eminent specialist on democracy, interprets the East European case in an almost diametrically opposite way from Putnam. Instead of retracing a millennium of history to discover where civic virtue has become rooted and where it is absent, di Palma champions the very recent East European experience of organizing against communism. The richness of the culture of dissent, he writes, may compensate for the fact that democratic Poland and its neighbors were starting out from an earlier stage of economic development:

> Though East European societies suffer from relative backwardness, the legacy of dissent may help them to escape the dire prophecies of the theorists of backwardness. By deciding to make civil society, rather than the state, the force behind Eastern Europe's regeneration, the dissidents have made an explicitly anti-Leninist choice. It is above all a cultural and indeed a moral choice.[24]

This new structure of normative thought could promote progress not by traditional developmental policies but by reconstituting citizens' relations with one another, that is, building networks of trust and cooperation. Di Palma holds out the possibility, therefore, that collective action can produce efficiency on the basis of a shorter but more recent and profound experience with solidarity and trust. This would not contradict Putnam's more general conclusion: "The fact that vertical networks are less helpful than horizontal networks in solving dilemmas of collective action may be one reason why capitalism turned out to be more efficient than feudalism in the eighteenth century, and why democracy has proven more effective than autocracy in the twentieth century."[25] Some of the data presented in the previous chapter, such as those on the urban-rural cleavage and on attitudinal differences regarding egalitarianism, suggest that the horizontal networks so important to the rise of Solidarity may not have survived the transition process.

Economic Models After the Command Economy

Before turning to economic changes in Poland in empirical terms, it is instructive to outline the general models of an economic system that were realistic options for any postcommunist system.[26] One of the many taxonomies[27] is that of the former Thatcher cabinet adviser and Oxford don John Gray, developed specifically to apply to postcommand economies. Gray identifies three principal Western models and three non-Western ones. The first Western model is the German social-market economy, often perceived in Eastern Europe as the postwar success story par excellence. The major theoretical assumption distinguishing this model is that the institutions of the free market are not the inexorable product of spontaneous economic activity but, rather, the result of institutional design and constitutional construction—very much as North has argued. Key ideas flowing from this assumption are, following Gray:

- market freedoms are not guaranteed by a policy of nonintervention, or laissez faire; they are created and protected by a competition policy that requires the constant monitoring, and recurrent reform, of the legal framework within which market exchange occurs.
- market institutions are justified not by their embodiment of any supposed structure of fundamental rights, but by their contribution to individual and collective well-being. They are therefore perpetually open to revision and reform by reference to this undergirding process.
- market institutions are not free-standing, but come embedded in other institutions, including those in which government acts to protect citizens from forms of insecurity that market institutions by themselves may create, or are powerless to prevent.[28]

This reluctant embrace of the free-market economy is also vividly captured in Taylor's stricture that "we can't abolish the market, but nor can we organize ourselves exclusively through markets. To restrict them may be costly; not to restrict them at all would be fatal."[29] Given the combination of German influence in Central Europe throughout history and the more recent East European experience of etatism linked to communist rule, the German social-market model seemed to be the most apposite to the case of East European states after 1989.

A second model is that of Swedish egalitarian social democracy. In its early phase, up to 1932, when the Social Democrats came to power, Sweden was characterized by limited government of a classical liberal kind. After 1932 and the expansion of welfarism, Gray stresses, "even at its most interventionist, Sweden was never as corporatist as the UK in the seventies; and for most of its recent history it has been more thoroughly capitalist in its productive institutions than most other Western countries."[30] The egalitarian model may have been well adapted to an ethnically and culturally homogeneous society that had never experienced full feudalism, in all these respects different from Eastern Europe. In addition, the high costs of welfarism reduce the likelihood that it can serve as a viable paradigm in a capital-starved state such as Poland.

The problem with the third model identified by Gray—Anglo-American capitalism—is that because it "is the result of a long, unplanned evolutionary development in which the common law played a large part, it is not readily exportable—especially to countries with very different cultural, legal, and political traditions."[31] The unplanned emergence of industrial capitalism in England followed centuries of agrarian capitalism. The large corporation at the heart of modern American capitalism is both difficult to reproduce elsewhere and possibly at odds with cultures in which municipal and cooperative sectors have flourished in the past. Anglo-American capitalism prospered under conditions of limited government; in Eastern Europe the strongest tradition is of popular rather than limited government. Gray sums up: "In an age of ethnicity and populism, reversion to the political models of the English-speaking world a century or more ago is an anachronistic and utopian project."[32]

One other Western model noted by Gray is the Chilean one of capitalist development under authoritarian dictatorship. This model is rendered unsuitable not only by the natural revulsion that many East European societies would feel for renewed dictatorship but by the fact that it is built on a preexisting legal infrastructure of market institutions—precisely what today's East European states need to construct.

For Gray, the three non-Western models have less applicability to the specific conditions in which Eastern Europe finds itself. The East Asian model posits strategic governmental intervention in the economy. In Japan, the Ministry of Trade and Industry has played a pivotal role in research and development strategy; in Taiwan, tariffs and subsidies promote industrial development; in South Korea, banks are key instruments of government policy; in Singapore and Malaysia, governments have played activist, interventionist roles in many different ways. Gray underscores, then, that the East Asian model requires the state to create successful market institutions and to remain constantly engaged in regulating capitalist development.

The Chinese model is based on even greater degrees of interventionism and authoritarianism than the East Asian and Chilean ones, and in addition it originated in market reform of an enormous agriculture sector. For Gray, in China "market institutions are most likely to be stable and successful if they do *not* replicate those of the West, but are instead molded so as to reflect the distinctive values and surviving traditions of native cultures."[33]

Finally, Gray identifies Atatürkist Turkey as a much-neglected non-Western model. Less for reasons of its distinctive economic policy than because of the efforts made by an authoritarian state to modernize and secularize society and to create the legal individual, this model is applicable only to the more backward regions of the postcommunist world.

From this typology we observe that at the crux of differing models of economic development lies the role of the state. Should it be expansive, regulatory, or minimal? In a number of respects, as Peter Evans has pointed out, the state has been asked to play contradictory roles in the economic sphere. Evans points to the dangers of a predatory state (as in Zaire) and contrasts it with the romanticized bureaucracy of Japan's Ministry of Trade and Industry. Although skeptical about even the latter, he concludes that a policy of less state intervention is a simplistic and misguided palliative. The fact is that enhanced state capacity *is* a requirement of effective economic policy, especially in promoting sustained structural adjustment:

> One of the prime virtues of adjustment programs is that they are very selective in the capacity they demand. Because they focus on the recalibration of a relatively small number of macroeconomic variables, they obviate the need for the massive regulatory apparatus that is required by less market-conforming strategies, to say nothing of the institution building required by state attempts to take on a directly productive role.[34]

Evans recognizes that "reconstructing the state is an amorphous and frustrating task, a project of decades if not generations." Yet "transforming the state from problem to solution"[35] has been the key challenge facing a government like that in Poland seeking to promote economic development.

One last consideration in this overview of economic models is the issue of the desirable sequencing of economic reforms. In addressing the specific case of Eastern Europe, the economist Richard Portes has identified some of the uncertainties involved:

> Should privatization accompany stabilization, or must it await the restoration of macroeconomic equilibrium and the arrival at reasonable relative prices? There seems no reason why "small privatization" of service establishments cannot go very quickly, except for any obstacles that restitution laws pose. One can make a strong case, however, that privatization of the large SOEs [state-owned enterprises] should follow financial restructuring ("cleaning out the books") and demonopolization, a centrally directed breaking up of large firms. Yet others argue that without privatization, there will be no supply response to lift the economy out of the depression that macroeconomic stabilization and price liberalization will induce.[36]

In the remainder of this chapter, I describe how Polish economic reform was attracted to different models, different state roles, and different economic sequencing over time. Some economic reform was still influenced by the market-socialist paradigms advocated by, among others, the Hungarian economist János Kornai.[37]

Other reformers wanted to go as far outside the Marxist tradition as possible and looked to the strategies developed by economists from the Chicago school, Harvard University, and the Hoover Institution.

The Balcerowicz Plan, passed by parliament in December 1989,[38] was clearly the product of neoliberal thinking espoused by prominent Western economists. Chief among them was Jeffrey Sachs, who outlined five aspects to rapid economic transition: economic stabilization, price liberalization, privatization, Western aid, and maintenance of a social safety net.[39] If the early Solidarity governments emphasized the first three aspects, by June 1994 the Strategy for Poland program advanced by SLD Finance Minister Grzegorz Kołodko marked a return to a social-market approach and gave more considered attention to the fifth. Kołodko promised to reduce the social costs of economic reform: "In the center of our strategy is the human being, not the money."[40] His plan was expected to generate 22 percent growth in GDP between 1994 and 1997. During this period, real wages were to increase by 11 percent, unemployment was to be cut by 10 percent, and the annual budget deficit was to be reduced to 2–4 percent of GDP. Wałęsa called the program the best he had seen in five years. These regular shifts in economic-policy course testify to the vibrancy of a marketplace of economic ideas in the country after decades of dogmatic central planning.

Socioeconomic Change

As in several other Soviet-bloc states, especially Hungary, important economic change in Poland began while the communist party was still in power. In February 1987 the United States lifted the remaining economic sanctions imposed on Poland as a response to the declaration of martial law in 1981, and shortly thereafter Party Secretary Czyrek visited Washington to discuss debt rescheduling and a new line of credit for Poland. Throughout 1987 and 1988 a stimulus-response model seemed to characterize relations between, on the one hand, the United States and international lending institutions such as the IMF and the World Bank (to which Poland was admitted in 1987) and, on the other, the increasingly reform-minded Polish government. Under Prime Minister Messner, first steps toward decentralization and price restructuring were taken.[41] One of the two questions in the November 1987 referendum asked for public approval for rapid economic changes over a two- or three-year period (the other concerned "deep democratization"). Two-thirds of voters—but only 44 percent of eligible voters—supported rapid economic change (the figures on democratization were slightly higher: 69 percent and 46 percent). In February 1988 the first move toward price liberalization was taken when food prices were increased by 40 percent and the cost of energy by 100 percent (locally produced coal rose by only 20 percent). In September 1988 impatient liberals within the party forced Messner's resignation. His replacement, Rakowski, introduced a series of reforms aimed at simulating market conditions for many commodities and extending greater autonomy to large firms, especially in conducting foreign trade. In November 1988 the Sejm adopted an economic consolidation plan that limited central planning and promoted private enterprise. In the first half of 1989, 1,302 joint ventures were registered, signaling both how serious the Rakowski government was about privatization and, more ominous, how eleventh-hour *uwłaszczenie* (appropriation) of state resources by the *nomenklatura* before the communist collapse was promoted. In short, it is clear that in the economic realm the transition was well under way before the roundtable talks.

Despite changes in governing coalitions, the Solidarity-based governments from the second half of 1989 to fall 1993 pursued similar economic strategies. These involved restricting the money supply, controlling hyperinflation while liberalizing prices (indispensable to moving from a state to market economy), keeping the budget deficit within certain limits (5 percent of GDP was the target), promoting currency convertibility (helped by the creation by Western institutions of a złoty stabilization fund), and developing incentives for private enterprise.

Poland's economic policy was grounded in an IMF formula adopted by Balcerowicz when he was appointed minister of finance and economic reform specialist in September 1989. A highly respected economist, Balcerowicz was not a participant in the roundtable talks and therefore had no direct input into the economic reform package agreed to at these talks.[42] In January 1990 he introduced a crash stabilization package popularly termed "shock therapy." Its core features were to be a balanced government budget, strict fiscal, monetary, and income policies, and convertibility of the złoty. In practice, these anti-inflationary measures were predicated on inducing short-term recession and lowering real income. IMF aid was made contingent on keeping close to the 5 percent target.[43] Balcerowicz's stabilization package also envisaged structural adjustment of the economy. Sweeping privatization would be a prerequisite of structural adjustment, and, indeed, a privatization law was enacted in July 1990 (after seventeen different drafts had been considered), followed in September by a law transforming 40 percent of state firms into public corporations owned by the treasury and private entities.

Although the economic data provided below can best suggest to us whether the initial pain inflicted by the Balcerowicz Plan was justified by the longer-term gains, we should not lose sight of the political criticism directed at radical reform. Sachs, rejecting such criticism, nevertheless recognizes the dilemma of such reform: "The utter political precariousness of economic reforms is, at first blush, a paradox. Why should something 'so good' feel 'so bad'?"[44] (To rephrase Sachs's paradox: Balcerowicz was able to carry out unpopular policies with public support.) From his social democratic advocacy perspective, Przeworski advances some answers to this question. A harsh critic of both the philosophy and the implementation of the economic reform, he argues that "the architects of reform were persuaded that their blueprint was sound—no, more: the only one possible.

They viewed all doubts as a lack of understanding, even a lack of responsibility."[45] Furthermore, "radical reform was a project initiated from above and launched by surprise, independently of public opinion and without the participation of organized political forces."[46] Przeworski also intimates that in December 1989, when the Balcerowicz Plan was introduced to the Sejm, it was presented with an ultimatum: The Sejm was "given sixteen pieces of legislation and told that it must approve the nine most important before the end of the month to meet the IMF conditions. As the parliament was continuing to debate, Wałęsa became impatient and suggested that the Sejm should simply give the government decree powers and be done with it."[47] For Przeworski, then, "The policy style with which reforms were introduced and continued had the effect of weakening democratic institutions."[48] Although his caricature of the top-heavy process of reform seems unassailable, it is debatable whether his conclusion about its adverse effect on democracy has been borne out.

In seeking to rein in the government's budget deficit, Balcerowicz was guided by a number of economic imperatives. One involved domestic factors. The economic policy of the communist government had failed because it tended to reward one and all—not just the productive employee or the competitive firm but also the malingerer or the unprofitable juggernaut steel works. In order to continue providing a social wage (welfare benefits) to citizens and also to permit large-scale bailouts of firms in financial trouble, the communist government allowed the national debt to accumulate and ignored rational economic considerations. Under communism, fraudulent claims for disability and sickness benefits were encouraged by a system ignoring traditional accounting methods. Even successive noncommunist governments remained hard-pressed to provide pensions and benefits claimed by some 8 million Poles—one-fifth of the population. A dispute within the Pawlak government in fall 1994 over whether to index these claims to rises in wages or to cost-of-living increases underscored the persistence of the problem of social transfer payments.

That Poland in the early 1990s has been transformed into a market economy with a corresponding social structure is beyond question, but there are problems with describing the transition to the market as an unqualified success. In 1990 alone, as many as 500,000 private firms were established, though perhaps half of these closed by the end of the year. By 1994 there were more than 2 million entrepreneurs in the country, and this despite the fact that a mass privatization program initially approved by the parliament in 1991 had been stalled for three years. Many large state-owned industrial plants had not been sold off. In March 1993 the privatization legislation that would have effected this change in property relations for over 500 major enterprises was defeated by an unusual coalition of Christian nationalist and secular social democratic parties. At this time, the U.S. Department of Commerce still classified Poland as a nonmarket economy. But the social democratic coalition government formed in fall 1993 continued the effort to sell off remaining state enterprises. In fall 1994 Prime Minister Pawlak signed legislation authorizing the privatization of more state enterprises, but shortly afterward he was accused of stalling, and Oleksy, his successor, had to renew the pledge to follow through with privatization of remaining large state industries. Even in a worst-case scenario of Poland's future, it is difficult to envisage reversal of marketization policy, if not of democratization.

Economic Growth

Already in 1993 some Western economists were hailing Poland's arrival in the postcommunist future. The country was the first in Central Europe to resume economic growth following the introduction of profound institutional and structural changes in 1989. It had the most privatized economy in the region, a buoyant stock market, vigorous consumerism, and reasonable prospects for the privatization of the colossal state industrial enterprises. By the end of 1991, exports to the EC had reached 60 percent of all exports.[49] Data for 1993 showed a 2.5 percent increase in GDP over a year earlier and industrial production up by 8.1 percent. In 1994 GDP growth was 4.5 percent and industrial production 15 percent higher than in 1993 (Table 6.1). Poland's was the world's best-performing stock market in 1993, even though only some twenty firms were listed and shares traded up to thirty-five times of a company's prospective earnings. Foreign investors were attracted to both the Warsaw stock market and Polish industry, investing US$1.59 billion in 1993 (for a cumulative total of US$3 billion). In 1994, however, the Warsaw stock market index fell by 19 percent as speculators became aware of company stocks' being overvalued compared with company book values.

TABLE 6.1   Selected Economic Indicators, 1994

Indicator	Percentage
Gross Domestic Product (growth rate)	4.5
Industrial output (growth rate)	15.0
Retail trade (growth rate)	11.3
Consumer prices (growth rate)	32.2
Inflation (rate of increase)	31.4
Budget balance (as percent of GDP)	−3.5
Unemployment (as percent of labor force)	16.0
	US$
Average monthly wage	304
Trade balance (in billions)	−0.8
Foreign exchange reserves (in billions)	5.8
Gross foreign debt (in billions)	38.7

Source: Business Central Europe, March 1995, p. 65.

Although investors were generally bullish on Poland, public opinion in the country in 1993 was less than bullish on the state of the economy (Table 6.2). A year later economic fears remained paramount for most Poles: 85 percent of respondents questioned in fall 1994 listed increases in food prices as their main fear, followed by increases in medical expenses (78 percent), rent (68 percent), and costs of children's education (50 percent). Fear of losing a job was cited by less than half the respondents (45 percent), suggesting that by 1994 job security was, paradoxically, less of a concern in Poland than in many Western countries.

In the short term, Balcerowicz's shock therapy produced large-scale unemployment, high inflation, a decline in industrial production (transport and construction sectors were an exception), and a drop in real income. Thus in the period 1989–1992, the cumulative four-year GDP fell by 17 percent, cumulative inflation was 175 percent, and unemployment increased by 13 percent.[50] But the Balcerowicz plan did achieve its most important objectives: restraining budget deficits and hyperinflation. In addition, it augmented trade with the West, led to an improved balance-of-trade account, cultivated a domestic capital market, and spurred foreign investment. Profitability, even in the public sector, was stimulated. Thus a 1993 World Bank report found that many state-owned enterprises had turned the corner: Better management, a sleeker and less costly labor force, and better product quality and assortment were important factors in generating earnings. Growth in the construction sector was particularly buoyant as infrastructural changes became a top priority, but the chemical, petrochemical, and electrical industries also spearheaded overall growth. By contrast, heavy industry—the mainstay of the socialist economy—soon withered. Coal output was down to just 60 percent of that recorded in the peak years of the 1980s, while steel output was halved. In short, structural adjustment policies had the overall effect of shifting investment from

TABLE 6.2   Hope Barometer: Respondents' Assessments of the Effectiveness of the Economic System (100-point scale)

Nation	Before 1989	1993	In Five Years
Poles	57	39	57
Belarus	75	15	42
Bulgarians	59	25	63
Czechs	44	55	81
Croats	28	2	71
Hungarians	74	29	69
Romanians	57	32	67
Slovaks	64	34	73
Slovenes	46	36	83
Ukrainians	76	4	42

Source: Polityka, no. 32, August 7, 1993, p. 20.

energy-intensive, labor-intensive, and raw-material-intensive industries to capital-intensive ones.

Employment and Income

In these early years of capitalism, Poland's economy faced problems of recession similar to those occurring elsewhere in the capitalist world. Nearly 3 million Poles (about 15 percent of the workforce) were unemployed. In 1994 about half of these had been without a job for more than a year. Among the hardest-hit sectors were those employing female labor: light industry, the educational system, the health service, and state administration. Nearly two-thirds of the nonmanual unemployed were women. Regional variations in the proportion of unemployed women were also perceptible; whereas in Warsaw 5 percent of women in the labor force were without work, in more rural Suwałki, Olsztyn, and Koszalin provinces the number was over 20 percent. To make matters worse, women's prospects for returning to the labor force were dramatically poorer than men's; the number of openings listed for women was one-seventh of what it was for men.[51]

Alarm over high unemployment is countered by claims that many Poles moonlight in second jobs just as they did during the communist period. In fall 1994 the Polish Market Economy Research Institute provided a report on workers employed unofficially in the economy. Thirty percent of Poles drew at least part of their income from illegal employment, which often paid wages twice as high as in the official sector. Undeclared income amounted to some US$7 billion annually—8 percent of Poland's 1994 GDP and 14 percent of total personal income. The Institute estimated that 46 percent of those claiming unemployment benefits were also receiving wages from unofficial work.[52] Although we need to be cautious in accepting the accuracy of data on such an elusive subject, it is clear that black-market labor is performed by a significant number of Poles and, increasingly, by visitors from the ex-Soviet republics.

According to the Main Statistical Office, in 1992 13 million Poles had a monthly income of less than 1.4 million old złoty. This figure represented the social minimum—a kind of poverty line. It signified that 39 percent of households were living in poverty in 1992 compared with 25 percent in 1991 and 20 percent in 1990. The purchasing power of a Polish citizen on an average monthly income declined markedly between 1989 and 1992. By 1992 the majority of Polish families spent half or more of their income on food. Following is a comparison of what an average income could buy in a month in 1989 and in 1992 (in parentheses): 1,017 (597) loaves of bread or 5,043 (820) bottles of milk or 201 (144) kilograms of cheese or 29 (19) men's shirts or 229 (80) train tickets for a 200-kilometer trip or 454 (159) theater tickets. In these years food prices increased fifty-six times, and consumer prices taken together rose at an annual rate of about 35 percent. In 1994 this rate fell to 25 percent. The market economy even produced something that the centrally planned economy never accomplished—a reduction in the consumption of meat.

In 1992 per capita meat consumption was 70 kilograms, below the level of 1980, when shortages of subsidized meat led to public protests and the emergence of Solidarity. Even as the quality and availability of meat improved, its consumption was likely to drop farther. Since the average monthly income was about US$200 (or 3.4 million złoty), not just meat but most of the benefits of capitalism—home ownership, holidays, most durable goods—were out of the reach of ordinary people.[53]

The socioeconomic standing of the family was of course greatly transformed by the transition to the market. The authors of one study drew the following contrast:

> The average Polish family in the era of real socialism accepted as certainty that employment might be poorly paid but it was there; that housing could be obtained through state allocation; that a mother who wanted to have a child could count on an entire system of benefits during pregnancy and upbringing of the child; that free medical care was guaranteed . . . , that the child could be left in a nursery or preschool; that the only school fees were voluntary contributions to the parents' association, that every interested young person who was at all intelligent could continue her studies.[54]

Since the transition to a capitalist economy, the picture has changed:

> Today the average Polish family has to recognize that it might find itself without any means of subsistence if its only provider were dismissed from work; that saving to buy a flat is almost impossible; that with a doctor under the threat of imprisonment for performing an abortion, a mother may have to give birth to a fifth or sixth child for whom, in the event of illness or disability, she could not afford to buy medicine or pay for an operation; whom she will never be able to take on a holiday or send to college; and it goes on.[55]

Downward economic mobility for many families has not always been accompanied by adverse changes in sociological categories. For example, survey data reported in early 1995 listed the three top-ranked occupations in terms of prestige as university professor (cited by 84 percent of respondents as a prestigious occupation), doctor (79 percent), and teacher (73 percent). Coal miners were ranked next (70 percent), but that was 11 percent lower than in a comparable survey carried out in 1987. The greatest losses in prestige over this period were for government minister (down 16 percent), factory director (down 15 percent), and priest (down 13 percent).[56] High-status professionals who suffer a reduction in their economic but not their social ranking may experience an especially deep sense of alienation and deprivation. Not only professionals but also former public servants such as health care workers and teachers have frequently been the first target of government-imposed belt-tightening. It is not surprising, then, that their strike action in spring 1993 led to the no-confidence measure (passed by a single vote) in Suchocka's government in late May, forcing new elections. Socioeconomic clout has shifted to new financial institutions—banks, insurance companies, pension funds, holding companies. Schools of business administration and management now attract the most talented young people, who previously might have gone into engineering or medicine. A separate issue is whether "the best and the brightest" had already emigrated from Poland sometime earlier. In a seven-year period ending in 1992, some 1.7 million Poles migrated to another country. Nearly half of them were between twenty-five and forty-nine, and many were well educated and in the professions. Even today, emigration still offers the best hope for socioeconomic advancement for many Poles.

In agriculture, farm incomes were halved between 1988 and 1992. Meat production dropped as demand fell. To exacerbate the plight of livestock farmers, in 1993 the EC banned the import of calves from former Soviet-bloc countries because of an alleged outbreak of foot-and-mouth disease. Only 20 percent of the country's private farmers has more than 10 hectares, and therefore only the former state farms are large enough to allow efficient modern farming methods. There are few buyers for them, however; domestic buyers are scarce, and foreigners need to obtain special permits from the Ministry of Internal Affairs before a sale can be closed. Still, in the western territories Poland acquired from Germany in 1945 there were some signs that large estates resembling those held by the former Junker class were reappearing.

Privatization

Before examining privatization policy in Poland, we need to disaggregate this generic, often casually used concept. A leading specialist on privatization in Eastern Europe, the United Nations economist Jozef van Brabant, has placed it in a broader context. Private ownership is neither an end, nor even a means, in itself:

> The key variable in bolstering economic efficiency in the PETs [planned economies in transition] through some form of privatization in a reliable, predictable, and sustainable manner is not ownership *per se*, but rather the market structures through which the assets will henceforth be allocated; ensuring that proper market structures come about is, therefore, a critical task. Pivotal is the relationship among ownership, competition, and the regulatory environment.[57]

Van Brabant distinguishes various objectives in privatizing a state-owned economy. Purely economic goals include improving economic efficiency, separating the role of government as producer from its other functions, strengthening a shareholding culture with private monitoring of enterprise performance, increasing the state's revenue from the sale of equity while reducing its expenditures by getting rid of loss-producing enterprises, developing financial markets, promoting competition, and removing inflation-producing monetary overhang,[58] that is, too much money chasing too few goods. Three important political goals of privatization are expanding liberties by restricting the role of government in economic affairs primarily to the enforcement of property rights, pursuing private property rights, thus supporting social stability and democratic consolidation, and removing politically appointed managerial structures and, conversely, engendering a "breakthrough of competent managers."[59]

Privatization involves a fundamental change in the ownership structure that political scientist Kazimierz Poznański identifies with termination of the state sector. One way in which this termination can be effected is the profit-oriented *custodian model,* which Poznański understands as involving the creation of holding institutions run by state officials that assume custody of public assets. Variously referred to as corporatization and commercialization, this model lays the basis for the creation of large-scale investment funds that will eventually transform ownership. This method was adopted in Poland but with at first limited success. A related *institutional-ownership model* involves giving control over the capital allocation of state enterprises to financial institutions such as banks, insurance companies, and retirement plans. These institutions will be driven by the profit motive and will initially serve as proprietary agents of state enterprises. Other privatization methods described by Poznański include the *labor-management model,* in which capital assets are transferred to employees, the corrupt *political-market model,* in which the majority of assets is made available to former high-placed communist officials, and the *foreign-agent variant,* characterized by ownership from outside the country. Poznański was very skeptical about the viability of the *universal-market model,* often romanticized by Western students of East European privatization, in which all citizens with the required minimum funds can buy shares in the state enterprises being sold off.[60]

Van Brabant provides his own list of privatization methods, several of which overlap with Poznański's. With *spontaneous privatization* managers entrusted with state assets are now able to take possession of them; the former *nomenklatura* begin to capture all property rights to the assets under their control. (The first Solidarity government sought to curb this form of privatization.) *Free distribution of state assets* principally involves a transfer of ownership to employees or a mass distribution of free shares (or vouchers) to the entire population, but it may also allow decentralized government agencies (such as municipalities) to obtain ownership rights. Often divestment through free distribution takes the form of the creation of special divestment, investment, mutual, or holding funds. Another form of privatization—more popular in the late communist period than the early capitalist one—is *state divestment of user rights* through leasing, franchising, and contracting out. In this way, private managers and investors take control of assets. But the most common form of privatization in Eastern Europe, as elsewhere, has been the *sale of state-owned assets.* This method can itself be disaggregated into a number of variants: sale through capital-market operations (such as a stock market) in which share prices fluctuate; a public offering of a block of shares but through closed bids, shares being sold for a fixed price; auction markets, in which assets are sold as a unit to a buyer; worker and management buyouts; and debt-equity swaps with banks, creditors, and foreign companies.[61]

Finally, adopting a sociological approach to the typology of privatization, instead of solely examining the method by which state ownership is terminated, David Stark enquires more generally whether market, bargaining, or administrative fiat was employed to transfer assets, whether such assets were transferred to corporations or to citizens, and whether financial ability or some other resources were needed to acquire state assets.[62]

In reviewing various typologies of privatization, my objective has been to highlight the intricacy of the process in Poland and elsewhere. Many Western accounts of the capitalist revolution in Eastern Europe adopt simplistic categories that do not do full justice to the scope of the subject.

I have referred to the rapid growth of the private sector in Poland since 1989. Growth has been particularly dramatic in the foreign-trade, retailing, and construction sectors, where it accounted for over three-quarters of sales. The government's green light for worker and management buyouts was important to the privatization drive, although the procurator-general reported that 10 percent of the initial spontaneous privatization involved *nomenklatura* buyouts.[63] Data for 1993 indicated that privatization had attained several milestones, surpassing 50 percent of GDP and slightly more of overall employment and accounting for 90 percent of sales in trade and 80 percent in construction. The most successful program was the "small privatization" of the approximately 125,000 retail outlets and small businesses operating as part of the state sector in December 1989. But private firms now range from street vendors and bazaar stalls to Curtis International, manufacturer of television sets, and Optimus, one of Europe's ten largest computer producers, with annual sales over US$100 million.

The 1990 privatization law was designed to transform large firms and conglomerates into state-owned joint-stock companies and limited-liability companies and, where necessary, liquidate and sell off their assets.[64] By 1994 some 2,000 of the 8,500 state enterprises had been privatized. though not many survived very long. Of the approximately 2,000 larger companies in existence in Poland in 1994, over 95 percent were new firms established exclusively by foreign capital or by foreign capital with a Polish partner. By contrast, only 3 percent were preexisting firms that had been purchased by private domestic firms or by shareholders as the 1990 privatization law had envisaged. It is striking that the centrally planned economy had established enormous corporations that had few takers under a free market and *not* the large ventures whose profile was so vital in a market economy. Not without reason does sociologist Jacek Kurczewski observe that "economic despotism was most efficient in plundering people engaged in private enterprise, and least efficient in direct productive action."[65]

The law set up a central agency to take charge of privatization—the Ministry of Ownership Transformations, more often known simply as the Ministry of Privatization.[66] Headed twice by Janusz Lewandowski (throughout 1991 under the Bielecki government, then from July 1992 to October 1993 under Suchocka), it promoted the free distribution of shares. In time, the argument that such a program was impractical led to a shift in policy toward "preprivatization restructuring," aimed at making state enterprises more attractive to purchasers in the medium term. The ministry's program of "quick privatization" of small and medium-sized firms, launched in July 1991, was its major success.

The politics of privatization were, naturally, affected by electoral verdicts. In 1992 the State Agency for Foreign Investment (Państwowa Agencja Inwestycji Zagranicznej—PAIZ) was established to promote investment in the country by matching potential Western investors with Polish enterprises on the selling block.[67] Financial backing for the agency's operations was to be provided by the West, specifically, the European Union's (EU's) PHARE program—initially designed to provide technical assistance but by 1994 also involved in direct investment projects. This external source of funding raised Polish suspicions about whose interests PAIZ would ultimately serve. In 1994 the Ministry of Privatization, now controlled by the left-leaning Pawlak government, turned down a nearly US$12 million grant from the EU to support the PAIZ, despite the fact that some US$4 billion in state assets were soon to be sold off as part of a renewed mass privatization program.[68] In October 1994, Prime Minister Pawlak announced that privatization of large state enterprises was being delayed because of technical problems in setting up investment funds (he needed to appoint a hundred candidates to their supervisory boards), as well as to await more opportune market conditions that would raise the value of state assets. Several weeks later, he gave the go-ahead for the privatization of 444 state industrial enterprises but held back another 20 for "strategic economic reasons" (these were all rural-based). He also warned that the process would be slowed down in 1995. Pawlak's hesitancy, which led to his replacement by Oleksy, reflected sensitivity to the political consequences of selling off state firms to foreign investors. Even with Oleksy's new reassurances, observers expressed doubts about the SLD-PSL coalition government's resolve to pursue large-scale privatization.

Privatization was the centerpiece of a strategy aimed at creating a market economy in Poland. It helped structurally to transform the economy into a market-based export-oriented one, it attracted foreign equity investment, and it could eventually provide considerable revenue to the Polish treasury. As outlined in the April 1993 mass privatization bill, shares in two hundred of the six hundred state or municipally owned enterprises, whose ownership and management was to be transferred to twenty national investment funds, were to be distributed to the population (though as of fall 1994 they still had not been). The theory was that individuals could activate their shares by paying a registration fee of about US$20. Share prices would subsequently be quoted on the Warsaw Stock Exchange, and shares would be tradeable over the counter. Central to the success of the investment funds were to be the fund managers, who had to convert the enterprises in their portfolios into profitable investments. A state selection committee was set up to appoint fund managers, and, surprisingly, even the postcommunist parties agreed that foreign fund managers and management consultants would help make the national investment funds succeed.

The 1993 Enterprise Pact signed by the Suchocka government, the business confederation, and trade unions requires enterprises privatized by other means to set aside up to 20 percent of their shares for their workforces, up to 10 percent to be given to employees and the remaining 10 percent made available for purchase by them at a 50 percent discount. Although some workers sit on the supervisory boards of such privatized companies, the legendary workers' councils of communist times have been abolished. In this way the pact drew Solidarity and other trade unions into the new market system and provided them with a platform for articulating views on macroeconomic policy. Ironically, the former procommunist trade union OPZZ, now headed by the political scientist Ewa Spychalska, was more supportive of the pact than Solidarity. It was also more reluctant than the Solidarity union, headed by Marian Krzaklewski, to push wage claims. It was the Solidarity union more than the OPZZ that contributed to bringing down the Suchocka government in 1993. Apparently its lingering idealism put it at odds with capitalist realities to which communist pragmatism helped it quickly to adjust.

Privatization was initially warily received by much of the Polish population, including those who had been staunch opponents of communism.[69] Many were aware of the dysfunctional aspects of privatization. John Gray graphically describes the chaotic side of this policy:

> In all the Communist states . . . the collapse of central planning has been accompanied by a process of "wild," "spontaneous," or "Hayekian" privatization—a process of privatization bizarrely akin to the unplanned emergence of market institutions postulated in F. A. Hayek's theorizings, but which, because of its extensive penetration and control by criminal elements, lacks many of the classical attributes of private property and voluntary exchange.[70]

The Polish sociologist Włodzimierz Wesołowski remarks that "unfortunately, present conditions favor the appearance of the traits of a lumpen-businessman rather than the reliable entrepreneur, since the system's shortcomings are being exploited by hucksters and incompetent people."[71]

The inevitable surge of bankruptcies caused by privatization can be interpreted in several ways. In 1992, 3,500 bankruptcy petitions were registered with the courts; in 1993 close to 2,000 occurred in Warsaw alone. Many small firms were forced out of business by the arrival of the multinationals (McDonald's, Unilever, and Levi Strauss), which put an end to the manufacture of knockoffs in Poland. Pirating of various copyrights (films, CDs, software) became so lucrative and widespread (Poland was the region's worst offender) that many Polish firms specializing in such products were forced to close. A 1994 law finally put an end to copyright piracy. It has been estimated, however, that up to 85 percent of bankruptcy cases are deliberate; costs are exaggerated and the remaining capital is transferred outside Poland. Ultimately, bankruptcy statistics may be an irrelevant indicator of the vibrancy of Polish capitalism.

International advice to Poland on privatization and other economic measures has never been in short supply. Major accounting, auditing, appraisal and legal firms have sent in "privatization commandos" to advise Western prospective buyers about Polish firms. Some Polish management consultant firms have been left out of this consultancy gold rush, even though their services would have proved considerably cheaper than those of a Western firm. Western companies moved in quickly after 1989 to revise auditing and accounting methods and standards to conform with EC practice and to prepare state-owned companies for privatization and sale to local and foreign investors.

The Reform of Banking

Privatization assumes a smooth-functioning and reliable banking system. Poland's banking system also had to be privatized and overhauled when a free-market economy was adopted. Banking reform originally began under the communists, when, in 1988, the nine regional branches of the Polish National Bank were hived off and groomed for their debut as the core of a commercial banking system. The privatization of Wielkopolski Bank Kredytowy took place in the following way: 30 percent of the shares were retained by the treasury; another 30 percent were offered to investment funds; 20 percent went on public offer, to be purchased by small private investors; 14 percent of shares were reserved for employees, and 6 percent were allocated to major foreign investors. The volatility of banking shares was illustrated in 1993 when a 30 percent public offering in Bank Śląski led to chaotic trading that included use of strong-arm tactics by street thugs to disperse small investors.[72] Insider trading was also widely alleged. In an investigation completed by the national inspectorate in November 1994, its head, Lech Kaczyński, found no wrongdoing in the privatization of Bank Śląski but did point to incompetence, especially on the part of successive finance ministers, that allowed inside traders to make small fortunes. Despite the obvious appeal of the public offering, at first no reliable strategic investor could be found for 45 percent of the shares. Another flaw in bank privatization was evident in the case of Bank Handlowy. With the end of communism, this state-owned bank lost its monopoly on foreign-trade financing, but in practice, even as a privatized bank, it still commanded a 60 percent share of this enormous sector. In the banking system as in other sectors of the economy, therefore, it did not necessarily follow that privatizing a state corporation broke up a monopoly or created perfect competition.

In addition to the former regionals, many private banks have been formed, with mixed success. Most of these are small and undercapitalized, and the government has encouraged them to consolidate. The greatest problem facing all banks has been the large number of nonperformance loans and bad debts stemming from unprofitable enterprises. Thus, about 60 percent of total bank debt is accounted for by 11 percent of Polish enterprises. So far, Polish commercial banks' low profits are the result of narrow interest-rate spreads (between deposit and lending rates), higher costs, and greater competition. Most banks are faced with heavy losses on loans to the fledgling private sector and have accordingly reduced lending to this capital-starved but risky sector. The long-term aim of bank restructuring is to improve banks' capacity to evaluate risks while helping finance the development of a dynamic private sector. As *Business Central Europe* put it, "Turning the banks from passive credit conveyors into sharp risk-assessors has been a priority."[73]

Efforts have been made by foreign concerns to prop up the Polish banking system. When in 1990 Western governments created a US$1 billion stabilization fund for the Polish currency, some US$600 million of this sum went unused. This amount, together with a US$450 million loan in 1993 from the World Bank, was set aside to restructure the banking system and provide banks with a reserve fund for dealing with bad debts. In 1993 the European Bank for Reconstruction and Development (EBRD) purchased a 28.5 percent stake in one of the former regionals, thus injecting US$12.7 million of new capital into the bank. To be sure, critics argued that the price of shares offered to the EBRD was too low. Western European commercial banks have now begun to buy stakes in their Polish counterparts; for example, the Dutch bank ING has bought part of Bank Śląski. Promotion of such industry partnerships is accompanied by restrictions on foreign banks' ability to open their own subsidiaries and branches. The French Banque Nationale de Paris, the German Dresdner Bank, and U.S.-based Citibank Poland are notable exceptions.

Pathologies of Early Capitalism

For critics of capitalism, the pathologies produced by capitalist transformation define the free-market economy. Certain types of capitalism of course generate more pathologies than others. Kurczewski contends that "a Darwinian model of social development has come to the fore in post-Communist Europe and seems to serve as a more or less explicit philosophy of the new political class.... The problem is that, however important the spirit of entrepreneurship is, the Darwinian model of capitalism applies neither to the realities of modern capitalism, nor to the Polish ethos."[74] Although dysfunctions are undoubtedly associated with capitalist transformation, especially its Darwinian variant, it is easy to exaggerate their impact and pervasiveness.

Violent crime has increased dramatically since the end of communism, though it has not reached the proportions in Poland that it has in Russia. In 1980 the police reported 589 homicides throughout the country. In 1990 the number had risen slightly, to 730. Two years later, however, 999 murders were committed in the country, far outstripping the rate of the previous decade.

White-collar crime has also risen dramatically. The new system has been rocked by financial scandals involving tax evasion or avoiding import duties, thereby robbing the state treasury of revenue, exploiting loopholes in the banking system through kiting operations, defaulting on exorbitant loans obtained through forged documents describing fictitious deals or through personal connections, and financial scams and outright fraud, including the setting up of bogus companies that rob people of their savings. Six supposedly self-made Polish millionaires were arrested between June 1992 and June 1993.[75] It is important here that laws and regulations were often unclear and encouraged abuse. Subsequent legislation has drastically reduced the amount of graft and corruption.

Some defenders of capitalism have endorsed quasilegal activity, arguing that Polish capitalism requires a concentration of capital in fewer hands even if it comes about as a result of unethical practices. This same logic should hold, of course, in welcoming the transformation of former communist apparatchiks into capitalist "entrepreneurchiks."[76] It would condone the appropriation of state-owned property by communists, and, indeed, in late 1994 Wałęsa seemed to acknowledge this when he claimed that efficiency overrode virtually all other considerations in the transition process. Poland's best-known entrepreneurchik is Jerzy Urban, now owner of the publishing house URMA and editor of the satirical weekly *Nie*. Many excommunists had a head start in bidding for firms to be privatized, either through insider information or because they had capital accumulated under communist rule. Although not illegal, the specter of communists' enriching themselves came to haunt capitalist Poland in the first years of the new system. In the first years of capitalist transformation, well-known intellectual dissidents, too, famous for their untiring, selfless crusade against communism in earlier decades, quickly enriched themselves when it became possible to do so. Five years after the democratic breakthrough, the moral outrage against abuse of society's trust by various types of entrepreneurchiks had largely dissipated.

But the largest financial scam that occurred in 1990–1991 had very little to do with the old elites. It involved two unlikely thirty-year-old businessmen, by training a doctor and a pianist, Bogusław Bagsik and Andrzej Gąsiorowski.[77] Accused of conducting a kiting scheme (or "oscylator") that robbed the banking system of over US$4 billion of illegally obtained interest, they managed to leave for Israel with US$35 million before they could be arrested. Second on the scandal list was David Bogatin, near-full owner of a private bank in Lublin, who was extradited to the United States on tax evasion and money-laundering charges. His dealings in Poland appear to have been within the law, and the action taken against him seemed to be prophylactic. Although ranked only sixteenth on the scandal list, Lech Grobelny could claim to be a scam pioneer. As head of a savings association, he suddenly left Poland with 32 million złoty of clients' deposits.

For many citizens, it is their own sense of economic inefficacy at a time of seeming economic opportunity that makes such financial scandals traumatic. The financial dealings of government ministers and parliamentary deputies in cornering shares purportedly offered to the public, purchasing state-owned companies for very low prices, and receiving kickbacks on government contracts have shocked the public no less. Egalitarian attitudes die hard, especially when new inequalities are perceived to result from corrupt practices.

Foreign Policy and the International Political Economy

Theoretically, the end of bipolarity should have increased both the importance of and the options for alliance management for individual states within the international system. In practice, options outside of Western political, military, and economic structures (most notably, NATO and the EU) are limited.

Foreign Policy

Regional Cooperation. Since 1989, a series of pan-European, regional, and transnational agreements have been concluded by Central European states. These range from participation in the fifty-two-state Organization on Security and Cooperation in Europe (OSCE) to establishment of the four-member Visegrad group. Let us consider how Poland seeks to forge international conditions favoring its economic development.

For Poland, bilateral accords with the reunified Federal Republic of Germany were especially significant. In October 1990 a border treaty was signed formalizing bilaterally what had been concluded at the two-plus-two negotiations. In June 1991 a treaty on good-neighbor relations was also signed. In a short time, Germany became the country's largest trading partner. In 1993 it accounted for 28 percent of Poland's imports and 36 percent of its exports. In addition, according to German calculations, in the five-year period 1990–1994 the country had provided Poland with US$12.1 billion in aid. This included US$1.7 billion in direct federal aid, US$3.2 billion in credits through multilateral debt restructuring, US$4.3 billion in debt relief, and US$668 million of its share (28 percent) of EU aid.[78]

In February 1991 a summit of Czechoslovak, Hungarian, and Polish leaders was held in Visegrad, on the Slovak-Hungarian border. Its objective was to coordinate regional activity so as to be consistent with European institutions and to forge trading relations on the basis of free-market economies. Although the CMEA's collapse naturally led to a reduction in trade within the former Soviet bloc, it did not follow that former member states such as Poland, Hungary, Slovakia, and the Czech Republic had to impose trade restrictions and quotas on each other. As Sarah Meiklejohn Terry writes, the meeting "was hailed at the time as a major breakthrough in Central European cooperation." But the Visegrad triad (Visegrad "group" after Czechoslovakia split in two) soon suffered from goal displacement. As Terry observes, "Instead of becoming an organization promoting intraregional cooperation as well as integration at the European level, the Visegrad process became fixated almost exclusively on the latter—in effect, it became a vehicle for coordinating Central Europe's 'road to Europe' while development of closer ties within the region languished on the back burner."[79]

In October 1991 another summit was held in Kraków. It produced a declaration calling for the Visegrad group's speedy integration into the European economic and legal systems. But the election in June 1992 of Vaclav Klaus as Czech prime minister was a blow to efforts at regional cooperation. Klaus saw little future for the Visegrad group as a form of regional partnership, and, especially on gaining entry into the EU, he advocated an individual country-by-country approach. Visegrad was to be primarily a consultative body serving to complement other multilateral bodies such as the Central European Free Trade Agreement (CEFTA). In January 1993 the four Visegrad countries agreed to create a free-trade zone.

CEFTA was organized in March 1993. Shortly thereafter, it signed a free-trade agreement with the European Free Trade Association (EFTA)—a step toward the creation of a European free-trade area. But this link also symbolized the lackluster trade performance of the Visegrad group countries with each other. Paradoxically, then, CEFTA trade links with EFTA were partly designed to promote trade within CEFTA.[80]

Beginning with Germany, Poland signed bilateral agreements that emphasized political and economic cooperation with every neighbor. The Czechs, as we have noted, seemed less interested in the idea of Central European solidarity than Poland. In turn, Slovakia was wary of too much Polish influence in the region. Trade agreements with Belarus and Ukraine were concluded, and in Ukraine's case even cooperation in military and defense-industry spheres was envisaged. A treaty with Lithuania was ratified only in 1994 after much wrangling over how past Polish-Lithuanian relations should be interpreted. Finally, Poland's border with Russia was now limited to the Kaliningrad district, but this technical detail made Russia's shadow over Poland no less visible. In sum, although efforts were made by all parties to maintain good-neighbor relations, it seemed that even small incidents—Poles' beating up Russian visitors at a train station, the blowing up of a bridge in Lithuania that was attributed to a Polish liberation front in the country never heard of before, a dispute about the property of the Ukrainian Uniate church in Poland—could create diplomatic consternation. At times it seemed that only outside institutions could prevent East Europeans from taking their quarrels with each other too seriously.

Western Europe. Poland joined the Council of Europe in November 1991 and signed the European Convention on Human Rights and Fundamental Freedoms that came into effect in January 1993. The treaty provides recourse to the Council of Europe's legally binding mediation where violations of civil rights are alleged. Polish governments also made clear their willingness to be bound by decisions of the European Commission and the European Court of Justice. Poland was also to be admitted into EFTA as a preliminary step to EU membership. The 1992 agreement between the EU and EFTA to create a common market indirectly reinforced the integration of Poland's economy with that of Western Europe. But the admission of Austria, Finland, and Sweden into the EU in January 1995 and their withdrawal from EFTA made Polish efforts to join the company of advanced industrial countries seem like taking aim at a moving target. Having received associate membership status in the EU in 1993, Poland formally applied for full EU membership in April 1994. The review process for applications was to begin, however, only in 1996.

Security and the West. A central foreign policy issue has been the alliance structure necessary to promote Poland's national interests. Table 6.3 shows how in-

TABLE 6.3   Fear Barometer: Others Feared the Most (percentages)

Nation	Minorities	Immigrants	Neighbors	Russians	Germans	Americans
Poles	35	41	62	63	68	11
Belarus	30	22	20	13	14	13
Bulgarians	46	0	61	5	3	4
Croats	57	28	62	34	3	6
Czechs	44	38	35	38	38	6
Hungarians	26	51	64	13	6	3
Romanians	60	16	67	62	13	10
Slovaks	53	23	46	26	21	5
Slovenes	13	61	60	3	3	14
Ukrainians	24	6	10	19	3	4

Source: Polityka, no. 32, August 7, 1993, p. 20.

grained Polish fears of neighbors Russia and Germany continue to shape popular attitudes. In response to pressure by Poland and several other regional states to obtain membership in NATO, in January 1994 a NATO summit proposed a Partnership for Peace (PFP) program to former Soviet-bloc countries as an alternative to full NATO membership. In the immediate aftermath of the breakup of the Soviet bloc, President Wałęsa seemed determined to press for full NATO membership as quickly as possible. The logic seemed to be that the end of the Cold War would produce a new type of bipolarity whereby the winning Cold War coalition would be expanded—with the addition of anticommunist Central European states—and the Cold War losers (Russia and most of the former Soviet republics) would be marginalized. But in August 1993 Russian President Boris Yeltsin suddenly reversed himself on Russian acquiescence to Poland's application for NATO membership, and since then the Russian government's opposition to an expanded NATO has hardened. The fact that the West has been sensitive to Russia's views on the subject has been a signal to Poland that the former Soviet bloc is not about to be divided into winners (the Central European states) and losers (the former Soviet republics). Indeed, some observers at the time went so far as to assert that "the West once again wants to make Moscow the sheriff of the Wild East."[81] The various tests of "Europeanness" that Poland and other aspirants to NATO had to pass in order to be deemed qualified for full membership were extensive: assessment of the strength of democracy, defense and foreign policy, military posture, and regional relations (such as ability to work together in the Visegrad group).[82]

The international relations specialist Charles Kupchan explains the reasoning behind the Partnership for Peace:

(1) Europe's uncertain strategic landscape necessitates a policy sufficiently flexible to adapt to ongoing change; (2) now is not the time to draw new dividing lines in Europe; (3) the West must seek to integrate the new democracies into its security

community without undermining NATO's military efficacy; (4) the activities resulting from NATO's outreach to the East must demonstrably bolster democratic reform; (5) NATO should design the PFP so as to enhance Western leverage over when
and how Russia uses force in post-Soviet republics.[83]

Some Central European leaders felt that the creation of the PFP and the criteria
that had to be met to obtain NATO membership were a ruse to drag out the
process of extending a Western security umbrella over the region. More cynical
observers believed that the unintended, or perhaps intended, consequence of de-
laying tactics was to allow a resurgent but pro-Western Russia to regain influence
over the region. From its inception, Poland was one of the leading critics of what
was seen as a halfway house for Eastern Europe. In mid-1994 Polish Defense Minister Kołodziejczyk attacked the PFP plan for not making clear how a state was to
move from partnership to NATO membership. Preliminary association with the
Western European Union (WEU)—an organization set up in 1954 to work closely
with NATO in ensuring security for states in the EC[84]—was put forward as one
further test for eventual admission into NATO. But Wałęsa and other Polish political leaders were dissatisfied with the West's step-by-step approach: From their
perspective Poland had first to join the EU, then integrate economically with the
West, then accept PFP and, furthermore, agree to an association with the WEU,
and only later receive firm Western security guarantees. Polish leaders felt that
economic and military integration with the West should be simultaneous. The
fact that, over five years after the fall of communism, obstacles to integration with
the West persisted began to erode popular support for the European idea. In seeking to reduce the chances that any one state (obviously, Russia) might feel isolated
or that new political or military blocs might form, the West had plausible reasons
for creating multilayered, multitiered regional and pan-European associations
with overlapping memberships. The danger was that carefully crafted and intri-
cate economic and alliance systems would prove too fluid, fudged, and unstable,
leading to both defection by individual states and disenchantment with pan-Eu-
ropeanism on the part of large sections of society.

In July 1994 U.S. President Bill Clinton visited Poland and announced a
US$100 million fund for carrying out joint military programs with democratic
partners in Central Europe. Shortly thereafter, small-scale but highly publicized
NATO exercises were held in Poland. In September 1994 an amendment put forward by U.S. Senator Hank Brown to a bill in Congress offered Poland, Hungary,
and the Czech Republic preferential terms for purchasing U.S. arms. These terms
were modeled on those already given to strategic U.S. allies such as Israel, Saudi
Arabia, and South Korea. By this stage the Polish government had to take comfort
from such small foreign policy victories.

In April 1995 the crucial issue of NATO expansion into Central Europe caused
renewed controversy when the Republican majority in the House of Representatives passed a resolution supporting the proposal. In turn, Russia threatened to
scrap both the START-2 (Strategic Arms Reduction Talks) and the Conventional

Forces in Europe (CFE) treaties that it had signed if Poland, the Czech Republic, Hungary, and Slovakia were admitted into the Western military alliance. The increasingly nationalist Yeltsin government did not seem willing to entertain compromise arrangements that would forego the stationing of NATO troops in these states while still providing them with a NATO commitment to defend them if they were attacked. Russia's recommendation that, instead of pursuing full NATO membership, Poland should return to its interwar foreign policy of maintaining equidistance between Russia and the West produced consternation in Warsaw; it was the flawed logic underlying just that policy that Polish historians held responsible for the dual invasion of Poland by Germany and Russia at the start of World War II. Russia also threatened to reevaluate the bilateral treaty it had signed with Poland in 1992 and its agreement to cancel each country's debt. While not overreacting to the Russian threats, Wałęsa continued to push gently for speedy admission into NATO, and even the recently appointed excommunist Prime Minister Oleksy visited NATO headquarters in Brussels to argue Poland's case. Nevertheless, the initial euphoria about the possibility of Poland's joining Europe and the West had all but vanished as Russian reassertion of what it regarded as its sphere of influence began to trouble Polish leaders.

The International Political Economy

Foreign Debt. If the security architecture designed to protect Central European states was intentionally equivocal, there was little confusion about the enormous role played by the global economy in shaping the region's economies. Poland has been facing immense foreign debt repayment obligations ever since Gierek initiated his economic opening to the West in the early 1970s. At the end of 1992 the country's outstanding external debt totaled close to US$50 billion, which represented 59 percent of GDP. Agreements signed in April 1991 with the Paris Club of foreign government creditors and in September 1994 with the London Club of foreign commercial bank creditors both reduced and rescheduled the debt, but the debt burden remains onerous. It is estimated that the servicing of Poland's Paris Club debt and new loans from international banks will add up to US$4 billion annually by the year 2005, as envisaged by the terms of the April 1991 agreement. The most important aspect of the agreement was a 50 percent write-off of Poland's official US$33 billion debt in two tranches if Poland held to the IMF policy guidelines. Initially the London Club banks showed reluctance to go beyond the 35 percent standard reductions associated with Brady-type debt restructuring agreements. Behind this thinking was an optimistic assessment of Polish economic growth. By this time some bank creditors had already written off much of their Polish debt or had traded it on the secondary market. Even here, however, creditors were encouraged by Poland's recent performance, and Polish paper rose in mid-1993 to 31 percent of its face value. In September 1994 an agreement on debt rescheduling with the London Club was finally concluded: 49.5 percent of

Poland's US$12 billion capital and accumulated interest debt was frozen, the remainder to be paid back over thirty years (amounting to about US$400 million annually), and Poland could purchase one-quarter of the total back at 41 cents on the dollar. Just as important, removing the stigma of debt would increase Poland's access to international capital markets. It would also be able to finance its budget deficit more cheaply, through the sale of bonds to foreign investors, instead of the hitherto highly inflationary method of borrowing from its own central and commercial banks.

The effective implementation by successive Polish governments of austerity measures (the term is rarely used because of its negative connotations) has helped the country to reach manageable levels of debt repayment—an outcome that the indebted communist government could not have hoped for. The top priority assigned to budgetary constraints has stimulated foreign equity capital inflows, led to the extension of standby loans from the IMF, and identified new projects to be financed by the World Bank and the EBRD.

Foreign Trade. The collapse of the CMEA trading system after 1989 and the change to hard-currency-accounted trade among regional states had an immediate negative impact on Poland's terms of trade.[85] Recession in the West made exporting even more difficult and led to negative current-account and trade balances. The Polish government sought to curb imports by imposing a 6 percent surcharge in December 1992 and permitting the złoty to slip through a "crawling peg" devaluation. Calls for more radical steps to devalue the currency and enhance Polish exports were a regular feature of political life in the early 1990s. Indeed, in late 1994 social democratic leaders attacked the National Bank of Poland's President Hanna Gronkiewicz-Waltz for being overprotective of the złoty.

From the last quarter of 1992 to the first of 1993, Poland went from a US$385 million trade surplus to US$370 million deficit. The high import elasticity of Polish industry, requiring imported components for its products, generated this sudden shift in the balance of trade. Polish consumers also played a part through increased demand for foreign-made consumer items. By 1994 exports were up once again, by 15 percent, while imports were down by 1.4 percent. Poland's trade deficit was thereby reduced from US$2.9 billion for the first half of 1993 to US$1.8 billion for the same period for 1994. But the potential for greater export-led growth remained; in 1993 Poland's exports per capita amounted to scarcely US$369, compared with US$1,251 for the Czech Republic, US$1,023 for Slovakia, and US$868 for Hungary. As noted earlier, Germany became the country's leading trade partner, followed by Russia and Italy. In January 1995 Poland and Russia signed an agreement in Moscow to settle their mutual debt dating from the Soviet and early transition periods. A "zero-plus" option was accepted that canceled both Poland's debt to Russia of 4.4 billion transfer rubles and US$2 billion and Russia's debt to Poland of 7 billion transfer rubles and US$366 million. The "plus" referred to the debts of Polish and Russian companies incurred in 1991 and 1992, the first two years of hard-currency trade. Russia agreed to pay Poland US$20 million in cash in exchange for Poland's transferring to Russia US$150 million in securities. It was unclear whether disagreement later in 1995 over NATO expansion might undermine the debt accord.

Foreign Investment. As did other former Soviet-bloc countries, the Polish government appealed for economic assistance and loans from the West. Studying only the credits earmarked for Poland (and therefore not always immediately forthcoming), in June 1993 the Polish Council of Small and Medium-Sized Businesses reported the following distribution of declared credits according to source: the World Bank (US$2.6 billion, 30 percent of all credits), the German government (US$1.6 billion, 18 percent), the French government (US$652 million, 8 percent), and the Italian government (US$468 million, 5 percent).

Foreign investment was limited up to January 1993; about 60 percent of the estimated US$7 billion in equity capital invested in postcommunist Central Europe went to Hungary. Polish leaders hoped for an average annual inflow of total foreign investment of US$2 billion. We need to proceed cautiously in estimating total foreign involvement in the Polish economy, for there is a difference between the actual amount foreign companies have invested directly in buying assets in Poland and the sums pledged in future foreign investment. Table 6.4 identifies the countries that have invested most heavily in Poland. Expectations of Western-style consumption patterns for a 40-million-strong market and expansion of trade in new consumer goods with eastern neighbors (the Baltic states, Ukraine, Russia, and Belarus) have helped fuel Western investment. After a slow start, U.S. capital represents about 36 percent of foreign investment, Italian 11 percent, and German and Dutch 8 percent each. For historical reasons, Germany has been cautious in investing in Poland, especially in regions such as Silesia and Pomerania that it lost to Poland after World War II. Charges of German revanchism would quickly surface should the "colossus to the West" be perceived as too hasty in acquiring stakes in Poland.[86]

TABLE 6.4   Capital Inflow into Poland, January 1991–December 1993 (percentages)

Source	Percent of Total Inflow
United States	36
Supranationals	12
Italy	11
Germany	8
Holland	8
France	6
Austria	4
Others	15

Source: "Survey: Foreign Investment," *Business Central Europe,* April 1994, p. 42.

By 1993, the three foreign corporations that had invested most in Poland were Fiat (US$180 million), Coca Cola (US$180 million), and International Paper (US$140 million). Two-thirds of foreign investment was in the manufacturing and mining sector and another 16 percent in wholesale and retail trade. Whereas the communist government had often reached an impasse with potential foreign investors over repatriation of profits, Solidarity governments were more sensitive to cries of a one-time sell-off of Polish assets. To examine the advantages and disadvantages of attracting foreign investment, let us review several cases of Western investment in Poland.

In the case of the largest foreign investor, Fiat, the Italian-based car manufacturer promised in October 1992 to invest up to US$2 billion over an eight-year period—a figure ten times higher than it had paid to buy the FSM car plant in Poland. Fiat retooled the Tychy plant for production of the popular Cinquecento, with 75 percent of production to be earmarked for export, and production of the Uno was to follow. This incremental approach reflected the reluctance of foreign companies to provide large-scale financing before testing Central European market conditions. Whereas General Motors concluded a US$25 million deal to buy 50 percent of the FSO car plant in Warsaw to assemble the Opel (the first unit being produced in November 1994), Ford backed out of plans to invest US$50 million in a car parts plant and turned to Hungary instead. Smaller automobile ventures in Poland included Mercedes's investment of US$12 million in a delivery van plant in WZM/Główno and Saab-Scania's 51 percent stake in a small heavy-truck plant in Słupsk. In 1994 both Peugeot and Volvo were still considering large joint ventures with Polish partners (the FSL/Lublin sedan works and the Jelcz truck factory respectively).[87] The extreme caution characterizing investment decisions was also affected by popular opinion, which was very suspicious about a sell-off of national assets to foreign interests. The revelation of one British-based consultant about the privatization process in Poland, reported by *The Economist*, would confirm the suspicions of many Poles: "Strategic sales to a foreign investor result in 'money being invested into the company, but at a point where it's at its lowest value; governments are thus in a weak negotiating position.'"[88]

Western companies seek involvement in the region not only because of lower labor costs but also to obtain market share and a springboard to the enormous Russian and Ukrainian markets. Global beverage, food, and soap corporations have become commonplace. Coca-Cola and PepsiCo had captured close to 70 percent of the carbonated-drinks market by 1994. With superior production and marketing techniques, they were able to drive many local producers out of business. Combining its beverage distribution network with its fast-food operations (Pizza Hut, KFC, and Taco Bell), PepsiCo's total investment in Poland up to 1998 was expected to reach US$500 million. In the electronics sector, Dutch-based Philips purchased a majority interest in Polam, a lighting equipment manufacturer, in order to compete for market share in the region with General Electric (purchaser of Tungsram in Hungary) and the Siemens subsidiary Osram (purchaser of Tesla in Czechoslovakia). In turn, the French electronics firm Thomson bought Polkolor, a manufacturer of color television tubes, to compete against Nokia (the Finnish group), Samsung of South Korea, and Philips.

Telecommunications was an industry in need of rapid modernization. At the end of 1991 Poland had one of the lowest rates of telephone line ownership in all of Europe: only 8 lines per 100 inhabitants, half of Portugal's total. While the Solidarity government decided that the international and intercity telephone network would remain in the hands of a state monopoly (Telekomunikacja Polska SA) and twenty local operators, it adopted a sectoral approach to industrial restructuring and collapsed five main telecommunications manufacturers into three companies. Each of the three systems suppliers was offered for sale, with two foreign companies encouraged to bid against each other for each. AT&T, Alcatel of France, and Siemens of Germany won bids and began investing in modernizing telephone-switching and transmission-gear manufacturers.[89] Their purchase of Polish state companies was a way for them to appropriate a one-third market share of Polish telecommunications. In return, each of the three companies controlling the industry was required to guarantee a 50 percent locally manufactured content level insisted upon by the government in order to help ancillary suppliers.

Problems most often cited in 1993 by foreign companies that discouraged investment in Poland included an inconsistent and unstable legal system (cited by 91 percent of respondents surveyed), unfavorable customs regulations (84 percent), high investment risks (77 percent), social conflicts and tension (72 percent), slow-paced and limited economic reforms (58 percent), excessive demands by trade unions (51 percent), wage demands (38 percent), and technological backwardness (34 percent).[90] Although central bank permission is at times still needed to repatriate profits (except those made on government bonds and treasury bills), this issue has vanished as a perceived stumbling block.

In early 1995 the *Economist* Intelligence Unit ranked Poland eighth of twenty-six transition economies of the former Soviet bloc in terms of its capacity for growth. It reported that "Poland's external debt burden, poor infrastructure, modest education levels and relatively high inflation rate may harm future growth."[91] Structural rather than cultural factors were cited, therefore, as the reason Poland ranked behind the three Baltic states, the three other members of the Visegrad group, and Slovenia. At the same time, this analysis suggests that future growth is now dependent on wise macroeconomic policies formulated by Polish leaders rather than on factors beyond their control.

Conclusion

In the past two chapters I have described the functioning of domestic political structures in Poland, the country's transformed economy, and the impact of the international system in consolidating change. Given the unprecedented scope of the undertaking—simultaneously introducing democracy into the polity and the market into the economy—the many achievements that have been recorded are remarkable. From a comparative perspective, it is obvious that Poland has a long way to go before integrating fully with Western Europe. Indeed, as long as the historical development gap between itself and the more advanced economies of the West is being narrowed we can speak of success, if not of any miracle.

Can we conclude that the process of democratic consolidation has largely been completed in Poland? In the introductory chapter I outlined some of the tests of such consolidation. One was that democracy had been successfully anchored when the major political forces agreed to be bound by outcomes determined by political institutions. This study has indicated that President Wałęsa found it especially difficult to adjust to the new political rules that he had helped to formulate but now seemed a fetter on his powers. By contrast, following their overwhelming electoral defeat in 1989 excommunists were among the first to understand the new rules of the game and how to take advantage of them. In general, however, the democratic process has become self-enforcing in Poland—virtually the entire political spectrum, including Wałęsa, has submitted to the outcomes the process has produced.

Formal criteria of democratic consolidation, such as holding at least two successive elections, providing for the alternation of parties in power, the renewal of government at regular intervals, and the replacement of at least one government by the main opposition party have all been met in Poland. Furthermore, the processual aspect—regular bargaining and compromise between insider and outsider groups about both procedure and policy—has been much in evidence as Polish party leaders have had both to build ruling coalitions regularly and to demonstrate their responsiveness to a society shaken by the scale of reform.

However comprehensive the analysis, it can never account for the x factors that can reverse the positive change that has been effected.[92] A global recession, Russian or even German revanchism, Central European bickering, nationalism, communism, and renewed authoritarianism at home are among the many variables that are unpredictable but remain crucial to the fate of Poland's democracy. Yet, it is in the nature of democracy to be open to greater uncertainties, and it is its responsiveness that usually permits it to overcome its adversaries.

To know certainty is to reach that whimsical island that contemporary Polish poet Wisława Szymborska calls *Utopia:*[93]

> The further you advance, the larger it opens,
> the Valley of Obviousness.
> If any doubt appears, the wind dispels it.
> The echo takes along a voice without being called
> and willingly elucidates the secrets of the world.
> To the right, a cave in which Meaning resides.
> To the left a lake of Profound Conviction.
> The Truth tears itself from the bottom and lithely
>   flows to the surface.

The valley is dominated by Unshaken Certainty.
From its peak there is a view down on the Heart
   of the Matter.
In spite of its charms, the island is uninhabited.

Notes

1. Charles Taylor, *The Malaise of Modernity.* Concord, Ontario: Anansi Press, 1991, p. 110. This book is based on the November 1991 Massey Lectures given by Taylor on CBC.

2. On the interaction between democratization and economic change, see Adam Przeworski, "Economic Reforms, Public Opinion, and Political Institutions: Poland in the Eastern European Perspective," in Luis Carlos Bresser Pereira, José Maria Maravall, and Adam Przeworski (eds.), *Economic Reforms in New Democracies: A Social-Democratic Approach.* Cambridge: Cambridge University Press, 1993, pp. 132–198. On the relationship between democracy and the capitalist state, see Graeme Duncan (ed.), *Democracy and the Capitalist State.* Cambridge: Cambridge University Press, 1989.

3. Leslie Elliot Armijo, Thomas J. Biersteker, and Abraham F. Lowenthal, "The Problems of Simultaneous Transitions," *Journal of Democracy,* 5, no. 4 (October 1994), p. 162. On the situation when social change is factored in, see Claus Offe, "Capitalism by Democratic Design? Democratic Theory Facing the Triple Transition in East Central Europe," *Social Research,* 58 (Winter 1991), pp. 865–892.

4. Leszek Balcerowicz, "Democracy Is No Substitute for Capitalism," *Eastern European Economies,* 32, no. 2 (March–April 1994), p. 42.

5. Leszek Balcerowicz, "Understanding Postcommunist Transitions," *Journal of Democracy,* 5, no. 4 (October 1994), pp. 75–89.

6. Robert N. Bellah, "The Quest for the Self: Individualism, Morality, Politics," in Paul Rabinow and William M. Sullivan (eds.), *Interpretative Social Science: A Second Look.* Berkeley: University of California Press, 1987, p. 378.

7. Stephan Haggard and Robert R. Kaufman, "Economic Adjustment and the Prospects for Democracy," in Stephan Haggard and Robert R. Kaufman (eds.), *The Politics of Economic Adjustment: International Constraints, Distributive Conflicts, and the State.* Princeton: Princeton University Press, 1992, pp. 319–320.

8. Haggard and Kaufman, "Economic Adjustment and the Prospects for Democracy," p. 321.

9. Haggard and Kaufman, "Economic Adjustment and the Prospects for Democracy," p. 324.

10. Haggard and Kaufman, "Economic Adjustment and the Prospects for Democracy," p. 341. See also their *The Political Economy of Democratic Transitions.* Princeton: Princeton University Press, 1995, and "The Challenges of Consolidation," *Journal of Democracy,* 5, no. 4 (October 1994), 5–16.

11. Haggard and Kaufman, "Economic Adjustment and the Prospects for Democracy," p. 349.

12. Haggard and Kaufman, "Economic Adjustment and the Prospects for Democracy," p. 350.

13. On the subject of consolidating economic reform, see Joan M. Nelson, "Linkages Between Politics and Economics," *Journal of Democracy,* 5, no. 4 (October 1994), 49–62.

14. Douglass C. North, *Institutions, Institutional Change, and Economic Performance.* Cambridge: Cambridge University Press, 1992, p. 83.

15. North, *Institutions, Institutional Change, and Economic Performance,* p. 98.

16. North, *Institutions, Institutional Change, and Economic Performance,* p. 92.

17. North, *Institutions, Institutional Change, and Economic Performance,* p. 99.

18. Friedrich Hayek, *The Fatal Conceit: The Errors of Socialism.* Chicago: University of Chicago Press, 1989, p. 7.

19. North, *Institutions, Institutional Change, and Economic Performance,* p. 140.

20. Introductions to this subject include Michael Thompson, Richard Ellis, and Aaron Wildavsky, *Cultural Theory.* Boulder: Westview Press, 1990. Also, Peter L. Berger, *The Capitalist Revolution: Fifty Propositions about Prosperity, Equality, and Liberty.* New York: Basic Books, 1986. Of course, Max Weber was among the first to describe the cultural context of capitalism.

21. Robert D. Putnam, *Making Democracy Work: Civic Traditions in Modern Italy.* Princeton: Princeton University Press, 1993, p. 157.

22. Putnam, *Making Democracy Work,* p. 171.

23. Putnam, *Making Democracy Work,* p. 183.

24. Giuseppe di Palma, "Why Democracy Can Work in Eastern Europe," in Larry Diamond and Marc F. Plattner (eds.), *The Global Resurgence of Democracy.* Baltimore: Johns Hopkins University Press, 1993, p. 266.

25. Putnam, *Making Democracy Work,* p. 175.

26. An excellent source for both theoretical and empirical studies of the various forms of capitalist transformation is the journal *Communist Economies and Economic Transformation* (previously known as *Communist Economies*). A more recent, specialized journal is *MOCT-MOST: Economic Policy in Transitional Economies.*

27. For example, John E. Elliot distinguishes between market and managed capitalism and between socialism and communism. See his *Comparative Economic Systems.* Belmont, CA: Wadsworth, 1985. Martin C. Schnitzer focuses on modified market economies, mixed ones, and centrally planned ones. See his *Comparative Economic Systems.* Cincinnati: South-Western, 1987.

28. John Gray, "From Post-Communism to Civil Society: The Reemergence of History and the Decline of the Western Model," in Ellen Frankel Paul, Fred D. Miller Jr., and Jeffrey Paul (eds.), *Liberalism and the Economic Order.* Cambridge: Cambridge University Press, 1993, p. 37.

29. Taylor, *The Malaise of Modernity,* pp. 110–111.

30. Gray, "From Post-Communism to Civil Society," p. 41.

31. Gray, "From Post-Communism to Civil Society," p. 42.

32. Gray, "From Post-Communism to Civil Society," p. 43.

33. Gray, "From Post-Communism to Civil Society," p. 46.

34. Peter Evans, "The State as Problem and Solution: Predation, Embedded Autonomy, and Structural Change," in Haggard and Kaufman, *The Politics of Economic Adjustment,* p. 177.

35. Evans, "The State as Problem and Solution," p. 181.

36. Richard Portes, "From Central Planning to a Market Economy," in Shafiqul Islam and Michael Mandelbaum (eds.), *Making Markets: Economic Transformation in Eastern Europe and the Post-Soviet States.* New York: Council on Foreign Relations Press, 1993, p. 35. David S. Mason has also cogently explained the "phasing" of economic reform in his *Revolution in East–Central Europe: The Rise and Fall of Communism and the Cold War.* Boulder: Westview Press, 1992, pp. 119–131. See especially his Figure 4.2, p. 121, on economic phas-

ing, which is adapted from Stanley Fischer and Alan Gelb, "The Process of Socialist Economic Transformation," *Journal of Economic Perspectives,* 5, no. 4 (Fall 1991), p. 102.

37. See Janos Kornai, *The Road to a Free Economy: Shifting from a Socialist System.* New York: Norton, 1990.

38. For a seventeen-point outline of the Balcerowicz Plan, see Adam Przeworski, "Economic Reforms, Public Opinion, and Political Institutions: Poland in the Eastern Europe Perspective," in Bresser Pereira, Maravall, and Przeworski, *Economic Reforms in New Democracies,* pp. 144–145. Przeworski bases his summary on *Tygodnik Solidarność,* January 5, 1990.

39. See Jeffrey Sachs, *Poland's Jump to the Market Economy.* Cambridge, MA: MIT Press, 1993.

40. "Squaring the Circle," *Business Central Europe,* July/August 1994, 19.

41. In his autobiography, Messner inevitably casts himself as a pioneer of economic reform. See Zbigniew Messner, *Kuglarze i księgowi.* Warsaw: BGW, 1993.

42. The head of the Solidarity group at the economic subtable of the roundtable negotiations was Witold Trzeciakowski.

43. For a critique of IMF structural adjustment policy, see Kevin Danaher (ed.), *50 Years Is Enough: The Case Against the World Bank and the International Monetary Fund.* Boston: South End Press, 1994.

44. Jeffrey Sachs, "Western Financial Assistance and Russia's Reforms," in Islam and Mandelbaum, *Making Markets,* p. 146.

45. Przeworski, "Economic Reforms, Public Opinion, and Political Institutions," p. 183.

46. Przeworski, "Economic Reforms, Public Opinion, and Political Institutions," p. 180.

47. Przeworski, "Economic Reforms, Public Opinion, and Political Institutions," p. 176.

48. Przeworski, "Economic Reforms, Public Opinion, and Political Institutions," p. 180.

49. See Bartłomiej Kamiński, "Emerging Patterns of Foreign Trade," in Richard F. Staar (ed.), *Transition to Democracy in Poland.* New York: St. Martin's Press, 1993, pp. 181–201.

50. Jean-Joseph Boillot, *Situation économique des pays d'Europe centrale et orientale en 1993 et perspectives 1994.* Paris: Centre français du commerce extérieur, 1994.

51. Henryk Domański, Krystyna Janicka, Anna Firkowska-Mankiewicz, and Anna Titkow, "Społeczeństwo bez reguł," in Andrzej Rychard and Michał Federowicz (eds.), *Społeczeństwo w transformacji: Ekspertyzy i studia.* Warsaw: IFiS PAN, 1993, p. 164.

52. *RFE/RL Daily Report,* September 30, 1994.

53. *Slowo,* July 5, 1993.

54. Domański et al., "Społeczeństwo bez reguł," p. 155, my translation.

55. Domański et al., "Społeczeństwo bez regul," pp. 156–157, my translation.

56. Reported on the Polish electronic news service *Dyrmalki,* January ·1995, compiled by Zbigniew Pasek.

57. Jozef M. van Brabant, *Privatizing Eastern Europe: The Role of Markets and Ownership in the Transition.* Dordrecht: Kluwer Academic Publishers, 1992. p. 148. The issues of economic competition and the regulatory environment in Poland would require separate study and expertise that cannot be provided in this book.

58. Van Brabant, *Privatizing Eastern Europe,* pp. 156–157. See his bibliography for a comprehensive list of works on the subject.

59. Van Brabant, *Privatizing Eastern Europe,* p. 158. The citation is from Anders Asland, "Principles of Privatization," in Laszlo Csaba (ed.), *Systemic Change and Stabilization in Eastern Europe.* Aldershot, England: Dartmouth, 1991, p. 22.

60. Kazimierz Z. Poznański, "Property Rights Perspective on Evolution of Communist-Type Economies," in Kazimierz Z. Poznański (ed.), *Constructing Capitalism: The Reemergence of Civil Society and Liberal Economy in the Post-Communist World.* Boulder: Westview Press, 1992, pp. 76–77.

61. Van Brabant, *Privatizing Eastern Europe,* pp. 211–213.

62. Reproduced with some variations in a number of publications. One source is David Stark, "Path Dependence and Privatization Strategies in East Central Europe," *East European Politics and Societies,* 6, no. 1 (Winter 1992), 17–54. See also Stark's chapter in Vedat Milor (ed.), *Changing Political Economies: Privatization in Post-Communist and Reforming Communist States.* Boulder: Lynne Rienner, 1993.

63. George Kolankiewicz, "The Reconstruction of Citizenship: Reverse Incorporation in Eastern Europe," in Poznański, *Constructing Capitalism,* p. 158, n. 8.

64. For a description of the legal framework regulating different types of company ownership, see Roman Frydman, Andrzej Rapaczynski, John S. Earle, et al., *The Privatization Process in Central Europe.* Budapest: Central European University Press, 1993, pp. 158–173. On the Polish case, see Frances Millard, *The Anatomy of the New Poland.* Aldershot, England: Edward Elgar, 1994, pp. 174–184.

65. Jacek Kurczewski, *The Resurrection of Rights in Poland.* Oxford: Clarendon Press, 1993, p. 5.

66. For an organizational chart of this Ministry, see Frydman et al., *The Privatization Process in Central Europe,* p. 179.

67. For an example of a PAIZ advertisement calling for Western partners, see "Financial Times Survey: Poland," *Financial Times,* June 17, 1993, p. v.

68. "Looking at Gift Horses," *The Economist,* September 17–23, 1994, 59.

69. On attitudinal, as well as technical and managerial, obstacles to privatization, see the illuminating analysis offered by van Brabant in *Privatizing Eastern Europe,* chap. 7.

70. Gray, "From Post-Communism to Civil Society," p. 33.

71. Włodzimierz Wesołowski, "Transformacja charakteru i struktury interesów: Aktualne procesy, szanse i zagrożenia," in Rychard and Federowicz, *Społeczeństwo w transformacji,* p. 126, my translation.

72. See Anita Blaszczak, "Jak zdobywano Bank Śląski," *Polityka,* no. 49 (December 4, 1993), 16.

73. "Kicked into Action," *Business Central Europe,* May 1994, 54.

74. Kurczewski, *The Resurrection of Rights in Poland,* p. 449.

75. In addition, several other millionaires "temporarily" left the country. This information is based on the annual survey "100 najbogatszych polaków" (The 100 Richest Poles) conducted by the weekly newsmagazine *Wprost.* See *Wprost,* supplement, June 20, 1993.

76. See Jacek Tarkowski, "Old and New Patterns of Corruption in Poland and the USSR," *Telos,* 80 (1989), 51–63.

77. For an account of the twenty biggest scandals, see Wojciech Markiewicz and Piotr Sarżyński, "Wielcy podejrzani," *Polityka,* no. 31 (July 31, 1993).

78. German Information Center, "German Support for the Reform Process in the Former Soviet Union and the Countries of Central, Southeastern and Eastern Europe," *Focus On . . . ,* March 1995, p. 4. The remaining aid was to cover the transfer ruble balance, or re-

payment of Poland's debt to the former German Democratic Republic. The exchange rate used in all calculations was DM 1.40 to US$1.

79. Sarah Meiklejohn Terry, "Prospects for Regional Cooperation," in Staar, *Transition to Democracy in Poland*, pp. 215–216.

80. For an analysis of CEFTA, see George Kolankiewicz, "Consensus and Competition in the Eastern Enlargement of the European Union," *International Affairs*, 70, no. 3 (July 1994), 485–487.

81. For an assessment of this view, see Adam Krzeminski, "Czy Zachód znowu nas zdradził?" *Polityka*, no. 49 (December 4, 1993), 1, 23, my translation.

82. For criteria related to NATO membership, see Theo van den Doel, *Central Europe— the New Allies? The Road from Visegrad to Brussels*. Boulder: Westview Press, 1993.

83. Charles A. Kupchan, "Strategic Visions," *World Policy Journal*, 11, no. 3 (Fall 1994), 112–113.

84. In 1991 three non-EU countries—Turkey, Iceland, and Norway—were admitted to the WEU.

85. For an analysis of regional trade and economic integration, see Andras Koves, *Central and East European Economies in Transition: The International Dimension*. Boulder: Westview Press, 1992, chaps. 4–8.

86. On German investment in Central Europe, see "Germany and Central Europe Survey: Ostpolitik Adrift," *Business Central Europe*, September 1993, 39–48.

87. Matthew Brzezinski, "East Europe's Car Makers Feel Sting of Capitalism," *New York Times*, April 28, 1994.

88. "Networking," *Business Central Europe*, February 1994, 27.

89. Ray Bashford, "Trying to Connect You—When We have More Lines," *Financial Times*, June 17, 1993, ix.

90. Jacek Bołdok, "Dżentelmeni mowią o pieniądzach," *Polityka*, no. 7 (July 10, 1993).

91. Reported in "Emerging-Market Indicators," *The Economist*, March 25–31, 1995, p. 116.

92. The extrinsic and intrinsic dilemmas facing new democracies are considered in Phillipe C. Schmitter, "Dangers and Dilemmas of Democracy," *Journal of Democracy*, 5, no. 2 (April 1994), 57–74.

93. Wisława Szymborska, "Utopia," translated by Czeslaw Milosz, in Czeslaw Milosz (ed.), *Postwar Polish Poetry*. Berkeley: University of California Press, 1983, p. 114.

Selected Bibliography

Although considerable scholarship has dealt with Poland's politics in the twentieth century, this list is limited to English-language books published about the postcommunist period, which remains less familiar to many students.

Błażyca, George, and Ryszard Rapacki (eds.), *Poland into the 1990s: Economy and Society in Transition*. London: Pinter, 1991.

Boyes, Roger. *The Naked President: A Political Life of Lech Wałęsa*. London: Secker and Warburg, 1994.

Connor, Walter D., and Piotr Płoszajski (eds.), *The Polish Road from Socialism: The Economics, Sociology, and Politics of Transition*. Armonk, NY: M. E. Sharpe, 1992.

Kamiński, Bartłomiej, *The Collapse of State Socialism: The Case of Poland*. Princeton: Princeton University Press, 1991.

Kurski, Jarosław, *Lech Wałęsa: Democrat or Dictator?* Boulder: Westview Press, 1993.

Millard, Frances, *The Anatomy of the New Poland: Post-Communist Politics in Its First Phase*. Aldershot, England: Edward Elgar, 1994.

Podgórecki, Adam, *Polish Society*. Westport, CT: Praeger, 1994.

Sachs, Jeffrey, *Poland's Jump to the Market Economy*. Cambridge, MA: MIT Press, 1993.

Slay, Ben, *The Polish Economy: Crisis, Reform, and Transformation*. Princeton: Princeton University Press, 1994.

Staar, Richard F. (ed.), *Transition to Democracy in Poland*. New York: St. Martin's Press, 1993.

About the Book and Author

A comprehensive analysis of politics in a young European democracy, this book describes the principal features of Poland's democratic system—the political institutions, parties, elections, and leaders that have shaped the transition from communism. Raymond Taras examines the complex Wałęsa phenomenon; the comeback of the communists; and the uneasy relationship between the presidency, parliament, and the prime minister.

Recognizing that democratic consolidation requires economic development, Taras considers Poland's economic performance under free-market rules as well as the related issues of privatization, foreign investment, trade, and integration into the global economy. Applying a regime-change framework that focuses on the sequence of crisis, choice, and change, he contextualizes Poland's political and economic transformation during the 1990s, describing the sources of crisis of the former communist regime and reviewing the political solutions considered by the embattled ruling elite and the restless Solidarity opposition. Throughout, Taras summarizes and tests a variety of theories governing democratic transition, institution building, and economic development, making an important contribution to the comparative study of democratic consolidation.

Raymond Taraś has taught political science at universities in England, Canada, and the United States and has served as a national fellow at the Hoover Institution at Stanford University. His publications include *Ideology in a Socialist State: Poland 1956–83, The Road to Disillusion: From Critical Marxism to Postcommunism in Eastern Europe,* and *Nations and Politics in the Soviet Successor States.*

Index

Third Republic, 19, 23, 161
  elections in, 186
  presidents/prime ministers of,
    176(table)
Thus Spoke Zarathustra (Nietzsche), 78
Timofiejev, Lev, 123
Tocqueville, Alexis de, on democracy, 3
Trade, 80, 81, 246, 250–251
Trade unions, 62, 98, 102–105, 126, 132
  privatization and, 241
Transition. *See* Democratic transition
"Transnational incompatibility" thesis, 221
Trybuna Ludu, 134, 148
Turowicz, Jerzy, 97
Two-plus-two negotiations, 57, 245
Tygodnik Mazowsze, 138
Tygodnik Solidarność, 142
Tyminski, Stan, 5, 166, 190, 191, 209,
    215(n51)

UD. *See* Democratic Union
Ukrainian Uniate church, property dispute
    with, 246
Unemployment, increase in, 234, 235
Union of Communists of the Polish Re-
    public "Proletariat," 145
Union of Labor (Unia Pracy, UP),
    164(table), 182, 197
  support for, 196, 199, 209
Union of Lublin (1569), 29
Union of Political Realism (UPR), 181. *See*
    also Union of Real Politics
Union of Real Politics (Unia Polityki Real-
    nej, UPR), 165(table)
Union of Social Democracy, 145
United Peasants' Party (Zjednoczone
    Stronnictwo Ludowe, ZSL), 64, 82,
    118, 132, 135, 141, 142–143, 177
UP. *See* Union of Labor
UPR. *See* Union of Political Realism;
    Union of Real Politics
Uprisings, nineteenth-/twentieth-century,
    28, 36, 37, 50–55
Urban, Jerzy, 81, 117, 119, 244
Urbanization, 72, 73
U.S. Department of Commerce, on
    Poland, 232

USSR
  economic relations with, 58
  military intervention by, 59
  threat from, 94
  See also Russia
UW. *See* Freedom Union

Valenzuela, Arturo, 171
Valenzuela, J. Samuel, on consolidated
    democracy, 1–2
Value system, 7, 85, 88, 95, 203, 211
  changes in, 15, 71, 82
Van Brabant, Jozef, on privatization, 237,
    238
Veterans' Association, 62
Veto power, compromise on, 137–138
Violence, 243
  politically motivated, 8
Visegrad group, 245, 247, 253
Voting
  apathy for, 194
  motivation for, 187, 188
  poll results about, 139(table)
  See also Elections

Wachowski, Mieczyłsaw, 177
WAK. *See* Catholic Electoral Action
Wałęsa, Lech, 5, 94, 101–102, 117, 123,
    130, 166, 195, 206
  coalition government and, 142
  democratic consolidation and, 244, 254
  dissatisfaction with, 199, 210
  Little Constitution and, 162, 169, 179
  NATO and, 247, 249
  presidency of, 175–177, 179–180, 181
  roundtable talks and, 125, 132, 136
  support for, 92, 189, 190, 191, 199, 200,
    209
Walewska, Maria, 35
Walicki, Andrzej, on Sarmatian ideology,
    26–27
Walters, Garrison, on middle class, 41
Warsaw ghetto, uprising in, 42, 45
Warsaw Pact, 58
Warsaw Stock Exchange, 240
Wealth, 119
  measuring, 75(table)